"Raskolnikov deftly shows how gender is staged in the context of allegorical debates on death and life. Raskolnikov's brilliance is to show how voices are split and allocated to various figures, often personified as male and female, and how these talking figures debate not only the place and meaning of the body, but questions of moral harm and the possibility of true knowledge. These debates are hardly philosophy in a recognizable sense, but they do engage philosophical questions through giving voice to various gendered characters. What emerges time and again is a self in a distanced relation to itself, often embattled, often split, for these dialoguing characters are and are not separate. What becomes clear throughout these debates is that the action involved is often capricious and arbitrary, and so the question of free will, of the efficacy of human action in the face of contingency, is posed again and again in a dramatic and dialogic genre whose action or plot lacks all signs of Aristotelian likelihood and probability. The book works in a subtle and surprising way to locate gender as a point of view, showing how personifications essential to the debate genre show the contours of gender and subjectivity as they are assumed through speech. This is a disorientingly smart and engaging text, essential to the early modern understanding of gender."

—Judith Butler, Maxine Elliot Professor at the University of California, Berkeley

"In *Body Against Soul: Gender and* Sowlehele *in Middle English Allegory,* Masha Raskolnikov offers a theoretically bold and historically responsive understanding of the self in medieval English allegorical literature. As a historical alternative to modern psychoanalysis, *sowlehele* allows her to make brilliant sense of Foucault's famous inversion of the Platonic dictum: 'the soul is the prison of the body.' As a literary preoccupation, *sowlehele* brings Raskolnikov closer than others have gotten to the strange operations of medieval prosopopeia. Persistently engaging and finely discriminating, Raskolnikov's book-long treatment of allegory exhilaratingly shows what is so abundantly productive and useful about this hoary form."

—Carolyn Dinshaw, professor of English and social and cultural analysis, New York University

"A fresh, smart look at some medieval English allegories that focus on the split self. Full of subtle readings and challenging insights."

—Barbara Newman, Northwestern University

In medieval allegory, Body and Soul were often pitted against one another in debate. In *Body Against Soul: Gender and* Sowlehele *in Middle English Allegory,* Masha Raskolnikov argues that such debates function as a mode of thinking about psychology, gender, and power in the Middle Ages. Neither theological nor medical in nature, works of *sowlehele* ("soul-heal") described the self to itself in everyday language—moderns might call this kind of writing "self-help." Bringing together contemporary feminist and queer theory along with medieval psychological thought, *Body Against Soul* examines *Piers Plowman,* the "Katherine Group," and the history of psychological allegory and debate. In so doing, it rewrites the history of the Body to include its recently neglected fellow, the Soul.

The topic of this book is one that runs through all of Western history and remains of primary interest to modern theorists—how "my" body relates to "me." In the allegorical tradition traced by this study, a male person could imagine himself as a being populated by female personifications, because Latin and Romance languages tended to gender abstract nouns as female. However, since Middle English had ceased to inflect abstract nouns as male or female, writers were free to gender abstractions like "Will" or "Reason" any way they liked. This permitted some psychological allegories to avoid the representational tension caused by placing a female soul inside a male body, instead creating surprisingly queer same-sex inner worlds. The didactic intent driving *sowlehele* is, it turns out, complicated by the erotics of the struggle to establish a hierarchy of the self's inner powers.

Masha Raskolnikov is associate professor in the Department of English at Cornell University.

INTERVENTIONS: NEW STUDIES IN MEDIEVAL CULTURE
ETHAN KNAPP, SERIES EDITOR

Body Against Soul
GENDER AND *SOWLEHELE* IN MIDDLE ENGLISH ALLEGORY

MASHA RASKOLNIKOV

THE OHIO STATE UNIVERSITY PRESS • COLUMBUS

Copyright © 2009 by The Ohio State University.
All rights reserved.

Library of Congress Cataloging-in-Publication Data
Raskolnikov, Masha, 1972–
Body against soul : gender and sowlehele in Middle English allegory / Masha Raskolnikov.
p. cm.—(Interventions : new studies in medieval culture)
Includes bibliographical references and index.
ISBN 978-0-8142-1102-1 (cloth : alk. paper)—ISBN 978-0-8142-9200-6 (cd-rom) 1. Allegory. 2. Body and soul in literature. 3. English literature—Middle English, 1100–1500—History and criticism. I. Title. II. Series: Interventions : new studies in medieval culture.
PR275.A4R37 2009
820.9'15—dc22
2009005373

This book is available in the following editions:
Cloth (ISBN 978-0-8142-1102-1)
CD-ROM (ISBN 978-0-8142-9200-6)
Paper (ISBN: 978-0-8142-5679-4)
Cover design by Laurence J. Nozik
Text design by Juliet Williams
Type set in Adobe Minion Pro

*This book is dedicated, with love and admiration,
to the memory of my father, Felix Raskolnikov (1930–2008),
and, in loving gratitude for her inspiration and support,
to my beautiful mother, Lenna.*

CONTENTS

Acknowledgments — ix

Introduction — 1

Chapter 1
Thought Enfleshed:
Philosophy and Psychology as Figured in Latin Allegory — 31

Chapter 2
Allegorizing the Split Self:
A Middle English Debate Between the Body and the Soul — 70

Chapter 3
"The Soul Is the Prison of the Body":
Pedagogy, Punishment, and Self-Love in a Middle English Debate — 105

Chapter 4
Defending the Female Self:
"Sawles Warde" and *Sowlehele* — 139

Chapter 5
Promising the Female, Delivering the Male:
Transformations of Gender in *Piers Plowman* — 168

Conclusion — 197

Appendix
In a Thestri Stude I Stod (I Stood in a Dark Place),
Translation by Masha Raskolnikov   203

Bibliography   207

Index   219

ACKNOWLEDGMENTS

Writing for an imaginary "ideal reader" is one of the conditions of producing a long piece of writing. This book began in an attempt to respond, using medieval literature as an archive, to Judith Butler's work on gender, embodiment, and, from my first semester in graduate school onward, the question of power's psychic life, always-already an allegorical situation; as I have moved forward on my own, it has been an honor to continue calling her my teacher. Anne Middleton has set for me an extraordinary and challenging example of scholarship and has given of her time, thought, and energy with an amazing generosity: she opened up the Middle Ages as a treasure trove for me, but without her guidance, I would still be lost in it. My work, both present and future, is inspired and informed by that of these advisers, both separately and in juxtaposition, in more ways than I can express.

This book's finished version owes a great deal to questions Steve Justice posed at its early stages. I would also like to thank Andy Galloway, Tom Hill, and Pete Wetherbee, whose examples have taught me how to be a colleague as well as a writer of books. Their insight, support, and suggestions were invaluable, as were those of my warm community of interlocutors and friends at Cornell University, particularly Laura Brown, Jason Frank, Roger Gilbert, Becky Givan, Sabine Haenni, Ellis Hanson, Molly Hite, Cary Howie, Rayna Kalas, Nick Salvato, Shirley Samuels, Lyrae Van-Clief Stefanen, Amy Villarejo,

Sara Warner, and Dag Woubshet, each of whom has taught me a great deal. I am grateful to Ethan Knapp for his enthusiasm for this book, which permits my study of the past to have a future.

I am lucky to have many friends to thank for reading and responding to this manuscript; thanks to Greg Tomso, Elizabeth Schirmer, and Holly Crocker for their sensitive reading of chapters and support along the way to writing them. I am also deeply grateful to Kate Washington for her thoughtful editing and suggestions for revision. In the larger community of medievalists, I also owe a debt of gratitude to Bridget Balint, Louise Bishop, Rita Copeland, Jody Enders, David Hult, Brenda Machosky, Barbara Newman, Bob Mills, Tison Pugh, Elizabeth Robertson, Emily Steiner, Nicolette Zeeman, and Katherine Zieman. This gratitude is partly for the pleasure of engagement and conversation, and partly because their work has in so many ways inspired my own. No acknowledgment is sufficient thanks for Katy Breen, my dissertation-writing partner. Her generosity as a reader has been, in itself, an extraordinary education, as has the privilege of listening to her think aloud through her own project. I was lucky to have had a rich, varied, and sustaining experience of graduate education at the Rhetoric Department at the University of California Berkeley: inside and outside that program, thank you, Gillian Harkins, James Salazar, Dale Carrico, Homay King, and Lon Troyer.

This book would not have been completed without the love and support of a large network of friends, although being in any one place meant missing those whose lives are based elsewhere. In my San Francisco life, thank you for the long, rich friendships, Kami Chisholm, Deb Cohler, Anastasia Coon, Debra Farrell, Alex Fraser, Sandra Lim, Sasha Merritt, Kate Morris, and Mazzy Thompson. For making my New York City life possible, and for years of wonderful conversation, thank you, Michele Gershberg, Cheryl Stewart, Enna Eskin, and Somjen Frazer. And, far away or close, it helps to be known by old friends: thank you, Ailsa Craig, Anna Korteweg, Emily Spring, Mark Freedman, Kristen Summers, Alec Badenoch, Sergei and Katia Kuznetsov, Alan Kanner, and Peggy Dieter.

I wish there were room here to thank all of the students, both graduate and undergraduate, who challenged me to think beyond myself: nothing has pushed my thinking forward as much as engagement with all of you. I would like to thank Caetlin Benson-Allott for choosing me as her mentor. Thank you, Jamie Friedman, Angela Furry, Tricia Har, and Misty Urban for being such able research assistants and advisees. Thank you, James Lee and Luke Terlak-Poot, Michael Barany, and the rest of the 2004 "Pleasure and Danger" seminar at the Telluride Association Summer Program, and thank you to the students who took various iterations of the "Bodies in the Middle Ages" class, enriching my life by their discussion and debate.

The writing of this book, and the dissertation that preceded it, could not have happened without the support of the Doreen B. Townsend Center for the Humanities, the Society for the Humanities at Cornell University, and the Mellon Humanities Seminar; financial support from the American Council of Learned Societies Fellowship; and the President's Council of Cornell Women Affinito-Stewart Grant. I am also grateful to the supportive listeners at the New Medievalisms Conference and the Medievalists' Writing Workshop, whose listening ears were invaluable as this book came together. An earlier version of the present study's fifth chapter appeared in the *Yearbook of Langland Studies* 2005 as "Promising the Female, Delivering the Male: Transformations of Gender in *Piers Plowman*," and some of my preliminary ideas about *sowlehele* were worked out in "Confessional Literature, Vernacular Psychology, and the History of the Self in Middle English" in *Literature Compass*.

Last and most important of all, I am so very grateful to have had the love and support of my family: my mother, Lenna Raskolnikov; my brothers, Alex and Marc; and my partner, Jennifer Tennant. Since childhood, my great-aunt Sophie Cherniavsky was my inspiration in seeking to live the life of the mind; I hope I have done honor to her memory, as well as to the memory of my father, Felix Raskolnikov, whose model I seek to follow as a scholar and a teacher.

INTRODUCTION

> *Soul:* I wish I could afford to live alone!
> What would I give to move my bed around,
> or moon about in music till eleven
> with none to care if I was off the ground?
> It would be Heaven!
>
> *Body:* I wish I could afford to live alone!
> What would a little privacy be worth!
> A place with a garden. O, a little earth
> to call my own![1]
>
> —"Debate of the Body and the Soul: A.D. 1949"

The contending forces that constitute a self have been named, variously, flesh and spirit; ego, id, and superego; appetites and rational will; body and soul. The connection between these forces is simultaneously quotidian and utterly mysterious. Often, the speaking "I" expresses its relation to the body as if it were a subject addressing a mysterious, unpredictable object. Although it's easy to say that we live our entire lives within or as bodies, the body itself (organs, arteries, strange liquids within) has no voice with which to express its materiality; its voice is produced by physical organs but expresses the thought of a nonmaterial being, variously called "soul," "self," or "subject" at different historical moments. That soul, the part that wields our voices, has depths that various kinds of soul-doctors, from psychologists to poets, must plumb, but its relationship with the material world has always been in question.

The works discussed in this book—medieval allegories that explore the relationship between the body and the soul—explore a kind of self whose very capacity for thought depends on placing these two hard-to-reconcile aspects of personhood into dialogue. In order to have such a dialogue, these works grant the Body a voice, while

---

1. Marcia Lee Anderson, *What Time Is It? And Other Poems* (Memphis, TN: Stafford Books, 1997), 30, lines 37–45. Further citations are parenthetical, with line numbers.

granting the Soul embodiment. The resulting dialogue is anything but harmonious: the self, as described in debates between the Body and the Soul, is often divided and self-critical to the point of beratement, as when the Soul lambastes the Body for indulging its appetites—a standard trope repeated in every poem in this tradition. Medieval Body/Soul debates ask questions about the origins of, location of, and preventive measures against sin, understood as the most significant disease from which a self could suffer. These works explore as well how the workings of power produce, prohibit, and delimit the possible manifestations of personhood.

Continuation of the medieval tradition of debates between the Body and the Soul was scattered after the Middle Ages: Andrew Marvell, W. B. Yeats, and Anne Bradstreet wrote much shorter versions of the debate, for instance. But, but among these few postmedieval examples, Marcia Lee Anderson's "Debate of the Body and the Soul: A.D. 1949" (this Introduction's epigraph) might best capture the nature of this relationship. In the poem, Body and Soul seem to share a squalid tenement. The Soul annoys the Body by playing "celestial" music until all hours. The sounds of the Body's "infernal plumbing" irritate the Soul and interrupt its attempts to meditate on spiritual matters. In the end, the Soul and the Body can agree only on moving out and finding their own homes apart from one another, homes described in terms that clearly show them to be, respectively, heaven and a grave. In other words, the nature of their conflict has so exhausted these two beings inhabiting the same space that this Body and this Soul can agree only on desiring death. The main difference between this modern poem and the medieval works it imitates lies precisely there. Anderson situates the two as living together, however unhappily: "Soul: I loathe this tenement. Such a façade / must have had a union architect. / It can't have been God" (Anderson, lines 1–3), whereas medieval authors imagined Soul and Body as possessing the capacity or desire to dialogue only after death has separated them.

Medieval debates between the Body and the Soul do not really belong to any doctrine or school. Instead, they seem to rely on some notion of common sense to produce persuasive didactic approaches to the self. This book inquires into what passes for psychological common sense in these medieval works, and into the ways received ideas are systematized in them, for isn't querying what it is that passes for common sense the very essence of contemporary cultural studies? Such allegories as the Middle English and Latin debates between Body and Soul, the Katherine Group's "Sawles Warde," and *Piers Plowman* take on philosophically and theologically abstruse topics such as the relationship between the soul and the body as if a good dose of common sense could really explain everything about materiality, discipline, and sin. Debates between the body and the soul and allegories like them dramatize the workings of the self through personification allegory, creating dynamic narratives where rather static concepts had been. In such debates, the body is literally *against* the soul, meaning both that the two are pitted against one another and that they are figuratively placed side by side, as partners inexorably bound together, either by ties of love or shackles of obligation (and often, in these poems, both).

Body/Soul debates stage the intertwined philosophical, theological, and psychological topics of human nature as a personal relationship, acting out the quotidian medieval struggle of mastering one's appetites or organizing one's sins for purposes of thorough confession. In their own contexts, such debates offer homely, commonsensical scenarios, all the better to render natural and inevitable the relationships of power and mutual contention within the self that they describe and, by describing, create. In these debates, allegory works as a privileged mode for thinking about power and hierarchy in the Middle Ages. For instance, in the thirteenth-century "Als I Lay in a Winteris Nyt," the most popular of the Middle English Body/Soul debates, Soul and Body bicker over why they occasionally missed church when they were living and united.[2] The Soul claims that it was trapped inside the Body and carried off to go hunting by its brute force. In its defense, the Body claims just the opposite, that it could not manage the smallest sound or movement without the

---

2. The debates that are considered to constitute the medieval English Body/Soul debate canon consist of eleven disparate versions that appear in twenty-seven different manuscript renditions. The taxonomic imagination of Francis Lee Utley, whose chapter "Dialogues, Debates, and Catechisms," in A. E. Hartung's *A Manual of the Writings in Middle English*, Vol. 3 (Hamden, CT: Connecticut Academy of Arts and Sciences, 1972), 669–745, helped confine the dialogues discussed within the boundaries that have kept debate poems apart from other forms of literature, linking them with the sermon tradition to which they are certainly related, topically as well as thematically. Utley devotes an entire section to Body/Soul debate, and his organization of the dialogues in chronological order lends an air of genealogical science to the traditional approach that reified them as an ever-improving subgenre, which includes a total of thirteen dialogues (he includes both Old English and Middle English), all ascending toward "Als I Lay in a Winteris Nyt," the poem I discuss in chapter 3. There are two Body/Soul debates in Anglo-Saxon—"Soul and Body I" from the Vercelli Book and "Soul and Body II" in the Exeter Book—along with some fragments from Worcester Cathedral. These, however, tend to be considered as part of the Anglo-Saxon canon and are not included in the few extant discussions of Middle English Body/Soul debates except as evidence of the topic's ubiquity. The "Body/Soul" tradition usually identified in Middle English poetry includes the 23-line Early Middle English "The Grave"; an address by the Soul to the Body (with the Body lying mute) known by its first lines as "Nou is mon hol and soint"; the two poems considered in the following two chapters; and the fifteenth-century "A Disputation Between the Body and the Worms," which, though not strictly a Body/Soul debate, seems to derive from that genre and is included, accordingly, in the Body/Soul debate section of John Conlee's *Middle English Debate Poetry: A Critical Anthology* (East Lansing, MI: Colleagues Press, 1993). In addition, there are a few fifteenth-century works, including a Body/Soul debate in the Porkington Ms. and both a prose disputation and a debate between the Body and the Worms in BL Addit. 37049. It might be remarked that only the two poems considered in chapters 2 and 3 are properly "debates" between Soul and Body, since only in these two does the Body "talk back" to the Soul.

Soul's help. The persistent question is about who has the power within the self, and, secondarily, about the nature and ethics of the relationship between its aspects. There is no resolution to this disagreement, only the inevitability of punishment, since both the Body and the Soul of the dead knight described in "Als I Lay" had refused to confess and repent in life. The sheer literalness of Body/Soul debates reduces the dualistic thinking that structured Enlightenment rationalism to the level of a sock-puppet farce, akin to a Punch and Judy show put on by a squabbling conjoined pair.

In modern times, the dualistic tendency to divide the soul (later "mind") from the body and to establish a hierarchy wherein the latter is deceptive and only the former has access to eternal truths has been called Cartesian. In studying medieval texts, one encounters a version of this dualism centuries before Descartes, but these categories are less rigid and self-evident, perhaps even playful. Of course, dualisms of different sorts existed in the Middle Ages: for instance, one form of it appeared in such revered texts as Romans 7:14–18, "I am of the flesh, sold into slavery under sin . . . nothing good dwells within me, that is, in my flesh . . . ."[3] In any translation, the grammar of Paul's sentence implies that "I" am a being distinct from but implicated in "my" own body; in his Letter to the Galatians, Paul enjoins Christ's followers to choose spirit over flesh, stating, "what the Spirit desires is opposed to the flesh; for those are opposed to each other, to prevent you from doing what you want" (Gal. 5:17–26). However important this dualism proved to be, another dualism, Gnosticism, which viewed the material world to be evil, was considered a heresy and persecuted; a number of later medieval heresies shared in this antimaterialist bias. The authors of Body/Soul debates seem to have kept the multiple dualisms in mind, blaming some evils on bodily appetites but carefully avoiding an outright condemnation of all flesh.

This dualist understanding of the self insists on the dueling nature of its components; thus, if medieval writers define the self as a soul yoked to a body, their interaction must be dramatized as conflict. As medieval thinkers imagined—and in so doing worked to discipline the possibilities for—the "self," allegory took up the function of organizing the conflicted relationship between bodies and souls. In other words, the allegories discussed in this book envision the self as divided into component parts and examine those parts and how they come together, at times characterizing their union as a kind of violence done to both. Despite the yoking of incongruous powers that it describes by positing the self through its parts, the psychological allegory of Body/Soul debate at times claims a retrospective vision of a whole being, an integrated

---

3. All citations from the New Testament are from the New Revised Standard Version Bible (NRSV) in the edition *The New Testament and Other Early Christian Writings: A Reader*, 2nd ed., ed. Bart D. Ehrman (Oxford: Oxford University Press, 2004).

self that may never have existed before its component parts were examined in this way.

In this book, I claim that at least some medieval allegories produce and express an immanent psychological theory, and that it is precisely the allegorical mode that enables a kind of flexible theorizing of the self that formal treatises cannot offer. What critics call, and teachers teach as, the genre of medieval allegory is not really a genre consistently concerned with obscure meanings, despite the fact that most writing about allegory assumes its figurative or hidden meaning is what matters.[4] The influential Latin allegories of the Middle Ages give flesh to various ideas and ideals, turning them into personified speakers, and dramatizing their actions to demonstrate a moral meaning or a theory about the world: If a personified speaker "wins" (most literally, in the pitched battle of Prudentius' *Psychomachia*, discussed in chapter 1), the idea that he or she personifies wins as well. This aspect of allegory is quite correctly understood as a function of allegory-as-personification and characterized by a trope that might or might not constitute a subsection of allegory—*prosopopeia*, a concept discussed in chapter 3.[5] As examples of this kind of medieval allegory, Body/Soul debates do not point to a hidden meaning. The Body in the debate represents all bodies and an individual's body at the same time, and also points toward sinners who may prioritize their bodily needs over the needs of the soul—honoring, in the author's opinion, the wrong part of the self. In some of the Latin and Anglo-Norman allegorical debates discussed in this book, this moral message is dramatized through gender difference: If Soul and Body are male and female, it becomes clear which of the two is meant to be in the wrong. In others, primarily in the Middle English tradition that includes "Als I Lay," the absence of gendered hierarchy itself becomes a marked issue, complicating any attempt to adjudicate between Soul and Body. The much better-known and more complex fourteenth-century work *Piers Plowman* brings these traditions together, making use of both ways to dramatize relationships between personifications over the course of its long narrative of self-seeking and soul-mending—what at least one scribe, in copying the Vernon manuscript, termed *sowlehele*.

4. Allegory, defined as extended metaphor or as something that means something other than what it says, is at least as old as the *Rhetorica ad Herennium*. "Allegory is a manner of speech denoting one thing by the letter of the words, but another by their meaning" ("Permutatio est oratio aliud verbis aliud sententi demonstrans") in Loeb Classical Library, trans. Harry Caplan (Cambridge, MA: Harvard University Press, 1954), 344–45. See Appendix I, "On the History of the Term 'Allegory,'" and Appendix II, "On the History of the Term 'Personification,'" in Jon Whitman's *Allegory: The Dynamics of An Ancient and Medieval Technique* (Cambridge, MA: Harvard University Press, 1987), 269–72.

5. For a study that focuses on precisely this aspect of allegory, reorganizing previous understandings of "allegory" as genre, see James J. Paxson, *The Poetics of Personification* (Cambridge, UK: Cambridge University Press, 1994).

Debates that literally pit body and soul against one another exist in a number of languages and are a useful index of regional and period differences in medieval allegorical writing, but they seem to have been particularly popular in England.[6] Middle English Body/Soul debates appeared in many kinds of manuscript contexts, from the small miscellany apparently compiled by John Norwood circa 1400 for his own personal use, to the Vernon and Simeon manuscripts, vast works that described themselves as devoted to *sowlehele*.[7] These debates were relatively short, and therefore comparatively simple, works, but they attempted to query, in a mostly systematic and certainly thoughtful manner, how the divisions of the self functioned.[8]

This book argues that allegorical personifications, particularly those of the soul and the body, participate in a narrative mode of doing psychology in the Middle Ages, anatomizing the self in a way that explicitly genders relationships between the self's different aspects. While this tradition can be traced back to the warring personified virtues and vices of Prudentius' *Psychomachia*, some of its richest examples come from didactic Middle English writings of the thirteenth and fourteenth centuries. I call these psychological narratives *sowlehele*, a Middle English term used here to describe a medieval phenomenon, which is discussed in detail in the next section. Works of *sowlehele* construct a notion of the self by dramatizing the relationships between its personified parts. In this book, I trace how works of this kind written in Middle English, a language

---

6. Theodore Batiouchkoff claimed that versions of the Body/Soul debate survive in Old and Middle English, Latin, Greek, French, Provençal-Catalan, Italian, Czech, "White Russian," Polish, Armenian, and Syriac, with prose exemplars in Latin, Old Norwegian, Old Icelandic, Old Castilian, and Hungarian, and that such debates probably originated in Egypt during the second millennium. See his "Le Débat de l'âme et du corps," *Romania* 20 (1891): 1–55; 513–78. Thomas Wright, in his *The Latin Poems Commonly Attributed to Walter Mapes* (London: Camden Society, 1841), lists Latin, Anglo-Norman, English, Greek, Provençal, French, German, "Netherlandish," Spanish, Italian, and Danish versions in the notes to his edition of the "Dialogus inter Corpus et Animam," which is discussed in chapters 1 and 3 under the title "Visio Philiberti."

7. The first was edited by Nita Scudder Baugh as *A Worcestershire Miscellany, Compiled by John Northwood, c. 1400. Edited from British Museum Ms. Add. 37, 787* (Philadelphia, 1956); the latter is one of the most studied medieval manuscripts and weighs at least fifty pounds. Yet the two have no fewer than twenty of the same pieces (poems, etc.) in common, almost all of them in Middle English. This is particularly noteworthy since BL Additional 37787, the small handbook, contains only twenty pieces in English and shares fifteen of those with the Vernon. Some of the works contained in the Vernon were edited as *The Minor Poems of the Vernon Manuscript* (London: Kegan Paul, Trench, Trübner & Co. for the Early English Text Society, 1892–1901), 37 and *passim*.

8. See the taxonomy by Francis Lee Utley, in "Dialogues, Debates, and Catechisms," in Hartung, *Manual of the Writings in Middle English*. Having divided the category "Religious and Didactic Dialogues" into (I) Supernatural Figures and (II) Abstractions, he finds thirteen dialogues (he includes both Old English and Middle English) under the general rubric "Death" and the specific rubric "The Debate Between the Body and the Soul."

that does not gender abstract nouns as male or female, were particularly free to experiment with allegorical gender in expressing tensions within the self, and therefore produced a unique kind of psychological thought.

Why does gender turn out to be central to this discussion of the psychological personifications of the self's parts? Because it is important—perhaps surprisingly so—to the authors of these allegories, particularly when they were dramatizing hierarchies within the self.[9] As an abstract concept, "the body" is neuter, but when it is personified, "Body" ceases to be an "it" and becomes a "he" or a "she." Functioning as a person means being designated as one or the other.[10] Much as in the interpellating moment when the doctor tells the newborn's parents "it's a girl," when an abstraction begins to speak in a medieval allegory it is immediately sexed, speaking *as* a female or *as* a male being.[11] The sort of narrative allegory that stages disagreements between abstractions is an excellent vehicle for enacting and reinforcing the realities of hierarchy, and assigning gender to allegorical persons becomes a virtue when it helps clarify relationships between concepts. But gendering abstract concepts female results in all kinds of problems within these allegories. From the authors' medieval perspective, populating the innermost self of men as well as women with female beings was a problem; so, too, extending the metaphor of Body and Soul as a married couple meant straying into the vexed realm of marital sexuality. *Sowlehele* allegory thus comes to figure an anxiety about conceptualizing aspects of the self and placing them in relation to one another.

In "Gender and Personification in *Piers Plowman*," Helen Cooper describes the situation of medieval personification allegory: Countless medieval allegories seem to have used female personifications to embody major

9. At the conclusion of Paxson's *Poetics of Personification*, he goes over several answers to the simple question: Why are so many allegorical personifications gendered female? Without solving the mystery, he nevertheless brings his own study to a close by suggesting further inquiry into the matter: "Personification, understood according to such a feminist program of critical analysis, might perhaps turn out to be at the figural heart of cultural issues regarding representations of sexuality and gender" (174). Such statements as these underlie the necessity for the present study.

10. While this could be substantiated by reference to the past few decades' work on the cultural abjection of nonconforming persons, at least some literary critics see this in looking at medieval allegory: "the very process of personification, of making into a person, invites that person to be imagined in human and therefore gender-specific terms, to be given actions and attributes appropriate to a woman, or, as most often in Langland, a man." Helen Cooper, "Gender and Personification in *Piers Plowman*," *Yearbook of Langland Studies* 5 (1991): 31–48, 34.

11. Louis Althusser, "Ideology and Ideological State Apparatuses (Notes Towards an Investigation)," in *Lenin and Philosophy*, trans. Ben Brewster (London: New Left Books, 1971). See also Judith Butler, *Excitable Speech: A Politics of the Performative* (New York: Routledge, 1997), for discussions of how the theory of the speech act can be read with Althusserian interpellation: Being named as something can be being made to *be* something, and of course performative speech acts can be understood as exceeding the limits of verbal speech.

concepts because most abstract nouns in Latin and the Romance languages are gendered as feminine. When English lost the gender structure that had characterized Anglo-Saxon, "for the first time in the history of Western culture, personification allegory was able to define the nature of the human form its concepts might take without grammatical constraint."[12] This study traces some of the effects of this freedom on the psychological work done by Middle English allegory, starting with the Latin- and Romance-language context, and proceeding through a number of thirteenth-century English allegories that made use of the lack of grammatical constraint Cooper describes, before returning to Cooper's analysis of *Piers Plowman* and a reexamination of its relationship to gender and the nature of the self.

Analyzing debates between the Body and the Soul and other allegories that participate in that tradition helps us define what was meant by "the soul" in the Middle Ages and understand it in relation (specifically, with "the body") rather than in isolation. To account for the soul as a full participant in the body-soul pairing brings up the issue of the self's composite nature. Such an accounting frames a relationship between parts of the person rather than isolating and, at times, idealizing the body in its inscrutability, as if it were possible to posit pure materiality as an object of study. Instead, I look at the idea of the self at a particular time and place, focusing on a specific tradition that was popular in England during the thirteenth and fourteenth centuries, in order to query how the self was being gendered, divided, and dramatized, to what ends and with what implications. Examining the medieval version of body/soul dualism promises to put the soul back where it belongs, into "body studies."[13]

Middle English allegory theorizing relationships between souls and bodies participates in the construction of a discourse about the workings of the person. I examine this range of discourses as a branch of medieval psychology that is a background neither to the modern self nor to contemporary disciplines of the self such as psychoanalysis and that does not fit comfortably within Latin philosophical and theological writings. Such an approach offers a return to the question of the self with a new twist, neither presenting a prehistory of that vague entity "the subject" nor describing the uncontested dominance of Latin clerical thought over all of medieval culture. Instead, it explores the varied and fertile literary and cultural development that I term *sowlehele*.

12. Cooper, 33.
13. What I call body studies was a wide-ranging field of study in the 1980s and 1990s: In medieval studies, it, and my work on the body, owes the greatest debt to the writings of Caroline Walker Bynum, particularly the essays collected in *Fragmentation and Redemption: Essays on Gender and the Human Body in Medieval Religion* (Cambridge, MA: MIT Press, Zone Books, 1992), and the volume *The Resurrection of the Body in Western Christianity, 200–1336* (New York: Columbia University Press 1995).

Introducing *Sowlehele*

In his index to the manuscript, one of the scribes who copied out the famous Vernon manuscript names this compilation "*Salus Anime* or *Sowlehele*." This study takes up the Middle English part of this term to account for certain uniquely medieval ways of describing and acting on the self. *Sowlehele* is a mode of didactic writing that makes use of allegorical narrative to educate sinners about the nature of their own sinning selves. Works of *sowlehele* anatomize the self—dividing it, naming its parts, and placing those parts in dialogue with one another. This term was regularly used in the Middle Ages, although not always to describe the writings considered works of *sowlehele*.[14] Present-day critics often understand *sowlehele* in terms of a hybrid of medical and pastoral uses, as a sort of figurative medicine; for instance, in an article about devotional poetry, Susanna Fein writes that "in reading this poem of 'sowlehele,' we swallow the medicine, and each time we reread the poem meditatively, discovering more of its embedded meaning, we increase the dosage and improve its effect."[15] The Vernon manuscript, which has the term *sowlehele* in its title, contains a range of works that have variously been understood as a collection intended for a monastic community, for novices, and for religious women. It contains many short devotional works, saints' lives, a number of debate poems, and several long works, including the "Northern

---

14. The *Middle English Dictionary* defines the word as meaning: "(a) Spiritual well-being; the health of the soul; the good of the soul; (b) healing of the soul, salvation; ben releved of ~, to be healed spiritually; (c) that which brings health to the soul; also, one who brings salvation; (d) pastoral care, cure of souls; (e) in oath and pious exclamation." In the MED, the first use of the word, in its meaning of "spiritual well-being," spelled "soule-hele or swolehele," is in a homily that appears in Vespasian D. XIV, published as *Early English Homilies from the Twelfth Century Ms. Vesp. D. XIV.*, ed. R. D-N. Warner, EETS 152. 1917 (New York: Kraus Reprint Co., 1971). An alternate spelling receives its own entry: *Soule-heil* is defined as "(a) The good of the soul; (b) healing of the soul, salvation," with its first use in a manuscript of an A-Text of *Piers Plowman*, "I haue walkid wel wide in wet & in dri3e and sou3t goode seintes for my soule hele." Dublin, Trinity College 213 (D.4.12) 6:19. Obviously, the word bears a relation to the Latin "cura animarum," but, like so many theological terms in vernacular translation, it takes on a life and a meaning of its own.

15. Fein describes the reading process in this way: "This poetry was not merely to be read (as we might be prone to think of reading as a simple straight-once-through process), but rather consumed in a metaphysical sense, so that it might bring "sowlehele" to the devout, penitent user. One needs to picture the meditant man or woman retreating regularly to a private spot, reading a text through many times over an extended period, quite likely committing it to memory, and pausing over its words and verbalized images to make connections, find patterns, discover signs and meanings, participate with compassion in its depiction of holy suffering, and absorb its objectified shape, that is, what it becomes when perceived whole rather than as a series of discrete signifiers" ("Herbs, Birds, and Cryptic Words for English Devotional Readers," *Essays in Medieval Studies* 15 [1998]: 35–44).

Homily Cycle," and an A-text of *Piers Plowman,* all of which lend themselves to meditative reading for the soul's benefit.[16]

Using the term *sowlehele* has the benefit of allowing us to think in medieval terms about psychology. After all, psychology claims to study the psyche, whereas *sowlehele* claims to heal the soul, a difference between studying an object and acting on it. The medieval term focuses on the performative aspect of works like the Body/Soul debates; works of *sowlehele* enact and produce the very thing they describe. All the works discussed in this study can be put in this category, whether they were written in Latin, French, or English, but the Englishness of the term privileges, as does this study, the Middle English tradition. The implicit audience for works of *sowlehele* consists of laypeople and the clergy that minister to laypeople. This is not a type of writing confined to the university or the monastery, but neither is it a set of "folk" theories about the self. It is popular in that it is intended *for* the people, but not necessarily *by* or *from* them. Works of *sowlehele* cross the artificially constructed boundary between the academic discipline of psychology and the cultural studies of quotidian understandings of the self. Moderns might recognize aspects of what we now call self-help in these works, although this study discusses works that might be called "literary" in a way that few modern self-help books aspire to be.

The term *sowlehele* describes works that produce a performative, didactic, and pastoral discourse aimed at explaining the self to itself. The discourse is performative in that it enacts the very relations it describes; it is didactic in that its overt intention is a pedagogical one; and it is pastoral, particularly in its thirteenth- and fourteenth-century manifestation, in that this discourse is intimately implicated in the work of confession. These three characteristics of *sowlehele* are sometimes subverted by two factors. First, as manifested in medieval personification allegory, *sowlehele* is a gendered discourse, one haunted by the possibilities of sexuality, whether it be manifested as courtly love, marriage, or, surprisingly, depictions of same-sex bonds. Gender and sexuality are everywhere and nowhere in the poems discussed in this book. The gendering of personifications is essential for positing hierarchy and describing the love and hate of the self for itself, but it often proves problematic for the didactic project being enacted in these poems. Second, the dramatic narrative drive of these works also sometimes seems to subvert the didactic and pastoral purposes. These poems are not sermons, after all. They enact an unfolding story, whose events may at any moment distract from the message or even overturn

---

16. For a detailed overview of the manuscript and its criticism, see J. Robert Duncan, "The Textual Context of the Vernon Manuscript" (PhD diss., University of Saskatchewan, 2000) and the collection of essays edited by Derek Pearsall as *Studies in the Vernon Manuscript* (Cambridge, UK: D. S. Brewer), 1990.

it, as when a reader might sympathize with the Body's arguments for its innocence and not move forward into the ultimate condemnation the poem suggests.

Using the term *sowlehele* gestures toward the concerns this book has in common with the new approaches to lay devotion that have so enlivened medieval studies over the past decades, yet shows how it approaches a somewhat different object of study: the relationship of the self to itself in the Middle Ages.[17] Works of *sowlehele* proliferated particularly in the wake of the decision to require annual confession of all practicing Christians. The Fourth Lateran Council of 1215 instituted a new requirement, generally known by its *incipit* as *Omnis utriusque sexus*. Each and every baptized Christian who hoped for heaven had to confess his or her sins at least once a year, a practice that had previously been reserved for the privileged few and for particularly spectacular sinners.[18] Confession as a practice antedated this historical moment, but the decision in 1215 anchored confession in time (as part of the annual cycle of the church year) and diffused it across all ranks. Numerous new texts were needed to aid in the organization and thinking of confession, texts written for priests and for literate laypersons in a number of modes. Laymen and women, specifically, needed guidance for the very important process of *preparation* for

---

17. See Jim Rhodes, *Poetry Does Theology: Chaucer, Grosseteste, and the Pearl-Poet* (Notre Dame, IN: University of Notre Dame Press, 2001), for a succinct summary of developments in the relationship lay populations and poets had to the significant theological debates of the fourteenth century, in the context of a study that never reduces poetry to a mere symptom of culture.

18. "All the faithful of both sexes shall after they have reached the age of discretion faithfully confess all their sins at least once a year to their own (parish) priest and perform to the best of their ability the penance imposed, receiving reverently at least at Easter the sacrament of the Eucharist, unless perchance at the advice of their own priest they may for a good reason abstain for a time from its reception; otherwise they shall be cut off from the Church (excommunicated) during life and deprived of Christian burial in death. Wherefore, let this salutary decree be published frequently in the churches, that no one may find in the plea of ignorance a shadow of excuse. But if anyone for a good reason should wish to confess his sins to another priest, let him first seek and obtain permission from his own (parish) priest, since otherwise he (the other priest) cannot loose or bind him. Let the priest be discreet and cautious that he may pour wine and oil into the wounds of the one injured after the manner of a skilful physician, carefully inquiring into the circumstances of the sinner and the sin, from the nature of which he may understand what kind of advice to give and what remedy to apply, making use of different experiments to heal the sick one. But let him exercise the greatest precaution that he does not in any degree by word, sign, or any other manner make known the sinner, but should he need more prudent counsel, let him seek it cautiously without any mention of the person. He who dares to reveal a sin confided to him in the tribunal of penance, we decree that he be not only deposed from the sacerdotal office but also relegated to a monastery of strict observance to do penance for the remainder of his life" (H. Schroeder, *Disciplinary Decrees of the General Councils: Text, Translation and Commentary* [St. Louis: B. Herder, 1937], 236–96; also in *The Medieval Sourcebook: Twelfth Ecumenical Council: Lateran IV 1215*. (http://www.fordham.edu/halsall/basis/lateran4.html).

confession: the organization of a coherent narrative about a life characterized by sin. Such texts included popular manuals and guides to sin and the self; they also included works of literature concerned with the nature of the self and how it became entangled in the web of sin in the first place. These provided an alternative psychological discourse to layfolk as well as to those priests who labored far from the dizzying heights of medieval theology.

Everyday people needed tools and models to help frame their own confessions and to help them think narratively about their own selves. Works of *sowlehele* were distinct in their practical transformation of academic philosophical, theological, and medical theories into narratives, in their emphasis on applicability, and, because they relied on personification allegory to understand the self, their dynamic use of character to advance plot. Jerry Root has argued that "confessional practice made widely available a technical language and an institutional apparatus dedicated to individual salvation. Together the technical language of confession and its institutional backdrop constituted a new cultural construction of the self."[19] My contribution concentrates on the specifics of this process as they are expressed in a particular poetic mode, that of allegories that stage debates between aspects of the self—a mode suited to discussing the embodied self and also to using the rhetorical and philosophical resources that are becoming available in Middle English.

As this book will argue, some specific aspects of English grammar—particularly its gender neutrality—make a real difference to the kind of allegorical disputation being written in the thirteenth and fourteenth centuries. Some English authors took advantage of the freedom afforded by not having most abstract nouns already gendered female, as they are in Latin and in most European vernaculars, to transform the tradition of populating the self with female allegorical figures. This made English-language allegories about the self distinctive and interesting, but that specificity does not render the kind of psychology being discussed in this book an exclusively English psychology. Just as in many medieval manuscripts Latin-language, French, Anglo-French, and Middle English texts were not rigidly segregated, there is no clear and distinct line one can draw to claim that only texts not written in Latin are capable of doing a certain sort of work.

What this book describes is a new twist on something that literary critics since (at least) Charles Muscatine's 1953 essay "The Emergence of Psychological Allegory in Old French Romance" have termed *psychological allegory*.[20] Muscatine's article makes its claim about the psychological allegory of the

---

19. Jerry Root, "*Space to Speke*": *The Confessional Subject in Medieval Literature* (New York: Peter Lang Publishing, 1997), 1.

20. See Charles Muscatine, "The Emergence of Psychological Allegory in Old French Romance," *PMLA* 68 (Dec. 1953): 1160–82.

Roman de la Rose. Closer to the Middle English corpus discussed in most of this study, Robert Ackerman's 1962 examination of "Als I Lay," the most popular Body/Soul debate, makes repeated use of the term *psychological realism*, which may derive from Muscatine's examination of psychology in allegory. More recently, Elizabeth Robertson's 1990 study of the Katherine Group also relies on the concept of *psychological realism*, specifically defined by Robertson as a quality of "texts [that] detail the circumstances of the everyday life of a specific audience, anchoresses, in order to explore the psychological conflicts inherent in that life."[21] There are others, of course, but these critics use such terms about works that will be discussed in subsequent chapters of this book. Like the literal dualism personified in the Body/Soul debates it examines, my study literalizes a conventional claim: that some medieval allegories are psychologically realistic. By literalizing it, I permit it to become the object of detailed examination. Body/Soul debates make literal the combination of contentiousness and connection implied by the conventions of how body/soul dualism is usually discussed, by staging a debate between the two. Considering these debates as works of *sowlehele* does not force them to exemplify a systematic philosophical or psychological approach, but permits them to function, perfomatively, as a significant way to theorize the self—an alternative to Aristotle, Galen, and theological debates and treatises about the soul.

In taking the psychology of allegory seriously, my study is vastly indebted to scholars such as Muscatine, Ackerman, Angus Fletcher, C. S. Lewis, and Michel Zink, as well as to Robertson and many others. At the same time, it attempts to refocus the "allegory as psychology" question on the specifics of confessional culture's approach to body, soul, and will. Additionally, this study strives to avoid treating the kind of psychology done by the allegories under discussion as realistic representations of how medieval persons actually thought, focusing instead on the ways in which psychological allegory prescribes and performs norms rather than describes persons.

A tension between contending forces such as soul against body is something that allegorical disputation captures particularly well. Such tension is also a central feature of almost any psychology, from Aristotelian faculties to Freudian ego, id, and superego.[22] Angus Fletcher's introduction to his influ-

21. Elizabeth Robertson, *Early English Devotional Prose and the Female Audience* (Knoxville: University of Tennessee Press, 1990), 3 and *passim*. See also Robert Ackerman, "The Debate of the Body and the Soul and Parochial Christianity," *Speculum* 37 (1962): 541–56.

22. Barbara Newman, as part of a discussion of "allegorical goddesses" that is crucial to this book's first chapter, writes that "it is a rare psychological theory that can dispense with personification figures. Psychologists of the most diverse schools, from Prudentius onward, have attempted to clarify inner conflicts by representing them as struggles for dominance among competing forces within the psyche." Newman, *God and the Goddesses* (Philadelphia: University of Pennsylvania Press, 2004), 43.

ential study *Allegory: The Theory of a Symbolic Mode*—in which he imagines allegorical personifications as something akin to obsessive-compulsives compelled to enact certain traits—claims that "we live in an age of psychological and psychoanalytic speculation, and we need to return periodically to earlier stages of that speculation, where perhaps we can find the starting point for both our more profitable and our more dubious explorings."[23] This project takes up Fletcher's challenge and extends it to a consideration of the psychology of gender in the allegorical representation of soul/body dualism.[24] Without making strong claims about how medieval persons actually lived their lives and thought about their selves, I attempt to trace how they were *instructed* to think about themselves, asking after the psychological norms and categories available to those ultimately unknowable medieval persons.

The representations of the self available to medieval thinkers were largely based on models developed in ancient Greece and, as such, could not account for some of the problems posed by medieval Christianity. The other major source for psychological thinking was, of course, the Bible. The Pauline letters in particular had a vast and complex influence (of course, these were also inflected by Paul's wide education in Platonic and neo-Platonic thought), but were never crystal clear about the nature of the self, generally using personal relations as metaphor for relationships between self and God or Christ and Church. Among the influential pagan psychologies, the most important is Aristotelian faculty psychology. This psychology names aspects of the self in terms of their activities: the term *faculty* is based on the Latin *facere*, "to do." Although the aspects of the self that are described vary with different commentators and with later medieval revisions, what the different faculties generally "do" is cause the body to remain alive (the "vegetative" faculty), to desire and to do good (the "appetitive" faculty), to perceive external stimuli (the faculty of sense perception), or to move the body (the "locomotive" faculty). This division of the parts of the self into forces capable of action undergirds much of how we comprehend medieval psychology.

23. Angus Fletcher, *Allegory: The Theory of a Symbolic Mode* (Ithaca, NY: Cornell University Press, 1964), 13–14.
24. Psychoanalytic theory examines depictions of the mind, not that religious remnant, "the soul," even if the Greek word *psyche* remains the discipline's name. It's possible to read the Body/Soul debate as a straightforward precursor to Freud. The expression of hysterical symptoms like psychosomatic illness could be understood as the scientific equivalents of the Body's speech in the debates, and the Soul's tutelary position could be understood as somehow similar to the complex, transferentially implicated position of the therapist vis-à-vis the patient. Instead, I argue that similarly schematic, similarly therapeutic, but actually quite different systems existed in the Middle Ages for organizing and helping the soul, the body, the self in the journey through life. This book asks after those systems, to the extent possible from the contemporary vantage point, in their own terms rather than in ours, a project already underway when Angus Fletcher posited the similarity between allegory and psychoanalysis in 1964.

Aristotle wrote about the relationship of the body and the soul in complex and contradictory ways. In *The Politics,* he famously wrote that women should be ruled by men: "it is clear that the rule of the soul over the body, and of the mind and the rational element over the passionate, is natural and expedient . . . again, the male is by nature superior, and the female inferior; this principle, of necessity, extends to all mankind . . . the one rules, and the other is ruled. . . . The courage of a man is shown in commanding, of a woman in obeying."[25] However, his most important work on body and soul, the *De Anima* (a work on which many medieval philosophers wrote commentaries, and quoted in their own arguments about the soul) made a complex claim: "that, therefore, the soul or certain parts of it, if it is divisible, cannot be separated from the body is quite clear. . . . Not that anything prevents at any rate some parts from being separable. . . . [I]t is not clear whether the soul is the actuality of the body in the way that the sailor is of the ship."[26] In other words, according to Aristotle, body and soul are *not* separable—except when they are. We might want to look at the results of these words, since the statements themselves are so confusing. Aristotelian theory, as understood in the Middle Ages, certainly seemed to see the body as a valid source of knowledge, but perhaps one that could be separated at some moments from the soul—an idea supported by Paul's statements about the flesh, in the aforementioned passages in his letters to the Romans, Galatians, and Ephesians.

Perhaps it was precisely the lack of clarity in Aristotle's statement, and even in his sailor/ship analogy (which appears in the twelfth-century Latin Body/Soul debate discussed in chapter 1, the "Visio Philiberti," and is also discussed in chapter 2 as part of a more extensive engagement with medieval philosophy), that made Body/Soul debate poems so important in the Middle Ages. After all, faculty psychology as imagined by Aristotle and reimagined by his medieval followers subdivides the soul or mind into faculties—even including some that pertain to bodily appetites—but never explains which part of the self is immortal. As a consequence, Aristotelian psychology fails to address the most urgent questions that Christians might want to pose in confession, questions that medieval persons, especially laypeople, might need answers to in order to construct a workable psychology: an understanding of the self that would be in line with the rest of Christian doctrine.

A second major theory at work in the Middle Ages was the medical model of the self, derived from Galen and his many academic followers or would-be followers. This is a largely physical model, with roots in the Stoic philosophical

25. Aristotle, *The Politics*, trans. Stephen Iverson (Cambridge, UK: Cambridge University Press, 1988), 7, 16.
26. Aristotle, *Aristotle's De Anima Books II, III*, trans. D. W. Hamlyn (Oxford, UK: Clarendon Press, 1968), at 413A3.

writings that claimed the soul was an imperceptible substance extant in every member of the body—that the soul was, in fact, a "mixing" of the body's humors.[27] Humoral theory is an ancient Greek medical view that described the body as a balance of four substances (blood, phlegm, yellow bile, and black bile). When these substances were out of balance, the body was ill. Medieval and early Renaissance medicine explained many problems and described the human personality in terms of the humors (melancholy was caused by an excess of black bile, and so on), although it is unclear how these bodily fluids could combine to form, or even strongly influence, the putatively immortal soul, sent from Heaven and only briefly inhabiting the body.

Humoral theory's skepticism about the metaphysical, though useful in some aspects of medieval medicine, did not respond to the fundamentally theological questions posed by seeing "the flesh" as one of the three great temptations, along with "the world" and "the devil." In other words, it is also too Greek for medieval Christianity. Some commentators found that it violated Aristotle's logic as well; because two (material) bodies could not occupy the same space at the same time, a material soul filling up a material body, though elegant and relatively practical, was an unsound proposition.[28] In a system fundamentally concerned with the search for salvation and the attempt to overcome sin, neither Aristotle nor Galen could offer a full account of the self's complex workings that would be satisfactory at the level of priest and parishioner. *Sowlehele* could not be accomplished by balancing the body's humors, but only by working on the memory in confession and the soul's control over the body in the renunciation of sin. Although these Greek thinkers were mediated for Christian culture by Cicero and then Augustine—and thence into the enormous trail of adaptations of his writings for all manner of purposes in Christian culture—they were still not suitable at the level of the everyday examination of one's own motives and actions necessary for the smooth functioning of a confessional culture.

A third major tradition of medieval psychology relates directly to the Aristotelian model, but with a Christian twist. This is Augustinian Trinitarianism,

---

27. See, for instance, "The Soul's Dependence on the Body," in Galen, *Selected Works*, ed. and trans. P. N. Singer (New York: Oxford University Press, 1997).

28. This account is largely derived from E. Ruth Harvey's *The Inward Wits: Psychological Theory in the Middle Ages and the Renaissance* (London: The Warburg Institute, 1975). According to Harvey, the history of medical descriptions of the soul (from the Stoics to Galen and on to Renaissance physicians) imagined it as a material element, composed of water or fire or blood. "However indispensable for the doctor, the material spirit was less satisfactory to the philosopher as a solution to the problem of the soul. It was argued that the soul must be in every part of the body imparting movement, life, and sensation to it; a material soul would then have to occupy exactly the same space as the body, which is impossible, for two bodies cannot occupy the same space at the same time" (31). Instead of a Stoic view of the soul, medieval theologians tended to adopt a post-Platonic one, which is strongly dualistic—the soul uses the body as a sort of "mortal dress" (32).

which divides the unified Trinity of God into memory, will, and understanding, and finds in the human mind a microcosm of this same unified trinity of capabilities. In works such as *On the Trinity,* Augustine produces a psychology out of his neo-Platonic theology, showing how, in order to reach God, the soul must learn about itself, for it is made in God's image. In some of his other writings, Augustine stages a highly personal accounting by the self of the circumstances and forces that have driven it to sin and, out of sin, toward redemption. Like *sowlehele* psychology, Augustinian Trinitarianism is a performative discourse that is at least sometimes (as in his *Confessions* and *Soliloquies*) produced in the form of a narrative. In essence, works of *sowlehele* democratize for general use that which Augustine performs as part of an exclusive, personal, and privileged relationship with God. This difference, however, is one that matters: The personal accounting of the *Confessions* proves unique in the history of medieval psychology, and not one that can be generalized to other writers. Trinitarianism proves too esoteric to be applicable to the pattern of sin and redemption in writings of pastoral care and lay instruction such as those that proliferated after the Fourth Lateran Council.[29]

Augustine and the long tradition following him adapted his teachings on Trinitarian faculty psychology to practical instances, but the closer to the needs of vernacular culture such traditions came, the less they retained their specific connections between human beings and the pattern of the divine Trinity.[30] The confessional tradition assumes that proper teaching precedes proper actions, and tends to proceed directly toward the particular and distinctive species of sins requiring understanding. That tradition, however, rarely suggests as directly as Augustine does that the individual penitent—especially the individual lay penitent—carries a model of the divine with her every thought, memory, and will.

29. See, for contrast, two works written before Lateran IV, Guibert of Nogent's *Monodiae,* a very odd imitation of Augustine that culminates in the history of the writer's abbey, and Abelard's *Historia Calamitatum,* which, for all its charm, delves none too deeply into the sources of sin.

30. Andrew Galloway, in his article "Intellectual Pregnancy, Metaphysical Femininity, and the Social Doctrine of the Trinity in *Piers Plowman,*" *The Yearbook of Langland Studies* 12 (1998): 117–52, makes a similar point; see 125. He also offers three "complexly overlapping spheres or cultural horizons of reception and dissemination of Augustine's Trinitarian ideas" (128), including that of academic commentators, Latin sermons on Trinity Sunday, and Middle English or Anglo-Norman homiletic materials and sermons. Particularly the third (but also the second) of these would have contributed to the body of texts that might be organized under the rubric of "*sowlehele.*" Interestingly, Galloway notes that the vernacular texts "usually treat the Trinity more cautiously and briefly, and (unsurprisingly) do not reproduce Augustine's most subtle psychological analogies" (131); indeed, *Piers Plowman* avoids making use of Trinitarianism for psychological purposes, because its author is more interested in examining "immediate social experience as well as social endeavor" (134). I cite this in support of my argument that, although Trinitarian psychology was clearly important in the Middle Ages, it did not necessarily reach the lay and the less-educated clerical audiences.

Each of these models—the Aristotelian, the Galenic, and the Augustinian—can account for the workings of the mind and certainly contain a place for emotion, or, to use the psychological term that distinguishes it from thought or action, *affect*. However, each of these models is very technical and complex, and the very proliferation of medieval works that did not make use of them may prove that they were ultimately more useful for theologians writing in Latin than for priests seeking to understand the souls of those they confessed. Partly in the course of transmitting such traditions to pastoral uses, and without always presenting rigid lines for its emergence, the Middle Ages could and did produce an alternative in works of *sowlehele*. Such works, rather than viewing all affect under the general rubric of the appetites, deal with the divisions within the self through a dramatic encounter between them. Works of *sowlehele* form an alternative, confession-oriented psychological mode to the more formal, Aristotelian-or-Augustinian mode, primarily written in Latin.

What makes the texts discussed in this book works of *sowlehele*, then, is that they served as part of the communication between priest and layperson—as part of a layperson's individual and private devotion, or a priest's search for models that might help communicate to parishioners—rather than as a discourse among members of the clerical class.[31] Body/Soul debates were being written for centuries before Lateran IV, but their popularity soared in the thirteenth century. My premise is that in the aftermath of Lateran IV, medieval Christians were faced with the formidable organizational task of making coherent narratives out of their lives.

This task was not immediately clear to all; it was almost fifty years later that the real proliferation of manuals intended to be helpful in the creation of these narratives began, and then there was no stopping them. The requirement to confess was a requirement on the memory, which—as Mary Carruthers's and Frances Yates's magisterial studies demonstrated some time ago—often relies on the vividness of imagery for its functioning.[32] The self and its sins had to be reified and organized into memorable categories. The categories proliferating out of the tradition of the French *Somme des Vices et des Vertus* (ca. 1279) by the Dominican friar Lorens d'Orléans, such as the Middle English *Ayenbite of Inwit* (ca. 1340) and the *Book of Vices and Virtues* (ca. 1375), may, at first,

---

31. Any list of such texts would have to include the *Pricke of Conscience*, *Handlyng Synne*, and the *Ayenbite of Inwit*, popular handbooks of sin that include stories as well as categories and subcategories of sinning; it would also have to include more explicitly literary works that stage the new interest in and understanding of the self, such as the debates between the Body and the Soul, the writings of the Katherine Group, and *Piers Plowman*.

32. See Frances A. Yates, *The Art of Memory* (Chicago: University of Chicago Press, 1974), and Mary Carruthers, *The Book of Memory: A Study of Memory in Medieval Culture* (Cambridge, UK: Cambridge University Press, 1990).

seem Borgesian in their complexity.³³ Medieval authors concerned with confession produced multiple, intersecting psychological systems. These systems were at once descriptive and normative. They described how a particular sin might be functioning in human life and, at the same time, served a delimiting, normative function organizing the range of sins considered possible, leaving some sins radically outside and beyond the pale.³⁴

In treating the psychological theories posited in these medieval works as deserving of study in their own right, this book aims to find an alternative to the fascinating but necessarily limited rubric of faculty psychology, which has long been used to explain virtually all medieval psychological thought. Faculty psychology and, to a degree, humoral theory were certainly important discourses for the Middle Ages, but they were not the only discourses, and they do not really explain the underlying thought that structures popular works like debates between the Body and the Soul. This book is not a psychoanalytic study of medieval psychology, although several of the models I discuss invite comparisons with Freud's more topographical models, such as the ego/id/superego. Neither does this study argue that the medieval works I discuss influenced later psychological models. Rather than viewing Body/Soul debates in the place of ancestors in some genealogical schema that delineates the history of psychology, I am ultimately concerned with literary analysis, specifically with analyzing the ways in which the dynamic narrative drive and characterizations in staged encounters between aspects of the self bring new dimensions to the work of *sowlehele,* and examining medieval popular culture, with its blend of piety and playfulness.

Despite the attention I pay to the historical context of medieval Christianity and to the contribution that reading medieval allegories as works of *sowlehele* makes to its history, these allegories are works of literature, not just historical

---

33. See Dan Michel, *The Ayenbite of Inwit or Remorse of Conscience*, ed. R. Morris, EETS Original Series 23 (London: Kegan Paul, Trench, and Trubner, 1866), and *The Book of Vices and Virtues*, ed. W. Nelson Francis, EETS Original Series 217 (Oxford and London: Oxford University Press, 1942). A genealogy of vernacular treatises on the vices and virtues is to be found in W. A. Pantin, *The English Church in the Fourteenth Century* (Toronto: University of Toronto Press, 1955), in a chapter titled "Manuals of Instructions for Parish Priests." See also Leonard Boyle, "The Fourth Lateran Council and Manuals of Popular Theology," in *The Popular Literature of Medieval England*, ed. Thomas Heffernan (Knoxville: University of Tennessee Press, 1985), 30–43, and Richard Raymo, "Works of Religious and Philosophical Instruction," in Albert Hartung, gen. ed., *A Manual of the Writings in Middle English*, 1050–1500 (New Haven: The Connecticut Academy of Arts and Sciences, 1986).

34. The obvious example here is the much-discussed prohibition on discussing even the possibility of homosexual desire/practice with parishioners in texts such as John Mirk's *Instructions for Parish Priests*, ed. Edward Peacock. EETS (London: Kegan Paul, Trench, and Trubner, 1868), but it is difficult to say what other life possibilities were foreclosed by remaining pointedly unnamed.

documents. Their narrative arcs—meaning that the relationships they depict take place over a period of time (however brief) and have an opportunity to develop—prevent these works from functioning as static didactic phenomena. Works of *sowlehele* are not just a simplification of faculty psychology, in part because my term describes a process of self-making and self-healing as much as a category of medieval writings. *Sowlehele* is allegorical writing about the self that lends itself to literary interpretation rather than a psychological, philosophical, and/or theological one because its analysis of the self necessarily relies on figural language, narrative temporality, and conventionally gendered language for discussing embodiment.

Homologies
WHAT GENDER DOES TO ALLEGORY, AND ALLEGORY TO GENDER

Examining the relationship between the body and the soul necessitates an awareness of the kind of metaphors that structured their relationship as a conflict.[35] Allegories portraying the self's internal hierarchies often used the rule of men over women to depict the relationship of soul and body. This is an Aristotelian homology, but it is also a conceit reiterated by Augustine, Jerome, and many others: Jerome wrote, famously, that "as long as a woman is for birth and children, she is different from man as body is from soul."[36] To understand spirit as male and flesh as female is already to enter the realm of allegory—after all, this move demands that one perceive material signifiers as pointing to a meaning beyond themselves.

But who's signifying whom? In statements such as Jerome's, "woman" seems to be functioning as a metaphor *for* bodiliness, and "body" seems to

35. For examples of some of the broad uses to which the metaphor of the body in the early modern period could be put, see Thomas Hobbes's *Leviathan*, ed. C. B. MacPherson (London: Penguin Books, 1982); Ernst H. Kantorowicz, *The King's Two Bodies: A Study in Mediaeval Political Theology* (Princeton, NJ: Princeton University Press, 1957); and the collection *The Body in Parts: Fantasies of Corporeality in Early Modern Europe*, ed. David Hillman and Carla Mazzio (New York: Routledge, 1997).

36. The full quotation is a little more forgiving, but it is the first section that gets cited again and again: "as long as a woman is for birth and children, she is different from man as body is from soul. But when she wishes to serve Christ more than the world, then she will cease to be a woman, and will be called man." St. Jerome, *Commentarius in Epistolam ad Ephesios III 5*, in PL 26: 567a, cited in Vern Bullough, *Sexual Variance in Society and History* (Chicago: University of Chicago Press: 1976), 365. See also Aristotle, *On the Generation of Animals*, Loeb Classical Library, trans. A. L. Peck (Cambridge, MA: Harvard University Press, 1953), 18. In Corinthians 11.3, St. Paul wrote that "Christ is the head of every man, and the husband is the head of his wife." See also Ephesians 5.22: "the husband is the head of the wife just as Christ is the head of the church, the body of which he is the Savior."

have become the thing being signified, the thing that femininity attempts to explain. Caroline Walker Bynum writes that "male and female were contrasted and asymmetrically valued as intellect/body, active/passive, rational/irrational, reason/emotion, self-control/lust, judgment/mercy and order/disorder. In the devotional writing of the later Middle Ages, they were even contrasted in the image of God—Father or Bridegroom—and soul (anima)—child or bride."[37] This mode of paired thinking is so ancient that it is virtually impossible to pinpoint its origins.

The medieval homology stating that body is to soul as woman is to man, and the demand for some conventional source for the eternal but loving conflict between both pairs, led medieval thinkers to an analogy: Not only are Soul and Body just like a man and a woman, they are also a husband and a wife. Such an analogy both posits a split (the Body loves its other) and mends that fissure in the same gesture. These things are united, albeit in a very medieval way, through and because of a hierarchal relationship. The homology also understands the necessity to discipline the speaking Body through the necessity of disciplining the chatty woman, and, perhaps, vice versa. The most famous of the analogies of body to wife is that of St. Paul in his Letter to the Ephesians (5:28–30): "Husband should love their wives as they do their own bodies. He who loves his wife loves himself. For no one ever hates his own body, but he nourishes and tenderly cares for it, just as Christ does for the church because we are members of his body." These words proved very influential. In *City of God*, Augustine argues that, since Adam and Eve were originally created to live together in a harmonious order of authority and obedience, a husband was therefore "meant to rule over his wife as the spirit rules the flesh."[38] It is not a great leap from this sort of analogy to allegories that stage the domestic squabbles between Body and Soul as the relationship of a

---

37. Bynum, *Fragmentation and Redemption*, 151. However, she then goes on to trace the great increase in "positive female figures" between the twelfth and fifteenth centuries, which she attributes to the desire, by male writers of devotional texts, to humble themselves, becoming subservient to Christ by becoming female: "the male writer who saw his soul as a bride of God or his religious role as womanly submission and humility was conscious of using an image of reversal. He sought reversal because reversal and renunciation were at the heart of a religion whose dominant symbol is the cross—life achieved through death" (171).

38. Augustine, *City of God*, trans. Henry Bettenson (London: Penguin Books, 1972), XV, 7. In Latin, "ubi intellegendum est uirum ad regendam uxorem animo carnem regenti similem esse oportere" (*De civitate Dei*, ed. B. Dombart and A. Kalb, 2 vols. Stuttgart: Teubner, 1981; 1993). Interpreting 1 John 2.15, Augustine understands "taking a wife" as an excessive attachment to the flesh. In his *Sermons on Selected Lessons of the New Testament*, Augustine describes the conflict of body and flesh as "just as if a husband and wife have a dispute with one another in one house; the husband ought to labor to this end, to tame the wife," translated in *A Library of Fathers of the Holy Catholic Church* (Oxford: Oxford University Press, 1845), 2:719. All of these are cited in John A. Alford, "The Role of the Quotations in *Piers Plowman*," *Speculum* 52 (1977) 80–99; see fns. 30 and 31.

married couple, and it is not surprising that allegory, a mode that gives voice and flesh to abstractions, can be used to capture the complicated interactions between such a pair.

Although Christianity has a reputation for body/soul dualism and for denigrating the body, which feminist critics often take up in deploring dualism, in fact the promise of bodily resurrection and faith in Christ's incarnation meant that the body was more respectable in Christianity than in other Mediterranean religions.[39] Philosophies declared heretical—like those of the Cathars, Gnostics, Docetists, Eutycians, and, earlier, the Manicheans (among others)—had argued that Christ was never enfleshed, but the Church Fathers asserted the human bodiliness of Christ, even as they decried venial sin, the sin of the flesh. The Council of Chalcedon, held in 451, declared that Christ was both fully human and fully divine.

Despite a high-level theology that knew better, the relationship that was used to explain the workings of the self in early works of *sowlehele* remained hierarchical dualism: good soul, uncomprehendingly trapped for a time in bad body. More often than not, the model of the body as debased also understood the body as feminine. Sometimes, however, perhaps because of the tendency of Latin allegory to present abstractions as "allegorical goddesses," it was the Soul that was female, lifted to the status of unattainable courtly lady vis-à-vis the Body as her rough and unworthy courtier. However, and this is a crucial point for understanding the poetry discussed in this book, designating the Body as *purely* "bad" remained theologically problematic. Avoiding the various antiembodiment heresies necessitated that depictions of the relationship between souls and bodies included at least a gesture toward love and cooperation between the two, or something other than all-out war within the self, although the inferiority of the body and flesh were largely beyond questioning. In some early poems (like the Old English homilies), working through the tensions between making sure that the Body was lower on the hierarchy and yet maintaining that Body and Soul love one another was not a priority, but in the works of later medieval *sowlehele* discussed in this book, these issues seem to have fired the imaginations of the poems' various authors, and became the basis for the kinds of elaborations and rewritings of a basic "Soul versus Body" model that took place.

To gender the soul female implicates Body/Soul debates in the tendency to produce idealized female figures as interlocutors for male philosophers. Such female figures get to transcend their gender rather than be debased by it. For later authors such as Jean de Meun, the gender of the female personifications

---

39. See St. Augustine, *City of God* XIV: 3, 550–51, for a discussion under the heading "the cause of sin arises in the soul, not in the flesh." See also Brown, *Body and Society*, and Caroline Bynum, *The Resurrection of the Body*.

of such abstract concepts as Reason permits some ironic play with the limits of their characters' female authority. Surprisingly, the strong heteronormative and sexist bias in the metaphors that figure the relationship of body and soul comes to be troubled and undone in the course of the centuries, specifically in the English language.

One of the reasons for this surprising turn is specific to the English language: the freedom from grammatical constraint referred to in Helen Cooper's article, mentioned earlier. In Latin writings, the selection of an allegory's sex or gender may seem arbitrary in the way that grammar is arbitrary—a given noun is, after all, feminine, masculine, or neuter in Latin. Our authors inevitably know this, and abstractions tend to be grammatically female, so they may as well be described as towering female figures. English, however, does *not* arbitrarily assign the male or the female gender to inanimate nouns like "chair" or to abstractions like "philosophy." Chairs or churches are neuter, and only *become* male or female when they begin to function as persons, to speak; thus, no grammatical necessity dictates that the English church be represented as female, since the noun had not implied this representation.

Curiously, Anglo-Saxon possessed a full set of noun genders, which all but disappeared in Middle English, although some lingering echoes of this grammar remained.[40] Middle English thus finds itself free of the grammatical constraints that shape the conventions of personification allegory in other vernaculars. A number of medieval allegories—from the Latin works discussed in chapter 1 to *Piers Plowman*, discussed in chapter 5—use grammar as a metaphor, often for the problems associated with gender and sexuality. It is clear from the use of grammar as metaphor in *Piers Plowman* that, at least for the poet we call Langland, grammar is capable of signifying at the level of ontology, and grammatical gender is far from arbitrary. At one point, one of the characters declares that the study of grammar is "the grounde of al," meaning by this, it seems, the ground of all education, and, through education, of discourse itself.[41] Grammar is capable of both describing and establishing hierarchies between speakers and is thus a way of *doing* philosophy through allegory, or of writing allegory philosophically.

Some debates written in English replaced the hierarchies created by the relationship between husband and wife in Latin and Romance allegories of

40. Charles Jones, in *Grammatical Gender in English: 950–1250* (London: C. Helm/Methuen, 1988), describes the persistence of noun gender's remnants in English, changing the story from one of loss to one of diminution. In his Introduction, he claims that "any comment available in standard handbooks on the history of English led the student to the assumption that grammatical gender was catastrophically and suddenly 'lost' from the language's rule system sometime 'around' the eleventh century" and argues, instead, that what he calls "echoes" of the gender classification of nouns endure for about 300 years.

41. *William Langland, Piers Plowman: The C-Text*, ed. Derek Pearsall (Exeter, UK: University of Exeter Press, 1994), XVII, 107.

Body and Soul with a multiplicity of other, frequently same-sex, models for hierarchy. Pointedly avoiding personifying either body or soul as female, they instead explored various forms of same-sex affiliation (teacher-student, foster brothers, mirror images) between male personifications in depicting the relationship of the self to itself. Such homosocial relationships model a same-sex power struggle within the self, which might be understood as both a depiction of certain misogynist norms (eliminating the female from the self) and an opening for contemporary critics to see the possibility for a queer reading. "Queerness" helps to describe, within the terms of this argument, the surprising turn away from loving and contentious differently gendered relationships to loving and contentious same-sex relationships within the self. The troubling of the heterosexual bonds between allegorical speakers, however, does not come out of any happy impulse on its authors' parts to liberate the stodgily normative Body-Soul relation of the Latin- and Romance-language tradition. Liberation from those languages is not the goal, although many critics (Muscatine, Ackerman) have implied that it is. Ridding the self of female personifications, in Middle English writings, works in the service of medieval misogyny. After all, one may assume (and, indeed, certain textual details discussed in future chapters demonstrate) that it was troubling for medieval authors to imagine the self as filled or framed by female persons or personifications, even ones subordinate to male rule. The necessity of overcoming this weakness seems to have trumped even the centuries-old conventions of personification allegory inherited from late antiquity.

Soul/Body Dualism from Foucault to Feminism

This study aims above all for an intervention in medieval studies; however, examining the prehistory of bodies and souls in relation to one another is a project that engages the energies of a variety of scholars in myriad disciplines, and complicating and deepening that broader field of inquiry is part of my aim here as well. Some of the credit or blame for rendering "the body" such a rich topic for scholars goes to Michel Foucault, whose *Discipline and Punish* and subsequent writings are crucial to the contemporary aspect of this project.

In his lifetime, Foucault never actually completed his project on the Middle Ages, and even if he had, the project had shown every sign of focusing on an earlier period than the one this study examines. However, his work has proven to be a continuing provocation and encouragement to medievalists and others interested in working out the genealogy of the modern self, which, for him, was always implicated in techniques for disciplining the body. This study of allegory and medieval poetry stands at the intersection of two related projects of Foucault—the project that he helped inaugurate of historicizing the body, and his later interest in the history of confession—two interests that Foucault himself never quite brought together. To think of body and soul intertwined, after Foucault, is to think of both as effects of the workings of power, acting to create the self as its effect. In fact, chapter 3 of this study examines Foucault's importance in theorizing *sowlehele* at some length. However, Foucault's work elided the specifically gendered dimensions of how power works to organize bodies and souls.

Femininity's association with embodiment goes back at least as far as Plato's *Timaeus* (the single Platonic dialogue that seems to have been available and popular throughout the Middle Ages), where matter is created in a female womb or "matrix."[42] Feminist critics have had a great deal to say about body/soul dualism as such, and particularly about what it has meant for women to be reduced to the synecdoche of the womb, to being merely and eternally on the side of "the body." At first, feminist scholars writing in the 1970s and 1980s turned the ancient association of woman with flesh into a project of valorizing the body and women, insisting that attention be paid to these two previously silent and denigrated entities.[43] This was a claim that posited the

---

42. The tradition of the *Timaeus* is rendered more complex and interesting in its rewritings within medieval allegory. Plato's cosmogeny is the only one of his dialogues to be disseminated in the Middle Ages, and it is the part of Plato that is meant when medievalists speak of medieval "neo-Platonism"; this can be unfortunate, since the *Timaeus* is an odd duck in the Platonic corpus and has very little to do with Plato's other, more interesting dialogues. However, it also happens to be the one that feminists such as Irigaray and Butler (and also thinkers such as Derrida) feel a particular need to discuss as one of the big justifications for sexism that resounded through the ages. An interesting article about the equation of woman with body in Plato, which, however, draws on Platonic dialogues that would not have been available for medieval thinkers to consult, is Elizabeth Spelman's "Woman as Body: Ancient and Contemporary Views" in *Feminist Studies* 8;1 (1982): 109–31. The *Timaeus* is essentially a "flat" allegory, one with very little temporal movement—it isn't a story but a description, an alternative cosmogeny. Arguably, the allegories that were written under its explicit influence (Bernardus' *Cosmographia* is an obvious example) add to this allegory the element of action, narrative—and thereby, temporality. With Bernardus, for instance, female characters are no longer just lying there being wombs for matter; they are acting, even if in odd ways.

43. In the "Introduction" to *Feminism and the Body* (Oxford: Oxford University Press, 2000), which contains many gestures of summarizing the discipline, Londa Schiebinger writes, "In the 1970s, feminists reinserted the body into history, bringing to light issues that had previously been considered too vulgar, trivial, or risqué to merit serious scholarly attention. ... The mind/body dualism that long underpinned Western culture made males the guardians of culture and the things of the mind, while it associated females with the frailties and contingencies of the mortal body. Females, subject to unruly humours, unpredictable hormones, and other forces, have been identified so closely with nature that nature itself is often called 'Mother Nature'" (1). Later, she writes, "In efforts to check the increasingly popular biological determinism, feminists in the 1960s introduced the term 'gender', distinguishing culturally specific forms of masculinity and femininity from biological 'sex,' construed as anatomy, physiology, and

body as the "real" and language as a mediating (productive, disciplinary) force, and created a distinction between "sex" (the putatively unalterable material embodiment as male or female) and "gender" (a linguistically mediated social construction, open to adjustment by cultural change).

This version of feminist theory about the body came to be reevaluated: The firm association of "woman" with "body" (and the understanding of "sex" as a true material ground for existence) demanded a language of authenticity and immediacy that trapped women into particular modes of life and understandings of themselves. In the 1990s, feminist critics such as Judith Butler and Elizabeth Grosz argued that the body is neither the passive object of cultural inscription nor the unmanageable and unknowable representative of prediscursive reality. The constructivist position in feminist theory maintains that the sex/gender distinction cannot hold because all that we can know about "sex" comes to us mediated through language and culture; the body and its materiality may or may not be "real," but the very question we ask about that reality comes courtesy of a discourse that posits the real and the linguistic/cultural as opposites, in a circular argument without end.[44]

The first chapter of Judith Butler's *Bodies That Matter* consists of a series of considerations about matter, materiality, and the connection between those things and the performative nature of sex and gender. As part of elucidating what materiality means for feminist theory, Butler turns to an originary moment for Western conceptions of the self, Aristotle's *De Anima*, citing the philosopher's view that "the soul is the first grade of actuality of a naturally organized body," and that they are as united as "the wax and the shape given to it by the stamp."[45] This language of the stamp, translated from the Greek *schema*, is a language of form, shape, and organization. Butler argues that a logical consequence of Aristotle's thinking is that matter does not and cannot exist without a schema or stamp. The schemata of bodies can be understood as "a historically contingent nexus of power/discourse." The consequence follows, just a few pages later, that not only cultural performance (gender, but I might also say the stuff of the soul) but also "sex" as an attribute of the body can and *must* be understood as performative.

---

chromosomes. The primary force of body history ever since has been to show that universal, transhistorical masculine and feminine bodies do not exist apart from culture" (2).

44. See Moira Gatens, *Imaginary Bodies: Ethics, Power and Corporeality* (London and New York: Routledge, 1996); Elizabeth Grosz, *Volatile Bodies: Toward a Corporeal Feminism* (Bloomington: Indiana University Press, 1994); Judith Butler, *Gender Trouble: Feminism and the Subversion of Identity* (New York: Routledge, 1990); and *Bodies That Matter: On the Discursive Limits of "Sex"* (New York: Routledge, 1993).

45. Butler, *Bodies That Matter*, 32, quoting Aristotle, "De Anima," *The Basic Works of Aristotle*, trans. Richard McKeon (New York: Random House, 1941), Bk. 2, ch. 1, 412b7–8.

This discussion of how matter *matters* is no neutral addition to the debate between idealism and "realism" that has raged for at least ten centuries: Butler's argument is ultimately in the service of a political point. According to her reading, Aristotle's thinking about the relationship of soul and body was radically rewritten by Foucault's critique of disciplinarity, where what Foucault, also, calls "the soul" functions as the "materialization" of the prisoner's body. The soul, Butler writes, "produces and actualizes the body,"[46] or, as Foucault famously expressed it, "the soul is the prison of the body."[47] The study of the soul—whether as psychoanalysis in the twentieth and twenty-first centuries or as viewed in relationship with the body in the Middle Ages—is a way into the knowable and describable experience of living in a body. The third chapter of the present study is concerned with this argument, particularly with its inherently medieval quality and how specific Middle English texts might be used to return to and rewrite these important concepts.

In important works that helped inaugurate "body studies," such as Elaine Scarry's *The Body in Pain*, the body's voicelessness is cause for concern, as if the body is a constituency with no vote in the democratic process. Critics of the constructionist position in feminist and queer theory find it problematic that if the body is understood as discursively constituted, it seems to lose some of its intractable realness by also being understood as a participant in language and culture. Such critics wonder if understanding bodily being as discursive will reduce claims about injury to the status of "mere" discourse, leaving no room to distinguish between symbolic and physical violence (the latter presumably far more serious than the former). I would suggest that medieval writings help show that such distinctions are already hard to come by.

The imagination of the later Middle Ages conceived all of this quite differently. Certainly, by the twelfth century, allegorical thinking (discussed at some length in chapter 1) saw the physical world and, indeed, historical events as standing in for and pointing toward less material, transcendent, divine realities. The discursive was never the merely discursive; it was the most real of realities. As the tradition of Body/Soul debates developed, the Body talked back to the Soul (as do, in other debates, subsections of the body such as the Heart, the Eye, the Hands, and so on), arguing in a markedly corporeal way, blending the discursive and the material in a way that seemed to be treated as largely unproblematic in other medieval writings.

Centuries before the experiments in bodily speech by such French feminists as Hélène Cixous and Luce Irigaray, the medieval body had already established its own scandalous speaking style (to paraphrase Shoshana

---

46. Butler, *Bodies That Matter*, 33.
47. Foucault, *Discipline and Punish*, 29.

Felman).[48] Indeed, the medieval body-as-woman was positively chatty, as some of the debates between the Body and the Soul discussed in this book will show. Unfortunately, chattiness is a negative trait associated with women in the Middle Ages, a trait that disciplinary works such as "Sawles Warde" seek to constrain. The metaphorical and allegorical language used to describe the nature of and relationship between souls and bodies is, as it turns out, a gendered one. This book examines the consequences of this gendered language both for the emergence of a self-consciously literary tradition of Middle English writings and for medieval understandings of the self.

Overview of Chapters

In order to trace the workings of *sowlehele*, this book reaches back to allegories that predate the Fourth Lateran Council and as far forward as the late fourteenth-century *Piers Plowman*. Chapter 1 explores works that were central to the history of medieval allegory in the Middle Ages, Prudentius' *Psychomachia* and Boethius' *The Consolation of Philosophy*. Prudentius and Boethius each set up a problem that increasingly troubled writers over the centuries following: Abstract concepts describing the qualities that inhabit the self speak in female voices and often inhabit female bodies. It seems odd to some later writers that such powerful roles are permitted to female figures. The last section of the chapter turns to two twelfth-century Latin debates between the Body and the Soul that can be read as responding to the problems of allegorical gender and proper hierarchies within the self. The two Latin Body/Soul debates—one anonymous, the "Visio Philiberti," and one by Hildebert of Lavardin, the "Liber de Querimonia"—repeatedly pose the question of how two elements as disparate in value and quality as soul and body could ever have been brought together, and how they might function in appropriate harmony.

Chapters 2 and 3 focus on two thirteenth-century Middle English debates between the Body and the Soul. Chapter 2 shows how "In a Thestri Stude I Stod" ("In a Dark Place I Stood") functions as a work of *sowlehele*, exemplifying how the poem's temporality contributes to its didacticism. In this debate, the Body talks back to the accusing Soul, refusing the Soul's theory that all sin is the fault of the flesh. I argue that the contending theories of blame that comprise this poem's matter are engaged in the production of a technology of *sowlehele* in part because other psychological models provided in the biblical,

---

48. Shoshana Felman, *The Scandal of the Speaking Body: Don Juan with J. L. Austin or Seduction in Two Languages*, trans. Catherine Porter (Ithaca, NY: Cornell University Press, 1983).

patristic, and ancient Greek writings about the soul that came down to the thirteenth century cannot fully account for this debate's dynamics.

Having begun to examine the possibilities of *sowlehele* as a model for understanding representations of the divided self, I then turn in chapter 3 to the surprisingly homosocial nature of the Middle English version of the relationship of the self to itself in the most popular of the medieval debates between the Body and the Soul, the thirteenth-century "Als I Lay in a Winteris Nyt," also known as "The Debate Between the Body and the Soul." This chapter exemplifies the workings of pastoral power in *sowlehele* writings and shows how that power sometimes cannot help functioning in a queer way. By comparison with its Latin and Anglo-Norman counterparts, "Als I Lay" makes use of the specific grammatical possibilities available to English-language writers by establishing both Soul and Body as male, eliminating the female personification of the Soul from the conversation, and portrays its Body/Soul bond as one based in powerful same-sex affect. The poem can be read to exemplify Foucault's famous phrase that "the soul is the prison of the body," but, I argue, "Als I Lay" also complicates his metaphor by portraying Body and Soul as locked in a queerly loving ambivalence.

Chapters 2 and 3 show how Body/Soul debates offer a performative theory of the self, both in the sense that they dynamically stage the different possible relationships within that self and in the sense used by philosophers of language that these poems work to produce the selves they describe. However, the relatively brief poems cited here are just some among many works to appear in manuscripts such as the Vernon to give instruction and occasion for meditation. The book's final chapters consider how the attempt to produce *sowlehele* functions in writings that are better known within medieval English studies. Chapter 4 looks at the early thirteenth-century personification allegory "Sawles Warde," a prose section of the collection known as the Katherine Group, in which the highly gendered tensions of ensoulment and embodiment are described for an audience of religious women. In a reversal of the dynamics in "Als I Lay in a Winteris Nyt," but not quite in a return to Prudentius' war of female vices with female virtues, this work is populated almost entirely by female personifications. "Sawles Warde" transforms the contentiousness of the Body/Soul debate into a domestic scene, imagining the self as a household besieged by danger. Within the home of the Body, Wit's wife, Will, threatens to stir up trouble, while visitors from without, such as Fear and Love of Life, undermine any sense in which this self might be considered hermetically sealed or safely closed off from the world outside its "house." This allegory is an instance of *sowlehele* as a mode of writing specifically aimed at disciplining women.

Chapter 5 turns from the explicitly female-gendered character of "Will" in "Sawles Warde" to *Piers Plowman*, where Will is instead figured as a man. In this concluding chapter, I consider *Piers Plowman* as a Middle English text that looks back to the questions of gendered representation in allegory posed by the early Latin allegories discussed in the first chapter. It is also a work that figures the problem of interdependence as an issue of gender and power, like yet unlike the thirteenth-century Body/Soul debates. *Piers Plowman* marks a crisis in the figurations of abstract ideas in female bodies (a tradition at least as old as Prudentius, if not Plato), a crisis intimately related to the development of *sowlehele* in medieval writings. It is a text that famously exceeds any and all generic descriptions, as it exceeds any pat conclusions reached by its own characters. However, reading *Piers Plowman* as a work of *sowlehele* opens up new ways of understanding the workings of gender, power, and discipline in the poem and, if it does not presume to resolve the questions it poses, helps resolve the questions posed by this book.

CHAPTER 1

Thought Enfleshed
PHILOSOPHY AND PSYCHOLOGY AS FIGURED
IN LATIN ALLEGORY

Barbara Johnson's published lecture "Women and Allegory" poses the question, "What does it mean to personify theory as a woman?,"[1] as part of a larger critique of how contemporary critical theory gets personified by its critics (frequently as "dead" or as "dying"). Johnson's discussion of allegory is prompted by an eighteenth-century allegorical painting that depicts "Theory" as a female form, prompting her to ask whether what we currently tend to call critical theory or poststructuralist theory is consequently a particularly female practice. This sighting of an allegorical image on the wall of the London Academy of Art represents one of those infrequent encounters between medieval literary studies and contemporary critical theory that enriches both, thanks to Johnson's use of an epigraph from Carolyn Dinshaw's *Chaucer's Sexual Poetics* that describes the convention by which the allegorical text is depicted as a veiled woman upon whose body various "masculine acts" of reading and glossing are performed. Johnson thus situates herself in relation to a centuries-old allegorical tradition

1. Barbara Johnson, *The Wake of Deconstruction*, in The Bucknell Lectures in Literary Theory; ed. Michael Payne and Harold Schweizer (Oxford: Blackwell, 1994), 53; the lecture that immediately precedes this one notes the necessity of personification as such in discussions of the so-called death of theory, asking, "What does it mean to treat a theory as an animate being? More precisely, what does it mean to personify deconstruction as animate only by treating it as dead, giving it life only in the act of taking that life away?" (17), without yet specifying how often that personified being is female.

and queries what it might tell us about the possibilities and limitations of what our culture imagines about women. How can women be irrational if Rationality is a woman? How can women be anything other than willful and capricious given that Will is a woman, too?[2] How is gender distributed and instituted in allegorical texts, and what are the implications of these institutions for thinking about the embodied, ensouled self? What, in short, is the gender of the allegorical Soul and Body in Latin-language works, those that most directly inform the Middle English tradition?[3] This chapter looks at how the use of female figures in some important medieval Latin allegories, including those of Prudentius and Boethius, installed gender hierarchy as an issue to be resolved in later medieval conceptions of selfhood.

One of the key preconditions of personhood in allegory is actually gender, since by beginning to speak, an abstraction ceases to be an "it" and clearly becomes a "he" or a "she." It is both a truism and an abiding mystery to present-day readers of late antique and medieval literature that allegorical representations of abstract concepts are almost always female. This is no accident, scholars note: At the most basic level, Latin and Romance languages tend to gender abstract concepts as feminine nouns, from the "goddesses" Natura and Ecclesia (Nature and the Church) to incarnations of the vices and sins like Luxuria or Superbia (Indulgence, Pride). Critics have often emphasized the view that the literary convention of a female tutelary figure, such as Boethius' Lady Philosophy, representing the abstraction Philosophia is an accident of grammar and therefore to be dismissed as *mere* accident.[4] Similarly, Johnson's essay

---

2. Ruth Mazo Karras describes an exemplum about a scolding wife and a drunken, misbehaving husband. In this case, John Bromyard reads the story as an allegory of humanity's relationship with God, with God as the ineffectively scolding wife, whose admonishment "man" ignores at his peril. Karras adds, "The theological moral does not prevent the story from reinforcing the image of woman as scold (or of man as drunkard). But if the scolding woman stands for God, can she be all bad?" (238). "Gendered Sin and Misogyny in John of Bromyard's Summa Predicantium," *Traditio* 47 (1992): 233–57.

3. James J. Paxson summarizes the problem of allegory in relation to gender toward the end of his *Poetics of Personification*, noting that although the argument from grammatical gender has a great deal of scholarly authority (he dates it back to Joseph Addison), "in the classical rhetorical tradition, the female body itself, as well as female social and cosmetic practices, are the figural images of figuration." James J. Paxson, *The Poetics of Personification* (Cambridge, UK: Cambridge University Press, 1994), 173.

4. This is particularly true of the critics who write about the Old French *Roman de la Rose*. The gender of Bel Acueil, a subsidiary love object for the narrator's quest, would be troubling and undercut the heterosexual love story with the possibility of homosexual attachment if it were not repeatedly emphasized that the gender of "Fair Welcome" is male *merely* by accident. See the discussions by Douglas Kelly (for the "mere accident") side, in *Internal Difference and Meanings in the "Roman de la Rose"* (Madison: University of Wisconsin Press, 1995), esp. 105–22, and Simon Gaunt's direct response to Kelly, in "Bel Acueil and the Improper Allegory of the *Romance of the Rose*," *New Medieval Literatures* 2 (1998): 65–93 (see especially 68 and 84–85). For general studies of female tutelary figures in the writings and imagery of the Middle

comes to an impasse: She discovers that Reynolds's painting closely echoes "Theory" in a Renaissance compendium of allegorical images by the painter Cesare Ripa, and is therefore not an original idea or invention by Reynolds. Ripa's *Iconologia*, in turn, is not making a comment on culture: He assigns genders to abstract nouns according to those nouns' grammatical gender in Italian. Like medievalists today, Johnson asks, is the odd appearance of this female figure at the Royal Academy of Art in London "mere" grammar, after all? Johnson concludes that the idea that grammatical convention underlies allegorical gender does not negate the possibility that such images "shaped the cultural messages addressed both to women and to men. It is just that the 'cause' of the cultural messages cannot easily be tied to intentions."[5] How these messages were shaped by the "mere grammar" of allegory and what they actually were remain questions.

Grammar alone cannot fully explain the prevalence of female personifications, but their dominating presence in medieval literature remains a familiar aspect of allegorical writing that deserves defamiliarization. Such figures are, of course, tokens: Lady Liberty on the New York City skyline does not guarantee American women's freedom, and it is unlikely that the existence of a Lady Philosophy in the realm of representation made any difference for medieval women wishing to learn philosophy.[6] Johnson doesn't quite tell us what difference the female representation of Theory makes. But she notes her existence, there on the wall of the London Academy of Art, and in medieval literature are her relatives Reason, Nature, Holy Church, and Scripture.[7] The oddness of these powerful female figures is this: They represent the very essence of

---

Ages, see Marina Warner's *Monuments & Maidens: The Allegory of the Female Form* (New York: Atheneum, 1985), and Barbara Newman's *God and the Goddesses* (Philadelphia: University of Pennsylvania Press, 2004), and her earlier work, *From Virile Woman to WomanChrist: Studies in Medieval Religion and Literature* (Philadelphia: University of Pennsylvania Press, 1995).

5. Johnson, *The Wake of Deconstruction*, 73.

6. Helen Solterer's *The Master and Minerva*, like Johnson's essay, begins with an allegorical depiction of a woman, this time a woman writing a response to a man's words. Solterer notes the important role played by figurations of women responding to, disputing with, and ultimately yielding to the authority of learned men. These women are only sometimes allegorical, but always useful as representations of (male) intellectual mastery: "If these texts include women in a version of the master/disciple disputation, they do so in a manner that ultimately counts them out. By projecting women as privileged mouthpieces of clerical wisdom, [they] make them party to clerical claims on the knowledge of women." Helen Solterer, *The Master and Minerva: Disputing Women in French Medieval Culture* (Berkeley: The University of California Press, 1995), 33.

7. Barbara Newman, in her book *God and the Goddesses* (see above), argues that these female tutelary figures represented the continuation of a pagan pantheon of female gods, which Christianity had all but erased (with the exception of Mariolatry). In other words, "allegorical goddesses" offer a challenge to a monotheistic male-centered Godhead, and, in the writings of mystics and certain poets, manage to do so without ever being accused of blasphemy.

rationality in a world where women are routinely equated with the irrational, the bodily, the appetitive, and, most especially, the capricious and badly disciplined will.

It is conventional to understand the European Middle Ages as a profoundly misogynist time and place (often figured as such in contrast to our own presumably more enlightened time). The medieval period left behind very few records of writings by women and produced a literature in which female characters appeared in almost exclusively romantic functions and almost never as full-fledged protagonists. Yet, within the Latin canon that informed all others, there existed this surprisingly self-conscious tradition of powerful, intellectually intimidating female figures, a tradition that did not fit with any assumptions that medieval society seemed to hold about women. Does this tradition subvert the famous misogyny of the Middle Ages, or does it recuperate and strengthen it? And must those options be the only ones for thinking about gender and allegorical embodiment?

This chapter looks at how the gender of allegory mattered to the Latin works that established the tradition of medieval allegory. As the rest of this book discusses, the female figures of Reason, Philosophy, and various Virtues that harangue and educate the narrators of allegory largely give way, in Middle English works written in the thirteenth and fourteenth centuries, to an economy of male-male instruction, an economy that reflects the "reality" of the pedagogical scene and also permits the female to be anxiously excluded from the psychological battles waged within the (male) narratorial subject. The Middle English works do not exist in a vacuum, however, and this chapter examines early Latin and later French works together, as interdependent strains of a single allegorical tradition that influences writers in medieval England, if only to reverse or transform certain tendencies in their precursors. The tradition traced here, however, cannot claim positive knowledge of direct influence. Granted, without the Latin models neither personification allegory nor its gender conventions would have become such significant issues in vernacular writings. Thus, this chapter does not adopt an evolutionary model which demonstrates that the discussion of the self in Middle English debates between the Body and the Soul had the allegories of Boethius and Prudentius as their ancestors. Instead, an examination of these important antecedents permits us to see how the tradition of female allegorical figures speaking with male narrators informs the way gender is written into the production of works from the Body/Soul debates to *Piers Plowman*. This, in turn, becomes the basis of this book's argument that understanding quotidian psychological thinking in the Middle Ages requires critics to consider how its underlying structures were affected by allegorical gender, a detail that only seems to be arbitrary in medieval allegories describing the self to itself.

Although a number of medieval works of philosophy are written as allegories, criticism for the most part makes the mistake of refusing to consider allegory itself as a philosophical mode; contemporary medievalists recognize and adhere to disciplinary boundaries that would not have occurred to the medieval writers we study. Contemporary writings about allegory have considered it as a psychological mode, at times by counterintuitively insisting on the psychological realism of some allegorical characterizations. Statements about the "psychological realism" of various medieval works imply that those works resemble present-day representations of the psyche, or even that they are in line with present-day psychological theories or, perhaps, simply with generally agreed-upon understandings of the self, things known by "common sense."[8] Philosophy and what we now call psychology were no more separable in medieval thought than allegory was from either of the other two. This chapter, therefore, examines works in which philosophy, psychology, and what comes to function as narrative drive or the development of events and characters over a period of time are all mixed together for purposes of what at least some medieval writers call *sowlehele*.

Prudentius
THE HISTORY OF ALLEGORY AS A HISTORY OF PSYCHOLOGY

When critics look at the beginning of medieval personification allegory, they turn to a fourth-century Latin poem, Prudentius' *Psychomachia*, the first fully developed personification-based narrative fiction.[9] The work's title is some-

---

8. An exception to this statement is the sensitive reading of allegory in general and the *Roman de la Rose* in particular by Michel Zink in "The Allegorical Poem as Interior Memoir," *Yale French Studies* 70 (1986): 100–126. Zink makes a connection between "allegory and subjectivity," which he distinguishes from "allegory and the expression of psychological realities" (101). But even when Zink considers the development of subjectivity in French romance, he understands psychology to mean something familiar from *this* century's psychological theories; he is looking for how "they" were really always just like "us," which is what Fletcher also does. Although this study does not call for a politics of radical otherness about the Middle Ages, I would like to suggest that we pay just a little more attention to how we understand their modes of representing the self as specific to their own moment: Zink does this when he makes connections between allegory and medieval theories about dreams and memory. See also James Simpson's *Sciences and the Self in Medieval Poetry*, which traces the different kinds of psychological hierarchy the two authors use in depicting the education of a single soul. James Simpson, *Sciences and the Self in Medieval Poetry: Alan of Lille's "Anticlaudianus" and John Gower's "Confessio Amantis"* (Cambridge, UK: Cambridge University Press, 1995), 13.

9. For instance, Jon Whitman also gives the *Psychomachia* as the first example of personification allegory in *Allegory: The Dynamics of an Ancient and Medieval Technique* (Cambridge, MA: Harvard University Press, 1987). Of course, "the technique [of allegorical personification] goes back at least as far as the figures on the shield of Achilles in *Iliad* 18, in which Strife,

times used to define the entire genre, and, along with *The Consolation of Philosophy*, the *Psychomachia* stands as a model for and origin of the tradition of allegorical personification in the Middle Ages.[10] This work inaugurates allegory's involvement with the unsystematic psychological thought that this study terms *sowlehele*. It also posits the intimate involvement of all medieval personification allegory with the doctrine of Christ's Incarnation. By making nonmaterial concepts appear as physical bodies, personification allegory was a way of thinking (in an acceptably nonblasphemous mode) about the complex implications of Christ's incarnation as a man. After all, in the beginning of the Gospel of John, the Word was made flesh; personification allegory repeats this process again and again, albeit with lowercase-letter words such as *will*, or *philosophy*. While the Word assumes male flesh in biblical narrative, abstract concepts tend to become incarnate in female bodies. The female allegorical personifications invented by Prudentius help inaugurate the odd tendency of allegorical personifications to engage in activities (in this case, waging war) that contradict any literal understanding of what women actually did or could do in that period. But these personifications do more than this: By standing in, by virtue of their femininity and also by their own admission, for fleshliness-as-such, Prudentius' virtues and vices permit Prudentius to work out the relationships between gender, psychology, allegory, and incarnational theology.

In the poem, personified virtues engage personified vices on a field of battle, the outcome in the virtues' favor clear from the start. The battle is waged in a series of one-on-one conflicts ending with the vices' defeat and concludes with the sisters Faith and Concord working together to build a temple in honor of Christ. The figure of Christ, whose incarnation in a human body and status as both human and divine are invoked repeatedly, is implicated in how

---

Uproar, and Fate are shown participating in a battle scene. More elaborately, Xenophon [in *Memorabilia* 2.1] shows Heracles forced to choose between Pleasure and Virtue, two abstractions personified as women"; see Martha A. Malamud, *A Poetics of Transformation: Prudentius and Classical Mythology* (Ithaca, NY: Cornell University Press, 1989), 55. More important and even more influential, Vergil's *Aeneid* 6 allegorizes various evils, and Statius' *Thebaid* has "gods, humans, and personified abstractions mix indiscriminately" (Malamud, *Poetics*, 56). Despite these examples of earlier allegory-like writing in Latin, Malamud joins most critics who discuss the history of allegory in saying that that "Prudentius appears to have created a new genre of poetry[;] . . . his choice of the sustained personification allegory directs the reader's attention to his treatment of characters not as people or as symbols whose meaning is always fixed, but as signs whose meaning is variable and inconstant" (Malamud, *Poetics*, 57). James Paxson offers an excellent summary of the critical tradition around the *Psychomachia*, which has often been underestimated as a "poetic or formal failure." See Paxson, *Personification*, 63.

10. Michel Zink's elegant definition of a *psychomachia* is that it is "understood in the broadest sense as a description of the movements and the conflicts within psychological as well as moral consciousness." See Zink, 100.

the poem posits the relationship between the body and the soul, between the material world and its transcendence. Not only does the poem subdivide the self into new categories; the *Psychomachia,* whose title is Greek for "battle of/ for the psyche," inaugurates a tradition of allegorical approaches to psychology that are neither formal nor fully systematized.[11]

From the beginning, the *Psychomachia* works to establish the dominance of the soul (a virtuous soul, of course) over the body, as if this dominance were not already a given. The supremacy of the soul is supported by analogies that connect it with the seemingly obvious dominance of the New Testament over the Old. Prudentius uses the Hebrew Testament as an allegorical prefiguration of the Gospels, performing his own act of *allegoresis* in the course of his personification allegory. The poem begins with a description of the life of Abraham, whose job is entirely one of prefiguration. This Old Testament patriarch stands in for the injunction "that every part of our body ... must be set free by gathering our forces at home," and an extended analogy follows between the rescue of Lot from Sodom as a predecessor for the rescue of the soul from sin.[12] The "setting free" of the body in the *Psychomachia* is accomplished by a (temporary?) defeat of fleshly appetite. Although the flesh is defeated, however, the logic of the poem demands the cooperation of victors and losers—Concord, the penultimate speaker, voices the paradoxical peace-making impulse within the warlike poem when she insists on looking for a way to coordinate and unite the warring aspects of the self, insisting that "where there is separation there is no strength."[13]

The achievement of a coherent, unified self seems to be the poem's goal, and to achieve this, Prudentius needs (allegorical) bodies. One line of development in the poem makes use of biblical patriarchs, but the more dominant theme—the poem's plot—hinges on a battle between embodied vices and

---

11. A key to understanding the poem lies in the question of its title: *Where* does the battle of vices and virtues take place? Is the *Psychomachia* a battle *within* the "psyche" (is the immaterial space of soul turned into a battleground for the damaged and killed bodies of vices) or is it waged *for* the soul, winner take all? Critics cannot decide, and the ambiguity enriches the poem. See Brenda Machosky, "The Face That Is Not a Face: The Phenomenology of the Soul in the Allegory of the *Psychomachia,*" *Exemplaria* XV: 1 (Spring 2003): 1–38. Machosky discusses what it means to understand the Greek title of this Latin work as a battle "for the soul's salvation" and points out that "the battle is for the soul, and yet occurs in the soul" (3, see also fn 6). The use of the Greek *psyche* resolves the tension between the Latin *animus* (as discussed later, largely intellect) and *anima* (largely, as Machosky puts it, "the principle of life" [4]) and the soul's "noumenal form," the passive division of the soul, which "responds to objects that assault the senses of perception" (20).

12. Prudentius, *Psychomachia*, ed. and trans. H. J. Thomson (Cambridge, MA: Harvard University Press, 1949), 279. In Latin on the opposite side of the page, "omnemque nostri portionem corporis ... domi coactis liberandam viribus" (lines 53, 55).

13. "Nil dissociabile firmum est," Prudentius, 333, line 763.

virtues that, for whatever reason (grammar, a distancing effect from any "real" scene of warfare, the pleasure of reversing the regular order of things), turn out to inhabit female bodies. These bodies are not just passive receptacles housing abstractions: They are flung about in battle and injured, their boundaries violated by other bodies.[14] To get to the point where concord between aspects of the self is possible, the poem's logic demands both the mangled bodies of the vices and the indomitable bodies of the virtues that did the mangling, a concord between flesh and spirit (with spirit, of course, functioning as a first among equals).

Perhaps because he had no clear models of extended personification allegory to draw from, Prudentius is remarkably self-reflective about the sort of fiction he is crafting, the type of allegorical writing inaugurated with the poem. He attempts to keep the behavior of his virtues consistent with their named natures, but, when pressed, he seems to choose the battle aspect of the allegory over maintaining the strict boundaries of his characters' identities. While virtues such as Patience triumph by enacting their virtuousness (Patience stands still and lets Wrath exhaust herself; perhaps uncharacteristically full of shame and expressing it as anger, Wrath commits suicide, leading to Patience's victory), other virtues seem to go against or at least beyond their function by committing graphic violence against the vices, as when Faith causes Discord to be torn apart bodily, or Sobriety goes a little over the top by making Indulgence eat her own bloody tongue as restitution for having lived on sweet and luxurious foods (the punishment that the vices suffer, by contrast, tends to fit their named natures perfectly, prefiguring Dantean *contrapasso*). When a meek female Virtue causes violent "bodily" injury to a Vice, Prudentius seems to worry about how a female character could act so violently. He worries more about the character's femininity than about the contradictory model of an incarnation of virtue committing truly grotesque acts of violence.

In one such encounter, something surprising and useful is going on at the intersection of gender and incarnation in Prudentius' allegory. Immediately following the violent sword-thrust with which the modest maiden Chastity kills "Lust the Sodomite," Chastity makes a victory speech comparing her achievement with that of Judith killing Holofernes, here imagined as the very spirit of lechery. Having committed an act whose violence contradicts her meek alle-

---

14. James Paxson observes that the graphic goriness of the battle scenes in the poem concentrate on violence inflicted on the teeth, tongue, and face: "Prudentius' focus upon the imagery of the destruction of the face, therefore, is a literalized reverse of prosopopeia. It is the symbolic dismantling of the trope by which the text invents the figural characters who inhabits its actantial narrative" (Paxson, *Personification*, 69). Paxson uses this aspect of the poem's carnage as a way into the exciting argument that this first personification allegory actually undoes personifications in the very place where they speak and personify, literally deconstructing the speaking self at the very moment of inaugurating medieval allegory as we know it.

gorical personality, Chastity must justify her own violence through reference of a biblical precedent. Prudentius seems fascinated by these moments when his characters violate their own named natures. Chastity must also emphasize just how far against her own necessary modesty she has gone, by pointing out that, yes, both she and Judith are women ("woman as she was [she] won a famous victory over the foe with no trembling hand").[15] Immediately after equating herself with Judith to justify her own violence, Chastity must then differentiate her own killing force from Judith's, and the two turn out to differ in the same way as the Gospels differ from the Hebrew Testament.

What is extraordinary about this passage follows immediately, through a surprising digression. Chastity ignores the bloody battle being waged around her to speculate, "but perhaps a woman still fighting under the shade of the [Hebrew] law had not force enough, though in so doing she prefigured our time."[16] She, a fighting female personification, is surprised that a woman could fight (perhaps because that woman is not a personification?) but moves to resolve this surprise by describing the "our times" that Judith prefigured. The transformation that marks the possibilities of regenerative violence in "our times" also goes to the larger, stranger argument that Prudentius seems to be making in writing the first personification allegory: the new possibilities for embodiment, for a new compact between soul and body inaugurated by Christ's incarnation as a man described by Chastity:

> Since a virgin bore a child, since the day when man's body lost its primeval nature, and power from on high created a new flesh, and a woman unwedded conceived the God Christ.... From that day all flesh is divine, since it conceives Him and takes on the nature of God by a covenant of partnership. For the Word made flesh has not ceased to be what it was before, that is, the Word, by attaching to itself the experience of the flesh; its majesty is not lowered by the experience of the flesh, but raises wretched men to nobler things.[17]

In this brief passage, we have moved from an act of violence by a woman to the contextualization of that violence within a biblical narrative, but now we have

---

15. Prudentius, 283, "famosum mulier referens ex hoste tropaeum non trepidante manu" (lines 64–65).

16. Prudentius, 283, "at fortasse parum fortis matrona sub umbra / legis adhuc pugnans, dum tempora nostra figurat" (66–67).

17. Prudentius, 284, "....post partum virginis, ex quo / corporis humani naturam pristine origo / deseruit carnemque novam vix ardua sevit, / atque innupta Deum concepit femina Christum.../ Inde omnis iam diva caro est quae concipit illum / naturamque Dei consortis foedere sumit. / Verbum quipped caro factum non destitit esse quod fuerat, Verum, dum carnis glutinat usum, / carnis, / sed miseros ad nobiliora trahente" (71–74, 76–81).

digressed—*because* the violence was a woman's, *because* woman is consistently equated with the flesh—into the realm of incarnational theology. What enables Chastity's digression? The female body, committing violence, is shown to have been sanctified by Mary's virgin birth and therefore licensed to struggle violently in the name of virtue, as Chastity has done. Mary is a typological antecedent for Chastity, just as Judith is Chastity's pre-allegorical antecedent, and these two "real" female bodies help justify the female form taken by Chastity. The purpose of this typological genealogy is to produce the Word incarnate as flesh through a female intervention, thereby sanctifying both (some forms of) femininity and corporeality, concepts so often yoked together.

In the preceding passage, the divine remains unchanged by its encounter with the female body, but the body is utterly changed by encountering the divine. The mode of personification allegory that he is inventing as he goes along enables Prudentius to think through the implications of a flesh that is both human and divine. At least for Prudentius, to say that "the Word was made flesh" is an essential utterance permitting allegorical writing. Personification allegory always makes the word into flesh, gives the concept its *prosopon* or face; and though Homeric literature prefigured this kind of allegory, it is essentially a genre invented in the centuries after Christ's life and death became significant to Western culture. It might be speculated, indeed, that this allegorical mode was invented in order to respond to the sheer surprising oddness of Christ's incarnation. Personification allegory is a mode so intimately connected with incarnation that its purview must also include the question of how *any* soul, by definition a transcendent, nonmaterial being, can come to be incarnated in *any* body.[18]

Even at its supposed point of origin, Prudentius' poem, this sort of allegory is centrally concerned with psychological questions such as the relationship of body and soul. In Boethius' *Consolation,* Lady Philosophy argues that "human souls are of necessity more free when they continue in the contemplation of the mind of God and less free when they descend to bodies, and less still when

---

18. Jon Whitman, in his book *Allegory: The Dynamics of an Ancient and Medieval,* offers a history of the connection between incarnational thinking and allegorical writing in terms of Origen's philosophy and its incorporation of "Jewish, Platonic and Gnostic legacies" (69). Casey Finch, in the introduction to his edition of the works of the *Pearl* poet (an author whose work is outside the purview of this study), writes something very similar about his reading of the intellectual context of *Pearl:* "The act of incarnation fuses the divine and the human into an absolute contiguity. Similarly, the didactic purpose of the *Pearl* poet depends on the way in which literal and figurative poles of language are collapsed in his poetics . . . but at the same time [. . .] the fundamental theological separation of the earthly and the divine, of horizontal and vertical language, is paradoxically underscored in this process." Casey Finch, *The Complete Works of the Pearl Poet* (Berkeley: University of California Press, 1993), 19. And later, Finch writes that what the reader of the *Pearl* learns is that "the physical is both separate from and a part of the metaphysical" (21).

they are imprisoned in earthly flesh and blood."[19] This represents a fairly common medieval view, but it subjects its proponents to the dangers of a Manichean dualism and must be expressed carefully, with full acknowledgment that soul and body must ultimately accept their union. In the *Psychomachia*, however, embodiment is described as itself capable of achieving a kind of sanctity. The body is clearly an effect of historical forces: After the Virgin Birth, it is different from what it had been before. In the narrative, Chastity tells the story of this transformation and, in so doing, also redescribes her own victory over Lust—the Virgin Birth, the birth capable of enacting such a transformation in the status of the flesh, is, for her, necessarily chaste, a birth accomplished without lust. Later in the *Psychomachia*, we are reminded that "Jesus mediates between man and God, uniting mortality with the Father so that the fleshly shall not be separated from the eternal Spirit and that one God shall be both."[20] The birth of Christ thus guarantees that the flesh, too, shall have someone who will speak for it in the court of heaven.

Brenda Machosky has argued that the whole point for Prudentius of inventing personification allegory and producing the *Psychomachia* had been "a need to present something that could not otherwise appear, the soul."[21] This is a wonderful phrase, partly because it is so counterintuitive. Is not the person of every human being, his or her gait and voice and personality, an appearance of the soul in the physical world? Are not the eyes, at the very least, the clichéd "windows of the soul"? But no: In the Middle Ages, the soul is far more mysterious and more difficult to manifest than that, especially if it is the soul in general ("Fight for Mansoul," as Thompson's Loeb translation titles the *Psychomachia*) rather than some specific person's soul.

The *Psychomachia* does the work of sanctifying the body as a vessel for divine Incarnation *and* for allegorical incarnation, as the proper vessel for the soul. However, all of this changes at the poem's end. There, the final dedication of the poem, addressed to Christ, explains:

---

19. Boethius, *The Consolation of Philosophy*, trans. V. E. Watts (London: Penguin Books 1969), 149. "Humanas uero animas liberiores quidem esse necesse est cum se in mentis diuinae speculatione conseruant, minus uero cum dilabuntur ad corpora, minusque etiam cum terrenis artubus colligantur." Latin text from *Boethius: The Theological Tractates and the Consolation of Philosophy*, ed. E. K. Rand, trans. H. F. Stewart and S. J. Tester (Cambridge, MA: Harvard University Press, 1973).

20. Prudentius, 333, "Utque homini atque Deo medius intervenit Iesus, / qui sociat mortale Patri, / ne carnea distent / Spritui aeterno sitque ut Deus unus utrumque . . ." (764–66). In "The Face That Is Not a Face," Machosky argues that "*spiritus* designates the conjoinment of the body and soul" (22), which permits her to argue that "the *persona* or mask of *spiritus* is *psychomachia*, the image of a soul in the figures of conflict," and goes on to argue that *spiritus* resembles Jesus in also being a persona, a "'face' which unites the divine with the mortal"(23), with the difference between them being that "God can be figured as Christ but . . . there is no figure adequate to the human soul" (30).

21. Machosky, 17.

> Savage war rages, hotly, rages within our bones, and man's two-sided nature is in an uproar of rebellion; for the flesh that was formed of clay bears down upon the spirit, but again the spirit that issued from the pure breath of God is hot within the dark prison-house of the heart, and even in its close bondage rejects the body's filth. Light and darkness with their opposing spirits are at war, and our two-fold being inspires powers at variance with each other, until Christ our God comes to our aid.[22]

As it turns out, in spite of the assertions of the good of incarnate existence, the body *is* the prison of the soul; actually, the heart is (the spirit is buried in the *carcere cordis*), and the flesh made of clay (*viscera limo effigiata*) is the prison where the soul (Prudentius alternates the two Latin terms for "soul," *spiritus* and *anima*, without apparent consistency) is incarcerated. The language of the prison house seems unavoidable, even in this poem, which had challenged that language early on.

Toward the end of *Psychomachia*, Man's nature is understood as double—body and soul warring with one another. The war between them rages within man's very bones, one of the few textual indications of the battle's location. Both sides of man's nature are in rebellion, and it is their split that keeps man from peace and joy. The thing Prudentius' virtues dread is division. Concord, whose very name demands unity, says "a divided will creates disorder in our inmost nature, making two parties in a heart at variance,"[23] even as this conflict guarantees both the narrative dynamism of the battle plot and the possibility that, divided from it, the good will overpower the bad. What is so odd about this process is that the poem had begun with a multifarious split—a battle between many speaking and acting characters with the stated aim of freeing the body—but it ends with dualism, as if the virtues' victory ultimately closes down the efflorescence of the self's many aspects. Along the way, however, the *Psychomachia* seems uncertain as to whether it is the bad body or the bad (divided) will that is at fault for the capacity for sinfulness that remains even after the virtues have slaughtered the vices.

Although it is not yet a debate between Body and Soul, this Latin poem is a battle *within* and *for* the soul staged in a manner that repeatedly thematizes the problem of embodiment. The body appears as both a site for corporeal

---

22. Prudentius, 343. "Fervent bella horrida, fervent / ossibus inclusa, fremit et discordibus armis / non simplex natura hominis; nam viscera limo / efigiata premunt animam, contra ille sereno / editus adflatu nigrantis carcere cordis / aestuat, et sordes arta inter vincla recusat. / Spiritibus pugnant variis lux atque tenebrae, / distantesque animat duplex substantia vires, / donec praesidio Christus Deus adsit . . ." (902–10).

23. Prudentius, 333. "Ergo cavete, viri, ne sit sententiai discors / sensibusin nostris, ne secta exotica tectis nascatur conflataodiis, quia fissa voluntas / confundit variis arcane biformia fibris" (758–61).

violence and a stage for female allegorical figures who are enfleshed enough to inflict hurt and to be hurt. Ultimately, the *Psychomachia* does not capture or represent a literal "psychology," but rather posits precisely the problem that the rest of this book addresses: that the formal theological and scientific psychology of the Middle Ages cannot and does not address the needs of Christian culture, which seems to have always-already been a culture of confession (compare St. Augustine, although in his day the word itself was closer to "profession of faith"), even if this tendency becomes formally institutionalized only centuries after Prudentius.[24]

Boethius
THE HISTORY OF PHILOSOPHY AS A HISTORY OF ALLEGORY

Personification allegory, which long predates the formalized university disciplines of debate, often figures philosophical thought as something spoken by the female personifications of abstract concepts to male interlocutors, who are often positioned as their students. There are obvious precedents for the philosophical dialogue in classical writing, from Plato to Cicero. Although the *Symposium* was not translated into Latin in the Middle Ages, and Socrates' take-no-prisoners female avatar Diotima was replaced by the apocryphal stories about Socrates' shrewish wife Xanthippe, Diotima's distant daughters—allegorical female figures offering lessons and correction to male thinkers—came to function as the structuring principle for works that crossed the divide between philosophy and literature, making massive contributions to both. The most significant of these figures is Lady Philosophy in *The Consolation of Philosophy*.[25]

Boethius' sixth-century philosophical allegory *The Consolation of Philosophy* had, if anything, even more influence than the *Psychomachia* on the continued use of female personifications to embody abstract concepts in medieval writings. Instead of staging an encounter between female beings embodying abstract concepts, it took a single larger-than-life abstraction, Lady Philosophy, and set her up in a pedagogical relationship with a human narrator. This

---

24. Michel Zink writes, although he does not develop this theme, that "In the Christian world, the psychological cannot be separated from the moral nor from the eschatological" (Zink, 105).

25. While *The Consolation of Philosophy* is generally considered a work of philosophy, it is written in the hybrid poetic style known as *prosimetrum*. This is a style of combining prose with poetry: Lady Philosophy voices a number of poems as part of consoling Boethius, which are interspersed with prose discussions between the two. See Bridget K. Balint, *Ordering Chaos: The Self and the Cosmos in Twelfth-Century Latin* Prosimetrum (Boston: Brill Academic Publishers, 2009).

hierarchical mode characterized a series of later medieval works, including the debates between the Body and the Soul, explicitly establishing the "didactic" dimensions of *sowlehele* through the paradigmatic pairing of teacher and student.

For medieval philosophers, thinking is something that happens in a situation that is at least figuratively dialogic, which means that thinkers are always nominally dependent on the figures of their interlocutors, often allegorical or allegorized as their students or their teachers. This is yet clearer from the later twelfth century on, as dialectical forms come to dominate the medieval university. The development of the *quaestio* and *quodlibet* modes, in which possible objections (from named or nameless other philosophers or philosophical positions) are listed and refuted, produces the fiction that the author is, at all times, responding to the objections and queries of an interlocutor—although such a person might not exist, or might well have written his treatise centuries before.[26] In philosophical treatises, the names of male authors become synecdochal for their own thought. For instance, it is still conventional to note, in the present tense no less, that "Aristotle says," or even that "Aristotle argues" (or "Barthes says," or "Barbara Johnson argues") when indicating some part of the written work attributed to that author. However, in allegorical philosophical dialogues, the author's thought is not always spoken by the figure that bears the author's name, even though we now discuss words spoken by Socrates as Platonic thought, and words spoken by Lady Philosophy as part of Boethius' philosophical system.[27]

26. Alastair Minnis defines the *quaestio* as a pedagogical process undertaken by a master, as if teaching a student. However, in his *Medieval Literary Theory and Criticism c.1100–c.1375: The Commentary Tradition*, ed. A. J. Minnis and A. B. Scott, with assistance from David Wallace (Oxford: Clarendon, 1988), he offers a brief and useful definition (212), and plentiful examples of entirely textual disputations that do not seem to have even the remotest origins in the classroom. The *quaestio* or *disputatio* seems to be a faux-oral form that performs a fiction of presence. The origins of the learned *quaestio* are, of course, in university lectures, where a professor's interlocutors (and straw-man questioners) would be his students, but the written form of such disputations certainly brings the dead as well as the living to philosophical account. The *quodlibet*, by comparison, seems to be a mode of topicality. Biannual disputational festivals (at Advent and Lent) would be open to the public and cover topics suggested by audience members; this was called an *a quodlibet* disputation. The improvisational answering of these questions constituted something of a public ordeal, and lists of both questions and answers were included in manuscripts. Anthony Kenny and Jan Pinborg, in a survey-type article, write that "both types of disputation, in the words of P. Mandonnet, were the academic equivalent of the medieval tournament-at-arms" ("Medieval Philosophical Literature" in *The Cambridge History of Later Medieval Philosophy*, ed. Norman Kretzmann et al. [Cambridge, UK: Cambridge University Press 1982], 22). For a survey of this model's development, see also Anthony Kenny's chapter on disputations in that same volume.

27. Helen Solterer, in *The Master and Minerva*, notes that one exemplary medieval master philosopher described himself as dedicated to the goddess of wisdom, Minerva; she notes in passing, "intellectual traditions in Europe had long typed knowledge as a woman (*scientia*),

In contrast with the male authors, the female speakers of medieval personification allegory are the embodied bearers of the authorial position: The words placed in the mouth of the figure that represents "the author" would not be sufficient without the words of the female personification, even if the author's actual position is worked out between the two protagonists. Lady Philosophy represents a major aspect of Boethius' philosophical enterprise, while "Boethius," the character in *The Consolation of Philosophy,* represents another. When medieval thinkers wanted to cite Boethius on fortune or predestination, they cited words that had been placed in the mouth of Lady Philosophy just as often as or, indeed, more often than they cited words spoken by the figure named Boethius in the *Consolation.*[28] Is Lady Philosophy anything more than Boethius in drag? Is she really permitted to be female? I argue that Boethius uses the sheer awesomeness of Philosophy's grand stature to make her into something more than himself, and that he makes her just female enough that her gender makes a subtle but significant difference, adding a sheen of philosophical irony to what she says. Here is the incredible oddness, which did not fail to strike the French and English writers of subsequent centuries who were influenced by Boethius: The authorial persona and its attendant authority is split between a female and a male character, or several of each.[29]

Medieval personification allegory grapples with a number of major philosophical questions at every turn. It can hardly help itself, since its origin and initial purpose were, in part, the writing of philosophy such as Boethius'

---

and its highest form, wisdom, as a female deity (*sapientia*)" (Solterer, *Master and Minerva,* 29). Solterer goes on to say that, for Abelard, "the bellicose and the feminine come together in the form of the disputation. Under the aegis of Minerva, verbal battles are to be waged. That Abelard chooses this goddess as mentor shows how the scholastic activity of disputing comes to be figured through women. But if intellectual mastery is represented in part through the feminine, where do women figure in?" The present study intends to contribute, in part, to the very long answer to this question in its own terms. Solterer's study is, finally, more concerned with French literature and with the figure of female respondents such as Christine de Pizan, and answers the question in terms of such "real" women; at the same time, it helps us understand, with fine nuance, not the unanswerable question of whether "real women" benefited or were harmed by these representations, but "how medieval debates over the injurious power of representation were articulated through gender" (Solterer, 216).

28. In a sense, Geoffrey Chaucer translated the "Consolation of Philosophy" twice: once as his relatively faithful *Boece,* and once when a crucial piece of Boethius' reasoning is translated as a speech by Troilus in *Troilus and Criseyde.* The former document, naturally, includes Lady Philosophy as a character, but the latter (far more famous and significant) puts Philosophy's words into Troilus' mouth, undoing the original transvestite drama, wherein Boethius wrote his own philosophical ideas as words spoken by this grand female figure.

29. Steven Justice has noted that "medieval commentators recognized the Boethian pedagogue as a faculty of the narrator's soul or of his literary activity.... Abelard says that Boethius speaks to Philosophy 'as someone speaking to himself'" ("Quasi... aliquis secum loquens," Peter Abelard, *Expositio in hexaemeron,* PL 178.760). "The Genres of *Piers Plowman,*" *Viator* 19 (1988): 296, fn. 27.

Consolation. But personification allegory was not developed as just a passive vehicle for something like the popularization of philosophy. Its form has an impact on its content in a number of significant ways, which even carry over into those vernacular allegories that are not explicitly concerned with philosophical matters.

The Consolation of Philosophy begins with Lady Philosophy driving away the Muses that had been consoling Boethius, dramatically staging a rejection of the arts in favor of her own philosophico-poetic artistry.[30] To drive away the Muses is to exchange one kind of female figure for another (another kind of swap of Xanthippe for Diotima), but it is also, in the context of this early moment in the *Consolation of Philosophy*, a statement about the allegory's genre refashioned in a dramatic mode. The first way personification allegory transforms philosophy follows directly from what was discussed earlier: Medieval allegories stage the scene of philosophy as a dramatic disputation, adding detail for emphasis, amusement, and, perhaps, as a reenactment of the pedagogical scene they so often reference. Philosophy is often written as a pedagogical mode, very obviously designed to impart or make memorable certain specific lessons (*memento mori* chief among those taught by the Body/Soul debates) and to translate theological concerns into a more dynamic mode. Given how many philosophical and theological treatises are written as dialogues (from Augustine's "On the Free Choice of the Will" or "The Teacher" to David Hume's *Dialogues Concerning Natural Religion*), it is clear that such translations do not necessitate simplification, but that the incorporation of narrative into the lesson or treatise transforms the pedagogical scene into one that asks questions about the nature and limits of pedagogy, of what kind of self there is and, therefore, what it can be taught.

In addition to its role as an important example of allegory's philosophical potential, Boethius' *Consolation of Philosophy* demonstrates a way in which allegory functions as a staging ground for an issue whose significance waxed and waned but remained persistently central in the Middle Ages: the debate about the limits and possibilities of free will in a God-ordered world. Personification allegory is such an apt mode for discussing this issue because of the specific limits imposed by allegorical characterization. Even a female Reason is not really free to be unreasonable, except in philosophical satire.

Allegorical characters do not have free will, but they often exist as a way of thematizing the limits of the will's freedom. The question of human freedom of will in a context of divine omnipotence and omniscience—the liberty to

---

30. For some of the discussions of Boethius' *prosimetrum* as poetry—discussions that tend to imply the joke that Philosophy did not drive the Muses away successfully, nor did she want to—see Seth Lerer, *Boethius and Dialogue: Literary Method in the "Consolation of Philosophy"* (Princeton, NJ: Princeton University Press, 1985), and Gerald O'Daly, *The Poetry of Boethius* (Chapel Hill: The University of North Carolina Press, 1991).

choose sin or salvation, known as *liberum arbitrium*—was a major philosophical and theological concern throughout the Middle Ages.[31] It appeared in allegory as the question of adhering or not adhering to generic conventions: Must a character named Kindness always be fully and adequately kind, a character named Sloth never, ever do anything that isn't characterized by laziness, and so forth? *The Consolation of Philosophy* culminates in a famous discussion of free will in the context of God's omniscience and foreknowledge of events in human history.[32] And yet the words about freedom of the will, attributed to Boethius, are spoken by an allegorical personification, Lady Philosophy, a character who must, of necessity, conform to her named nature and enact philosophical thinking at all times. She persuades Boethius that God functions on an eternal plane, where time functions differently and things that happen in a certain causal order for human beings have always-already occurred to a divinity who lives in an eternal present. The section of the work that deals most explicitly with the problem of the freedom of the will is repeatedly separated out and cited (most famously by Chaucer in Troilus' despairing monologue in *Troilus and Criseyde*).[33]

Lady Philosophy is *the* prototypical tutelary allegorical figure, setting the pattern for many to come, from Bernardus Silvestris' Noys to Langland's Holy Church. Boethius does not have to highlight the irony that his *Consolation of Philosophy*'s Lady Philosophy is utterly bound to speak philosophically and wisely—that she is not free to do otherwise. Other medieval authors think through this problem for him, and stage it again and again in their allegorical disputations.[34] Lady Philosophy speaks at great length, after all, about a human free will that she herself is utterly denied by her named nature's predetermined imperative to be wise and decorous, and, indeed, pointing out such constraints seems to be part of Boethius' project in the *Consolation*. Lady Philosophy even

---

31. For a clear summary, see John M. Bowers, *The Crisis of Will in "Piers Plowman"* (Washington, DC: Catholic University of America Press, 1986).

32. See Chaucer's *Boece* in *The Riverside Chaucer*, 3rd ed., ed. Larry D. Benson (Boston: Houghton Mifflin, 1987), 395–470. See also Rita Copeland, *Rhetoric, Hermeneutics and Translation in the Middle Ages: Academic Translations and Vernacular Texts* (Cambridge, UK: Cambridge University Press, 1991), 142, in which Copeland argues that the *Boece* aims to replace the Latin *Consolation* as the academic referent of Chaucer's own *Troilus*, in the same way that Chaucer aims to replace Boethius as an *auctor*.

33. See Geoffrey Chaucer, "Troilus and Criseyde," in *The Riverside Chaucer*, ed. Benson, Book IV, lines 953–1085. This passage paraphrases and adapts prose 2 and 3 in Boethius' *Consolation of Philosophy*. In the Explanatory Notes to this passage, Stephan A. Barney points out the striking and witty omission by Chaucer of Boethius' defense of the will's freedom, leaving this Boethian passage, and Troilus, in a philosophically unnecessary state of despair about the inevitability of fate ("Troilus and Criseyde," in *Riverside Chaucer*, Bk. IV, l. 1048).

34. In his translation of *The Consolation of Philosophy* into Anglo-Saxon, King Alfred renames her "Wisdom," a male character. See *King Alfred's Version of the Consolations of Boethius Done into Modern English, with an Introduction*, trans. W. J. Sedgefield (Oxford: Oxford University Press, 1900).

tells Boethius, who wonders about this freedom, that "it would be impossible for any rational nature to exist without it."[35] Although she is the very personification of a rational nature, however, Lady Philosophy is fully delimited by her name.

This delimitation by name is something that critics of allegory have seen as problematic. Angus Fletcher worried that "an allegory of Justice, for example, will omit the contingencies that make a nonrepressive, tolerant justice so difficult to achieve. It omits the human detail."[36] Continuing to think about the particular example of Justice, Gordon Teskey wondered, "what sort of body does Justice have?"[37] He perhaps answers his own question when he restates it a few pages later: "What is the stuff out of which Shamefastness is made? She is made of her gender."[38] Perhaps this is true of Shamefastness, but can this be true of every single female allegorical personification, and does the "gender" that makes up the substance of these personifications change from figure to figure?

The complicated negotiation of gendered embodiment within a discourse of universals is evident even in *The Consolation of Philosophy*'s early medieval dialogue. The bodies of allegorical figures can be described in terms of how they take up space, what they are wearing, how beautiful or terrifying they might appear. But a basic aspect of how they must be described is through the gender their bodies take on. When Lady Philosophy enters the cell where Boethius is poetically lamenting his fate (and drives away the Muses that had been keeping him company), she is described as "awe-inspiring... her eyes burning and keen beyond the usual power of men."[39] Philosophy's height seems to change over time, and on occasion she seems to pierce the very sky and, inconveniently, become "lost to human sight."[40] Unlike many of the

---

35. Boethius, *Consolation of Philosophy*, Bk. V, prose 2, 149, l. 3. "Est, inquit; neque enim fuerit ulla rationalis natura quin eidem libertas adsit arbitrii" (*Anicii Manlii Severini Boethii Philosophiae consolatio*, ed. Ludovicus Bieler, *Boethius, Opera I* Corpus Christianorum, Series Latina, 94 [Turnholt, 1957]).

36. Angus Fletcher, *Allegory: The Theory of a Symbolic Mode* (Ithaca, NY: Cornell University Press, 1964), 29, fn. The same example is also taken up in Gordon Teskey's *Allegory and Violence* (Ithaca, NY: Cornell University Press, 1996).

37. Teskey, *Allegory and Violence*, 21. Teskey goes on to argue that "the event of self-predication, whereby Justice is said to be just, leaves a residue that is not justice but the thing in which Justice must inhere in order to be true of itself."

38. Teskey, 23.

39. Boethius, trans. Watts, 35. "oculis ardentibus et ultra communem hominum valentiam perspicacibus" (Colore vivido atque inexhausti vigoris, quamvis ita aevi plena foret ut nullo modo nostrae crederetur aetatis, statura discretionis ambiguae; Boethius, ed. Bieler, *De consolatione Philosophiae*, Bk. I, prose 1, l. 5).

40. In Boethius, ed. Bieler, "Nam nunc quidem ad communem sese hominum mensuram cohibebat, nunc vero pulsare caelum summi verticis cacumine videbatur; quae cum altius caput extulisset ipsum etiam caelum penetrabat respicientiumque hominum frustrabatur intuitum."

female figures that followed her, Philosophy is not described from head to toe, a rhetorical trope called *effictio* and used to excellent effect in the romances of the Middle Ages for ladies both beautiful and loathly. Philosophy's highly symbolic dress, though described at some length, is hard to visualize. The color of what she is wearing is difficult for Boethius to determine, because in order to emphasize the neglect that philosophy suffers in his age, her raiment seems to be covered in dust, and has been torn "by the hands of marauders."[41] Despite all of this pointed avoidance of physical specificity (unto a sort of surreal vision of a body constantly in metamorphic flux), the sole stable *physical* quality of Lady Philosophy is her gender.

Lady Philosophy embodies the contradictions of female personification in a way that later readers seemed to notice. Besides the way in which Jean de Meun's Reason and, later, William Langland's Holy Church respond to this convention, translators of Boethius dealt with the problem posed by her femininity—in one famous case, by the simple process of eliminating it. King Alfred, in his Old English translation of Boethius, took it upon himself to regender her as the masculine (and also less overtly scholarly) Wisdom (Gesceadwisnes), whereas "Boethius" becomes Mind (Mod). Of course, we cannot know why this was done, but it is hard to miss that this is a switch that makes the space of philosophy male only. Centuries later, *Piers Plowman* enacts a similar sort of switch when a female character named Anima in that poem's B-text version becomes, in its C-text recension, a character named Liberum Arbitrium: curiously, both Lady Philosophy/Wisdom and Anima/Liberum Arbitrium are characters who discuss the possibilities and limits of the will. A key aspect of these Old and Middle English transformations of the discussion of free will is that they are conducted by male speakers, a product, as the rest of this book argues, of a desire to eliminate the feminine from psychological models of the self. In the tradition to which both Alfred and Langland are responding, however, Philosophy is female and bound to her named nature beyond any freedom to choose or deviate. Given that medieval femininity was fenced in by constraints, using a female personification to figure a lack of freedom seems only natural; using that female being to figure a lack of freedom *and* to discuss the complex limitations and possibilities of free will in the abstract, universal sense is an ironic paradox bordering on brilliance.

The problem of Philosophy's free will or lack thereof can be understood, in part, through the medieval debate about predication, a debate that Boethius

---

De consolatione Philosophiae, Bk. I, prose 1, l. 2.
41. Boethius, trans. Watts. In Bieler, "Eandem tamen vestem violentorum quorumdam sciderant manus et particulas quas quisque potuit abstulerant" (*De consolatione Philosophiae*, Bk. I, prose 1, l. 5).

freely entered into in another of his philosophical works, this time a non-allegorical one—his commentary on Porphyry's *Isagoge*.[42] The problem of predication is the question of whether, as Plato and neo-Platonists would argue, there exists a universal quality, say, "chairness," that transcends the particulars of any given chair. Thinkers such as the fourteenth-century philosopher William of Ockham maintained, on the contrary, that "universals are nothing more than names—naturally significant general concepts, primarily, and secondarily the conventional signs corresponding to them."[43] Predication was a major issue to medieval thinkers. Whether universals did or did not exist outside of philosophical debates, allegorical writing guarantees that they *do* exist as literary categories.

In personification allegory, names *are* precisely one and the same as the categories they describe, with the word *Justice* naming and describing the character Justice. Personifications of abstract concepts *are* these concepts in their universal expression, and yet by being brought into a narrative scene, they exit the timeless realm of abstraction and begin to function in the sublunar, mortal world. They take up bodies, and so might be imagined to suffer the limitations that bodily capacity poses. Grammar or convention or the history of dualism compels personifications to take up female bodies, thus becoming susceptible to a limitation that complicates their functioning as a universal. This complication, of course, is an effect of this highly gender-inflected culture: Barring a burning bush, anything that speaks is a "he" or a "she," and being a "she" never manages to be neutral, even if, as Boethius established in the sixth century, she is Philosophy.

Vernacular Readings of Latin Allegory
THE *ROMAN DE LA ROSE* AND HOW GENDER MATTERS

Despite a powerful discourse that considers the gender of allegorical personifications as the arbitrary accident of Latin grammar, medieval authors were not entirely blind to the implications of their practices around gender. Even if Prudentius and Boethius were quite subtle in the ways they played with the

---

42. I am referring here in very shorthand form (because to give the discussion justice would be a chapter in itself) to the debate that was inaugurated by *Isagoge* and continued through the fifteenth century; the first few centuries of this debate are well encapsulated in Paul Vincent Spade's edition of *Five Texts on the Mediaeval Problem of Universals: Porphyry, Boethius, Abelard, Duns Scotus, Ockham*, ed. and trans. Paul Vincent Spade (Indianapolis, IN: Hackett, 1994).

43. *The Cambridge History of Later Medieval Philosophy*, ed. Norman Kretzmann et al. (Cambridge, UK: Cambridge University Press 1982), 434.

gendering and embodiment of personifications, by the twelfth century Jean de Meun had noticed and humorously deplored some of the implications of using female figures to represent the reasonable, the rational, and the philosophical.

The *Roman de la Rose* demands to be read as a psychological allegory, and, insofar as it contains a series of characters that seem to represent the different states of mind possessed by a single person, it is one (even if not a work of psychological aid as such). The psyche being allegorized is not the male narrator's, however, and this poses a problem. The poem is an anatomy of a female being, the Rose, whose being, as Guillaume de Lorris informs us early on, represents that of a lady whose identity is being concealed. The different manifestations of the Rose encountered by the Lover are aspects of the self that deal with the social world only. The *Roman de la Rose* contains nothing that would tell us about the relationship of the Rose's will to her soul's immortality, about her psyche apart from its relational aspects. Consequently, the *Roman de la Rose* does not offer a psychology that can be used to describe and diagnose the relation between the different sins of a single confessing subject, say, or what a woman or man is in the privacy of his or her own soul—the battle of an individual's personal *psychomachia*. Such a description is not the poem's intent, and for the purposes of this study, these limitations prevent it from being usefully read as a work of *sowlehele* in the way that debates between the personified Body and Soul of a single being might be, even if they are written in Latin.

In his portion of the *Roman de la Rose*, during a pivotal scene that parodies the teacher-student model made famous by Boethius, Jean de Meun playfully works through the implications of using female allegorical figures to advance a (male) author's intellectual agenda through a marked exaggeration of one character's femininity. In this scene, the Lover hears the lessons of Reason, Jean de Meun's version of Lady Philosophy. But *this* Reason, who should be advising the lover to be reasonable, per her named nature, is gradually overwhelmed by the Lover's attractiveness and offers herself as his paramour, a replacement for the Rose after which he quests. She is, of course, in the process offering him the option of being a lover of the rational, but the flirtatiousness of the tone is hard to miss:

> Nevertheless, I don't want you to live without a friend. If it pleases you, turn your attention to me. Am I not a lady beautiful, noble, fit to serve a worthy man, even the emperor of Rome? I want to become your friend, and if you wish to hold to me, do you know what my love will be worth to you? . . . I am the daughter of God, the sovereign father who made and shaped me so.

> See here His form, and see yourself in my clear face. No girl of such descent ever had such power of loving as have I, for I have leave of my father to take a friend and be loved.[44]

This moment is a late and highly stylized development in the tradition of female speakers in medieval allegory, a moment of vernacular response to already established tendencies in the Latin authorities.

The thirteenth-century personification allegory of the *Roman de la Rose* represents a crucial step in the development of medieval psychological allegory, even if it is too busy being ironic to enact what Middle English scribes were to call *sowlehele*. Particularly in Jean de Meun's continuation of Guillaume de Lorris's allegory of love, the poem both synthesizes and parodies a huge swath of the Latin intellectual (and allegorical) tradition, while also actively engaging in the philosophical debates of its time. But despite Guillaume de Lorris's promise that his allegory will represent the whole of the art of love, despite many characters' attempts to advise the narrator in surviving overwhelming emotion, this psychology is not intended for healing. Even so, Jean de Meun's playfulness about allegorical gender (in the case of Reason, and in the queer figure of Bel Acueil, a male entity personifying a woman's initial welcoming to a man) shows that contradictions like the one between the purported irrationality of women and a female Reason were clear to at least some medieval authors.

The strong associative link between "woman" and "body" was discussed in the Introduction; it is both literalized and upended by Jean de Meun. Female forms were considered apt vessels for Philosophy or Reason for reasons beyond Romance grammar: By becoming personifications, what were abstractions like "philosophy" actually gaining? It at least seems that they are gaining a (female) body to inhabit, in a world where flesh was endlessly analogized with that which is gendered female. To equate the body with femininity is to place it very low on any epistemological hierarchy. This had worked for as long as the source of all true knowledge was divine illumination, an Augustinian concept immensely influential throughout the Middle Ages. However, with the

---

44. Guillaume de Lorris and Jean de Meun, *The Romance of the Rose*, 3rd ed., trans. Charles Dahlberg (Princeton, NJ: Princeton University Press, 1995), 166–67. "Ne porquant si ne veull je mie / que tu demeurges sanz amie. / Met, s'il te plest, en moi t'entente. / Sui je pas bele dame et gente, / digne de servir un preudome, / et fust enpereres de Rome? / Ci veill t'amie devenir; / et se te veuz a moi tenir, / sez tu que m'amor te vaudra? / . . . Si avras en cest avantage / amie de si haut lignage / qu'il n'est nule qui s'i conpere, / fille Dieu, soverain pere, / qui tele me fist et forma. / Regarde ci quele forme a / et te mire en mon cler visage. / N'onques pucele de parage / n'ot d'amer tel bandon con gie, / car j'ai de mon pere congie / de fere ami et d'estra amee." Guillaume de Lorris et Jean de Meun, *Le Roman de la Rose*, ed. Felix Lecoy (Paris: Librarie Honoré Champion, Editeur, 1985), ll. 5765–93.

rediscovery of Aristotle's *De Anima* in the early thirteenth century, it suddenly appeared that an authority (*the* authority) had argued that the bodily senses were also a crucial source of knowledge. Aristotle's interest in the body as a source of knowledge sponsored a movement in Latin-language philosophical circles that may have prompted Jean de Meun, ever the most ironic of vernacular commentators on philosophical trends, to remember that the new scientific/philosophical interest in the body might have some impact on the conceptual understanding of "woman," long equated with it.

By the thirteenth century, to give the entire notion of "the body" over to the realm of femininity, symbolically at least, is to relinquish a necessary source of knowledge. This did not mean a wholesale turn toward studying the ancillary problem of "women," of course—rather, it tended to result in a decoupling of "woman" and "body," for many but not for Jean de Meun. According to Sarah Kay's analysis of the epistemology of embodiment in the *Roman de la Rose*, it is as if Jean de Meun half-jokingly offers the following new take on the workings of dualism: "If women are to body as man is to mind, and the body is a necessary source of knowledge, then women are a necessary source of knowledge." This seems to justify Jean de Meun's explicitly sexual rewriting of Guillaume de Lorris's romantic quest for the love of the Rose, and its profound interest in getting inside the Castle where the Rose is imprisoned, if even by the back door. The philosophical quest for knowing a woman and the sexual quest for "knowing" a woman are one in Jean's continuation of the *Roman de la Rose*.[45]

Jean de Meun is not necessarily alone in seeing the humor in medieval personification allegory and its generic conventions. Guillaume de Lorris's section of the *Roman de la Rose* also tweaks the intersection of philosophy, psychology, and allegorical narrative, as is evident in another pivotal but small detail: how characters do or do not possess free will given their allegorical names, a question addressed earlier in terms of Boethius' Lady Philosophy. In Guillaume's portion, early in the poem, a character named Dangier (usually translated as Resistance) makes a small concession to the Lover. When he is caught and reprimanded by Shame and Fear, he is angrily reminded that he ought to behave as standoffishly as his name implies:

> "How can you sleep at a time like this?" she said, "with all this misfortune? . . . Have you been lying down now? Get up immediately and stop up all the holes in this hedge; be kind to no man. It doesn't agree with your name for you to do anything but make trouble. If Fair Welcoming is

---

45. Sarah Kay, "Women's Body of Knowledge: Epistemology and Misogyny in the *Romance of the Rose*," in *Framing Medieval Bodies*, ed. Sarah Kay and Miri Rubin (Manchester, UK: Manchester University Press, 1994; New York: St. Martin's Press, 1994), 211–35, 232.

open and sweet, you are to be cruel and violent, full of offensive words that wound."[46]

She goes on to tell a proverb about how a buzzard cannot become a sparrow hawk, transparently explaining that Dangier, a "villain," cannot rise above his station no matter what he does. Dangier is an example of an allegorical character who stretches the limits of his named nature until forced to snap back into its confines: Insofar as he is a person, and subject to persuasion and charm, he can be nice to the Lover, but insofar as he is an allegorical figure for the Rose's reluctance to yield to the Lover, he must not. Dangier's will is not entirely free because he is an allegorical character; but of course the will of a serf subject to a lord is not entirely free, either. The difference is of both scope and the nature of allegorical characterization as a literary conceit.

What permits Jean de Meun to play in this way with the contradictions that structure medieval thinking is the conceptual flexibility medieval allegory affords. This form has the capacity to respond to shifts in philosophical thinking, like the one referenced previously, in a very literal way, by dramatically staging how the implications of such philosophy *work*. When allegorical figures speak, argue, or even do battle with one another, they are staging a way of thinking about the self by thinking about embodiment. Notions such as Philosophy or Liberty move from existence as abstractions to taking on some sort of body, as well as a moment in time and a voice.

Staging Body/Soul Debate in Latin Allegory

Even before Guillaume de Lorris and Jean de Meun had created their witty critique of allegorical gender and the mode's ability to limit character's free will, the tradition of using female figures to represent abstractions had persisted from its inauguration by Prudentius and Boethius. Philosophical allegory experienced a particular flowering in the twelfth century, with a group of thinkers inspired by Plato's *Timaeus* and one another.[47] This group included

---

46. Dahlberg, 77; "Comment dormez-vous à ceste hore, / Fet-ele, par male avanture? . . . Levés tost sus, et si bouchiés / Tous les partuis de ceste haie, / Et ne portés nului manaie: / Il n'afiert mie à vostre non, / Que vous faciès se anui non. / Se Bel-Acueil est frans et dous, / Et vous, soies fel et estous, / Et plains de ramposne et d'outrage: / Vilains qui est cortois, c'est rage . . . ." Lecoy, 3814–15; 3828–36.

47. For some of the other late antique/early medieval works that also took up the convention of female tutelary figures, see Martianus Capella's *The Marriage of Philology and Mercury*, written in the early fifth century (available in English as *Martianus Capella and the Seven Liberal Arts*, trans. William Harris Stahl and Richard Johnson, with E. L. Burge [New York: Columbia

not only those who were directly linked with the cathedral school of Chartres but also those who picked up and extended their interest in humanist studies and literary applications of Platonizing philosophy.[48] Among their many other accomplishments, the twelfth-century thinkers and poets whose writings and sometimes lives have often been linked as the "Chartrians"—Bernard of Chartres (although, apart from John of Salisbury's quotations, his verifiable works are lost), Thierry of Chartres, Gilbert of Poitiers, William of Conches, and John of Salisbury—laid the foundation for a merging of philosophy, psychology, and literary allegory. In what follows, this book steps away from the chronological sequence of famous and influential works, *Psychomachia–Consolation–Roman de la Rose,* to examine works that are considerably less famous but deal very directly with the matter of how the self is organized, through staging debates between the Body and the Soul.

The debated and useful notion that such a thing as a Chartrian "school" existed contributed importantly to another idea, something of a commonplace in contemporary medieval studies, that the twelfth century "discovered" the individual, to use the title of Colin Morris's study. More recently, however, the argument that it was individuality that the twelfth century discovered has come to be replaced with the contention that what was discovered, or perhaps reformulated, in that era was something more like psychology, or rather ways of talking about the self both descriptively and normatively.[49] This "discovery"

University Press, 1977]), and Theodulus' extraordinarily popular school text, the *Eclogues,* a debate between Alithia (Truth) and Phronesis (Intelligence). See *Ten Latin Schooltexts of the Later Middle Ages: Translated Selections,* ed. and trans. Ian Thomson and Louis Perraud (Lewiston, NE: Mellen Press, 1990). Considerations of space and the demands of arguments do not permit a discussion of these works and their influence.

48. Whether there were "Chartrians" in the sense of writers linked to one another is very much a matter of debate. For the premier study of what it would mean to write as if this were a coherent group, see Winthrop Wetherbee's *Platonism and Poetry in the Twelfth Century: The Literary Influence of the School at Chartres* (Princeton, NJ: Princeton University Press, 1972). For an argument against the existence of such a school, see the chapter entitled "Humanism and the School of Chartres," in R. W. Southern, *Medieval Humanism and Other Studies* (Oxford, UK: Blackwell, 1970), 61–85. For a defense of the "Chartrian" thesis, see Wetherbee, "The School of Chartres," in *A Companion to Philosophy in the Middle Ages,* ed. Jorge J. C. Gracia and Timothy B. Noone (Oxford, UK: Blackwell, 2003), 36–44.

49. Some of the milestones in the critical literature on the twelfth-century invention of something like the self, decade by decade, would include Colin Morris, *The Discovery of the Individual 1050-1200* (London: SPCK, 1972); Caroline Walker Bynum, "Did the Twelfth Century Discover the Individual?," in *Jesus as Mother: Studies in the Spirituality of the High Middle Ages* (Berkeley: University of California Press, 1982); and David Aers, "A Whisper in the Ear of Early Modernists," in *Culture and History, 1350-1600: Essays on English Communities,* ed. David Aers (New York: Harvester Wheatsheaf, 1992). Such work takes up the provocative notion that the very idea of selfhood has a history, an idea with which Michel Foucault is often credited. In the 1980s, some significant scholarship in Renaissance studies claimed that the individual was being invented in the Renaissance, and critics such as Aers took issue with that, even as the

can be described in terms of its contribution to twelfth-century science. In *Sciences and the Self in Medieval Poetry*, a study that examines two psychological allegories that offer the narrative of a single self's development, James Simpson has shown how John Gower's *Confessio Amantis* as well as Alan of Lille's *Anticlaudianus* function as "psychological allegories of the individual soul."[50] Simpson goes on to write that "both poems are structured around a psychology, and both imply a very subtle psychology of learning, which profoundly modifies the scientific content of either poem. It is central to the argument of the whole book, then, that both poems are coherent psychological allegories, anatomizing and representing the education of a *single* soul." Twelfth-century writers were certainly doing more than setting the stage for the specifically vernacular version of *sowlehele* psychology of the Middle English debates between the Body and the Soul, but those thirteenth-century debates would not have been possible without the kind of thinking about the soul and the body that was being done in the neo-Platonic allegories of the twelfth century.

The earliest standalone Body/Soul dialogues on record seem to have been written in Old English, not Latin, as sermons and homilies. "Body/Soul dialogue," however, may be a misnomer for these Old English works, "Soul and Body I," "Soul and Body II," and the "Worcester fragments": Before the twelfth century, no Body actually offers counterarguments to the Soul's accusations or, it seems, talks back at all.[51] The earliest work that took the Body's speaking

---

hope for finding a clear moment when the notion of the individual was invented faded and, I believe, came to be replaced with a series of complex eruptions of rhetorics of selfhood, none of which could claim originary status. Ultimately, the irresolvable questions about how and when our notion of the self came to exist may be partially resolved through close inquiry into the disciplinary discourses (like psychology, of the medical, theological, and *sowlehele* varieties) that emerged to both describe and normalize whatever it is that persons were thinking they were.

50. Simpson, *Sciences and the Self,* 13.

51. The division and personified conflict between body and soul was also developed in the tradition of Christian legends and homilies, visions of dead bodies whose souls lament as they are dragged away to hell or rejoice as they are lifted up to heaven—a tradition that exists in both Latin and the vernacular. Theodore Batiouchkof has written about the early Christian origins of the Body/Soul legend ("Le Débat de l'âme et du corps," *Romania* 20 [1891]: 1–55; 513–78) and Louise Dudley about the connections between this legend and the Egyptian Book of the Dead (*The Egyptian Elements in the Legend of the Body and the Soul* [Baltimore: Bryn Mawr College Monographs No. 8]. However, the most proximate sources for the debate are homilies: Eleanor K. Heningham has argued that Body/Soul debates can be traced to the homilies of one Ephraem Syrus, d. 375 ("The Precursors of the Worcester Fragments, *PMLA* 55 [1940]: 299n]). See also two important Latin sources, the Nonantola version of the Body/Soul legend, originally edited by Batiouchkof as an appendix to his article about Body/Soul debates (see 576–78 of that article) and a pseudo-Augustinian homily, Sermon 49 of the collection *Sermones Ad Fratres in Eremo* (edited in the *Patrologia Latina* 40: 1332–34). The last two have been edited, and information about sources assembled, by Michael J. B. Allen and Daniel G. Calder, ed. and trans., in *Sources and Analogues of Old English Poetry: The Major Latin Texts in Translation* (Cambridge, UK: D. S. Brewer, 1976). See also Douglas Moffat, *The Soul's Address to the Body: The Worcester*

role seriously and is therefore considered in this study as a Body/Soul debate was written in Latin around 1100. Hildebert of Lavardin, Archbishop of Tours, produced an allegorical debate between a narrator named Hildebert and his soul called the "Liber de Querimonia."[52] Hildebert may have been drawing on a much older tradition of sermon literature but fusing it with the conventions of the Latin personification allegory and the philosophical work done by the disputational mode. The only other early debate of this kind, the twelfth-century Latin "Royal Debate," also known as "Nuper huiuscemodi," is preserved in a single manuscript and organized as a series of very long set-piece speeches rather than as dynamic interchange.[53]

It is unclear whether Hildebert's personification allegory was the first or one of the first full-fledged debates between the Body and the Soul, but it was certainly part of a very early moment in the history of this homiletic trope's emergence as a popular literary/didactic hybrid genre in which the Body really did talk back to the Soul. Hildebert's work also provides the most direct and fruitful link back to the allegorical traditions of Boethius and Prudentius. Certainly, Hildebert was known to be in correspondence with the best minds of his day (including Anselm of Canterbury, Hugh of Cluny, and Bernard of Clairvaux), and may have been particularly well-positioned to observe and influence the way in which thinking about the body/soul relation in the homiletic tradition (speaking Soul, silent Body) may have become unsatisfying. He was also quite aware that there was another, Boethian tradition to draw from to create his own work, and he did so.[54] This study does not attempt to

Fragments, ed. Douglas Moffat (East Lansing, MI: Colleagues Press, 1987), and *The Old English Soul and Body*, ed. and trans. Douglas Moffat (Cambridge, UK: D. S. Brewer: 1990).

52. According to Bridget K. Balint's dissertation on the "Liber de Querimonia," the *Cosmographia* appears in three of the twenty-two medieval manuscripts that contain Hildebert's allegorical debate between Hildebert and Anima, which represents a number of scribes thinking that the two works went together nicely. See Balint, "Hildebert of Lavardin's 'Liber de querimonia' in Its Cultural Context" (PhD diss., Harvard University, 2002), 90; see also n. 65.

53. Eleanor K. Heningham, editor of the so-called Royal debate, argues for the Royal's primacy as the first Latin debate to stage a disagreement between the Body and the Soul. According to her research, it is likely that the "Royal" was a major source for the "Visio Philiberti," which, in turn, was a major source for the thirteenth-century English Body/Soul debates discussed in the next chapter. Heningham was unaware of the existence of Hildebert of Lavardin's work, and it is not clear how she would have positioned her argument had she taken his dialogue into account: She dates the "Royal" to the first half of the twelfth century, but there is no evidence proving it earlier or later than Hildebert's; my chapter discusses Hildebert at more length simply because he is the link between the Boethian tradition and the Body/Soul dialogues. The "Royal" debate, also known by its incipit as "Nuper huiuscemodi," is edited and introduced by Heningham in *An Early Latin Debate of the Body and Soul* (Menasha, WI: George Banta Publishing Company, 1937).

54. The preceding, like most of my factual information about Hildebert of Lavardin (and a useful translation of his allegory), comes from Balint, "Hildebert of Lavardin's 'Liber de querimonia.'" Balint, *Ordering Chaos* (2009), is the revised version of this dissertation. The Latin

trace a tradition of influence, although Bridget Kennedy Balint has argued persuasively that the "Liber de querimonia" "stands at the head of a stream of body-and-soul debates composed in Latin during the twelfth and thirteenth centuries."[55] Instead of engaging this claim and the developmental model such engagement would entail, this study looks at selected resonant moments in the history of the kind of disputation that was being used as medicine for the soul. Hildebert's poem certainly was that, and more. According to Peter Orth, the debate's editor, Hildebert's version of the Body/Soul debate survives in twenty-two manuscripts, which would be a great many if it were a Middle English work but is not so many for a work written in Latin by a significant figure in the Church hierarchy. While Hildebert's poem seems to have been disseminated far better than the roughly contemporary "Royal Debate" (extant in a single copy), it was certainly not the most popular example of its type. The reasons for this are, most likely, contained in the allegory's rather surprising and convoluted plot, which revolves almost entirely around the politics of allegorical gender.

Hildebert of Lavardin's "Liber de Querimonia" is a hybrid of the homiletic Soul's lament and the scene of a narrator consoled by a tutelary female figure embodying some abstraction. This new strain of poetry depicting the contents of the self as divisible into a Body and Soul was written in part as tribute to the dialogic allegorical structure of the *Consolation of Philosophy*, which, according to Balint, was the central influence on the text in terms of vocabulary and style. Like Boethius, Hildebert uses the *prosimetrum* form, alternating poetry with prose. Like Boethius' *Consolation*, Hildebert's "Liber de Querimonia" imagines the soul as a lady arrived to lecture to a hapless narrator bearing the name of the *prosimetrum*'s author. Hildebert's narrator, rather than being imprisoned, has been absorbed in rebuilding his house, which had fallen down as a result of a fire (this circumstance and the Soul's lamentations about its lack of proper lodging may be allegorical gestures toward an ultimately underdeveloped "body as castle" trope, discussed in a different context in chapter 4).[56]

The "Liber" establishes itself as both like and unlike the surviving Old English homilies containing an address by the Soul to the Body. Instead of being a hulk of mute, dead flesh, the figure representing bodiliness is a living

---

edition of Hildebert's allegory appears as Peter Orth, ed., *Hildebert's Prosimetrum De Querimonia und die Gedichte eines Anonymus* (Vienna: Osterreichische Akademie der Wissenschaften, Arbeiten zür mittel- und neulateinischen Philologie 6, 2000).

55. Balint, *Ordering Chaos*, Appendix II, 174.

56. Balint, *Ordering Chaos*, Appendix II, 174. "Incendio domus mea corruerat et reficiendi studio sollicitus anhelabam: ligna cedi preceperam, quadrari lapides et expensas operi provideri; totus eram in hoc et omissis pontificalibus negotiis, quo in loco ponerem fundamenta, quantum palatia extenderem, nunc intuitu, nun arundine metiebar" (Orth, 1–5, 989A).

narrator named Hildebert. Perhaps because Hildebert of Lavardin is using his own name as that of the narrator, the Body makes cogent and reasonable arguments in its defense, using skilled rhetoric. Hildebert objects that the Soul "ascribe[s] the entire cause of your corruption to the exterior man.... [Y]ou have used the body as your accomplice, [...] as a master uses a slave, or as an artisan a tool.... Why then do you paint another, an innocent, with the dye of your crime?"[57] Naturally, the Soul still wins the argument, citing the authority of the Church Fathers, specifically the narrative of the Fall and the equation of Eve with the sinful flesh: "Our flesh was tempted, woman was tempted ... because of the flesh inciting and the spirit incited as though by her husband and spouse, that first transgression came to be."[58] Eve, the "woman" here, represents the original "wife" side of the pair being imagined; that "wife" is the body, or the flesh, and it is also, in the context of this dialogue, Hildebert, the narrator.

In his *prosimetrum*, Hildebert of Lavardin, like Boethius before him, makes use of his tutelary figure's gender as a way of making a philosophical point: Whether one reads the work as an interpretation of Boethius or an innovation similar to Jean de Meun's coquettish Reason depends on what one thinks of the *Consolation of Philosophy* as a work of self-conscious literary art. However, whether imitating a subtle point unsubtly or differentiating himself from Boethius, who missed the implications of his own writing, Hildebert assiduously addresses himself to the problem posed by having the top tier of the hierarchy permanently occupied by a female figure. By the personification allegory's end, he effectively inverses the genders of his speakers, and his Soul establishes herself as "husband" to the unruly and appetitive "wife," Hildebert's narrator, Hildebert. Late in the *prosimetrum*, after Hildebert has become Anima's "proud" wife, the allegory's last lines look back at its beginning with horror in this way: "A monstrosity [comes about]: the flesh becomes husband, the spirit, wife."[59] The situation being described as monstrous toward the allegory's end is actually a perfectly apt description of the quasi-Boethian situation (the spirit gendered female, the body somehow gendered male, and

57. Balint, *Ordering Chaos*, 181. "Hinc autem specialiter moveor, quod totam corruptionis tue causam exteriori ascribis homini visa..." (19–21).... "Tu autem ad ea, [que tibi ipsi noxia sunt], ita ministro uteris corpore sicut dominus servo, sicut artifex instrumento" (Orth, 80, 995C–996A).

58. "temptata est enim caro, temptata est mulier ... ut ex subigente carne et subacto spiritu velut ex marito et coniuge primum illud gigneretur delictum ... (Balint, *Ordering Chaos*, 184; Orth, 85, 998A–998B, 31, 35–37).

59. Balint, *Ordering Chaos*, 190. In Latin, this line is: "Inque creando nefas caro fit vir, spiritus uxor" (Orth, 95, 11, 1004A). The phrase "proud wife" occurs in this passage: "... in the manner of a strict regimen or the stern and scrupulous admonishment of a husband to his proud wife." Balint, *Ordering Chaos*, 186. In Latin: "... quam vel egro dicta vel superbe coniugi severior et morosa mariti correctio" (Orth, 90, 118, 1001A).

the two apparently married to one another) that began the "Liber de Querimonia." The speaker's initial gender and marital arrangement is to be retrospectively understood as a terrible perversion, while, for a contemporary reader, the fact that the genders of the *prosimetrum*'s two protagonists prove to be exchangeable cannot help seeming strangely, startlingly queer. This queerness may support the argument made in Tison Pugh's *Queering Medieval Genres* about Hildebert of Lavardin as a poet who queers medieval genres, although Pugh's argument concerns Hildebert's lyrics and does not touch upon this debate.⁶⁰

According to Balint's succinct summary of the gender problem plaguing the "Liber de Querimonia": "In Hildebert's universe, the soul must be masculine in order to be virtuous; in order to reclaim virtue, Anima, the fallen bride of Christ, must assert authority over Hildebert, and the most effective way to do so is to be *vir* to Hildebert's *uxor*."⁶¹ The narrator, Hildebert, must undergo a conceptual sex-change in the course of the allegory in order for a proper hierarchical relationship to be established between himself (as Body) and his own soul. He does so, tells us that he's doing so, and notes the strangeness of so doing.

60. Tison Pugh's chapter on Hildebert of Lavardin and two other Latin poets in *Queering Medieval Genres* (New York: Palgrave Macmillan, 2006) discusses a contradiction in Hildebert's poetic corpus. Among Hildebert's lyrics, there are some praising same-sex love (these are set in a classical past) and others sternly condemning sodomy. Indeed, in the poem "De malitia saeculi," Hildebert characterized same-sex desire as the "sexual incarnation of the fallen world ... [which] can only be conquered by the flesh being ruled by the mind." The poem reads, "Et, vice mutata, caro jam nimium dominata / Mentis ad imperium, det sibi servitium," which Pugh translates as "Turn things around again, and let flesh, which has excessively dominated, / Give service to the command of the mind" (Pugh, *Queering*, 36). Pugh is quoting and translating *Les Mélanges poétiques d'Hildebert de Lavardin*, ed. Barthélemy Hauréau (Paris: Pedone-Lauriel, 1882), 68–69. This Hildebert, who insists that the same-sex loving flesh be conquered, closely resembles the author of a marriage model for Body/Soul relations, but seems to contradict the Hildebert of the boy-love poems "Cum peteret puerum" ("When He Sought the Boy") and "Phoebus de interitu Hyacinthi" ("Phoebus on the Death of Hyacinth"), which are discussed in Pugh, 33–34. Pugh argues that, though his poems about boy-love may or may not tell us something about Hildebert's real and hidden desires, the celebration as well as the condemnation of sodomy in his poetic corpus exists because medieval writers "could have believed that same-sex acts were both good and bad, both salvific and damning [because] ... a significant strand of biblical teaching emphasized that the mighty and powerful shall be lowered and the weak and helpless raised in the kingdom of heaven" (25).

61. Balint, "Liber de Querimonia," 66. Balint notes, "If we had begun with an appearance of a personified, female *caro* to a soul named Hildebert, all conflict would have been averted. As it is, though, the author reestablishes body and soul in their proper places by demoting Hildebert to wifely status, and restoring the soul to superiority by reassigning its grammatical gender and its status within the marriage metaphor," 64. Somehow, readers of the allegory cannot help thinking in the subjunctive about all the problems Hildebert *could* have avoided—but surely he didn't avoid them for a good reason. See also Balint's more complex revisiting of this argument, *Ordering Chaos*, 89–92.

There are a number of words for "soul" in Latin, many of which are used interchangeably, in arbitrary or in deliberate fashion. The main difference between them seems to be the gender of the nouns: In addition to *anima* (f), there are *animus* (m) and *spiritus* (m). Barbara Newman gives a very clear description of the convention of including only Anima in personification allegory:

> The semantic fields of *anima* (f.) and *animus* (m.) overlap, but *animus* is more commonly linked with the "higher" mental faculties—mind, spirit, purpose, imagination, courage, will—while *anima* is linked with the vital breath and the "lower" faculty of quickening the body. One might have expected medieval writers, with their well-known preference for the mental over the corporeal, to personify and valorize the *animus* rather than the *anima*, but they almost never did.[62]

In medieval Latin debates between the Body and the Soul, the Soul is most often referred to as "anima," which is also true of the Latin titles given in manuscripts to Middle English, Anglo-Norman, and Old French Body/Soul debates. In addition to *corpus, corporis* (neut), the most frequently used word for "body," there is also *caro, carnis* (f). These last two should map nicely onto the body/flesh distinction, with the feminine noun standing in for the fallible flesh, but, in practice, these are often used interchangeably. Latin-language authors, therefore, have a wide latitude in organizing the gender dynamic of the relationship between body and soul, and yet the most common form remains very stable.

The most standard definition of the soul's relationship with the body is given in a well-disseminated pseudo-Augustinian text, *De Spiritu et Anima*, most likely written by a Cistercian monk. The definition this treatise offers has become standard, even if the text it appears within never quite enters the philosophical canon: "The soul is a substance which participates in reason and is so fashioned as to rule the body" [*animus est substantia quaedam rationis particeps, regendo corpori accomodata*]."[63] This tag seems to have been quite

---

62. Newman, 36.
63. A. V. C. Schmidt discusses the *De Spiritu et Anima* as a possible source for the Liberum Arbitrium section of *Piers Plowman*, citing its usefulness as "a kind of encyclopaedia of psychology, which was widely read in the Middle Ages. This highly eclectic work attempts to synthesize Platonic, Aristotelian, and Biblical ideas. . . . [Such works] formed one of the chief sources, if not *the* chief source, of psychological doctrine and terminology" A. V. C. Schmidt, "Langland and Scholastic Philosophy," *Medium Aevum* 38.2 (1969): 144. Schmidt offers a brief analysis of *De Spiritu et Anima*, William of Thierry's *De Natura Corporis et Anima*, and Cassiodorus' *De Anima*. According to Schmidt, these works were such useful sources for psychological knowledge because they were "noncontroversial" and "accessible," and used a less technical

common. What is distinctive is that its choice of terminology for body and soul [*animus* (m) and *corpus* (n)] is *not* used in the literature that reflects this definition with the most clarity—Latin Body/Soul debates, with Hildebert's "Liber de Querimonia" as just the earliest example.

It would have been far simpler to begin with a dominating, perhaps masculine Soul (*animus* or *spiritus*) who would justly rule over the narrator/Body. If the Soul were masculine, the Body could even be either *caro, carnis* (f), the Soul's subservient wife, or *corpus, corporis* (neut); it would not necessarily matter. Later medieval English authors do just this, positing a masculine Soul's domination of a masculine Body and fully excluding the feminine—this, in fact, is the literary/linguistic development traced in the next two chapters. Hildebert, however, seems too committed to his Boethian *modus operandi* to begin the work with this simple arrangement; instead, he achieves the proper gender hierarchy in an incredibly convoluted manner whose progress makes up most of the matter of the "debate."

Why set up the task of achieving the "correct" gendered hierarchy to be so difficult? Not only does it prove morally unacceptable; it also seems to necessitate a lengthy discussion of female sexual sinfulness. Somehow, the heterosexual dyad of husband and wife seems to suggest, to Hildebert-the-author's apparent discomfort, ongoing conjugal relations taking place within the self. Sex is a specter haunting this debate, as indeed it seems to haunt the rhetoric of all Body/Soul debates (notwithstanding the fact that sex with another aspect of oneself can, at best, be understood as narcissism). In Hildebert of Lavardin's rendering of this problematic theme, Anima's lament to Hildebert, at the allegory's beginning, is entirely about sexual sin: She complains, at some length, about having been prostituted by her own servant girl. In the "Liber," whether because it is early or because it is idiosyncratic, that servant, the sinful *ancilla*, is the third character, a silent ill-doer in the Hildbert/Anima dialogue.[64] And yet, as the allegory proceeds and it turns out that Hildebert is the Body of this put-upon Anima, his defensiveness and his eventual regret make it seem as though he is shouldering the blame for Anima's mistreatment. In terms

---

language. Surprisingly, he contrasts the accessibility of these encyclopedic works with "the later disputation-form of the scholastic writers" (which debates rather than merely asserting a set of theories). *De Spiritu et Anima* is available in English translation, appearing in *Three Treatises on Man: A Cistercian Anthropology*, ed. and with an introduction by Bernard McGinn, Cistercian Fathers Series 24 (Kalamazoo, MI: Cistercian Publications, 1977). *De Spiritu et Anima* appears in this collection under the title "Treatise on the Spirit and the Soul," translated by Erasmo Leiva and Sr. Benedicta Ward SLG.

64. Balint notes that "the popularity of this metaphor [*domina/ancilla*] to represent a proper hierarchical relationship cannot be overstated" and cites examples from Augustine's *In Epistolam Joannis ad Parthos X*, Geoffrey of Vinsauf's *Poetria Nova*, and Peter Damien's *Lettre sur la toute-puissance divine*. Balint, PhD diss., 7n.

of fault or guilt, Hildebert-qua-Body and the servant girl seem to become a single being, as if Body and Flesh, which begin as separate characters, come to be viewed as a single, sinning whole—but somehow this union permits the normative, divinely sanctioned economy of a "proper" marriage of Soul and Body (with the Soul as husband) to exist.

In the years that followed the writing of Hildebert's allegory, a tradition of Latin Body/Soul debate came into being. Some debates survive in single manuscript copies, such as the one that Hans Walther, its editor, titled "Streit zwischen Korper und Seele" (also known by the incipit "Conpar mea nobilis") and the "Altercacio Carnis et Spiritus" (incipit "O Caro, cara vilitas"), analyzed thoroughly and well by Michel-Andre Bossy in a 1976 article in *Comparative Literature*.[65] In both poems, the flesh and sexuality are inextricably linked, and the Soul is simply disgusted by the Body's propensities, instead of being in any way implicated in them by marriage or partnership. In a way, these poems can be seen as participating in the tradition of Hildebert's "Liber"; they might also, in naming the Body as sinning flesh, be somewhat guilty of a Manichean rejection of the bodily that other Body/Soul debates adamantly refuse. The Body/Soul debate with the greatest dissemination, however, was a peculiar thirteenth-century poem usually referred to as the "Visio Philiberti."

The "Visio Philiberti" is a hugely popular poem that richly deserves an entire study of its own. It survives in at least 131 manuscripts, making it a Latin-language best-seller, and this plentitude alone apparently poses such an immense challenge to editors and critics that it has hardly ever been edited or studied, a gap that Neil Cartlidge has recently started to remedy with his 2006 *Medium Aevum* article.[66] In the limited terms of this study, the poem

65. Michel-Andre Bossy, "Medieval Debates of Body and Soul," *Comparative Literature* 28 (1976): 144–63, 154. "Conpar mea nobilis" is edited, along with "O Caro, cara vilitas," in Hans Walther, *Das Streitgedicht in der Lateinischen Literatur des Mittelalters*. Vol. 5, Pt. 2 of *Quellen und Untersuchungen zur Lateinischen Philologie des Mittelalters* (Munich: Oskar Beck, 1920).

66. Neil Cartlidge argues, quite persuasively, that there are probably many more copies in addition to the 131 identified by Walther (Walther claims to have identified 132, but Cartlidge points out that one among that number is a placeholder for a missing and unexamined manuscript). Neil Cartlidge, "In the Silence of a Midwinter Night: A Re-Evaluation of the *Visio Philiberti*," *Medium Aevum* 75: 1 (2006): 24–46. There are several fairly similar versions of the "Visio Philiberti." The more popular, with 131 copies (incipit "Noctis sub silentio") has been edited by Thomas S. Wright as part of the collection, *The Latin Poems Commonly Attributed to Walter Mapes* (London: Camden Society, 1841). Attribution to Walter Mapes has always been questioned and has largely been debunked in the twentieth century. However, a very similar poem, with the incipit "Vir quidam existerat dudum hermita," was edited by Edelstand du Méril in *Poésies populaires antérieures au XIIe siècle* (Paris, 1843), 217–30. There is an also an older edition by Theodor Georg von Karajan, in *Frühlingsgabe für Freunde älterer Literatur* (Vienna, 1839). The "Visio Philiberti" appears in partial form on the verso (164v) of a manuscript, the Cotton Caligula A xi, which contains a copy of *Piers Plowman* B that begins on the following recto (f. 165r). However, I have been unable to determine with any certainty whether both

represents a different, although related, strain of thought about the Body and its position vis-à-vis the Soul, a richly philosophical representation of this relationship as evinced, in part, by the long critical tradition of (falsely, scholars now think) attributing the authorship of the "Visio Philiberti" to significant British philosophers, particularly Robert Grosseteste.[67]

The "Visio Philiberti" is introduced by a passage that shows up in only certain redactions, as a vision by a pious monk. The scene of disputation portrayed in it is framed by an external narrator, whose frightened and repentant response to the vision telegraphs the poem's didactic intent. Yet the poem is less like a homily than like a philosophical debate: Soul and Body both make masterful use of a number of rhetorical devices in addition to the conventions of *ubi sunt* (enumeration of lost possessions and status) and other necessary elements of didactic deathbed situations. The gender of the Body does seem somewhat flexible. It is first addressed as "O *Caro* miserrima," but when the Body responds to the Soul it is described, apparently by that third-person observer, as "*corpus* caput erigit."[68] Ultimately, however, the "Visio Philiberti" and many subsequent debates turn from the husband/wife model to a same-sex economy of social differentiation and do not spend much time playing with the "corpus/caro" or "animus/anima/spiritus" distinctions. In the single descriptive model of the Body and Soul's relationship that the poem offers, the Body describes itself as an *ancilla* and then, as a virtual synonym, as *pedissequa* to the Soul's (badly behaved) *domina* (who explains that God gave her the Body as a handmaiden).[69] This same-sex hierarchy is very clear and needs

---

poems were written in the same hand and whether there was any scribal intention to link the works together.

67. This was the attribution proposed by Hans Walther (in *Das Streitgedicht*) and is regularly mentioned by the few critics who discuss the poem, but Cartlidge says that the suggestion "outruns the evidence" (Cartlidge, "A Re-Evaluation of the *Visio Philiberti* 42, n. 21). While such attribution is nothing like a secure ascription of the poem to any particular author, it is one of the oldest and most consistent aspects of the reception history of a poem that has received little critical attention beyond such attribution, and it functions as a sort of vote of confidence in the poem rather than a genuine evaluation of its qualities.

68. Wright, "Dialogus Inter Corpus et Animam," in Thomas Wright, *The Latin Poems Commonly Attributed to Walter Mapes*, ll 9 and 94; italics mine.

69. Wright: "et ut ancilla fierem tibi me donavit" (113); "si velle spiritus in opere ducatur / per carnem pedissequam suam, quid culpatur?" (130–31). Cartlidge, in a discussion of the Body's arguments in its own defense, finds these characterizations of the Body-as-handmaiden unconvincingly humble, arguing that these "images of its subordinacy are far too artful and overdrawn to appear as anything other than hypocritical" (Cartlidge, "A Re-Evaluation of the *Visio Philiberti*," 34). However persuasive they might have been intended to be in terms of the actual debate between Body and Soul, *ancilla* and *domina* are the terms that name their relationship, as affirmed by the Soul when she counteraccuses the Body of treachery, calling her *familiaris proditrix* ("household traitor," 156), as Cartlidge himself notes, a "distinctively 'feudal' concept" (Cartlidge, 34).

no reversing: Social class seems to have a more stable basis than the gender of allegorical beings.

In place of a disputational scene in which a female personification of philosophy or reason lectures a male interlocutor, Soul and Body, both female, struggle with the fact that they are one but separate (this contrasts with Hildebert, who initially had trouble recognizing the stern Anima as his own soul). Michel-Andre Bossy notes that it differs from other Latin Body/Soul debates by presenting itself "less as a disputation between separate speakers than as a dialogue-in-monologue."[70] This sense of one being warring with itself, rather than two quite separate beings in dialogue, is the particular achievement of the "Visio Philiberti" as a work of psychological theory rather than an improved-upon, more amusing homily or a new spin on Boethius or Prudentius. As Cartlidge argues, rather than glibly recapitulating medieval dualism, the complex interactions between Body and Soul "testify not to a 'mentality' or an alternative theology, but to the instinctive recognition on the part of creative artists in the Middle Ages that theology is necessarily too complicated and too heavily qualified to be translated, without adaptation, into forms that are also dramatically effective or aesthetically appealing."[71] This poem is not a transcription of any particular school of medieval theology or psychology into dialogue form; it is a work of Latin *sowlehele,* which means that it attempts a balance between the didactic and the dramatic. Sometimes, the attempt of the "Visio Philiberti" to be "dramatically effective and aesthetically appealing" queers the scene that the poem describes, positing it as a scene of same-sex affection.

In its first speech, the Soul accused the Body of having tainted it, of having dragged it (certainly a physical metaphor) toward crime: "you always dragged me towards ill-doing / and so we will always be in sad sorrow."[72] When the Body responds, it does so in the language of seduction instead of the language of force: "the flesh seduces the soul," she says, and, seduced, the Soul follows the flesh "like a bull led to the slaughter."[73] What may seem to a modern reader a boggling moment of queer figuration—of a female being corrupting another female being—is certainly not intended to be so. The phrase "like a bull led to the slaughter" works to disrupt this queerness, since *"ductus"* (led) marks the bull's masculinity, all the more so since *"bos"* (bull) *can* be a neuter noun

---

70. Bossy, "Medieval Debates of Body and Soul," 144. Michel-Andre Bossy also writes that previous scholars had "slighted the dramatic suppleness and individuality of [these] works in order to pigeonhole them in a rigid stemma" (150).

71. Cartlidge, 27.

72. "Semper ad scelera pessima traxisti / unde semper erimus in dolore tristi" (Wright, "Dialogus Inter Corpus et Animam," 36–37).

73. "Eorumque blanditiis caro seducit animam / quam a virtutum culmine trahit ad partem infimam, / quae statim carnem sequitur ut bos ductus ad victimam" ("Visio Philiberti," in Wright, *The Latin Poems Commonly Attributed to Walter Mapes,* 107–9).

but isn't functioning as one here. However, the analogy with the bull is just that, an analogy. The female Soul is seduced *as if* it were nothing more than a male ox. Can this reading be intended by the author? Probably not. I'm sure that, instead, the economy of seduction in this passage is rendered in same-sex terms precisely to avoid the dangerously matrimonial language of such works as the "Liber de Querimonia." Intentionally evoking same-sex relations or not, this queer moment is the only instance of either party in the debate using the language of seduction. In what proves to be a common tactic in Body/Soul debates, the poem quickly turns away from any mention of love between the two parts of the same being toward the discourse of discipline, as if the latter were ever entirely free of any touch of the queer.

The Soul's response makes use, quite precisely, of the model where the Soul comes to be figured as the prison of the Body, in Foucault's famous formulation, a language whose transformation back into love in the English tradition becomes the topic of this study's third chapter:

> When I wanted, flesh, to castigate you,
> With hunger or wakefulness, or to tame you with a whip,
> Soon the vanity of the world began to idolize you,
> And drove you to become empty with trivialities.
> And thus you took the mastery (*dominium*) from me,
> You were my familiar betrayer (*proditrix*).
> Through the enticements of the world you dragged me after you
> And sweetly submerged me in the filth of sin.[74]

In this passage, which is the closest to actually discussing the relationship between the two beings that are really one (and is radically different from its Middle English counterpart, as discussed in chapter 3), the Body seems to have been merely distracted from the Soul's attempts to punish/teach it. The language of "dragging" (*traho, trahere*) and of betrayal is what the Soul uses. It is only the detail that the Soul is submerged in sin "sweetly" (*suaviter*) that might suggest some joy being taken in the dragging process, but this sweet submersion is very different from the Anima/*ancilla*/Hildebert relationship of the "Liber de Querimonia." Refusing the model of a queer heterosexuality of Hildebert of Lavardin's allegory, the poems I discuss in chapters 2 and 3, in an apparent attempt to get away from the problematic and sexualized language of a marriage between Soul and Body, take up the queer same-sex model set up in the "Visio Philiberti."

74. "Quando te volueram, caro, castigare / fame vel vigiliis, vel verbere domare, / mox te mundi vanitas caepit adulare / et illius frivolis coegit vacare. / Et ita dominium de me suscepisti / familaris proditrix tu mihi fuisti / per mundi blanditias me post te traxisti, / etin peccati puteum suaviter mersisti" (Wright, "Visio Philiberti," 151–58).

The Performative Work of Allegorical Debate

The relationship of soul and body is something that is being imagined and reinvented throughout the Middle Ages, but fully articulated literary considerations of this relationship thrive particularly in the thirteenth century—the century of the Fourth Lateran Council—and they thrive at the intersection of didactic literature, allegorical poetry, and pedagogical discipline. Together, debates between the Body and the Soul, and other descendants of the *psychomachia* tradition, contributed to the formation of a way of thinking that was never as simple a dualism as these poems' titles would suggest. Latin debates between the Body and the Soul dealt with the issue of the self through disputational allegory, which permitted them to engage the fused philosophical and psychological issues that all medieval personification allegory highlights. Allegory also permitted such debates to stage the problem of the self in terms of the gender of its component parts, a surprising development that may have had more to do with the history of allegorical conventions than with the philosophy or psychology of the person.

Personification allegory functioned as a major mode of "doing" psychology in the Middle Ages, giving guidance to those who, though seeking to understand the nature of the self, would find the more formal tools and tropes in academic treatments of the self excessively abstract or irrelevant. Medieval allegory mixes the philosophical and the psychological and permits them to play off one another, never "dumbing down" the ideas in question, but rather putting them on the stage, using performative utterance to create and delimit the self and its possibilities. J. L. Austin's well-known definition of the performative emphasizes social consent to an utterance that does what it says. Allegorical personification performs in this sense, "doing" philosophy by "being" Philosophy, while also the using more conventional definition of performance as something staged. Personification allegory functions as a performative psychological theory, and specifically as a theory that performs the relationship between the body and the soul.

Throughout this chapter, I have been wary of any claim that allegorical gender is based "merely" on the ancient structures of Romance grammar, which genders abstractions as feminine. In some of the earliest Body/Soul debates written in Latin, especially Hildebert of Lavardin's "Liber de Querimonia," and particularly in how the "Liber" differs from the later and far more popular "Visio Philiberti," the playful work of gender in allegory becomes very clear. These works connect the Latin and the vernacular traditions by interweaving personification allegory, philosophy, and psychology. The informal quality of body/soul and afterlife theology that characterizes Latin Body/Soul debates, particularly the "Visio Philiberti," marks them as works of *sowlehele*. In these works, perhaps, we have proof that grammatical gender is more plaything than straitjacket to the nimble minds of Latin-language authors. The complex and often startlingly queer work of setting up hierarchy between Body and Soul through gender is possible because of the richly useful incarnational inherent to the Latin words for "soul" and "body," although Middle English finds its own ways to create this play without gendered nouns, as the poem "Als I Lay in a Winteris Nyt" discussed in chapter 3 shows.

The convention of female tutelary figures guiding hapless narrators and/or battling evil within the self helps to install something that is figured as female into the very center of a certain conception of selfhood, as a voice that speaks within. The debates produced in this tradition had very different levels of circulation—from the considerable, popular dissemination of Boethius' *Consolation of Philosophy* or the "Visio Philiberti" to the relative obscurity of Hildebert's "Liber de Querimonia." The English works discussed in the following chapters make use of similar tropes and figures even as they mold the notion of the self into new and different shapes and hierarchies. All of the Body/Soul debates—Latin, Old French, and Middle English alike—share a central concern with how the hierarchy that places the Soul in the dominant role is to be maintained at every level of the allegory, with how to depict the utterly joined quality of the Soul/Body relation with a minimal possibility for slipping into a depiction of sexual sin between them. The Middle English debates, "In a Thestri Stude" and "Als I Lay in a Winteris Nyt," are able to do so in a language free of whatever arbitrarily grammatical constraints Romance languages possess, because, although remnants of noun gender remain for centuries, Middle English authors are not in any way bound to gendering abstract nouns as feminine. This permits works of *sowlehele* to excise even the same-sex feminine relationship of "Visio Philiberti" and to work through the hierarchies of male-male power relations, setting up a homosocial world where the love that must of necessity exist between Soul and Body expresses the ambivalent and complex politics of medieval love between men. In the following chapters, I return to the Latin Body/Soul debate tradition as well as to Prudentius and Boethius as part of understanding works as diverse as a *psychomachia*-like allegory for anchoresses and a quest to know the truth by a person who oscillates between being a man named Will and a personification of the will.

This chapter began with Barbara Johnson's gesture toward the history of representations of women in allegory and, with that gesture, how the Middle Ages inhabit certain modern forms of thought. The medieval allegories discussed here did not constitute a sort of passive womb waiting for modern critical theory to inseminate it with meaning, like the *chora* of the *Timaeus* waits for the demiurge to create matter. My hope is that Johnson's encounter with Dinshaw's analysis of allegorical reading, and with early modern allegory in general, was something more than merely accidental, just as Johnson and I both hope, without certainty, that all those female allegorical figures are the products of something more telling about the status of the female body in culture than "mere" grammatical norms.

In her essay, Johnson ultimately understands the workings of personification as intimately similar to the discourses of positionality within identity politics, of speaking "as if" and "for" given groups, whether minoritarian or majoritarian. She points out the problem of allegorical reference in the political sphere: Dominant groups see themselves as "personifications of the whole—humanity, reason, law, truth—not personifications within a *psychomachia* for control of the social text" (73). In other words, one danger of allegory is that it will totalize and simplify instead of dramatizing the complexity of conflicts between groups that might or might not be fully represented by persons bearing the labels of identity politics. Personification endows an abstraction with a body and a voice; but, as in seminal feminist works such as Denise Riley's *Am I That Name?: The Category of "Women" in History* and in Johnson's writings on allegory, questioning the validity of how an allegory refers and of the relationships it elucidates is also a crucial political activity.

Johnson's description of the political sphere as a "a *psychomachia* for control of the social text" reimagines the conceptual capacities of the *psychomachia* and uses the language of allegory to transform, as the chestnut goes, the personal into the political. This analysis seems, to me, beautifully to promise that the work we do in seeking to understand the politics of personification in the Middle Ages both is important in and of itself and might prove applicable to discussions of modern souls and bodies. The chapters that follow are an attempt to read medieval allegory, the politics of gender, and the institutions of both philosophy and psychology in a way that neither chooses body over soul or modern over medieval, nor maps these onto one another. Like the optical illusion in which what looks one minute like a rabbit appears to be a duck the next, these chapters work on seeing complex things in multiple ways. Given time, it is possible to see both images and even to play with their necessary interdependence.

CHAPTER 2

Allegorizing the Split Self
A MIDDLE ENGLISH DEBATE
BETWEEN THE BODY AND THE SOUL

A dead Body lies upon a bier. Above stands its Soul, lamenting all of the sins committed in life by the self now split into spirit and corpse. Instead of lying mute as the remonstrations rain down, the Body responds, entreating the Soul to leave it alone with its suffering, to leave off its lamenting. The Body seems willing to rot in silence as punishment for its misdeeds in life, but the Soul—expecting punishment for the sins that Body and Soul had committed while still joined—continues to complain and to accuse, drawing the increasingly reluctant Body into argument. At last, the Body, cold in anticipation of the grave's chill, refuses to squabble further; the pitiless Soul, however, continues to preach at its intractably silent and prone mate, concluding the dialogue-turned-monologue with a sermon on Christ's sacrifice and the biblical signs of doomsday.

What does it mean to separate two aspects of a self and allow them to speak to one another, to accuse and blame and squabble in the extremity of death? The plot recounted in the preceding paragraph is that of the thirteenth-century debate known as "In a Thestri Stude I Stod"[1] ("In a Dark Place I Stood"), a poem that represents

---

1. The Latin rubric that prefaces this debate is "Hic incipit carmen inter corpus & animam" (at least in the Bodleian Ms. Digby 86), but it is conventionally known by its English incipit. It is listed in the Index of Middle English Verse as #1461. I am basing my discussion on John Conlee's edition of the poem as it appears in Oxford, Bodleian Library Ms. Digby 86 (*olim* Bodl 1687), fols. 195v–200r in *Middle English*

an inquiry into the nature of the self through an allegorical staging of debate between its component parts. Although, as the previous chapter discussed, debates between the Body and the Soul such as the "Visio Philiberti" would have been available in England to the Latin-literate since the early twelfth century, in the later thirteenth century a particularly large number of such debates appeared in English. In these works, the problems of gender, discipline, love, and hierarchy had to be worked out in order to communicate the poems' dual messages, both the direct, didactic lesson about repenting while there is still time, and the subtext about teaching penitents about how their innermost selves work.

Understanding "In a Thestri Stude" and other Body/Soul debates as instances of *sowlehele* psychology opens up their philosophical and literary complexity more effectively than reading them as mere dramatizations of the psychological systems of Aristotle or Augustine or of "faculty psychology" as a general category. With these Middle English Body/Soul debates, this book moves away from figurations of the self through female personifications, common in Latin and Romance-language allegories. In this English version, as exemplified by "In a Thestri Stude," both Body and Soul are clearly male, and I turn now to the construction of masculine gender performance as an aspect of *sowlehele* psychology in thirteenth-century English writings.

Debate poetry organizes personification in a dynamic mode. In examining it, we can observe just how one specific strain of the English textual tradition has represented the relationship between souls and bodies as the building blocks of selves, selves that are being brought into being through relationship with one another. Reading the disputations between Body and Soul in this and the following chapter helps us comprehend the concept of person, the limits of allegory, and the rhetoric of embodiment at this moment in the development of Middle English disputation.

Body/Soul debates are consistently referred to as works that were very "popular" in the Middle Ages. Despite this trope of "popularity," these poems have been called popular far more often than they have been studied. For instance, on the first page of his full-length study of debate poetry, Thomas Reed, Jr., calls Body/Soul debates an "inexhaustibly popular medieval subject," but his study does not discuss these debates at any length.[2] The two English

---

Debate Poetry: A Critical Anthology (East Lansing, MI: Colleagues Press, 1991). Two other versions of the poem are extant, one in Cambridge (Trinity College Ms. B.14.29 [*olim* 323] fol. 29v) and one in London (British Library Ms. Harley 2253, fol. 57v). My translation of the poem into modern English appears as an appendix to this book.

2. Thomas Reed, Jr., *Middle English Debate Poetry and the Aesthetics of Irresolution* (Columbia and London: University of Missouri Press, 1990), 1. Reed's study is the first published full-length examination of Middle English debate poetry as such (which makes its lack of interest in Body/Soul debate all the more regrettable), and one of the first full-length studies

Body/Soul debates discussed in this chapter and the next appear in ten manuscripts between them, which constitutes a respectable number (by comparison, there are only sixteen surviving manuscript copies of Chaucer's *Troilus and Criseyde,* the work that medieval audiences considered his masterpiece). The popularity of the English take on the Body/Soul debate can be understood as an effect of the new interest in didactic literature following the Fourth Lateran Council's injunction to confession, *Omnis utriusque sexus.* Unlike the Latin works discussed in the preceding chapter, works of *sowlehele* written in Middle English could be read by a wide audience, possibly including women. This poem's final section on the signs of the Last Judgment mark it as a work intended to teach laypeople about sin, its consequences, and the afterlife. "In a Thestri Stude" was not popular by accident; it was tapping into a powerful need for texts explaining the self to itself.

Thirteenth-century Body/Soul debates such as "In a Thestri Stude" perform the didactic, descriptive, and literary work that mark them as both examples and particularly interesting developments of their historical moment. In part, this is because a number of additional debates are capable of serving as reference points to compare them with, like the Latin debates discussed in the previous chapter. Surviving works about Body and Soul in Old English and Early Middle English debates include graveside lamentations by the Soul (with the Body described as passive audience) that considerably predated 1215. However, it does not seem coincidental that the most elaborate and complex poems in this mode were most popularly diffused (and most likely produced as well) in the later thirteenth century. Factors other than the Fourth Lateran Council and its aftermaths must have contributed to these poems' production and popularity, or there would have been no Body/Soul debate tradition at all predating 1215. But confessional culture, with its vast demand for guides and handbooks, took up the mode that was already in place and made of it something new and genuinely innovative.

"In a Thestri Stude" participates in this effort to craft a workable, applicable model of the self for use in thinking about sin and redemption, borrowing

---

of any medieval debate poetry, sharing that honor with Hans Walther's *Das Streitgedicht in der lateinischen Literatur des Mittelalters* (Munich: 1920). My study, on the other hand, is an inquiry into the possibilities of some poems that organize their psychological thought through debate. In that, it may be closest to extant studies of specific works that are usually categorized as "debates"—*Wynnere and Wastoure* and *The Owl and the Nightingale* have proven popular subjects—where the focus on these specific works leads their authors to readings of other debate poems in terms of their relevance to their objects of study. See, for instance, Kathryn Hume, *The Owl and the Nightingale: The Poem and Its Critics* (Toronto and Buffalo, NY: University of Toronto Press, 1975); Nicholas Jacobs, "Typology of Debate and the Interpretation of *Wynnere and Wastoure*" in *Review of English Studies* 36 (1985): 481–500; and Thomas Bestul, *Satire and Allegory in Wynnere and Wastoure* (Lincoln: University of Nebraska Press, 1974).

from Latin writings to create something new. Its assumptions, "mistakes," and reinterpretations of doctrine participate in *sowlehele* psychology. The poem works out its own version of psychology by performing its understanding about the specific nature of the relationship between the soul and the body in a didactic context: Personification *does* what it describes, in the manner philosophers of language term a performative speech act. In some ways, the poem can be understood as part of the appropriation of Latin learning for vernacular uses, since it translates aspects of theological psychology and of Latin Body/Soul debate but adapts them to the limitations and possibilities of the English language. In other ways, which include its dualism and its omission of a clearly stated provenance for the will, "In a Thestri Stude" poses a challenge to Latin learning. Scholarly theological and philosophical ruminations on the nature of the self—St. Augustine's work on body, soul, and will, discussed later, serves as the privileged example—prove insufficient to explain this poem.

Although Soul and Body (at least, at the poem's beginning) could be those of *any* dead person, the narrative details in the Soul's lamentation of a life ill-lived tell us that the dead person had been a proud nobleman who had loved to hunt. This character is both a conventional "type" and, to an extent, an individualized person with his own detailed history. Not incidentally, as soon as this corpse acquires a history, it becomes gendered, a nobleman rather than a noblewoman. By themselves, the words *body* and *soul* (and the alternative terms for soul used in the poem, like *gost* and *mynde*) don't indicate the speakers' genders: The fact that the dead person whose pieces are now interacting with one another had been male comes out in the details about his misspent life. "In a Thestri Stude" offers a vision of the self that does not rely on gender difference to establish the nature of the relationship between body and soul, which conventionally requires the clear dominance of the soul. This Middle English psychological allegory imagines the different aspects of the self as staunchly, clearly male, a possibility that Latin- and Romance-language allegories could not entertain thanks, among other things, to the gendering of abstract nouns as female in those languages.

What does it mean to create a literal Soul—a concept of the soul that has its own voice and, to a degree, its own individuality? How do we understand the sheer circularity of the *essence* of person being itself *possessed of* personhood? What does it mean to bring this Soul into discursive being by giving it a voice but not marking it as female the way Latin allegories do? Instead of envisioning the soul as an elevated female principle to be venerated like a tutelary allegorical figure such as Boethius' Lady Philosophy, the Soul of "In a Thestri Stude" is neutrally male. Its participation in the category "male" functions as the unmarked and universal common denominator between the debaters, since the Body, too, seems to be male in this dialogue. The apparent maleness of both debaters avoids the issues of heterosexualized hierarchy within the self encountered by Hildebert of Lavardin in his debate. Figuring both Body and Soul as male also seemingly excises the problematic traces of the feminine from within the self, as Latin-literate medieval readers may have encountered it in the *ancilla/domina* pairing of "Visio Philiberti" and in other psychological allegories featuring personifications of powerful female figures. "In a Thestri Stude" depicts relationships within the self as occurring between male beings, seemingly evading the possibility that heterosexuality (and with it, sexuality as such) might enter the scene. Yet, without the "obvious" hierarchy offered by the wife/husband analogy, "In a Thestri Stude" cannot assume and must work to establish the clear superiority of Soul over Body. In one of few published discussions of the poem, Helen Philips writes that "the genre of Body and Soul debate itself centers on the doctrine that human identity involves two entities that ultimately belong to different realms of being and will separate from each other to face different fates," and she emphasizes the "furious acrimony" of the Middle English debate, which differentiates it from its Latin counterparts.[3] I would argue that this acrimony is a result, in part, of the absence of the clear gender or class hierarchies that characterized the two Latin Body/Soul debates discussed in the previous chapter. With "In a Thestri Stude," we have exited the mannered and convention-bound world of female "allegorical goddesses," where hierarchy is always-already clearly understood, and entered a homo-social world, such as a classroom or a monastery, of male beings jockeying for power against other male beings where hierarchy is uncertain and either character could end up on top.

"In a Thestri Stude," like Body/Soul debates generally, produces its narrative through disputation, a practice more common to classrooms than confessionals. However, the Body claims repeatedly that it would prefer to remain silent in awaiting its own punishment, even though the disputational situation itself prohibits it from keeping still.[4] In this "debate poem," the *act* of debating seems to have been forced on one of the opponents rather than willingly engaged in by an equal. Although the Body and the Soul begin by speaking in alternating four-line stanzas, the Body speaks less than half the lines of the

3. Helen Philips, "Dreams and Dream Lore," *Studies in the Harley Manuscript: The Scribes, Contents and Social Contexts of British Library Ms. Harley 2253*, ed. Susanna Fein (Kalamazoo, MI: TEAMS, 2000), 254.

4. Gordon Teskey, in *Allegory and Violence* (Ithaca, NY: Cornell University Press, 1996), writing of "the disorder with which and out of which allegory works," suggests that "under the regime of polysemy"—which, in his account, characterizes allegory—"anything that appears to escape or to resist the project of meaning—passion, body, irony—is interpreted as a further extension of meaning" (30). Although the Body/Soul debates discussed in this chapter do not form a part of the canon—Teskey is mainly writing about Dante and Spenser—to which Teskey attributes the capacity to know the chaos of allegory for what it is, the symptomatic attempt to force meaning on and speech out of the Body in this dialogue seems in line with his thinking.

poem, in part because the Soul has a monologue that begins at line 53 and continues for approximately fifty lines, to the poem's end. Forced to acquire a voice to defend itself from the Soul's accusations, the Body nevertheless falls back into its materiality and, once it has said its piece, refuses to debate any further. Even if, as the Soul's words suggest, it might not be aware of the full theological context of its situation, the Body, taking its turn, indicates that it knows its own fate clearly enough.

Although "In a Thestri Stude" offers clear moral warning, insisting that wrongdoing is severely punished, it also presents a meditation on the nature of the self and of sin, on the provenance of the will, on how a life can be understood when viewed in retrospect. Debates between the Body and the Soul, in any language, are often self-reflexive about their form, perhaps as a consequence of their way of splitting the self into speaking pieces through allegory, as the preceding example of the reluctantly speaking Body suggests. This poem can also be understood as part of the development of personification allegory as a tool for thinking about the parts of the person; the complicated division of labor between Body and Soul being debated in this poem invites introspection while offering to organize the shape this introspection will take. This chapter's examination of the kinds of narration, temporality, and voicing this poem performs will help work through the poem's peculiar sort of psychological didacticism, aiming to understand the ways in which the psychological models provided in the biblical, patristic, and ancient Greek writings about the soul that came down to the thirteenth century both can and cannot account for this debate's surprising dynamics. What follows is a discussion of the implications of the depiction of the split self in "In a Thestri Stude" drawing on a close reading of the poem. I then address the way in which this poem can be read as a particular kind of psychological allegory, arguing that the poem's form and content are both implicated in the history of allegorical representations of the self, and develop some of the implications of what it means to imagine that self's parts as all male, with maleness functioning as a human universal as well as a specified human history.

Temporal Beings

From the poem's first, titular line, the poem's narrator is located in a specific albeit unspecified place, a dark that gives inexplicable access to the dead being and its parts: "Hon an βester stude I stod an luitel strif to here" ("In a dark place I stood, a little argument to hear"; "In a Thestri Stude," 1–2).[5] The poem's

---

5. In translating the Middle English phrase, I have preserved the awkwardness of the

"little strife" takes place at an interstitial moment between the lifetime when Soul and Body were united as a single person who made choices, owned possessions, and acted as a unified being (and, as such, confessed and possessed a faith) and the moment of dissolution that will follow after the dialogue ends. In the dialogue's aftermath, the person that Body and Soul had been when alive is utterly sundered. The broken parts suffer separately and continue to function apart, only tentatively awaiting reunion at Judgment Day.

The narrator of the poem makes a single full appearance, in the work's first line, as the "I" who stands in the dark place. This first line locates the narrator spatially but provides neither context nor body for this speaker, and what follows does not clarify whether the narrator stood in this place in order to hear the argument, or overheard this argument by fortuitous accident. Is this hearing, in other words, an act of the will or a vision sent by divine intervention? The fact that this poem is *not* a dream vision, as so many medieval allegories are, is noteworthy.[6] If it were a vision seen in a dream, the Body and the Soul of the narrator would *also* be split, the Body sleeping and the Soul witnessing a dialogue. As it is, someone whose body and soul are still united becomes a witness—whether by choice, by chance, or by divine intervention—to the dissolution of someone whose Body and Soul have separated and are struggling with one another. The narrator-as-eavesdropper, standing in darkness, offers little commentary on what is overheard, but that one line situates and frames the debate that follows as a drama mediated by an observer.[7] In that sense, the dialogue is theater, performed for an audience of one. In that sense as well, the duality of having two active speakers in a debate is somewhat undermined, because a third party is observing and thereby triangulating the powers at play. This triangulation is echoed, as I discuss in a subsequent section, in the absent presence of a solution to the debater's problems: the faculty of the will, which would seem to be the most plausible solution to the problem of guilt's provenance that the poem's debaters are trying to solve.

Body's self-referential "mi" and "me," which underline the Body's continued tendencies toward greed, even in death. Citations from the poem will henceforth include line numbers only.

6. Helen Philips notes that it may as well be one: "The speeches and debates of Body and Soul take place in a realm beyond that of normal human time and space, but, as is common with medieval literary visions, they are not necessarily explicitly designated as dreams.... [T]he dark place in which the narrator stands at the beginning of 'In a Thestri Stude' is unspecific and suggests not only the nighttime when dreams come and the darkness of the grave, but also that indefinite mental area where vision and allegory are enacted" ("Dreams and Dream Lore," 253–54).

7. This detail differentiates this particular debate poem from those that appear as proto-dramas, lacking a framing device and organized exclusively as exchanges between speakers, and causes this poem (as well as its near-contemporary, "Als I Lay on a Winteris Nyt") to read as if it were a dream vision, offering the obvious comparisons to the far more elaborate and complex (and also simply later) works such as *Piers Plowman* and Chaucer's *Parliament of Fowls*.

Of the two debaters witnessed by the narrator standing in his or her dark place, only the Body is situated in space: "þer hit lai on þe bere" ("there it lay on the bier"; 2). Only this story's third character, the Soul, makes its appearance exclusively as a speaking voice; this Soul is referred to by both the Body and itself as "gost" throughout the poem, and three times as "wrecche gost."[8] "In a Thestri Stude" proceeds as a discussion between Body and Soul without much apparent narratorial intervention, with the exchanges that follow limited to one four-line stanza per speaker until the lengthy final monologue. At first, it is the narrator who establishes the speakers, repeating the formula "þo spac the gost" (3 and 13) or "þo spac the bodi" (9 and 17). However, as the argument between Body and Soul develops, the Body and Soul themselves, rather than the narrator, begin to inform the reader of who is speaking, by beginning their brief speeches by addressing one another. One knows it is the Soul speaking when the speaker's angry reply begins with the word "Body." For example, the Soul tells the Body, "Bodi, thou hauest liued to longe" ("Body, you have lived too long"; 20). This device contributes to the many ways in which the very structure of the dialogue thematizes the Soul and Body's interdependence. Like "Dame Sirith," which accompanies this dialogue in one manuscript (Digby 86), "In a Thestri Stude" comes to resemble a play in rhyming verse, performative in the sense of being theatrical as well as of bringing into being the parts of the self it names.

The poem never *quite* becomes a play, however. Although scribes sometimes insert marginal notes or use red or blue ink for one line or along the margin to mark a change between one speaker and the other, this is ultimately more a means of assisting the oral reading that any medieval work would entail than an essential gesture, since each speaker either refers to his interlocutor or to himself in the first line of each speech, invoking the identity of the listener as a means of establishing the identity of the speaker. The dramatic mode of the disputation thus remains firmly in the narrative dialogue mode. It is based on brief exchanges rather than narrative description. Consequently,

8. *Gost* is a word that goes back to the 1100s—it appears in the Bodleian Homilies—that means, according to the *Middle English Dictionary*, "(a) The soul of a dead person; also, the spirit of Christ descending into hell; (b) a damned soul, whether in hell or returned to earth; also *fig.* an emaciated or tortured person; (c) a dead body . . . and 3(a) The soul of man, spiritual nature; the soul as distinguished from mind, the emotional nature; the life principle in man." In the Anglo-Norman version of this sort of poem, the author seems to have had trouble imagining a creature that is always and entirely a voice as the representation of the Soul, and instead portrays it as "de petite figure estoit la criature / e estoit la chaitive tote verte comme chive" ("the creature was a small figure / and that fellow was all green as a chive," lines 7–8) ("Un Samedi Par Nuit," in Thomas Wright ed., *The Latin Poems Commonly Attributed to Walter Mapes*, London: Camden Society, 1841, ls. 16). See chapter 3 for an extended discussion of this work, and also chapter 5 for a discussion of *Piers Plowman* B's Anima, whose surreal physical presence is more like the Anglo-Norman "criature" than the invisible voice of the Middle English soul.

Soul remains intertwined with Body in the dialogue's form. In other words, each speaker's self is established, to signal the reader as to who is speaking, by establishing who its Other is.

The third presence, our increasingly silent narrator, completely ceases to speak by line 20, yielding the floor to Soul and Body. One might wonder if this is partly because his (or her) own integrity as a whole being, a Body and a Soul that are united and working as one, is undermined or at least threatened by the separability of these two. Another possibility, one to which I will return, is that the convention of this dialogue demands that there be two—and no more than two—presences in the darkness. Although the "I" of "In a Thestri Stude" is that of the narrator, the dialogue he recounts demands his silence in order to work as a dyadic (rather than triadic) structure. Limiting the number of speakers in this rather pointed way is part of what makes this poem so different from a simple dramatization of theological psychologies of the self and its parts. It is a simplification of those far more complex structures, certainly, but it is also an effective didactic dramatization.

The Soul of "In a Thestri Stude" is a taunting, mocking one, whose first question to the Body—"wi liggest βou nou here?" ("Why are you now lying here?"; 4)—pretends that death as such is a punishment for the Body's sins, rather than an inevitable end to which all mortal bodies (and souls) tend. The Body shows a similar ignorance of mortality: "I vende mi worldes blisse me wolde euere I-last," it replies ("I thought my worldly bliss would last forever for me"; 10), in a line where the repetition of "my" and "me" seems to emphasize the false pride of individualism, since it is coming from one half of what had been a whole being. The Body had lived, we discover in reading the debate, in a sort of eternal present. The Soul, however, whose speech detailing the largely terrible events of "Domesday" occupies more than a third of the poem, after all debate has been concluded, seems to exist in both the retrospection of regret and dread of a future it knows through prophecy, and never shares the same moment in time as the Body.

Throughout the dialogue, the Body's dread of its fate is manifested in the specific details it offers about the debaters' present situation, offered to counter the details the Soul offers about their past life together. In response to the Soul's taunting question, "Wer is βI muchele pruide, βI ve[i]r and βI gris / βine palefreis ane βI steden and βi pourpre pris?" ("Where is your overweening pride, your rich furs / your palfreys and your steeds and your purple opulence?"; 14–15), the Body answers, "ibounden beβ mine honden, min eien aren me hud" (my hands are bound, my eyes are hidden"; 19). Whatever limits have been imposed on it by the fact that its Soul is gone from it seem to be forcing the Body to think in the present, rather than to see the present as a continuity with the past—while the Soul, bearer of the intellect of this now-dead man, demands to narrativize their predicament, seeking explanations for the arbitrariness of individual human action and of human suffering.

As they are represented in "In a Thestri Stude," Body and Soul are so separate that their temporal locations are out of sync. If the poem is performatively producing a certain notion of the self by naming its parts and having them speak, that self is being given a disjunctive temporality. The poem allegorically enacts the disjunctive time of the self as part of its theorization of a split and disunified subject. The interdependence of the Soul and Body pair is made obvious by this division. Without the Body, the Soul doesn't have a grounding in the present; without the Soul, the Body cannot imagine the passage of time. Both the desire to imagine the two united and the impossibility of their union are staged by their dialogue. The psychology of the poem is not limited to *what* the Soul or the Body says; it is also inherent in *how* each says it.

Philosophers and theologians wonder how spirit and flesh can coexist, being so different; one answer this particular poem gives has to do with the two not really coexisting after all, because they do not function on the same temporal plane. Allegory has the opportunity to enact temporal disjunction as a detail of character development and yet, by making it a detail rather than the point of the poem, to avoid making too much of this difference. Body and Soul meet, after all, in their dark place, and although they cannot come to an understanding—in part, because of the psychological effects of living in different perceived times—it can be shown that one of them is right and one is wrong, that there is a better and a worse time to be inhabited for purposes of *sowlehele*.[9]

The narrator establishes the scene of the debate and, essentially, sinks into the background. However, one intervention by the narrator seems intended to establish that the Soul is right and the Body is wrong, an apparently gratuitous signpost declaring a premature winner. Following the Body's first retort to the Soul's accusations (the Body simply notes that it had expected its worldly bliss to last forever and that it is now bound to the earth by its own sins), the narrator remarks, setting up the Soul's reply: "þospac þe gost mid rute red after ful" ("Then the Soul spoke with right counsel instead of foul"; 13). One way to read this intervention is as a simplifying didacticism: This is a debate, but the winner is known in advance. But this intervention occurs in line 13, nothing

---

9. Philips also notes the importance of temporal distortion in the poem: "The message of the urgency of penitence and reform that is expressed through this device of the soul trying to penetrate didactically the body's unresponsiveness is also expressed through a manipulation of time (past, present, and future) in the text.... Since Body and Soul signify two aspects of those who receive the teaching, the fictional 'now' of their exchange represents the future of the living audience. It is that time after death when bodies and souls can speak in some symbolic, archetypal space about their real theological relationship, seen now tardily in its full clarity for the first time" (258).

like it appears later in the poem, and its force is ultimately lost. The Body does not debate the Soul in any conventional way, by making logical claims about its innocence. Instead, the "counsel" that the narrator has described as "foul" consists of a series of statements by the Body about its condition: It cannot escape the place where it lies, it awaits its own dissolution, worms treat it as prey, its new house is made of mere mud, and its woe is enough that it cannot be more, no matter how much the Soul chides it. These are not arguments of the kind made by philosophers in the course of a real debate, but they are arguments of a kind just the same. The Soul speaks of consequences and shared histories, the Body states the bald facts of agony, voicing the suffering of matter rent from spirit and stranded in its own materiality.

Although its tone is accusatory in a much simpler sense (sins were committed, punishment is coming), the Soul's accusations against the Body also constitute a lament rather than an argument about the nature and division of blame. It is the Soul who details hell's dooms and who will endure its pains, although the suffering that awaits the Soul is, according to its own doctrine, the fault of the Body. It is also a lesson. The Body was the one who thought that its worldly bliss would last forever. (The fact that a Body could "think" or "surmise" at all is in itself an oddness that characterizes the poem.) The eternal present of the Body's conception of time has joys and dangers, and the dangers are significant. *Sowlehele* allegory takes its narrator outside space and time to experience *memento mori* as a dark place. The limits of temporal joy are evident at the moment of death; the ignorance of one who is unaware of them is being corrected by the Soul for the Body's and also for the reader's benefit.

Fallen Characters

In its accusations and laments, the Soul taunts the Body with all the things he has lost, as if only the Body had owned lands and enjoyed the hunt, as if the Body, without the participation of the Soul, has passed false judgments ("false domes to deme, to chaungen two to fiue"; "False judgments to judge, to give two in exchange for five"; 7) and stolen from the poor ("poure men to βreten, binimen hem here heritage"; "threaten poor men, deprive them of their inheritance"; 31).[10] These apparently arbitrary details perform an expository function: They tell us that the corpse must once have been a male member of the nobility, locating him as something more specific and identifiable than a sort of Everyman composite figure, although these details are far from offering the

10. The tone of the Soul's complaint, from the first accusatory verse onward, is similar to the tone of complaint poetry of this period, including the quasi-legal plaint of Pees against Wrong in *Passus* IV of the C-text of *Piers Plowman*.

reader anything like a conventional literary "character." Philips connects this detail, made manifest in the Soul's *ubi sunt* (literally, "Where are they now?") taunts to the Body, to the genre of "mutability literature"—a literature about how the mighty must inevitably fall—which, she writes, "is one of the areas of medieval culture that provides a vehicle for criticism of the rich and powerful."[11] The social "fall" of the Body from greedy nobleman who mistreated his subjects to a corpse lying cold and miserable in the small, uncomfortable "house" of the grave charts its movement from "false" elevation to "true" debasement. The man had been guilty of pride, had owned a fine house and horses—all of which this individual had enjoyed entirely too much. All of these actions and possessions are listed as though they pertained exclusively to the Body, and implied no involvement on the Soul's part, although it is also clear that the Soul was present to witness every act—and the Soul seems to enjoy detailing all these lost riches.

Both Soul and Body, but *particularly* the Body, have moved to a lower place in the social hierarchy upon death. In this way, this English poem might recall the "Visio Philiberti," discussed in chapter 1, in which the Body is represented as the (female) servant of its mistress, the Soul, although the Latin Body is always *ancilla,* and the Body only becomes "lowe" as the consequence of a fall: "ful lowe shalt thou fallen for all thin heie parage" ("you have fallen so low, for all your high status"; 32), and again, "Ful louue shalt though fallen for alle thine bores" ("so low shall you fall for all your high bowers"; 47). Within the male same-sex hierarchy of "In a Thestri Stude," the Body is not figured as a servant, but as a fallen nobleman, an echo of postlapsarian humanity more generally. Insofar as the Soul's *ubi sunt* passage enumerates the kinds of possessions and powers the dead man held, it becomes clear that *both* Body and Soul lament a precipitous fall in status as part of mourning their (collective) death.

The Body, perhaps because it cared deeply about social status, repeatedly calls the Soul "wrecche," a common general term of abuse whose literal meaning emphasizes its object's poverty. A wretch is a bad man, but, specifically, a *poor* bad man, which is not what the nobleman had been in life but seems to be what the Soul has become in death. The Body repeatedly tells the Soul to "wende awei nou, wrecche" ("go away, you wretch," 25; and again, "wrecche gost, βou wende awei," 33), until the Soul responds that "Uuas I neuere wrecche bote βoren βin heuele redes" ("I was never a wretch but through your evil counsel"; 37). The Soul emphasizes the sense in which the Body is the more fallen of the pair by acting as the Body's guide to the ways of death, offering instruction about hell and its pains while keeping itself remote from involve-

11. Philips, 256.

ment with the choices and chances that had characterized the life of the person they had been together.

Although the pious reader would presumably get the message that caring too much about material goods is a symptom of fleshly lust, it is quite clear that this Soul is unjustly denying its own involvement and guilt. Present-day readers might even psychologize its behavior as being "in denial." The Soul can't possibly be as sinless as it claims to be. Indeed, the speaking Body is present in this dialogue in part as a tool for overcoming the Soul's hypocrisy and overcoming its claim to be genuinely separate from desire. Even as it insists on its own "superior" position, the Soul—lamenting that it awaits punishment for the Body's sins—is implicated in the acts of its inferior. The Soul is forced to "descend" to the level of the bodily just as the man who used to unite Soul and Body as one is forced to "descend" into a poverty he had once despised. Most of the burden for this loss is borne by the Body, whose newfound poverty is made quite clear in the dialogue: It complains that, lacking its prior rich clothes, its sides are cold where it lies.

The Soul preaches to the Body as if it were a priest telling a dead or dying person what awaited him or her. If it were truly a priest, of course, the Soul would be speaking from a position of authority and with some objective distance, using more explicitly the language of confession and penance. The Soul, taking on a preacher's role, is in an oddly self-reflective position, since it is actually engaged in telling the Body about the fate that awaits its own self—after all, death is the fate of *all* bodies, while hell, the Soul's next destination, is reserved for sinners. The Body would be rotting now no matter what it had done in life; but the Soul implies that it is an innocent, being taken to hell in punishment for another's sins, much like Christ, whose role in the dialogue I discuss later.

The Body is wholly given over to the caprices of the natural world, to its own bodiliness. As the unlocated narrator listens in the dark, the Soul piles detail upon detail in reconstructing the shared past and dreading the separated future of the now-split self. The Body, in its turn, refuses to budge from its present state, manifesting a will surprisingly different from that of its own Soul, and willfully, arbitrarily, insisting on silence. However, the Body seems aware of an *immediate* future for itself—a vividly physical future, its own dissolution. In a transparently didactic gesture by the poem's author, the Body seems capable of understanding that other bodies will also meet its fate. As the Soul taunts that it will no longer be able to commit the unjust and bullying acts it had enjoyed in life, the Body responds:

Wrecche gost, thou wen away, hou longe sal βis strist laste?
Wormest holdeβ here strif and here domes faste;

I-mad hoe habbeβ here lotes mi fles for to caste;
Mony fre bodi schal rotien, ne bid I nout nou βe laste." (25–28)

Go away now, wretched ghost, how long shall this strife last?
Worms are holding their own strife, rendering their own stern judgments,
They are casting their own lots for my flesh;
Many free bodies will rot, I shall not be the last.

Here, the Body begs to escape the debate that compels its speech, asking the Soul to leave it to the impinging worms. These "worms" are anthropomorphized as rational persons (capable of passing judgment on the Body) and imagined as being, at the time of the dialogue, in the process of casting lots. This gambling echoes the Gospel account of the Crucifixion, and the brutal materialism of soldiers casting lots for Jesus' garments: Even in its biblical allusions, the Body is bound to the mundane and worldly rather than to the transcendent. Like Jesus' garments, flesh is regularly figured as a garment for the soul, but here, the "my" of "mi fles" references the Body's entire being, rather than a discardable object. To itself, the Body is merely the object of the worms' callous gambling, not the creature on the cross whose body as well as soul will be resurrected. Personification gives the flesh-garment speech, and what seems like fear of its own incipient partition. Is the Body exonerating itself in this allusion to biblical suffering, or is it simply echoing in its own abasement the humiliations heaped upon Christ, whose very humiliation enables mankind's redemption and the promise of eventual bodily resurrection, even for such bodies as this, at a future time beyond the Body's own capacity to imagine?

In the end, the Body refuses to speak further, because, as it says, no matter how much the Soul chides it, its woe is enough that it cannot be more. With the important exception of its prophecy that it shall not be the last body to meet this fate, the Body seems largely confined within its own present. The underlying assumption behind its words might be that the bodily as such has no history except insofar as it is registered and mediated by the Soul, which is the part of the self that is capable of grasping consequence and temporality. The Body's silence, of course, is just the opening the Soul then needs to launch into its long monologue on the signs of Doomsday, an event located in the future but capable of fulfilling everything about the past.

"In a Thestri Stude," like all debates of this tradition, asks questions about selfhood that render the obvious answers less than obvious. In place of and anterior to a self engaged in projects of self-fashioning, defined as a negotiation between presenting the self to the world and the constraints imposed on such presentation, this poem offers the self as something that is being performed relationally, and in continual flux—a contentious, interdependent self based equally in the material and the spiritual worlds, split and adversarial and somehow unimaginable as the ethical whole, although it apparently functions as one for purposes of punishment.

The Poem's Medieval and Manuscripts Contexts

Although every generation reads the Middle Ages anew, and historical distortion is as fruitful as it is inevitable, we must continue to ask after what medieval writers and readers *thought* they were doing, as far as we can determine it. Having read "In a Thestri Stude" as a modern reader might, we can also ask how the poem might have been read by its Middle English audience. One way to answer this question is to examine the manuscript tradition, the choices made by scribes and compilers that expressed their own notions of where this poem might fit in the world of medieval writing. As with "Als I Lay in a Winteris Nyt," this poem appears in manuscripts that combine the didactic with the pleasurable, *sentance* with *solas*. As a piece of writing, "In a Thestri Stude" serves (mostly) the same didactic needs as countless even less canonical devotional texts that list vices and virtues and prepare the parishioner for a proper confession. But this particular work is not always found next to the devotional materials, just as it is seldom grouped with other "debates," even though contemporary scholarship studies it as such. (See John Conlee's influential edition/collection of medieval debate poetry, which includes a rich selection of Body/Soul debates.)[12] Insofar as scholars try to figure out the intended uses of a medieval work by its manuscript location, "In a Thestri Stude" is rather confusing.

The debate appears in three manuscripts: Oxford, Bodleian Library, Ms. Digby 86 fols. 195v–200r; Cambridge, Trinity College Ms. B.14.39 fol. 29v; and London, British Library, Ms. Harley 2253, fol. 57 v. Although this is fewer than some other debates ("Als I Lay" appears in seven), Chaucer's *House of Fame*, for instance, also survives in no more than three manuscripts. Although "In a Thestri Stude" is seldom placed next to lyrics, romances, or other, more obviously "protoliterary" works in the manuscripts where it appears, the poem was being placed next to satires of higher learning and understanding in the vein found in "Goldiardic" Latin poetry, works of amatory rhetoric, and even works resembling French fabliaux, such as "Dame Sirith." Unlike "Als I Lay," which is more or less clearly positioned in a way that confirms its relationship with what medieval writers often termed as texts devoted to *sowlehele*, "In a

---

12. Conlee, 1990.

Thestri Stude" is found right after a French debate between two ladies about love and fidelity in Digby 86,[13] whereas in Harley 2253, the manuscript featuring the famous Harley Lyrics, it is next to a poem on Jesus' descent into hell.[14] These two manuscripts represent two very different understandings, indeed, of where the work belongs, thoroughly testifying to its complexity.[15]

Digby 86 works as a representative example of how "In a Thestri Stude" seems to function in its manuscript context. It is not a work of high theology or philosophy; instead, it is dropped into a popular context where its didactic effectiveness echoes that of some other works, but where it also interacts with works written in a less didactic mode.[16] Along with "In a Thestri Stude," Digby 86 contains several other debate poems, including "Dame Sirith" and "The Thrush and the Nightingale"—works primarily concerned with heterosexual amatory matters, and therefore including female characters and/or discussions of women. Despite the relatively secular nature of the poems in the vicinity of "In a Thestri Stude," Digby 86 cannot be mistaken for an entirely secular collection, either. The manuscript begins with lists of the Seven Sacraments and the Ten Commandments in Anglo-Norman, and a few turned pages after "In a Thestri Stude" would bring a reader to a rather lengthy text of "Orationes devotae" in Latin.

Works like "In a Thestri Stude," with their inevitable *ubi sunt* passages enumerating all that a given life contains and all that death has now taken away, serve as warnings and reminders, and are therefore perhaps well placed

---

13. The debate that immediately precedes "In a Thestri Stude" is the Anglo-Norman love debate ("Ci commence lestrif de ii dames"), one of the relatively few instances in which the actual term *amour courtois* is used in medieval literature, according to Neil Cartlidge, who cites the lines "Mes quant ele ad lez lui soun courteis ameour, / Meuz en poest counsentir feble meinteneour" (55–56), in "Aubrey de Bassingbourn, Ida de Beauchamp, and the context of the 'Estrif de deus dames' in Oxford, Bodleian library Ms. Digby 86," *Notes and Queries* 47:4 (London: December 2000): 411–15. For a discussion of this poem, see also Marilyn Corrie, "Further Information on the Origins of Oxford, Bodleian Library, Ms. Digby 86," in *Notes and Queries* 46: 4 (London: December 1999): 430–34. The contrast between a courtly love debate and "In a Thestri Stude," an allegorical debate wherein the traditional female personifications are avoided in favor of male/genderless speakers, is a sharp one.

14. The manuscript also contains some saints' lives and fabliaux in Anglo-Norman, as well as the Harley Lyrics, dated from around 1340, and is sometimes described as one scribe's opinion of what is "best" in the Middle English and Anglo-Norman literary works available at the time. Consequently, the genres of this anthology range very widely.

15. The poem's third manuscript appearance is in Trinity College B.14.39, formerly Cambridge Ms. 323, a mixed Latin/English manuscript (with some French, but not much), which begins with a poem about how a scribe, addressed in the second person, was going to learn how to write and avoid sin at the same time. The work in English that precedes "In a Thestri Stude" is titled "Hawe on God in [to?] Warchipe"; so here, as in the Harley manuscript, "In a Thestri Stude" is being included in a *sowlehele* context.

16. According to John Conlee, "Digby 86 is the handiwork of the Dominican friars of Worcestershire; it contains more works in French than in English, and more secular works than religious ones" (Conlee, 238).

in the midst of the relative frivolity of other debates, such as the one that precedes "In a Thestri Stude" in Digby 86; its sharp contrast with works like that courtly debate echoes the way its male same-sex pairing changes the traditional use of female personifications to represent abstractions discussed in chapter 1. In Digby 86 as well as the other manuscripts where it appears, "In a Thestri Stude" appears with works both devotional and amatory. It seems to me that such a mixed vernacular textual environment would be particularly useful in fostering the kind of playful philosophical inquiry that characterizes the poem.

The question that "In a Thestri Stude" insists upon is this: Whose fault is it that the Soul, denied heavenly bliss, is carried off to hell at the poem's end? The death of this Body, in itself, seems to be no one's fault, but the suffering of the Soul begs the question of guilt. This question is a relatively new development in the tradition of Body/Soul debates. The two Anglo-Saxon versions of the debate included in the Exeter and the Vercelli manuscripts and the fragmentary Old English work (whether rhythmical prose or verse is unclear) from Worcester, preserved in a thirteenth-century manuscript, all feature a Soul confident that it is in the right, and that the Body's appetites are solely responsible for the punishments that the Soul now has to endure.[17] This arrangement may have struck its readers as rather unfair: It is as if the Soul, like the Christ himself, is innocently suffering for the Body's trespasses. This analogy must have been sufficiently clear that it manifests itself in "In a Thestri Stude," as this chapter discusses in a subsequent section.

The surviving Anglo-Saxon poems "Soul and Body I," "Soul and Body II," and the "Worcester fragments" are not really dialogic works like the debates discussed in this book. The Body lies mute throughout the Soul's speech, and a description of its dissolution is the only response offered on its behalf. The intractable materiality of the silent Body of Anglo-Saxon poetry is particularly striking in the Vercelli Book's second Soul/Body poem, in which the Soul is that of a formerly virtuous man and will not suffer hellish torments, unlike the sinful souls in most of the tradition's poems. *That* Soul comes to praise the Body, but notes, with some regret, that the Body's fate in death, which will continue until the two reunite on Judgment Day, remains exactly the same as it would have been had it sinned throughout its life.

The silent Body in the Anglo-Saxon poems bears a semblance to the many

---

17. For studies devoted to these poems, see Douglas Moffat, *The Soul's Address to the Body: The Worcester Fragments* (East Lansing, MI: Colleagues Press, 1987), and Douglas Moffat, ed. and trans., *The Old English Soul and Body* (Cambridge, UK: D. S. Brewer, 1990). On the Anglo-Saxon homilies in context, and for a summary of debates about their interpretation, see chapter 4 of Samantha Zacher's *Preaching the Converted: The Style and Rhetoric of the Vercelli Homilies* (Toronto: The University of Toronto Press, forthcoming).

homilies and sermons that reference the trope of the Soul's accusation of the Body after death. Such nondialogic works put all the responsibility for the choices made by the living man or woman onto their bodies, and so, perversely, the dead sinner's self becomes very clearly associated with its physical form, understood as that part of the self that acts. Poems such as "In a Thestri Stude" and "Als I Lay" feature a Body that disputes this model of Body-as-sole-actor, which sins and goes on sinning while a trapped Soul, which apparently has nothing to do with a person's day-to-day choices, protests within. In pre-thirteenth-century Body/Soul debates in English, the Soul is merely the preacher, standing on the outside to offer smug or distressed commentary, powerless to act. Meanwhile, the silenced "I" of man awaits Judgment Day (that day whose warning signs and events the Soul's final speech details), when it will once again be able to speak and shall—because, in this model, the Body *is* the seat of the self—be the one answerable to God for both Soul and Body. The monologic quality of the Old English poem avoids the question that will become central to Middle English Body/Soul debates and was key, as we have seen, to the Latin tradition of the same: the question of guilt's proper assignment.

A Psychology of Dissolution

At the close of the dialogue, a man's body will be devoured by worms, but as it opens, the Body possesses a Soul's capacity to reflect and to have opinions. At the dialogue's end, as well, a Soul will proceed to hell, having apparently gained some of the Body's faculty to suffer, to act, and, most of all, to be acted on by violent means. "In a Thestri Stude" draws no distinction between the parts of the Soul that will set off on this journey: Every part of the Soul disputed by the medieval philosophers of so-called faculty psychology—"agent intellect," "sensitive soul," "vegetative soul," and so on—will go to hell together.[18] Faculty psychology is the general term for medieval psychological theories derived, in part, from a reading of Aristotle's *De Anima*; its adherents would understand the soul as separated into functions that work together to varying degrees, establishing a part of the soul as the section that has desires and appetites and

---

18. I derive this thumbnail summary of faculty psychology in part from the chapters on "The Potential and Agent Intellect" and "Criticisms of Aristotelian Psychology and the Augustinian-Aristotelian Synthesis" by Z. Kuksewicz in *The Cambridge History of Later Medieval Philosophy*, ed. Kretzmann, Kenny, and Pinborg (Cambridge, UK: Cambridge University Press, 1982), and from Elizabeth Ruth Harvey's *The Inward Wits: Psychological Theory in the Middle Ages and the Renaissance* (London: The Warburg Institute, 1975). I discuss the problem of the will in the context of faculty psychology in a later section of this chapter.

sinful pleasures. That part of the soul was deemed "lower" than other parts, and therefore more readily corruptible—and it might be so implicated in the life of the body that it would remain behind at death.

The debate between the Body and the Soul is located in a particular moment, as the narrator stands in the dark listening, before the Soul departs for hell and the Body is buried. This moment is one that is poised between wholeness (that of the man that was, now dead) and the final dissolution of the union between Body and Soul (even though that separation is also a moment or interval, in the sense that it will end on Judgment Day, when Soul and Body are reunited). To a medieval philosopher thinking in terms of faculty psychology, this dissolution would contain a contradictory sort of implied wholeness, because, in the debate's situation, all of the Soul's faculties are speaking as one. The tension inherent in the Soul's speeches—that is, the tension between a rigid division of labor among aspects of the self and the ambiguity about where the guilt for the individual's sins lies—arises from the generic demands of the poem's debating allegory as well as the debates of the medieval theologians who never quite agreed on how to synthesize the Aristotelian and Augustinian ways of dividing up the aspects of the self.

"In a Thestri Stude" ignores and, by ignoring, manages to highlight the ways in which Body/Soul debates make no sense. Ontologically, the Body cannot speak or think; those are not faculties that pertain to it. The Latin "Visio Philiberti" seems to be the only Body/Soul debate in which the Body, trying to place blame for their mutual misdeeds on the Soul, asks it whether a Body could so much as speak if it were without an animating Soul. In fact, the Soul ought not be able to feel, absent sensory input from the Body, and yet it is clear that it fears the physical pains of hell, where it will achieve enough embodiment that it will be able to experience heat and pain.[19] Caroline Walker Bynum, discussing the doctrinal disputes around purgatory and bodily resur-

---

19. Augustine, for one, seemed confused by the generally held belief that souls experience incredibly physical tortures in hell: "Now since this cannot happen until soul and body have been so combined that they cannot be sundered or separated, it may seem strange that the body is said to be killed by a death in which it is not abandoned by the soul but remains possessed of soul and feeling, and endures torment in this condition. For in that final and everlasting punishment . . . we correctly talk of the 'death of the soul' because it no longer derives life from God. But how can we talk in this case of the death of the body since it is deriving life from the soul? For otherwise it cannot feel the bodily torments which are to follow the resurrection" (St. Augustine, *City of God*, Bk. XIII, ch. 2. Trans. Henry Bettenson [London: Penguin Books, 1972], 511). In Latin: "Quod cum ante non fiat, quam cum anima corpori sic fuerit copulata, ut nulla diremptione separentur; mirum videri potest quo modo corpus ea morte dicatur occidi, qua non ab anima deseritur, sed animatum sentiensque cruciatur. Nam in illa poena ultima ac sempiterna . . . recte mors animae dicitur, quia non vivit ex Deo: mors autem corporis quonam modo, cum vivat ex anima? Non enim aliter potest ipsa corporalia, quae post resurrectionem futura sunt, sentire tormenta" (*De civitate Dei*, ed. B. Dombart and A. Kalb, 2 vols. [Stuttgart: Teubner, 1981, 1993], 1:557–58.

rection, noted that "preachers, hagiographers, and schoolmen saw nothing fundamentally inconsistent in depicting the bodily tortures of disembodied spirits although they sometimes admitted it was odd."[20] Body/Soul debates such as "In a Thestri Stude" are precisely those texts in which the "oddness" of disembodied spirits' experience of torture is being worked out and worked on, and being turned into allegorical narratives with psychological aims.

A debate such as "In a Thestri Stude" is, among other things, a philosophical inquiry, an inquiry far less formal than those of hagiographers or schoolmen but one that is flexible and nuanced enough to permit interrogation of the oddness of spirits undergoing bodily suffering, and the even greater oddness of the speaking Body. One reason for the poem's productive muddling of concepts may be quite simple: To rigidly posit soul/body dualism was, after all, to participate in the Manichean heresy. Even though Western Christianity often slipped into a sort of demonization of the bodily, during the Middle Ages and afterward, the fact of Christ's incarnation and the sanctification of the bodily persisted, as we have seen in Prudentius' *Psychomachia*. To posit a Soul and a Body that share certain qualities and are even capable of loving one another, as we will see in chapter 3, is to heighten drama, to stage an interesting thought experiment, and to avoid any hint of a heretically rigid dualism.

The relationship between Body and Soul, which forms the drama at the center of the poem, is riven by the urgency of the question: Which part of the self must assume responsibility for sin committed in life? Knowing whom to blame for the Body's and Soul's collective doom seems crucial to both, even though they now exist on the far side of life, in a time when all they can do is look into a future composed entirely of punishment for their past. If the Body had been figured as sinful and lustful female flesh, it would have been easy to say that it bore the responsibility for trapping the Soul within it as in a prison. If a clear dynamic of dominance had been established from the start, in which the Soul would have been leading and directing the Body's actions as a ghost in the machine, their sins would have clearly been the Soul's fault. "In a Thestri Stude" lacks these simple solutions. Philosophically speaking, what the dialogue really needs is a third debater, the will. Since at least Augustine, medieval philosophers had believed that sin originates in the will (or, possibly, in the willing aspect of the soul), rather than in the body as such. However, there are a number of reasons, including linguistic ones discussed later, for omitting the will from this dialogue, including the conventional rhetoric for dialogues and debates (which holds that they contain two and only two speakers) and an old, pre-philosophical tradition of splitting the self into two and only two parts. A

---

20. Caroline Walker Bynum, *The Resurrection of the Body in Western Christianity, 200–1336* (New York: Columbia University Press, 1995), 281.

number of overlapping conditions, as well as a desire for narrative elegance, seem to require that, in "In a Thestri Stude," the will, and attendant guilt, are passed back and forth in a quarrel about where they belong.²¹

Body/Soul debates such as "In a Thestri Stude" thematize the tension between Aristotelian understandings of their relation, in which the soul is seen as the form of the body, and the view that the body is a shell animated by the soul, associated with Plato and medieval neo-Platonism. The neo-Platonic version, generally linked to Plotinus, posits higher and lower souls, and only the lowest soul interacts with the body. Medieval Aristotelians, too, divided the soul into its component faculties, but they were also guided by Aristotle's own writing into a productive confusion about the relationship of soul and body.

In an influential passage in Aristotle's *De Anima* (in the Latin version produced by William of Moerbeke, available to medieval readers by the 1270s, according to Ivo Thomas, who introduces its modern edition), Aristotle wonders about the separability of soul and body:

> Therefore it is evident enough that the soul is inseparable from the body—or certain parts of it, if it naturally has parts; for it is of certain bodily parts themselves that it is the act. But with respect to certain of its parts there is nothing to prevent its being separate, because these are acts of nothing bodily. Furthermore, it is not clear that the soul is not the "act" of the body in the way that a sailor is of his ship.²²

21. How much well-known medieval writers such as Chaucer and Gower knew about scholastic theories of the self remains an unresolved debate in itself, and we know infinitely less about the anonymous author of "In a Thestri Stude." One view, held by one of the few critics who have written about Body/Soul debates, argued that neither a background in the Church Fathers nor formal theological training was available to the anonymous authors of these poems; they draw instead, he maintains, on "common sense," partaking of the debates of their times (which had much larger concerns in mind, like the resurrection of the body). Robert W. Ackerman, "Debates of the Body and Soul and Parochial Christianity," *Speculum* (1961): 541–65. For a more recent and optimistic approach to just how aware medieval poets might have been of the burning theological issues of their day, see Jim Rhodes, *Poetry Does Theology: Chaucer, Grosseteste and the Pearl-Poet* (Notre Dame, IN: University of Notre Dame Press, 2001).

22. *Aristotle's De Anima in the Version of William of Moerbeke and the Commentary of St. Thomas Aquinas*, trans. Kenelm Foster and Silvester Humphries (London: Routledge 1951), 174, II.i.242–44 (according to the traditional divisions within editions of Aristotle, this section would be numbered II I 413a 7–9 in any modern edition of the Greek text). Thomas Aquinas, in his commentary, clarifies—to a degree. "As to Plato's opinion that the soul is the act of the body not as its form but as its mover, he [Aristotle] adds that it is not yet clear whether the soul is the act of the body as a sailor of a ship, i.e. as its mover only" (*Aristotle's* De Anima, 178). James of Venice made an earlier (but apparently unedited) translation of the *De Anima* that, according to Dod, was "widely circulated in the thirteenth century" Bernard Dod, "Aristoteles Latinus," *The Cambridge History of Later Medieval Philosophy* (Cambridge, UK: Cambridge University Press, 1982), 46. See also Dod's "A Table of Medieval Latin Translations of Aristotle's Work," pp. 74–79,

The analogy of a sailor sailing a ship is a metaphor of containment—the soul carried through space by the body, contained within it—but this figure is itself working in the service of a technological metaphor. The ship might be thought to be the act of the sailor because the sailor directs its movement, but Aristotle seems to assume that it is the sailor who is the act of his ship, and, therefore, permits the possibility that consciousness is a function of embodiment. The double negative of Moerbeke's version mires us in Aristotle's confusion, which even Aquinas (and the several other philosophers who, according to Edward Mahoney in the *Cambridge History of Later Medieval Philosophy,* commented about and used this analogy) could not fully clarify.[23] The relation between soul and body is so unclear, in fact, that most Christian philosophers concerned with salvation subdivided and redivided the soul (which already came down to them somewhat subdivided and complete with faculties, from both the Platonic and the Aristotelian traditions) to make it clearer which part stays behind and which part goes to Heaven or to hell—a division that "In a Thestri Stude" simply ignores, at the price of other kinds of confusion.

"In a Thestri Stude" foregrounds the complexity of drawing distinctions between form and content and renders them difficult to maintain by giving a voice to the Body and rendering the Soul vulnerable to what is portrayed in the poem as a physical form of suffering—the heat of hellfire. Thus, while such poems are rich in their implications for histories of psychology, their richness is also that they form a neglected aspect of the history of allegory through the complicated nature of their personifications. They are useful in demonstrating the ways in which allegory (in its many modes) and personification (in its endless variety) were places for performing intricate and ambivalent thinking about the self in the England of the later Middle Ages.

If "In a Thestri Stude" were a debate written by philosophers, whether some stripe of Aristotelian or neo-Platonist or some adherent of the slightly different Augustinian interpretation of the divisions of the self—if, in other words, this was an orthodox work of philosophy—the speaking parts would be almost endlessly multiplied; subsections of subsections of the soul's being would be brought in to speak their parts. This is, incidentally, something that seems to happen at a particular moment in *Piers Plowman,* as discussed in chapter 5: Anima in B.XV and Liberum Arbitrium in C have moments of stating *all* of their names and all of their functions at once, and the confusion of these moments in both the B and C versions is an important indicator of

---

of that same article, which lists 144 surviving manuscripts of James of Venice's translation and 268 surviving manuscripts of William of Moerbeke's.

23. Edward Mahoney, "Sense, Intellect and Imagination," in Norman Kretzmann et al., eds., *The Cambridge History of Later Medieval Philosophy* (Cambridge, UK: Cambridge University Press, 1982), 612, fn 42.

how poorly this sort of direct application of faculty psychology to a latter-day *psychomachia* really works. What is particularly interesting about "In a Thestri Stude" is that it is *not* such a poem, and yet it does not lack for careful philosophical thought on the topic of division and subdivision of the self.

Even without going into the full complexity of a philosophical treatise, a working definition of what a soul or what a body is needs some explanation of where desire, appetite, action, and choice are located. "In a Thestri Stude"—a work of *sowlehele* largely intended to be useful rather than philosophically interesting and not committed to a particular school or view of what human beings are—*still* sees the self as profoundly characterized by inner rifts and tensions. The problem of guilt, the poem's central disputed matter, begs the question of the will's location, since the will functions as a sort of third party to the dialogue, passively being passed back and forth between the debating pair.

How to answer the question of guilt that the dialogue poses so urgently? Rather than choosing between blind obedience to an Aristotelian or Augustinian reading of the debate and an assumption that the author was ignorant of patristic writings, I want to seek the middle ground, or perhaps the entirely *other* ground, that the poem makes available. Medieval writings about psychology set out a series of theological explanations of the relationship between soul and body that cannot fully account for the sort of relationship depicted in this poem and, as we will see, in "Als I Lay." As a consequence, although I have tried to understand the poem in Aristotelian terms, and am about to turn to examining it in terms of St. Augustine's writings about the will, I ultimately find these authorities insufficient. My concern, therefore, is not just with whether this debate is or is not Augustinian in its psychology of the will, but rather with the ways in which it uses the abilities of the vernacular to think through problems that Augustine had considered and other schools of philosophy and theology were also considering at that time. The real problem, as it turns out, is not just including the will but also translating "will" into English.

The Problem of the Excluded Will

"In a Thestri Stude" functions as a debate precisely because it elides the problem of the will: If the provenance of the will were crystal clear, Body and Soul would have nothing to argue about, and yet will, though never mentioned, is ever-present. Instead, the poem hinges on the difficulty of theorizing the capacity for free choice that medieval philosophers call *liberum arbitrium*. This is one of the keys to understanding the peculiarities of style and form that characterize the poem, and perhaps even the diversity of the works placed beside it in manuscripts. While "In a Thestri Stude" permits certain fairly conventional rhetorical gestures that also occur in sermons and homilies (the preaching on the signs of Doomsday, for instance, and the *ubi sunt* formula), it also offers an opportunity to think through the distribution of powers and punishments among the faculties that make up the self.

The attempt to understand the relationship of soul and body to the will and, ultimately, to salvation occupied a great deal of space in medieval philosophy and theology, including some crucial chapters on this topic in Augustine's *City of God*.[24] There, Augustine explains that "the first death consists of two, the death of the soul and the death of the body; so that the first death is the death of the whole person, when the soul is without God and without a body, and undergoes punishment for a time."[25] What is this "whole person," and what comprises such a person? As we shall shortly see, even Augustine is not entirely sure. Here, Augustine embeds his discussion of what death separates and destroys in a discourse on the first human beings and the meaning of their disobedience in the Garden of Eden:

> [There] the soul, in fact, rejoiced in its own freedom to act perversely and disdained to be God's servant; and so it was deprived of the obedient service which its body had at first rendered. At its own pleasure the soul deserted

---

24. In his introduction to *Three Treatises on Man: A Cistercian Anthropology* (Kalamazoo, MI: Cistercian Publications, 1977), Bernard McGinn summarizes the debates surrounding Augustine's views about the relationship of body and soul, which seem to have changed a great deal over his lifetime—and even over the course of the argument made in *City of God*. McGinn believes, with O'Connell, that Augustine initially accepted but eventually rejected Plotinus' neo-Platonic model of higher and lower souls in favor of a biblical view, which McGinn characterizes as "the historical materiality of man" (8). McGinn concludes that Augustine "failed to systematize the two understandings of man to which he was heir" (9). He also notes that misreadings of Augustine on this matter were common, and often considered orthodox in the Middle Ages. According to Beryl Smalley's summary account of Augustine's view on this matter, *The Study of the Bible in the Middle Ages* (Oxford: Clarendon, 1941), Augustine "defines man as 'a rational soul which uses a body,' with the accent on the transcendence of the soul; so the spirit transcends the letter; their connexion [sic] is tenuous and artificial, depending on the mechanical rules of allegory" (10). The definition Smalley attributes to Augustine is Plato's (from I Alcibiades 129 e), and was cited by Plotinus, as McGinn points out (McGinn, 8). That tenuousness of the body/soul connection—like the arbitrariness of the relationship between the signifier and the signified—would have left the Soul and Body of "In a Thestri Stude" with nothing to say to one another at their journey's end.

25. St. Augustine, *City of God*, Bk. XIII, ch. 12, trans. Henry Bettenson (London: Penguin Books, 1972), 522. "Quonium prima constat ex duabus, una animae, altera corporis: ut sit prima totius hominis mors, cum anima sine Deo et sine corpore ad tempus poenas luit; secunda vero, ubi anima sine Deo cum corpore poenas aeternas luit." Augustinus Hipponensis, *De Civitate Dei*, CL. 0313 SL 47, ed. B. Dombart and A. Kalb. Corpus Christianorum, Series Latina (Turnhout, Belgium: Brepols, 1955).

its superior and master; and so it no longer retained its inferior and servant obedient to its will.²⁶

This moment, one of many when Augustine positions himself in the ongoing debate about the status of the Soul/Body relation, is particularly interesting in the connection it implies between servitude and selfhood. The Soul is God's servant, and is disobedient and thus, punished, loses its disciplinary grip over the one who once was the servant's servant, the Body. Even more relevant to this discussion is how Augustine's discourse highlights the absence of a significant third element from the Middle English Body/Soul debate—the will.

The poem's view of the workings of the will and the sinful appetites differs in a fundamental way (either through rejection or through ignorance) from the descriptions of the appetites in medieval philosophy and in the complex of theories that this chapter has termed faculty psychology. One basic way in which it differs is that medieval philosophy was fascinated by the role of the will in sin. By the fourteenth century, some philosophers "sought to attribute to the human will a wide variety of cognitive activities that included judgment, evaluation, and a sort of discursive reasoning."²⁷ By this time, the Will might have merited a role of its own in an allegory (as, arguably, it does, in both "Sawles Warde" and *Piers Plowman*, discussed in the second half of this study), and the absence of a character named Will to blame in "In a Thestri Stude" is a problem as well as a driving force in the poem—without Will to blame, Body and Soul try to figure out which of the two parts of the self is at fault. Of course, everything to do with the different powers of the self was hotly debated throughout the Middle Ages, and a plethora of theories were advanced—but it is clear that our anonymous author was not trying to deal with these large issues head-on, even if he or she was asking similar questions. The ways in which "In a Thestri Stude" deviates from faculty psychology might be understood as the product of ignorance on an author's part, or of imagined ignorance on the part of the author's intended audience, but the fact remains that they offer a somewhat different view from the one readers of medieval psychological writings might expect.

26. Augustine, *City of God*, Bk. XIII, ch. 13, 522. "Jam quippe anima libertate perversum propria delectata, et Deo dedignata servire, pristino corporis servitio destituebatur: et quia superiorem Dominum suo arbitrio deseruerat, inferiorem famulum ad suum arbitrium non tenebat" (Augustinus Hipponensis, *City of God*).
27. John Bowers, *The Crisis of Will in Piers Plowman* (Washington, DC: The Catholic University of America Press, 1986), 53. A footnote on this page indicates that this notion was anticipated by Peter John Olivi (1248–98). Bowers's study offers a wonderfully succinct summary of the development of the Christian doctrine of the will from the letters of Paul through the writings of St. Augustine and the philosophy of Thomas Aquinas; see especially his chapter 2, "Complexities of the Will."

The status of the will is never named as a problem by either speaker in "In a Thestri Stude," and yet it is undoubtedly the series of willed acts performed by the now-dead knight that pose such a problem for the Soul's salvation. But what part of the knight performed those acts, and is that the same part that now bears responsibility for them? The Soul of "In a Thestri Stude" seems to accuse the Body of having possessed the will and the appetites of the person now dead; the Body chose wrongdoing, and the Soul, allegedly innocent, could do nothing to stop it. Now that the Soul is being punished, it can take revenge only by taunting the Body on its bier.[28]

The dyadic structure of "In a Thestri Stude," and the consequent necessity of more than one occluded third party or term (the narrator as well as the will), testify to a linguistic problem Middle English authors encountered in an interesting way: the difficulty of translating a Latin philosophical vocabulary into the vernacular. Just as the term *Soul* is ambiguous (is it *anima* or *spiritus*, the "rational" or the "sensitive" soul that is speaking to the Body?), it is difficult to express will in its volitional rather than its futural sense in English. Even if this sense of the word *will* exists (as it does, even in Old English, in the verb *willan*), it does not map fully onto the Latin philosophical vocabulary. After all, it is possible to "have all one wills (wants)" or to say "I will (intend to) do this"; the word will can translate as sexual desire, power of free choice, or intent, but it is not exactly the same thing as the verb *volo, velle, volui* or the noun *voluntas, voluntatis*. *Voluntas* indicates the desiring part of the soul, often translated as "will," but the English word *will* is also used to translate *liberum arbitrium*, the freedom of the will in general, and turns out to be less precise than either of the Latin terms.[29] This is a matter of available English

---

28. Anne Middleton has noted that the real problem in Middle English may be not the lack of a term for "free will" or "free choice" (*liberum abitrium*) but the way in which the term *free* is associated with the term *noble*, a sociolegal status distinct from bond-man or bond-servant (Anne Middleton, private communication).

29. The meaning of *voluntas, voluntatis* and its relationship to Middle English literature are most clearly presented in James Simpson's discussion of *Piers Plowman*: "Christian philosophers inherited from classical philosophers a division of the soul into a cognitive power and an affective power: into a part of the soul which thinks, and perceives the truth on the one hand, and a part which feels, and desires the good, on the other. Common Latin terms for these two basic parts of the soul are *ratio* for the thinking part of the soul, and *voluntas* for the desiring part. When these terms are translated into the vernacular, there are different words used for both of them, but 'will' is the term most often used in Middle English for *voluntas*. In a late fourteenth-century text, *The Cloud of Unknowing*, for example, the author states that the soul has 'two principal worching myghtes, reson and wille' (ed. Phyllis Hodgson, London: Oxford University Press, EETS. 1955, p. 115). He defines 'resoun' as a 'myght thorough the whiche we departe the iuel fro the good, the iuel fro the worse, the good fro the betir, the worse fro the worste, the betir fro the best' [116]; and 'wille' he defines as a 'myght thorou the whiche we chese good, after that it be determined with reson; & thorow the whiche we loue God, we desire God, & resten us with ful liking & consent eendli in God [116]." James Simpson, *Piers Plowman: An Introduction to the*

vocabulary and usage only, since, clearly, most if not all English authors were reading Latin works, even if not necessarily works of Latin philosophical debate about the nature of the will. "In a Thestri Stude" does not use the Boethian language of free will, which becomes so important in later English writings. Although Thomas Usk, in the late-fourteenth-century *Testament of Love*, manages to distinguish between free choice and free "arbitrement," a century earlier (and earlier, also, than Chaucer's translation of Boethius and his *Troilus and Criseyde*, with its consideration of the role of the will), "In a Thestri Stude" does not deploy this language.[30]

In Middle English, the word *will* means both the act of choosing and, potentially, the thing that is willed.[31] This sense of the will does not function successfully as a philosophical term, and, lacking such a term, the allegories that contain discussions of the will or of the self's capacity for free choice (and allegorical characters very much invite such discussions) perform complex maneuvers *around* the problem of willing and choosing. The Latin *voluntas*, however, is always a part of the self and never refers to that outside thing being desired, and perhaps this is why medieval philosophers tended to think in terms of the more separable, abstractable term *liberum arbitrium* when considering the freedom of choice some faculty of the soul possessed. At any rate, neither of the Latin terms *voluntas* or *liberum arbitrium* exactly coincides with the scope of the other, and neither precisely coincides with the scope of the English term *will*.

"In a Thestri Stude" is marked in multiple ways by the problem of the will. The capricious choices the self makes in life (for which the Soul blames the Body) reflect its freedom to exercise the *liberum arbitrium*, the free choice of the will—a freedom that expresses the often capricious freedoms of the self as arbiter. These are aspects of the poem's mode of personification that mark its attempt to *do* psychology informally and in the vernacular, performing psychology as a byproduct of philosophy, literature, pedagogy, and preaching. "In

---

B-text (London: Longman, 1990), 95, citing Hodgeson, 1944.

30. See Thomas Usk, *The Testament of Love*, ed. R. Allen Shoaf (Kalamazoo, MI: Western Michigan University [TEAMS], 1998).

31. The *Middle English Dictionary* lists both: "1(a) The appetitive and volitional faculty of the soul;—often as contrasted with reason, imagination, etc.; also in fig. context; also person.; volition; also, the soul in its appetitive operations." And "3(a) That which one wants or requires, a desire; also in prov. expressions; also, that which suits one's pleasure; don (werken) ~; haven ~." I thank Steven Justice for a useful discussion on this topic. Hannah Arendt notes this about the English word *will*: "The strange ambivalence of the English language, in which 'will' as an auxiliary designates the future whereas the verb 'to will' indicates volitions, properly speaking, testifies to our uncertainties in these matters." "These matters" are the way in which the will is "our mental organ for the future as memory is our mental organ for the past," an understanding that, Arendt notes, she does not share with the large number of philosophers who see "the will" as an illusion. Hannah Arendt, *The Life of the Mind* (New York: Harcourt Brace Jovanovich, 1978), 13.

a Thestri Stude" is a work whose fundamental conflict and narrative development are both created out of the building blocks of philosophical, theological, and didactic thought. Because it inhabits thought in a dynamic way, it cannot be reduced to "merely" enacting philosophical ideas, but making philosophy speak is part of what the poem accomplishes.

"In a Thestri Stude" permits the Soul to put the blame of earthly sin on the Body instead of on the will, but according to Augustine, it is not the Body's lusts that corrupt the Soul. Rather, it is something that Augustine can locate *within* the Soul—the will. In his *Confessions,* Augustine considers the problem of the will at some length. "The mind gives an order to the body and is at once obeyed, but when it gives an order to itself, it is resisted," he writes, and we might consider the Body/Soul debate as a kind of corrective to this model.[32] In explaining how the mind might not be able to control the self, Augustine has recourse to the concept of the will (in just the place where the Soul reverts to blaming the Body):

> The mind orders itself to make an act of will, and it would not give this order unless it willed to do so; yet it does not carry out its own command.... For the will commands that an act of will should be made, and it gives this command to itself, not to some other will. The reason, then, why the command is not obeyed is that it is not given with the full will.... So there are two wills in us, because neither by itself is the whole will, and each possesses what the other lacks.[33]

Augustine's two wills name a fissured, split self centuries prior to the Body/Soul debate's emergence as a genre. One can speculate that the possibility of, indeed the necessity for, debate poetry as a genre comes out of this passage. Augustine seems to be theorizing that debate as a practice is always-already located in the *voluntates* (literally, "wills") since they are always at least double if not multiple. However, Augustine's description of the split will depicts a process that remains internal to what medieval readers would call "the Soul" and therefore avoids the entire tricky question of the Body so oddly addressed by "In a Thestri Stude," where the Body is assumed to have something like a will of its own.

---

32. Augustine, *Confessions,* Bk. VIII, ch. 9, trans. R. S. Pine-Coffin (New York: Penguin Classics, 1961), 172. "Imperat animus corpori, et paretur statim: imperat animus sibi, et resistitur." Augustinus Hipponensis, *Confessionorum libri tredecim* CL.0251. Corpus Christianorum, Series Latina (Turnhout, Belgium: Brepols, 1955).

33. Augustine, *Confessions.* "Imperat animus ut velit animus, nec alter est, nec facit tamen.... Quoniam voluntas imperat ut sit voluntas, nec alia, sed ipsa. Non utique plena imperat, ideo non est quod imperat.... Et ideo sunt duae voluntates, quia una earum tota non est, et hoc adest alteri quod deest alteri" (Augustinus Hipponensis, *Confessionorum libri tredecim*).

One solution to seeing the will as an excluded character whose presence would have solved the dilemma of blame that exists in all Body/Soul debates would be to understand the "rational will" as standing in an equivalent relationship to sinful passions and appetites as an ideal Soul stands to its appetite-ridden Body. Robert Pasnau's chapter on human nature in the *Cambridge Companion to Medieval Philosophy* contains a telling passage in which Pasnau explains Augustine's writings on the will in terms of Augustine's own reading of Galatians 5:17: "The flesh lusts against the spirit and the spirit against the flesh." Pasnau writes that "although the Pauline text suggests that spirit and flesh are matched in an even fight, medieval authors tended to view the relationship between the will and the passions as asymmetrical, inasmuch as only the will could give rise to voluntary actions."[34] Unnoticed in this analysis is the slippage from the language of "flesh and spirit" into the language of "the passions and the will"; this slippage owes much to medieval commentators who, trying to avoid Manichean dualism, chose to understand "flesh" as "depraved will."[35] Medieval authors seem to have equated the body with the passions or appetites; a will capable of controlling the passions or choosing among them would stand in the same relation to the passions as the soul does to the body. Even though the rational will has primacy, Pasnau concludes, "not even St. Paul could keep his flesh from lusting against his spirit. To make sense of that influence, the flesh was viewed as doing its work indirectly, by shaping how the mind conceives of a situation."[36] A debate of Soul with its Body could thus be analogous to a debate between the will and the passions, even though the Middle English debates featuring a character named Will tend to characterize him (*Piers Plowman*) or her ("Sawles Warde") or the neuter "it" ("Wit and Will") as at least bumbling and at most dangerously in need of stern discipline.

To discuss the figure of the will in "In a Thestri Stude" is to discuss something that isn't present in the poem as a voiced character, but instead as a philosophical problem that the poem never succeeds in solving. The exclusion of the will from the Body/Soul dialogue is an effect of a literary (as well as a lexical or grammatical) choice. Debate poems are almost always structured as dialogues with *two* speakers taking their turns. The Body/Soul tradition

---

34. Robert Pasnau, "Human Nature," in *The Cambridge Companion to Medieval Philosophy*, ed. A. S. McGrade (Cambridge, UK: Cambridge University Press, 2003), 223.

35. McEvoy gives the example of St. John Chrysostom's gloss on Galatians 5:17, stating that St. John Chrysostom "counters their [the Manicheans'] interpretation by claiming, quite legitimately, that Paul uses 'the flesh' habitually to mean not the body as such but the depraved will, so that the blame rests not upon the physical body but upon the slothful soul." James McEvoy, "Grosseteste on the Soul's Care for the Body: A New Text and New Sources for the Idea," in *Aspectus et Affectus: Essays and Editions in Grosseteste and Medieval Intellectual Life in Honor of Richard C. Dales*, ed. Gunar Freibergs (New York: AMS Press, 1993), 45.

36. Pasnau, 223.

never strays from this dyadic organization, but by confining itself to a dualist model, yet trying to avoid a heretical dualism that utterly condemns the flesh, it becomes committed to a dual-power analysis of the living individual, and to an unresolvable debate about guilt. Having split the self into Body and Soul, the author is presented with a theological problem: Which of these two has actually chosen the actions that the two of them have performed in their mutual history of tenuous unity? Is the Soul (with no subsplit available that would permit a "higher" and a "lower" soul to struggle for dominance) entirely imprisoned in the Body's wants, its "depraved will"? Or does the flesh ventriloquize the willful choices made by its spirit's volitional powers? The neither/nor nonanswer given by "In a Thestri Stude" and other poems in the Body/Soul tradition is philosophically unsatisfying, but it points to a somewhat satisfying solution: These poems are not dramatizations of philosophical stances about the relationship of the body and the soul, but rather appropriations of those stances for purposes of *sowlehele*. They are works whose narrative dynamism works in tension with a performative, didactic, and pastoral discourse aimed at explaining the self to itself, making selective use of medieval philosophical concepts but turning them to their own uses, as a rhetoric aimed to both emotionally and intellectually move and thereby educate a lay public.

Christ's Body, Christ's Soul

There is a moment near the end of "In a Thestri Stude" that helps make clear both the difference and the proximity between theological psychology and the psychology of *sowlehele*. This moment comes at the transition point, the break where the poem changes. The Body has petulantly refused to speak further: "βei βou chide nit and dai, ne sege ich the namore" ("Though you chide me night and day, I will say no more to thee"; 52). In response, the Soul reprimands the Body, accusing it of having never thought of God while living:

> Bodi, wi neuedest βou βe biβout, βe wile βou mighttest i-wolde
> Hof him βat makede ous alle of nout, wat hauest βou him I-holde?
> For hore sunnen and nout ffor his his fles he solde;
> Blodi he was on rode I-don, so the profete hous tolde. (53–56)

> Body, why did you never think, while you had the power to have chosen to do so
> Of him that made us all out of naught, of all that you owe him?
> For our sins and not for his he gave his flesh;
> Bloody was he on the cross, so the prophet tells us.

The Body had already alluded to the Crucifixion in the image of the worms casting lots, and the Soul had, in the immediately preceding speech, promised or threatened to call on Jesus: "To Jhesu will ich callen, he be mi socours" ("To Jesus will I call, he [will] be my salvation"; 48). Here, however, the Soul accuses the Body of having grievously forgotten about Christ. In fact, despite the earlier allusions, it may be that both of them have. There seems to be no hope for salvation in what the Body or the Soul utter in this dialogue. The slightest ghost of hope is retrospective: The Soul asks the Body why it hadn't, when it had the chance, thought of Christ, because the moment after death is too late. There is, in this moment, an element of simple didacticism, as well as an "I told you so" sort of schoolyard taunt and the fundamental confusion of faculties (Why was it the Body who should have done the thinking?). But, most of all, there is, at last, a way out of the Body/Soul dyad in this moment, through an invocation of a flesh that isn't the Body's.

Line 55—"for hore sunnen and nout ffor his his fles he solde"—stands out in the poem, and not only for the awkwardness of its doubled "his." Christ's flesh, as that which is sacrificed for the good of humankind, is the only flesh explicitly mentioned in the poem besides the Body's. The doubled "his" can almost be understood as a separation; "his sins" and "his flesh" are so different from one another, because Christ's flesh has not sinned, that each needs its own "his" to mark it. Is he giving his flesh or selling it? The verb "sellen" can mean "to give" or "to sell" in Middle English; the *Middle English Dictionary* lists usage for the former as early as circa 1130 and the latter as early as circa 1200. My translation emphasizes the first of these meanings without, however, being certain that the distinction can be fully and firmly maintained, or that the author of "In a Thestri Stude" would want to maintain it. In this dialogue, Christ stands in a relationship to his own flesh that is not unlike that of the Soul in relation to the Body, except that his flesh is much more valuable, and far more meekly unresistant to being given or sold than one suspects this poem's Body would be. The difference is that Christ's flesh obeys him, as does his will, whereas the dilemma of the human split will is that it struggles between good and evil, splitting the human self in multiple ways.

Theologically, Christ's two natures do not map exactly onto a Body/Soul distinction. As early as the First Council of Nicea in 325 it had been firmly resolved that Christ was *not* merely a divine soul clothed in a human body, since the union between the earthly and the divine that he represented was more complete than such a dualism implies.[37] Nevertheless, the possibility of

---

37. For discussions of the role that representations of Christ's nature played in medieval culture and written texts, see Miri Rubin, *Corpus Christi: The Eucharist in Late Medieval Culture* (Cambridge, UK: Cambridge University Press 1991); Sarah Beckwith, *Christ's Body: Identity, Culture and Society in Late Medieval Writings* (London: Routledge, 1993); and Caroline Walker Bynum, *The Resurrection of the Body in Western Christianity, 200–1336* (New York: Columbia

owning and thereby selling the flesh is a reflexive relationship, and Christ's reflexive relationship to his flesh participates in an economy that *resembles* that of the Soul/Body debate, modeling the ideal relation of mastery over the Body that should be available to a more perfect Soul.

Christ himself is the original personification allegory—"verbum caro factum est" ("The Word made flesh"; John 1:14). In the grammar of line 55, "his fles he solde," the poem also offers the fundamental principle of its own allegorical construction—a relationship of a divisible two rather than an indivisible two-natured unity or a relationship of three. In this context, Christ and his flesh can be understood as an exemplary split self being offered as a contrast to the split and self-berating selfhood of the dead knight. Christ is interesting in the context of this poem in that he is *two*—a self complete with detachable, sellable flesh, not just human melded with divine and *not*, most emphatically, the sublime triune complexity of the Trinity's triply split self. To think in threes—which would mean to include the narrator or the will in the dialogue, in the case of "In a Thestri Stude"—would be to involve oneself in that great, formal edifice, and our author neatly avoids such pitfalls by opting for Christ's soul and body rather than the language of the Trinity.

The last section of the poem details the prophesied signs of the coming Judgment Day, "domesdai," a day both terrible and wonderful in that it will see the Soul's reunion with its Body. When the dead shall rise up, they will be judged, the Soul tells the Body, using the word *dome* that had previously appeared in details about the evil judgments rendered by the nobleman they had been when together. The Soul's narrative and the poem conclude with all souls going to heaven (presumably, all souls that are judged as good, although the Soul doesn't specify) and with Satan banished. The Soul itself sighs, somewhat surprisingly (given that the prospect of being reunited after Judgment Day has just been discussed): "alas; / Wo werthe that ilke stounde, bodi, that thou boren was" ("Alas. Woe was that time when you were born, Body"; 105–6). Even after one hundred–odd lines of this poem, it remains unclear whether the "you" that the Soul addresses in these words is really separate from the "I" that speaks, and the irony produced by this confusion is very evident. In fact, this ironic confusion marks the place where readerly pleasure, pleasure in the functioning of well-written figures, would presumably be produced in this poem of doomsday and of death.

The Split Self of *Sowlehele* Psychology

The encounter between Soul and Body discussed in this chapter offers scenes

---

University Press, 1995).

of disputation, accusation, and (to an extent) confession. The self portrayed in Body/Soul debates like the one I have discussed is one that comes into being through a disputational and disciplinary relationship. It is retroactively constructed, referred to in the past tense after it has already ceased to exist. Personification is used, in medieval allegories, as a means of embodying abstract ideas. In Body/Soul debates, the abstraction being embodied is that of the split self itself. What the disputation performs is the splitting of what had been one (dead mute, and representable as real) person into two speaking, allegorical ones. The allegorical debate recalls a formerly living being—the dead man whose life is under discussion in the poem—producing his life as something real while bringing to speech two of his aspects. This process is how this debating allegory aptly figures the contradictions of allegorical embodiment, its arbitrariness yet necessity, its timelessness, which is nevertheless also its historicity.

"In a Thestri Stude" exists as a node on a complex intertextual network. Along one axis, it can be understood as part of a history of English sermons and homilies depicting Soul/Body conflict. Seen in this way, the innovation of the poem lies with the scandal of the Body that talks back, rather than lying prone and dead as the Soul rehearses its many regrets at the bier.[38] Along another axis, it is possible to argue that "In a Thestri Stude" was not directly influenced by the vernacular traditions of English writings at all, since the Old English works on the Soul berating the Body had very little dissemination compared to works in the Latin tradition, such as the extraordinarily popular Latin "Visio Philiberti."

With this in mind, we can look at "In a Thestri Stude" in terms of its vernacular innovation, at how it brings the theological problems that the "Visio" assumes into a new sort of focus. Along yet another axis, compared with other vernacular Body/Soul debates written at roughly the same time, it is a shorter and somewhat less sophisticated work than "Als I Lay" or the Anglo-Norman "Un samedi par nuit" (both discussed in the following chapter), but it is also a little earlier than either. The information to be gained by looking at "In a Thestri Stude" along with its vernacular counterparts is the odd detail of how many of these debates were being produced in England, or at least were retained in manuscripts that both contain English-language poetry and have ended up in British libraries.[39]

---

38. Scholars agree, as Ackerman succinctly puts it, that "The Old English Soul's Address is not in any sense a source of the Desputisoun." Ackerman, 543.

39. The most elaborate, or perhaps just the best-preserved, versions of the Body/Soul debate (the versions in which the Body makes an active and philosophically complex defense of itself, actually engaging the Soul in real dialogue) all seem to originate in England, although the placing of the "Visio Philiberti" in England has been disputed. It has been a critical convention

Throughout the Body/Soul debate tradition, whether in Old English, Anglo-Norman, Latin, or Middle English, a tension between linked yet separated beings and the hyperbolic literalness of their personification are these poems' two fundamental rhetorical gestures—the two jokes that make such poems work, rendering them popular enough to be written and rewritten in all those versions in all those different languages. The dialogic situation of poems such as "In a Thestri Stude" is not premised on a notion of self and other, founding the self through some sort of dialectical relation, although the poem might be read in concert with such notions. It is, rather, a genre of dialogue that queries the very location of the fissure within that peculiar unit, the self, asking just what the division of labor within the self might be, wondering just what the fissures within look like and how it is that they are produced and policed. Words such as *self* or *person* are relatively inadequate for describing the conjunction of Body and Soul, in their separated dialogic state and, possibly, even in the state to which they retroactively refer, the unity they seem to have had within the man who is now dead.

What sort of psychology does this poem offer? It is a psychology after the fact, after death has determined the end of the story and no further suspense about outcome is possible. It is a psychology wherein the notion of the self is an anterior one—the man who once united this particular body and soul is a person whom the reader never encounters except in retrospective narrative by the two parts that death has rendered capable of separating and squabbling. The events, pleasures, and faults of this man's life are narrated, with some nostalgia, by the Soul: The man they had been had been full of physical vigor, but the dead Body cannot "lepen to leiken ne to rage / Wilde beres to beten, to binden leounes sauuage" ("[neither] leap to play or to rage / to beat wild bears nor to bind savage lions [to your will]"; 29–30). They are shown to be inessential by the set piece of the *ubi sunt* speech, the lament about all that had been loved and lost in life. Even so, certain inessential aspects of that particular man have clearly dropped away to permit him to play the didactically necessary role of Everyman. Perhaps, the poem suggests, the whole cannot be mourned, had

---

to associate this purported popularity with Robert Grosseteste, and, for a time, to attribute authorship of the most popular Latin Body/Soul debate to him, noting that he did clearly author a philosophical allegory, the influential *Chateau d'Amour*. Although the attribution of the "Visio Philiberti" has been discredited, Grosseteste did make a number of arguments about the Soul's care for and love of the Body that were both controversial and influential in their day, and may have contributed to the intellectual environment within which Body/Soul debates were being written in England. See James McEvoy, "Grosseteste on the Soul's Care for the Body: A New Text and New Sources for the Idea," in *Aspectus et Affectus: Essays and Editions in Grosseteste in Honor of Richard C. Dales*, ed. Gunar Freibergs (New York: AMS Press, 1993), for a discussion of Grosseteste's sometimes controversial work, which focused on the love that, specifically, Jesus' soul had for his body.

never *been* a whole, and only seems to have existed after it has been sundered and can be inferred in retrospect.

"In a Thestri Stude" makes literal in its form *and* in its content many of the issues that are significant to Middle English debate poetry and to allegorical writings in Middle English in general. Analysis sheds light on the way in which the relationship between materiality and mind was being thought of and some of what could be done with such thinking, and it participates in revealing the kinds of philosophical and theological vocabularies available to English authors of the thirteenth century and subsequently.

This chapter has argued for the significance of the split self of Body/Soul debate, not necessarily as a unique work of art worthy of entrance into a literary canon, but as a work that literalizes certain kinds of thinking about the nature of the self that do not map onto the psychological theories we tend to assume were the only ones operating in the Middle Ages. The speakers of this disputation—not mere embodiments of then-current ideas, but clearly vehicles for a process of working through some truly contentious concepts—turn out to be particularly apt at considering the complex role played by the oft-troubling emergence of a conception of the will's freedom in medieval discussions and depictions of selfhood.

CHAPTER 3

"The Soul Is the Prison of the Body"
PEDAGOGY, PUNISHMENT, AND SELF-LOVE IN A
MIDDLE ENGLISH DEBATE

> *The soul is the prison of the body.*
> —Michel Foucault

"For a long time," wrote Foucault in his storyteller's voice in *History of Sexuality, Volume One*, "the individual was vouched for by the reference of others and the demonstration of his ties to the commonweal (family, allegiance, protection)."[1] In other words, according to this account, once upon a time the individual was vouchsafed by position within a hierarchy. This "before" section of Foucault's story thus posits a simpler time prior to subjection, specificity, individualization.[2] Although we might take issue with this portrait of "before," it may not be necessary to accept it unquestioningly to fully appreciate the richness of the "after": "Then, [after 1215] he was authenticated by

1. Michel Foucault, *The History of Sexuality: An Introduction, Volume One*, trans. Robert Hurley (New York: Vintage Books, 1978), 58–59. This volume was originally published in France as *La Volonté de Savoir* (Paris: Éditions Gallimard, 1976).
2. While many of Foucault's methods and claims have been indispensable to historians and theorists of early modern sexuality, he has also been much criticized for the ways in which he imagined the sexual discourse of the Middle Ages as unitary. Karma Lochrie, in "Desiring Foucault" (*The Journal of Medieval and Early Modern Studies* 27:1 [1997]: 3–16), suggests that Foucault's work on the Middle Ages is troubling, that "the nostalgic, naturalized, felicitous expression is as strange and inhospitable a formulation as the alteritist one of a unitary discourse marked by obedience, avowal and self-decipherment" (10), and warns of a possible "carceral effect" Foucault's writing on the Middle Ages might have; however, she agrees to salvage the "spirit, if not the letter of Foucault" in asking questions such as "[C]ould pleasures refuse the erotic idioms of medieval texts and modern readers and 'travel' without becoming simply illegible and insignificant?" (13).

105

the discourse of truth [that] he was able or obliged to pronounce concerning himself. The truthful confession was inscribed at the heart of the procedures of individualization by power."[3]

Here, Foucault was not describing anything so triumphant as a rupture preceding the birth of modern subjectivity. In fact, he insisted in his late interviews on the striking and surprising *continuities* with Greek ascetic practices that his readings uncover, and detailed how confession had existed as a practice prior to becoming a required annual event. Rather than positing the birth of a new beast slouching toward Enlightenment to be born, Foucault offered an account of new *processes* of individualization arising out of old—processes that emerge through an institutional demand for a certain kind of dialogue, the confessional interaction that constitutes the matter of pastoral care. In the specific context of medieval England, such processes can be termed *sowlehele*, and one privileged example of *sowlehele*, the Body/Soul debate known as "Als I Lay in a Winteris Nyt," can exemplify as well as complicate Foucault's story.

Writings that might be categorized as *sowlehele* arise out of the demands for clarification of the nature of the self in the context of medieval confessional culture. The unpublished fourth volume of *The History of Sexuality*, detailing the history of that culture, was to have been titled *The Confessions of the Flesh* (*Les Aveux de la chair*), but the kind of confession discussed in this chapter concerns the interplay of the flesh's confessions with those of the soul in a situation where the two debate with one another after death.[4] This concern with the body's interaction with the spirit permits a sharpening of the concept of *sowlehele* through an encounter with Foucault's late thought about self-constitution. Bringing Foucault's engagement with confession together with the split self of Body/Soul debate and its specifically medieval take on psychology offers a new way of understanding something Foucault seems to have had some difficulty with: how and where the private psyche meets the social world; how to describe its constitution as productive as well as subjectivating; and how to describe its actions without ignoring either its own agency or the inevitability of various kinds of "power" acting on it.

3. Foucault, 58–59.
4. Foucault refers to *Les Aveux de la chair* as "a second volume in the same series . . . [that] deals with Christian technologies of the self. And, then, *Le Souci de soi*, a book separate from the sex series, is composed of different papers about the self . . ." in "On the Genealogy of Ethics: An Overview of Work in Progress," in *Michel Foucault: Beyond Structuralism and Hermeneutics*, ed. Hubert Dreyfus and Paul Rabinow (Chicago: University of Chicago Press, 1982), 231. Thus, according to this 1983 interview, *Care of the Self*, presently in publication as the series' volume II, was actually conceived as being volume III in the series. The materials examined in this volume are also discussed in "The Subject and Power," which appears in the Dreyfus and Rabinow collection, too, and in Jeremy R. Carrette's *Foucault and Religion: Spiritual Corporality and Political Spirituality* (London and New York: Routledge, 2000), as well as a collection of Foucault's late essays selected and edited by Carrette, *Religion and Culture: Michel Foucault* (New York: Routledge, 1999).

In his *History of Sexuality, Volume One (La Volonté de Savoir)*, Foucault was focused on the institutionalization of confession in the thirteenth century. But he was still thinking about the constitution of the desiring subject and not, as later, about the intimate co-imbrication of the social and the psychological. With the series' second and third volumes, Foucault had turned to examining the history of subjection—the constitution of selves by and through relations of power—through practices of care for the self, of which confession was to be one significant instance. What this book terms *sowlehele* would be an example of such practices, rendered specific to its English-language context and time, but of course this is not what Foucault worked on. That said, in interviews, Foucault promised that his fourth book was going to be about the Middle Ages, although his interest was largely in describing how early medieval Christianity organized subjection in the context of divine law, confession, and penitence.

As Foucault worked on the multivolume *History of Sexuality*, his thought shifted from understanding confession as a form of institutional control of the self toward a view of confession as a form of self-constitution intimately involved with the workings of (external, social) powers on the subject. "The self," he writes, "has ... not to be discovered but to be constituted, to be constituted through the force of truth."[5] Foucault argued that the very thing that we might take as a given, the speaking "I," has a history—and its history lies, at least in part, in the relationship between penitent and confessor. Critics have often understood Foucault's examination of confession as a veiled critique of psychoanalysis, through comparisons between the scene of psychoanalysis and the confessional. We might, instead, think about these later writings as inquiring into historical *alternatives* to modern psychoanalytic theory, of which *sowlehele* might be one. Foucault's work connects contemporary critical theory and medieval cultural studies with the history of psychology at the nodal point of confession and the constitution of the self therein.

In several of his dialogues, Plato referred to the body as the prison house of the soul.[6] Foucault famously reversed this formulation in *Discipline and Punish*: The soul, he wrote, is "the prison of the body," and, simultaneously, something that is "produced within the body by the functioning of a power that is exercised on those punished."[7] Metaphors of spatiality are productively

---

5. Michel Foucault, "About the Beginning of the Hermeneutics of the Self (1980)," in *Religion and Culture: Michel Foucault*, 168. See also other essays in that volume.

6. Plato, *Phaedo* 81d, *Phaedrus* 250c. In *Cratylus* 400c, Socrates attributes this definition of the body as the prison of the soul to the Orphic poets as part of a discussion of how to define "body." *Collected Dialogues of Plato*, Bollingen Series LXXI, ed. Edith Hamilton and Huntington Cairns (Princeton, NJ: Princeton University Press, 1989).

7. Michel Foucault, *Discipline and Punish: The Birth of the Prison*, trans. Alan Sheridan (New York: Random House, 1979), 29. [Originally published as *Surveiller et Punir: Naissance de la Prison* (Paris: Editions Gallimard, 1975).]

muddled here. The soul is figured as external to the body, surrounding it as a prison would, while simultaneously emerging from within, centered inside the body's enclosure.[8] Foucault's language avoids choosing the soul *or* the body to function as an authentic core supporting a stable notion of the self, while keeping a dynamic tension in play between the two. Foucault's theory lacks only an allegorical dialogue to clarify how the concepts of "body" and "soul" work to both constrain and produce one another. This chapter examines one such dialogue.

The Body/Soul debate "Als I Lay in a Winteris Nyt" produces a particular version of the self for purposes of *sowlehele* through a series of performative speech acts, including the *prosopopeia* of the speaking body, discussed later, and a mourning for lost unity by a split subject whose duty in life had been to establish a proper hierarchy between the aspects of the self. The debate is explicitly concerned with the disciplinary relations—relations of hierarchy, love, and power—that most intimately characterize the subject of confession in relation to pastoral power. Having considered a similar poem, "In a Thestri Stude I Stod," in chapter 2, I now build on that reading by taking up this longer and better-known English Body/Soul debate and reading it against its analogues in Latin and Anglo-Norman. This examination of "Als I Lay" through the interplay of difference from and similarity to its analogues shows how the workings of texts that perform *sowlehele* are consistent in their approach to self-discipline as well as how the resources of the English language make the Middle English poem distinctive.

The exact date of composition for "Als I Lay" is unknown, but it first appears in manuscripts of the mid to late thirteenth century.[9] The poem is also

---

8. Judith Butler offers a similar analysis of the same passage in Foucault, albeit in the service of a very different argument, when she writes about it that "the soul is figured as itself a kind of spatial captivity, indeed, as a kind of prison which provides the exterior form or regulatory principle of the prisoner's body." Judith Butler, *The Psychic Life of Power: Theories in Subjection* (Stanford, CA: Stanford University Press, 1997), 85. See also Butler's characterization of the consequences of this confusion: "The transposition of the soul into an exterior and imprisoning frame for the body vacates, as it were, the interiority of the body, leaving that interiority as a malleable surface for the unilateral effects of disciplinary power" (86–87).

9. "Als I Lay in a Winteris Nyt" appears in seven manuscripts, mostly large miscellanies and anthologies; Laud Misc 108 (Bodl. 1486) fols 200r–203r (verses 1–48, 185–642 only); Auchinlech Ms. (Advocates 19.2.1), fols. 31vb–34vb; Vernon Ms. (Bodl. 3938), fol. 286rc; Digby 102 (Bodl.1703), fol. 136 r; BL Ms. Royal 18.A.x. fol. 61v; BL Addit. Ms. 22283, fol. 80va (verses 1–198 only); BL Addit. Ms. 37787, fol.34r. It is listed in the Index of Middle English Verse as #351. I am basing my discussion on Conlee's edition of the poem as it appears in Laud Misc 108, with supplementary readings from the Auchinlech Ms. in *Middle English Debate Poetry: A Critical Anthology* (East Lansing, MI: Colleagues Press, 1991). I have also consulted Thomas Wright's edition of the poem, in *The Latin Poems Commonly Attributed to Walter Mapes* (London: Camden Society, 1841). There is also an edition by Wilhelm Linow, "βe Desputisoun between

commonly known in the critical literature as "The Disputation Between Body and Soul," evidence of its role as *the* Body/Soul debate, standing synecdochally for the entire tradition in the minds of critics who organize anthologies or write about these debates. To take the example of a lesser-known miscellany, Laud 108, we find that "Als I Lay'" is included among works such as the *South English Legendary, King Horn,* and *Havelock*—works that combine religious instruction with narrative pleasure. At over 600 lines, this poem is longer than any other Body/Soul debate and quite a bit longer, as well, than most poems that tend to be described primarily as "debate poems." This poem's length is due, according to its editors and critics, partly to the many "confessional" details it offers. It also offers a larger quantity of gruesome detail (putrefaction, the tortures of Hell, etc.) than most debates. The claim that this poem can stand in for the tradition is mingled with what may seem like a very different contention: that this debate is the best example, indeed the culmination, of the debate form, or at least of the small subgenre of Body/Soul debate (either all such debates, or possibly just these debates as they were written in Middle English). No lesser critic than George Kittredge called it "the best embodiment of the theme in any literature."[10] Even so, though several editions were produced in the nineteenth and early twentieth centuries, it has not been the subject of much critical attention among medievalists over the past fifty years.

The plot of "Als I Lay" is not very different from that of "In a Thestri Stude I Stod": A body on a bier is confronted by its own soul, who chastises it for a life ill-lived. Over the course of an *ubi sunt* passage intoned by the Soul, the enumeration of many lost possessions describes the life of a wealthy knight. The Soul both accuses and preaches to the Body, and the Body eventually answers back to upset the Soul's apparent certainty that all fault for a life lived in sin lay with the sinful flesh. In answering, the Body argues that it had been like a mute beast, and the Soul had infused it with its own will, and, consequently, all sins were the fault of the Soul's mismanagement. The Body's counteraccusation is much more philosophically coherent and affectively complex than any other response by a speaking body in the Middle English tradition, and so is the Soul's response. Much of this chapter focuses on the specifics of the emotions with which both characterize the relationship between them. Over the course

---

βe Bodi and βe Soule," *Erlanger Beitrage zur Englischen Philologie* I (1889). A translation of this poem appears in John Gardner, *The Alliterative Morte Arthure: The Owl and the Nightingale and Five Other Middle English Poems* (Carbondale, IL: Southern Illinois University Press, 1973).

10. G. L. Kittredge, "Introduction," in *Debate of the Body and the Soul,* modernized by F. J. Child (Boston: R. E. Lee Company, 1908),quoted in Sister Mary Ursula Vogel, *Some Aspects of the Horse and Rider Analogy in "The Debate Between the Body and the Soul"* (Washington, DC: Catholic University of America Press, 1948), 1.

of the debate, that relationship is figured successively as that of penitent and confessor, student and teacher, brother and brother. While much of what the Body and Soul say is motivated, within the poem, by the rhetorical demands of the disputational scene—with details of their relationship being stated to prove the Body's or the Soul's innocence of the wrongs done by the knight they had been—a kind of excess builds up as relationship piles upon relationship. This excess offers a set of immanent theories about the kinds of relationships that might exist between spiritual and material aspects of the self, producing *sowlehele*. As a byproduct or intimate condition of the possibility of this excess, the poem also describes, as if inadvertently, several kinds of loving homosocial interdependence that might exist between men.

"Als I Lay" begins to appear in major miscellanies at the end of the thirteenth century, and ultimately appears in more surviving manuscripts than any other work classified as a Middle English "debate poem." Whatever the actual date of its composition, that relative popularity helps us understand it as an example of the writings about the confessing subject that was produced in the aftermath of the Fourth Lateran Council. Although Body/Soul debates have received little critical attention in the second half of the twentieth century, there is one invaluable article on "Als I Lay." Robert Ackerman's "*The Debate of the Body and the Soul* and Parochial Christianity" situates the poem within the context of vernacular and Latin works of pastoral care.[11] Ackerman reads "Als I Lay" as a work worthy of attention in itself, for its specific rhetorical quality, and also as a work that "realizes the spirit of the popular Christianity of its day," arguing that the debate's implicit theological stance (regarding the Soul's relation to the Body, resurrection, guilt, and punishment) is one that reflects lay piety and participates in parochial didacticism.[12]

As I do, Ackerman considers "Als I Lay" as a significant bearer of the traces

---

11. Robert Ackerman, "*The Debate of the Body and the Soul* and Parochial Christianity," *Speculum* 37 (1962): 541–65. A relatively recent but fairly technical article about "Als I Lay" argues that the poem's didactic effect is partially achieved by reference to the Augustinian concept of the "second death," which punishes through "an eternal mutual antagonism between the reprobate's body and soul caused by the intermutative effect of their postmortem cohering." Liam O. Purdon, "'Als I Lay in a Winteris Nyt' and the Second Death" in *Mindful Spirit in Late Medieval Literature: Essays in Honor of Elizabeth D. Kirk* (New York: Palgrave Macmillan, 2006), 46. The two articles represent a debate that this book tries to elide: Ackerman insists that the author of "Als I Lay" is not aware of, or at least not using, conceptions of sin and the soul from medieval philosophical writing; Purdon argues that "Als I Lay" is structured by the thought of St. Augustine. To argue that "Als I Lay" is a work of *sowlehele* cleaves more closely to Ackerman's position, but, as previous chapters have shown, that is not the same as accusing the poem of being simple, folksy, or unlearned. The version of lay piety represented in "Als I Lay" seems to me closer to the theologically sophisticated but poetically and narratively driven one discussed by Jim Rhodes, in his book *Poetry Does Theology* (Notre Dame, IN: Notre Dame University Press, 2001).

12. Ackerman, 544.

left by the Fourth Lateran Council of 1215 and its requirement of annual confession. However, Ackerman's commitment is also to proving that "Als I Lay" is a superior work of literature—superior, for instance, to the "Visio Philiberti," the Latin Body/Soul debate that may well have been the Middle English poem's most immediate source. Ackerman's close, comparative reading of the Latin and Middle English debates is invaluable, but he misses the opportunity to consider the implications of the "humanizing transformation" from the purported stuffy clerkishness of the "Visio Philiberti" that he claims for the vernacular version. Ackerman's rhetoric emphasizes the homely, down-to-earth vividness of Middle English, but he does not really explain why this should be more valuable in a literary evaluation than what he characterizes as the more explicitly philosophical Latin version. He lists three things that are "new" in "Als I Lay," meaning not present in the "Visio Philiberti": a brief reference to witchcraft; references to the rituals of Matins, Mass, and Evensong; and interest in the trinity of "the world, the flesh, and the devil." Every other difference that he lists is one of quantity (*more* discussion of putrid corpses in the expanded English version, *more* enumeration of prideful living in the knight now dead). However, perhaps because of the limitations of a journal article, Ackerman eschews extended discussion of what his own argument implies: that "Als I Lay" can be fruitfully read through a poetics of *sowlehele*.

Although the actual term *sowlehele* is not used in "Als I Lay," a close analogue is: Enumerating how it never listened to its orders, the Soul tells the Body, "I bad the βenke on soule-nede / Matines, masse, and euesong" ("I bade you to think of 'soul-need,' / at matins, mass, and evensong").[13] To read "soul-need" as a category of piety is to understand this utterance as the kind of instruction that the poem explicitly offers by way of lament. Had the Body listened to the Soul's injunction, the two would not now be damned. To take these lines more literally is to notice that the Soul is asking the Body to have kept to a rigid schedule of fulfilling needs explicitly designated as not its own—the needs, in fact, of the Soul. Also, it is to notice that the Soul is claiming it could influence but not cause the actions the Body took, a claim that the Body disputes throughout the poem. Transforming the abstract obligation to pray into a personified soul with its own needs and demands is a paradigmatic gesture of *sowlehele* didacticism, but that very didacticism, having created a character named Soul who can be judged as a personality within the poem, also undermines the abstract force of the law by its very narrative concreteness. The Soul comes off as a bit of a demanding whiner, even if, by all accounts, its claims against the Body are correct.

13. "Als I Lay in a Winteris Nyt," lines 233–34, in John W. Conlee, *Middle English Debate Poetry: A Critical Anthology* (East Lansing, MI: Colleagues Press, 1991). Henceforth, line numbers only will be used for quotes from "Als I Lay."

What Ackerman's analysis points to (but does not describe) is a work of allegorical personification in English that attempts to think about the human self in *both* disaggregation and relationship. He calls this, as many critics of Middle English literature do, the particular sort of "psychological realism" evinced by vernacular writings, but the "realism" he is describing is that of our contemporary psychological notions, or, rather, our contemporary version of "common sense."[14] For instance, it might seem like common sense to see that the Soul who laments that "soul-nede" was not met could be construed as a "realistically" whiny figure. But such a reading sets a trap for the bad or overly literal reader, who would then miss the appropriate didactic lesson. This study continues Ackerman's work, but asks, What is the specific nature of the sort of "common sense" on the subject of psychology being produced by works like this in the thirteenth century, and what does it do to our analysis of this work if we assume that it *is* worth studying (because Ackerman has helped establish it as such) and move forward into examining what *kind* of common sense it is representing? In other words, what kind of "homely realism" *is* this, exactly?

At poem's end, the Body is left to rot, and the Soul is carried away and tormented by devils in Hell. Neither is vindicated; neither convinces the other of the justice or coherence of its point of view, and both endure ignominious infliction of suffering apart (at least until Judgment Day, when they will be reunited and begin to suffer together). This is an effect of the dramatic situation of the disputation—both parts of the dead knight are eventually going to hell, neither is going to turn out to be "right," and even if the Soul at times stands in for a sort of priest or teacher, it does so imperfectly. Poetry organized as a debate between two personified abstractions necessarily deals with the problematic relationship between the abstract and the concrete, the bodily and the spiritual, world and Word. Body/Soul debates in general thematize the distinction between form and content but render them difficult to maintain by giving a voice to the Body and rendering the Soul vulnerable to what is portrayed in the poem as a physical form of suffering—the heat of hellfire. In what follows, a close reading of "Als I Lay" shows how it functions as a work of effective *sowlehele,* and how its affect-rich portrayal of the love between the Soul and the Body exceeds its ostensibly didactic mission. That love exists to some degree in most versions of the Body/Soul debate in Latin and the vernaculars. In Middle English, it gets coded in a variety of ways discussed later, but each of these ways depicts male same-sex interdependence. That queer relationship, of male beings bound together for all time, shows how *sowlehele* can and often must be read as queer in its Middle English manifestations.

14. Ackerman, 564.

Voice and *Prosopopeia* in "Als I Lay in a Winteris Nyt"

"Als I Lay" is a poem in two unequal parts: The first concerns the debate of the Soul and the Body; the second, shorter section details the tortures experienced at the (inconclusive) conclusion of that debate when a legion of demons descends on the Soul to begin its eternal punishment. The poem begins: "Als I lay in a winteris nyt / In a droukening bifor βe day / Vorsoβe I saugh a selly syt: A body on a bere lay" ("As I lay on a winter's night / in the darkness before day / Forsooth I saw a wondrous sight: a body lay upon a bier"; 1–3). These opening lines suggest that the poem is a dream vision, although it might also be a vision seen in a dazed state during the night. In the third line, the narrator describes what he sees, the "selly syt," without ever indicating that he (if it is a he) is sleeping. At the close of the debate, the narrator is still lying wherever it is that he lay, although now covered in a cold sweat and promising God to live a better life henceforth.

Is this a dream vision, and why—in a poem that generally expands on its sources—is this detail left unclear and unelaborated? Staging the debate as a waking vision might have seemed most likely to qualify it as a prophecy worth heeding. The Latin Body/Soul debate that seems to be a source, or even *the* source, for "Als I Lay" is explicitly titled "*Visio* Philiberti," and its beginning clearly establishes it as a dream. The Middle English poem resists this clarity, leaving open the possibility that this debate is the allegory-like *somnium*, in need of interpretation.[15] By not specifying that it is a dream, the poem may also take on a more mundane quality, as if seeing souls speak to bodies were ordinary or at least possible.[16] In addition, something about the confusion between sleep and waking in "Als I Lay" works to code, right from the start,

---

15. The *somnium* is one of the five kinds of dreams according to Macrobius' influential classification scheme, and it is defined as an "enigmatic dream... that conceals with strange shapes and veils with ambiguity the true meaning of the information being offered" (Ambrosius Theodosius Macrobius, *Commentary on the Dream of Scipio*, trans. William Harris Stahl [New York: Columbia University Press, 1951], 84–85). The classification of all dreams is as follows: "All dreams may be classified under five main types: there is the enigmatic dream, in Greek *oneiros*, in Latin *somnium*; second, there is the prophetic vision, in Greek *horama*, in Latin *visio*; third, there is the oracular dream, in Greek *chrematismos*, in Latin *oraculum*; fourth, there is the nightmare, in Greek *enhypnion*, in Latin *insomnium*; and last, the apparition, in Greek *phanatsma*, which Cicero, when he occasions to use the word, calls *visum*." Macrobius, 87–88.

16. Something like this is noted in Christopher Cannon's analysis of "The Owl and the Nightingale": "*No one has fallen asleep*," he writes, describing the beginning of that poem (italics his). "The absence of this crucial predicate for a dream vision also means that this poem not only presents bird speech as unremarkable, but it insists that an owl and a nightingale actually have something to say." Christopher Cannon, *The Grounds of English Literature* (Oxford: Oxford University Press, 2004), 113–14.

the productive confusions enacted by the rest of the poem between a Soul surprisingly corporeal, especially when being tortured in hell, and a Body possessed of philosophical thought and a voice, locked in a particularly tense relationship even by the standards set by other Body/Soul debates.

Unlike the Soul of "In a Thestri Stude I Stod," who concludes the poem by essentially turning into a preacher and offering a sermon on Judgment Day (that day when Soul and Body will be reunited), "Als I Lay" concludes with the Soul borne away by a thousand devils to hell. Over a hundred lines detail the ways in which the Soul is tortured, painfully up on a Hell horse's spiked saddle and set upon by devils "opon the sadil he was sloungen / As he scholde to the tornement" ("upon the saddle he was slung / As if he were riding to a tournament"; 545–46). After riding in the hunt for a while, predator becomes prey when the Soul is flung off the saddle and chased by the hounds "as a tode" ("like a toad"; 555). The punishment is appropriate for one who had been a knight in life but had been unable to reckon properly with the fact of embodiment, with the Body in its animal capacity. This moment might actually be a manifestation of pointed and ironic pedagogical aptness on the part of the poem's devils: Riding a devil horse as punishment might be an image that a former knight would be particularly equipped to understand.

As in other Body/Soul debates, the poem's first speech is a volley of accusations the Soul launches at the mute Body. The Body is accused of having sinned so much through greed and appetite in life that it now deserves its punishment: rotting in the grave. Although other Body/Soul debates mention that virtuous bodies, too, meet this unsavory fate, here the Soul seems to think that bodily decay is simply and entirely a punishment. This puts *all* of the arbitrary details of the Body's embodiment in the service of moral admonition. The Soul is angry that the Body's appetites have damned them both, and now the Soul will have to suffer unbearable tortures in hell. It is evident that part of the punishment that the Body receives after death is to become the object of the Soul's mockery, to hear the Soul's *ubi sunt* lament, and to understand that, in being sundered from the Soul, it has lost the whole world. It is just this argument, however, that the Body eventually turns against the Soul: If the Body is nothing without the Soul, is it not the Soul who ought to be considered the responsible party when guilt is being attributed? Given the poem's final section, where the Soul's suffering at the hands of devils is detailed and the abandoned Body's is not, "Als I Lay" seems, surprisingly, to accept at least some aspects of the Body's argument and, at the very least, to conclude in a draw between the two opponents. Such an understanding, however, is necessarily preliminary: The poem is framed by a debate about guilt, but its middle seems less about guilt and more about specifying the loving interdependence between the self's parts.

As it begins its speech of accusation against the Body, the Soul seems to believe that it is in one of those Body/Soul debates in which the Body's guilt can simply be assumed and will be tacitly accepted by the silent flesh. The Soul's *ubi sunt* speech is more than 120 lines (in a poem not much over 600 lines long) of uninterrupted accusatory monologue, which details possessions, friends, and even a wife, the latter two both singularly unsorry to see this person dead on the bier. The Soul's speech does not concentrate on cataloging the dead one's social world alone. It enumerates, as well, pleasures taken and injustices done, imputed to the Body's appetites and clearly the results of the dead knight's will. The *ubi sunt* formula, here, permits the Soul to provide details that make the person who is now dead specific, individual, capable of unique (albeit ubiquitous) forms of sin. Foucault cited "individualization" as one of the effects of the new confessional technologies; this Body/Soul debate features a far more obviously individualized dead knight than earlier English and Anglo-Saxon Body/Soul debates, but the narrative thus created posits a self through negation, as that which is no longer, that which is now lost, that which deserves punishment. "Als I Lay," like "In a Thestri Stude I Stod" before it, represents a moment when the literal/material (body) smashes up against the figurative/linguistic (soul), and both come away with pieces of one another. In the process of moving through "Als I Lay," the Soul acquires a literal physical form, and the Body acquires (but, somehow, also loses) a voice.

Narrating the lost life that had been, the Soul details items such as the lost home (now a grave) and the lost clothes (now a shroud), but all seem to act merely as a lead-up to the most surprising and poignant of the Body's losses: the voice. The Body loses access to making use of the voices of others, the Soul points out, including those "tragetours" (magicians?, actors?) who used to "bere thi word ful wide / and maky of the rime and raf" ("bear your name / words far and wide / and make rhyme and verse about you"; 57–58). Earlier than that, however—in fact, quite early in its *ubi sunt* catalog—the Soul demands to know "[Where is] "thi lede that was so loud?" ("your voice that was so loud"; 22).[17] This line, which is not highlighted as the most important

---

17. The *Middle English Dictionary* defines "lede" in ways that conflict with the context of this translation. Lede is defined as "1. (a) Law, ecclesiastical system, order 2. (a) Customs, ways; also, behavior." It also defines the same word as "1(a) A person, a man (b) in pl.: subjects, followers, retainers; an army; sg. servant; as form of address to an inferior: 'My man'; (c) a prince, lord; God; as form of address: sir; (d) ?a lady; (e) the human race, mankind; also, one of the human race, a human being; ~ werk, human operation. 2. (a) A people, nation and 3. Land, landed property, landholdings." In my disagreement with the MED, I have consulted two translations of the poem. John Gardner's reads "boast" for *lede*, and F. J. Child reads "voice." See John Gardner, *The Alliterative Morte Arthure: The Owl and the Nightingale and Five Other Middle English Poems* (Carbondale: Southern Illinois University Press, 1973), 161, and *The Debate of the Body and the Soul*, trans. F. J. Child (Cambridge, UK: John Wilson and Son, 1888), 10.

by any means (the Soul goes on listing the knight's losses and documenting his life for another hundred lines), nevertheless grows in importance over the poem's course, because it names something "Als I Lay" accomplishes that very few other poems of the tradition have. It is also repeated, in a way: The Soul tells the Body that "hi mouth is dumb, thin ere is def" ("Your mouth is dumb, your ears are deaf"; 246). The Soul thus enumerates the ways in which the Body has lost access to its own senses in being sundered from the Soul.

The *Rhetorica ad Herennium,* long attributed to Cicero and one of the most popular rhetorical treatises of the Middle Ages, defines how the category of "voice" functions in relation to allegory in the Middle Ages.[18] It defines the trope of *prosopopeia* (which it terms the somewhat less used Latin *conformatio*) as that which "consists in representing an absent person as present, or in making a mute thing or one lacking form articulate."[19] The absence mourned here, I would argue, is the wholeness that never was, a single being, indivisible or at least undivided. Instead, Body/Soul debates, in whatever language, install the split of the subject into its entire history, whether detailed by the Soul claiming to have been a passive observer or by the Body claiming to have been an automaton. In "Als I Lay," the two mourn their lost unity rather than deploring it. The structure of any Body/Soul poem, therefore, is that of *prosopopeia*—aspects of a dead knight, normally incapable of speech, brought into dialogue with one another. In "Als I Lay," as in few poems of the tradition, when the Body does lift up its head and speak, its voice—a groaning, ghostly voice—seems loud enough to rebut the Soul.

The Soul's accusations argue that the Body, by virtue of being bodily, is the carrier of sin, an accusation that relies on the assumption that embodiment implies materiality, and materiality implies appetite and sin. However, a pure version of this view—embodiment as purely evil—would be Manichean,

18. Gordon Teskey, writing of the politics of allegory, suggests that "the very concept of the body as something that has a private interior and a public exterior is created by the voice. It is the voice that gives the body an inner sanctum where deliberation can occur and whence speech can issue[;] . . . without voice the body is meat" (*Allegory and Violence* [Ithaca, NY: Cornell University Press, 1996], 124). The politics of the self as discussed in this chapter permit the body to have a voice, but never permit readers to forget the body's proximity to meat, the tentativeness of its possession of a voice.

19. *Rhetorica ad Herennium*, Bk. IV, trans. and ed. Harry Caplan (Cambridge, MA: Harvard University Press, Loeb Classical Library, 1954), 66. James Paxson offers an excellent reading of this passage as a definition that also renders the term almost impossible to define; see his *The Poetics of Personification* (Cambridge, UK: Cambridge University Press, 1994), 14–15. According to Paxson, Quintillian's *Institutio Oratoria* is to be given credit for first naming the trope of personification *prosopopeia*. His study argues that what literary critics tend to subsume under the category "allegory" should rightly be termed "personification." While I am using *prosopopeia* in this chapter to name the explicit thematization of speech by a literally inanimate being, Paxson's study traces the history of the trope back to the etymology "prosopon + poein," "to make a face" (Paxson, 18), seeing it as a far larger category.

dangerously heretical, and contrary to the incarnational philosophy underpinning Christian belief. Whereas medieval works, including those Old English Body/Soul debates in which the Body lies silent and accused, occasionally seem to slip into this view, in "Als I Lay," the Body is given the opportunity to respond persuasively and defend itself thoroughly. Its speech is also marked, right from the start, as both spectacular and spooky:

The bodi βer it lay on bere	The body, there it lay upon the bier
A gastlich βing as it was on,	A ghastly thing as it was
Lift up his heued opon βe swere;	Lifted up his head upon its neck;
As it were sike it gan to gron	[And] began to groan as if one who is sick.

(139–42)

This transition from the Soul's speech to the Body's recapitulates the poem's fourth line ("a body on a bere lay"), and, in effect, begins "Als I Lay" again. The Soul's enumeration of the dead knight's life had relied so heavily on lists of the typical things all who are dead must lose (love, joy, possessions) that its speech was almost ordinary. The Body's slowly rising head—why detail that it raised its head "upon its neck" if not to slow down the process of its rising?—returns the reader forcibly to the horror of dead things speaking. The Body's utterance, however, is neither pathetic nor horrifying; it is surprisingly reasonable.

Unlike the Body of "In a Thestri Stude I Stod," whose response to the Soul is largely a complaint, pointing to the profoundly different worldview possessed by flesh without its spirit, this Body seems to understand time and causation in the same way as the Soul, or a whole human philosopher, might. The Body responds by arguing that the Soul was granted the knowledge of good and evil even before birth. The Soul was responsible for all the choices the self, now dead, had made in life, the Body argues, and its knowledge renders the Soul responsible for the well-being of the self that death has divided:

For God schop the aftir His schaft	For God shaped you after his image
And gaf the bothe wyt and skil;	and gave you both wit and skill;
In thi loking was I laft	in your keeping [*lit*: looking, *imp*. guidance, direction] was I left
To wisse after thin oune wil	to direct/teach according to your own will

(185–88)

The Body's response insists that the Soul had a pedagogical, rather than a pastoral, romantic, familial, or friendly, responsibility to guide it (although all of these options are attempted by one debater or the other over the course of the poem). At this point in the dialogue, this view of authority seems fully in line with conventional representations of feudal lordship: The Soul was a paternal figure imbued with the knowledge and responsibility to guide those who are less fortunate.

Here, *prosopopeia* is a voice that marks the rhetorical transformation that is taking place when (normally) mute matter begins to interact in the world of the dream. This version of the *prosopopeia* is perhaps closest to the one mournfully described by Paul de Man as that which "makes accessible to the senses, in this case the ear, a voice which is out of earshot because it is no longer alive."[20] In both ancient and contemporary formulations, *prosopopeia* makes a process rather than a product into a trope. In itself, this trope's presence at the very heart of the poetry of disputation underlines the ways in which the subject that it describes is one engaged in an uncertain process of becoming, rather than a stable or unitary entity.[21] *Prosopopeia* is undergoing an ironic twist: The two voices that speak, those of the Body and the Soul, are audible to one another because both are equally dead. This doubled *prosopopeia* is audible to a single other party, the poem's narrator.

The workings of *prosopopeia* in the poem are complicated, somewhat, by the Soul's repeated figuration of the Body as a sort of beast, usually a horse.[22] Immediately before the Soul names the loss of its voice among its many losses, it compares the Body to a lion: The knight used to ride high on his horse, "as a lyun fers and proud" ("as a lion, fierce and proud"; 20). But even though, in

---

20. Paul de Man, "The Epistemology of Metaphor," in *Aesthetic Ideology* (Minneapolis: University of Minnesota Press, 1996), 24.

21. The voice played a significant role in medieval preaching and in pedagogy as well. Kenny and Pinborg point out that the prolegomena to textbooks often included a note on the significance of oral instruction, frequently citing Pliny's statement that "the living voice affects the intellect much more than the reading of books." The selection Kenny and Pinborg give, taken from Radulphus Brito, ca. 1300, goes on to gloss the Pliny passage, "And he [Pliny] gives the following justification for his contention: the teacher's pronunciation, facial expressions, gestures, and whole behavior make the pupil learn more and more effectively, and what you hear from another person is situated deeper in your mind than what you learn by yourself" (Radulphus Brito, *Proemium in Parva Mathematicalia*, Ms. Bruxelles, B. Royale 3540–47, f. 2f, cited in Anthony Kenny and Jan Pinborg, "Medieval Philosophical Literature," in *The Cambridge History of Later Medieval Philosophy*, ed. Norman Kretzmann et al. [Cambridge, UK: Cambridge University Press, 1982], 16).

22. In a published 1948 dissertation on the subject of this poem, Sister Mary Ursula Vogel examines "Als I Lay" in terms of what she describes as an ancient analogy, that of the Soul/Body being compared to a rider and his horse. In her analysis, Vogel also argues and demonstrates that the poem does not fit well with Thomistic doctrine in depicting the split and independent soul and body, a neo-Platonic conceit she attributes to Augustine; but it does accord with St. Thomas Aquinas's philosophy in according most of the blame for the knight's damnation to the Soul. See Vogel, *Some Aspects of the Horse and Rider Analogy*.

its pride, it enjoyed riding on a horse and being known as a great knight, the Body also *was* a horse, or, rather, became one in the process of yielding to sin. The Soul describes its relation to the Body as a pedagogical one—"To teche were βough me bi-taught" ("You were taught to learn from me"; 217)—and it names the rival teacher—"the qued" ("evil"; 218)—and notes that "Wiβ βi teβ βe bridel βough laught" ("with your teeth you caught the [evil's] bridle"; 219). This is not a simile. In life, the Body was not *like* a horse; it acted as if it *were* a horse, and is transformed into a horse by the Soul's performative speech—or by the devil's seduction. Within the same few stanzas, the Soul also describes the Body as having ignored its teachings when, in its youth, it "renne aboute and breyd wod" ("ran about and brayed like a madman"; 228). This bridle-bearing Body described by the Soul in its counteraccusation is less than human, and the previously loud voice has become an animal noise, a madman's shout, and might not deserve the dignity of a hearing in the context of the debate. This, however, is the Soul's rhetoric.

The Body fully responds to the Soul by reinvoking and turning the rhetoric of animal innocence around. It wishes that it never *had* become human: "I schole haue ben dumb as a schep . . . That et and drank and lai and slep" ("I would have been dumb as a sheep / That ate and drank and lay and slept"; 281–82). It goes on to argue that, if this were so, it might have been slain but it would not have gone to hell after death (an assertion that contradicts the Soul's lament that it, alone, is going to hell while the Body rots in comparative peacefulness). In the context of the poem's debate, these two rival sets of claims seem to cancel each other out: The Body continues to be permitted to debate, since it is *not* understood as simply or primarily an animal physicality, and the Soul is still not unequivocally to blame for the ills that have befallen this ill-matched pair. However, the question of the status of the Body's voice has been rendered in a manner that continually troubles the poem.

This study is invested in returning "body studies" to the concept of the soul, but in the Middle Ages, the problem was quite the opposite. "Soul" was all: "Als I Lay" (along with a very few other poems) explicitly brings the concept of the body into *sowlehele* psychology. The Body's voice, when it reasserts one, is a groan, "as it were sike it gan to gron" ("began to groan as if one who is sick"; 142). This spooky groan reinforces the vulnerability of bodies, how they are subject to illness and physical pain. And yet, even if it speaks as one who is sick, the Body's rebuttal insists on the interrelatedness of Soul with Body, and on the Body's essential humanity. It claims that the relationship between these two characters is—and has always been—love and fellowship, complaining that "me thought min hert brast / When deth so diolfuli me drap" ("it seemed to me that my heart had burst / When death so cruelly took me"; 147–48). The Body of "Als I Lay" and its analogues frequently resorts to a sort of irony to point to its own bodiliness—after all, the Body is the one who possesses the heart, and it is likely that (at least in the understanding of medieval medicine) the heart did, precisely, burst at the moment that death came to it. But beyond the joke that the Body is embodied, through the Body's words the claim is made that, in this relationship, it is the Soul that has callously and cruelly neglected the Body's well-being. The love and fellowship asserted by the Body has, among its other functions, the capacity to defy the Manicheanism that one might read into the rigid slash that divides "Body" and "Soul" in the term I am using in this book, "Body/Soul debate." The Body's speech insists that Body and Soul are joined, in love if not as a single being, and that their relationship, and relative guilt, must be worked out from that perspective.

The extraordinary thing about the Body's voice—simultaneously described as lost and yet, somehow, made present as part of the dialogic situation of "Als I Lay"—is how it contradicts, or perhaps just radically reworks, the famous discussion of voice in Aristotle's *De Anima II*. In that much-commented-upon text, Aristotle (who has been discussing the different senses and their relationship to the soul) states quite explicitly, "Voice is the particular sound made by something with a soul."[23] Aristotle expands on this a little:

> Voice is the sound of a living thing. No inanimate being utters voice, though, by analogy, the flute and the harp are said to "speak"; and, so, too, other inanimate objects which sound with duration, harmony and significance. The resemblance arises from voice also having these qualities. [. . .] It is necessary that air enter when [an animal] draws breath. Hence a striking by the soul (in these parts) upon air inhaled through the windpipe is voice.[24]

However, traditionally, animals do not have souls yet have something like voices, which leaves open the possibility that the Body is a kind of speaking animal. Bartholomaeus Anglicus, in his *De Proprietatibus Rerum*, talks about the voices of birds and animals as well as of rational men.[25] In "Als I Lay," the voice is not the sole provenance of the Soul, but is rather shared equally. As an authorial decision, this one, first and foremost, permits the dialogue to

---

23. D. W. Hamlyn, trans. and notes, *Aristotle's "De Anima" Books II and III* (Oxford: Clarendon Press, 1968). Essentially the same wording is used in W. S. Hett's 1935 Loeb translation of *De Anima*, and in Richard McKeon's *Basic Works of Aristotle* (New York: Random House, 1941).

24. *Aristotle's De Anima in the Version of William of Moerbeke and the Commentary of St. Thomas Aquinas*, trans. Kenelm Foster and Silvester Humphries (London: Routledge, 1951), II, 466–69, 476–77.

25. Bartholomaeus Anglicus on the voices of animals is discussed, translated, and quoted in Cannon, *The Grounds of English Literature*, 117. Cannon consulted and translated Bartholomaeus, *De proprietatibus Rerum* (Basel: Ruppel, ca. 1468), fols 8v–9r.

happen. If the Body genuinely couldn't regain its voice, this poem would be no different from the Old English graveside lamentations of sinless or sinning souls.

Whereas the discourse of confession presumed that there is a soul to be penetrated and explored for its innermost secrets, "Als I Lay" figures the body as an *additional* vessel of secrets and assertions, one that might be compared with the psychoanalytic model of the unconscious but does not fit comfortably into Freudian parameters. The self's conscience or its will, the part of greatest concern to moral thought, could be imagined to belong anywhere, or even split in half, since it could be contained within the body *or* the soul. Neither Body nor Soul in "Als I Lay" constitutes an individual in and of itself, and the "truth" they produce, in dialogue, is profoundly undecidable. No one "wins" the disputation, although this disputation is implicated in establishing and, possibly, destabilizing a hierarchy between its two speakers.

In an article that suggests uses for Foucault's late thought on confession in an analysis of the psychoanalytic scene, Judith Butler points out that the production of the voice can belong to the body: "speaking is a bodily act. It is a vocalization; it requires the larynx, the lungs, the lips, and the mouth. Whatever is said not only passes through the body but constitutes a certain presentation of the body.... [S]peaking is a sounding forth of the body, its simple assertion, a stylized assertion of its presence."[26] Butler's reading of the physicality of speech is contrary to the Aristotelian model, but closer to the kind of speech heard in "Als I Lay": a speech that confesses the Body's actions and constitutes a postmortem action by the Body. Butler is writing about the psychoanalytic scene, which is quite different from the medieval vision discussed in this chapter but shares with it an interest in confession, self-constitution, and what it means to converse, if only with oneself. The *prosopopeia* of the speaking Body and Soul is, at its core, a sort of analysis of the "powers" that make up the self as it is understood in *sowlehele* psychology. It is also the discourse of the individual coming into being through narrative—in this case, a narrative in which power is exercised by one aspect of the self over another.

Negotiating Responsibility
GENDER AND PEDAGOGY IN THE THIRTEENTH CENTURY

The *Cambridge History of Medieval English Literature* contains an article by Rita Copeland and Marjorie Curry Woods about the intersection of "Class-

---

26. Judith Butler, *Undoing Gender* (New York: Routledge, 2004), 172. "Bodily Confessions" is the revised version of a paper given at the American Psychological Division Meetings (Division 34) in San Francisco, CA, in 1999.

room and Confession" in the thirteenth century. This article is premised on the argument that "both on historical grounds and in cultural terms, pedagogical texts and classroom practices have their natural counterparts in confessional texts and practices."[27] Copeland and Curry Woods discuss the way in which the idea of *disciplina,* defined as "the regulation of knowledge and the regulation of the self, whether through the rigors of the classroom or of penitential practice," linked pedagogical and pastoral discourses and acted in the lives of thirteenth-century persons.[28] This is clearly medieval studies done in a Foucauldian vein. "Als I Lay," too, uses the language of the classroom to enact the work of educating the penitent for confession. Although didactic works are not generally known for their subtlety, as this section will show, this allegory uses figures drawn from pedagogical *disciplina* in order to enact confessional discipline.

One way in which the discourses of classroom and confession were linked in the Middle Ages was through the education of clerics, the process of disciplining schoolboys and forming their characters. In the late 1950s, when the coeducation of boys and girls still seemed new, Walter Ong inaugurated a discussion of the ways in which medieval and Renaissance classroom discipline and the learning of Latin functioned as a "puberty rite." Drawing on then-current anthropological studies, Ong made a case for understanding the distinction drawn between Latin and vernacular as a distinction between the all-male environment of the school and the world of home, family, and mother.[29] More recently, and with a great deal more detail, Ralph Hanna discusses the formation of what he calls "a Real Man" in English schooling during the Middle Ages, a contentious situation between master and student in which the student is regularly beaten.[30] Although Hanna's reading is primarily concerned with evaluating the roles of female allegorical personifications in *Piers Plowman,* the allegory discussed in chapter 5, the tools and tropes of his analysis

---

27. Rita Copeland and Marjorie Curry Woods, "Classroom and Confession," in *The Cambridge History of Medieval English Literature,* ed. David Wallace (Cambridge, UK: Cambridge University Press, 1999), 376. The texts discussed in this article include only one disputation—the prose *Dives and Pauper*—and the article does not deal with any works that dramatize confession in a problematic way, as "Als I Lay" does. Copeland and Curry Woods cite a number of discussions that suggest priests and parishioners participated in a system of pastoral power, and "the template which could provide the pattern for their (the priests') role was often to be found in the situational context of the classroom" (400).

28. Copeland and Curry Woods, 377.

29. Walter Ong, "Latin Language Study as Renaissance Puberty Rite," *Studies in Philology* 56 (1959): 103–24.

30. Ralph Hanna III, "School and Scorn: Gender in *Piers Plowman,*" in New Medieval Literatures, Vol. III (New York: Oxford University Press, 1999), citing Whittinton, a basic book by the thirteenth-century grammarian John of Garland, EETS, OS 187. See J. N. Adams, *The Latin Sexual Vocabulary* (Baltimore: Johns Hopkins University Press, 1982), 14–15.

illuminate the depiction of pedagogical discipline and gendered hierarchy in "Als I Lay."

According to Hanna's reading of the surviving records of a grammar school at Wotton (established in 1384, much later than "Als I Lay" first appeared in a manuscript), the formation of the "real" man depends on a kind of *disciplina* that relies on the beating of boys. In other words, he describes corporal punishment as an inherent, essential part in the formation of medieval masculinity (or, at least, of clerical masculinity). Thus far, Hanna is fully in accord with Ong's analysis. In Hanna's more linguistically specific account, the struggle of wills between master and student tends to be resolved through reliance on the *virga*, a word whose polysemy Hanna notes—the whip or rod that is referred to in schoolboy exercises as "my maysters doughter." No doubt, *virga* evokes *virgo* ("virgin"), in the minds of at least ill-trained Latinists, which accounts in part for that reference. According to Hanna, "the whip is the one girl in a boy's life (and his master's accomplice)."[31] The polysemy grows even more confusing when we note that *virga* was a word current in the Middle Ages both for the whip or rod used to beat schoolboys and, like *rod*, for penis.

Discussing a woodcut popular in printed grammar texts, Hanna describes an illustration. It depicts a "transaction between master and boys. The conscientious instructor is separated from his admiring flock not just by the book, that source of expertise which he passes on, but also, surmounting all, by the corrective rod."[32] The rod is described in typically antimarriage schoolboy exercises punning on *virga/virgo* (and written by these same masters) as the one girl that boys *should* or *do* have contact with; of course, the word for rod, the thing schoolboys fear, is also a word for a significant aspect of the schoolboy's anatomy. One might even suggest that it is the possession of a penis that permits a child to become a schoolboy and become subject to the corrective rod; it is certainly what defines him as a possible candidate for "clergie"—the learning that leads to ordination.

Although the status of having been whipped as a boy is that which characterizes a Real Man, Hanna goes on to argue, the humiliation of being whipped demasculinizes the nascently masculine young boy, producing, if nothing else, some real rage against the castrating female, both whip and wife. While, for Hanna, this explains something of the misogyny of medieval texts, this story of quasi-castration by an object that bears the name of "penis" also describes a kind of split within the boy's self, between his punishable nature and an aspect of his bodily self. *Disciplina* functions, in Hanna's account, as the mechanism of a kind of splitting, a dividing of self from self, rendering ambivalent the relationship between the boy and that aspect of himself that bears the name of

31. Hanna, 221.
32. Hanna, 220.

virga—and which both qualifies him for and subjects him to specifically *clerical* discipline.

In "Als I Lay," we have observed the manner in which the means of correct training is exemplified in the Body/Soul relation, in life (especially in childhood) but also after death, in that moment of remonstration. The boy grows into a man through his encounter with disciplinary pedagogy as well as through the practices of confessional subjection and the complex process of splitting, self-beratement, and self-love that seems to be its not entirely negative consequence. The speaking woman—the *virga*, here imagined as Lady Philosophy or any other tutelary female figure—is noteworthy largely by her absence from the scene of "Als I Lay": The dialogue's world excludes female allegorical personifications. Significantly, the split self of this Middle English allegory is engaged in a particular *kind* of dialogue—not, say, a discourse of courtly romance or the kind of tutelary scene featuring an "allegorical goddess," but a discourse of a complex kind of self-love. Although it is easy to see that the term *self-love* might have something to do with what psychoanalysis has termed *narcissism* and (as countless critics have pointed out) linked explicitly with homosexuality, this medieval poem seems to be actively and literally staging this dynamic. We might not be able to understand that the self can have love for itself without recourse to twentieth-century terminology, but this poem enacts such love in its own way, and "narcissism" doesn't begin to describe it.

Insofar as Body and Soul are posited as separate from one another in order to enable *any* Body/Soul debate, their dialogue tells a story of a complicated love and partnership between two entities that are fundamentally one, who love and hate themselves by loving and hating each other. Hildebert of Lavardin staged this through a marriage metaphor; the author of the "Visio Philiberti" imagined it as the intimate relationship of mistress and servant. All of these retain the female element. Middle English allegories, such as "In a Thestri Stude" and "Als I Lay," tend to posit relationships within the self as purely male. (A significant and illuminating exception is "Sawles Warde," discussed in the next chapter.) "Als I Lay," more than its slightly earlier Middle English counterpart, posits the relationship between these male aspects of the self as love, and becomes implicated—intentionally, or only in the retrospective eye of the beholder—in a kind of queer self-love. (Indeed, it seems to ask, is not the very notion of love, not only discipline, of the self for itself fundamentally "queer"?)

It is also marked by another sort of queer hierarchy whose queerness is best understood in contrast with the poem's analogues: "Un Samedi Par Nuit"—an Anglo-Norman poem that exists in a single manuscript (Ms. Cotton Julius A. VII), and may have been a source for the Middle English one—and the very popular "Visio Philiberti." "Als I Lay" is roughly twice as long as the "Visio Philiberti," but, as we have seen, the Latin poem is the basis of many of its rhetorical moves, and the popular Latin debate may also be the basis of "Un Samedi Par Nuit." All three poems describe a graveside disputation between a Body and a Soul, in which blame is passed back and forth; all three of these poems subdivide the self in order to better understand it; and all three function as works of *sowlehele*. There are, however, differences that matter between these related poems—largely, differences in how they manage the gendering of hierarchy and the specifics of interdependence. The differences between the Middle English poem and its counterparts in other languages are symptomatic of the particular ways in which writers who chose to write in English or to translate into that tongue chose to describe the confessional subject's constituting parts.

In "Visio Philiberti" (as discussed more fully in chapter 1), the Body is the Soul's *ancilla,* deserving and demanding better training and more punishment:

Deus te creavit,	God created you
et bonam et nobilem,	good and noble,
sensuque dotavit,	and endowed you with senses,
et ad suam speciem pariter formavit,	and shaped you in his image,
et ut ancilla fierem	and as a maidservant
tibi me donavit	he gave me to you,
ergo si tu domina creata fuisti...	therefore, if you were created as the mistress...

"Visio Philiberti" (110–14)

The Latin poem also establishes a static relationship of class hierarchy, with the Body playing the role of servant, but without the romantic coding of courtly love. There is a brief moment of same-sex corruption, when the Body admits that "the flesh seduces the soul." And, seduced, the soul is rendered animal-like and follows the flesh "like a bull led to the slaughter."[33] For most of the poem, however, the hierarchy between Corpus and Anima is based in class difference, and the moment of corruption stands out specifically as a terrible, perhaps even terrifying, reversal of the proper order (as in the other, less popular Body/Soul debate, Hildebert of Lavardin's "Liber de querimonia," in which the Soul is briefly, "shockingly" stuck in what is coded as the improper role of wife to Hildebert/Body's "husband").

33. "Eorumque blanditiis caro seducit animam / quam a virtutum culmine trahit ad partem infimam, / quae statim carnem sequitur ut bos ductus ad victimam" ("Visio Philiberti," 107–9), discussed in context in chapter 1 of this study.

There is a moment of class distinction in "Als I Lay" as well, but it serves mostly to clarify that both speakers in the dialogue are clearly marked as male. It is very brief: In describing the suffering caused by the Body, the Soul says "I βolede βe and dide as mad / To be maister, and I βi cnaue" ("I suffered you and did as I was made / letting you be the master, and I your servant"; 335–36). In contrast with the mostly stable class difference between Corpus and Anima, the Middle English poem cannot seem to find *one* consistent way to organize the "obvious" hierarchical superiority of the Soul, and is left with presenting multiple options to describe the relationship of Soul and Body, options that permit ambivalence regarding relative guilt or innocence, and a narrative frame capable of affecting the poem's moral and didactic effect: teacher/student, rider/horse, brother and brother, master/servant.

In "Un Samedi Par Nuit," "L'ame" appears "estoit issue, ce me ert vis tote nue / En guise d'un enfant" ("The soul was sitting, to my view it seemed entirely nude / In the likeness of a child . . .").[34] One wonders, at first, whether this is the innocent little child within a sinning man, or whether the Body, coded as female because it is flesh, has somehow given birth to its own soul as its child. However, the dialogue reveals that, here, "un enfant" is a term for young female figure, a figure capable of being inserted into an amatory discourse.[35] She is referred to as "petite figure" ("Samedi," 7), and sternly addresses the Body in the masculine, calling it "chaitif maleurez" ("miserable wretch," "Samedi," 26). At the level of the courtly discourse of the Anglo-Norman version, the Body plays bumbling suitor to the Soul's fine lady.

As a suitor, the Body is gendered male, and subordinate to the (female) Soul insofar as both participate in a discourse of courtly love, which reverses the usual hierarchy of the sexes in favor of courtly service:

Je ere jadis ten serf,	I was once your serf,
par toi iere vermef;	To you I seemed as vermin;
je ere ton soumier,	I was your pack-horse,
T estoies ma dame,	You were my lady,
Si me carchas la soume,	Thus my carcass bore a load

---

34. "Un Samedi Par Nuit," in Thomas S. Wright, ed., *The Latin Poems Commonly Attributed to Walter Mapes* (London: Camden Society, 1841), lines 5–7.

35. This kind of language is common to medieval English as well—*A Pistil of Susan* features the word "fode" to describe both children and young women, indiscriminately, to the point that it can be difficult to tell which of the two protagonists (the poem features both a child and a young woman) is being discussed. First edited by Hermann Varnhagen in *Das altfränzosische Gedicht* Un Samedi Par Nuit *Erlanger Beitrage zür englischen Philologie*, Vol. 1 (Leipzig, 1889). The other editions are *Poésies populaires latines antérieures au douzième siècle*, ed. Edélstand Du Méril (Paris, 1843), and Theodor Georg von Karajan, ed., *Frühlingsgabe für Freunde alterer Literatur* (Vienna, 1839).

que je ne puis soufrir,	which I could suffer no more,
le quer me fist partir.	the heart of me went away.
(161–64)	

The difference between Body and Soul is a difference of social class as well as of gender, although courtly love poetry could use the figure of hard labor to express the courtly work noblemen might do for the ladies they serve. To have the Soul represented as female organizes the text of that debate in the terms of gendered hierarchy, and the Soul impersonates an allegorical goddess/harsh mistress to the Body, who is playing the *chevalier*. This is, in part, a result of the gender of the nouns for soul and body in Anglo-Norman. In languages in which nouns are gendered, *ame* and *anima* are female, and this establishes a seemingly natural hierarchy within Body/Soul poems in these languages. In Middle English, in which nouns are altogether uninflected by gender, other, less "natural" or socially defined hierarchies than those between males and females need to be established when hierarchy appears necessary. In the particular case of Body/Soul debates, the lack of noun gender helps produce a particularly interesting set of competing discourses for same-sex hierarchy.

Models of Love and Interdependence

As it turns out, figurations of same-sex interdependence are at the very heart of medieval English confessional culture. The Middle English Body's speech, in which it responds to the Soul's accusations, rejects the position of sinner silently hearing a list of its sins. In it, the Body steps, briefly, outside the bounds of the poem's narrative situation, and foregrounds the didactic genre in which the poem is written—in effect, pushing against the confessional nature of the scene. The *form* of "Als I Lay" is very obviously didactic—but here, the Body makes it clear that the relationships of the poem's protagonists, the relationships that form its *content*, are also based on a didactic association. The Body, refusing blame for the wrongs of the knight it had been, argues that the Soul was entrusted, in effect, with being the Body's teacher and it therefore should not be blamed for its actions:

Ne toc I neuere wyche craft	I never knew any craft
Ne wist I hwat was guod nor il,	Nor did I know what was good or evil,
Bote as a wretche dumb and daft,	But was like a wretch, dumb and deaf
Bote as thou taughtest ther-til	Except when you taught [me otherwise].

(189–93)

This description of the Body/Soul relationship *by* the Body marks a significant turn in the poem, a turn toward a more explicit (and yet more confused) discourse on the Body and Soul hierarchy. Had Body and Soul been "squabbling," rebutting one another's arguments as equals? That would be wrong, especially if the Soul is the Body's confessor. No, says the Body, emphatically. One is the other's master, and therefore the responsible party when guilt for a life ill-lived is being divided up.

When the Soul counters the Body's refusal to be blamed for the dead knight's sins, it does not entirely deny the image of itself as teacher but, rather, complicates it. Both Soul and Body were born of woman, says the Soul, and fostered together, and the Body carried the Soul about (as a stronger sibling might bear a weaker) since the Soul could take no actions by itself.

Abouten, bodi, thou me bar;	Around [the world], Body, you bore me;
Thou mostist nede, I was withoute	You needed to, I was without
Hand and fot, I was wel war.	Hand and foot, as I was well aware.
Bote as thou bere me aboute	Unless you carried me about,
Ne might I do the leste char;	I could not do the least of tasks;
Thorfore most I nede loute,	Therefore, I necessarily had to bow down
So doth he that non other dar.	As one who dares do nothing else.
Of a wymman born and bredde,	Of one woman born and bred,
Body, were we bothe tvo:	Body, were we both, the two of us:
Togidre fostrid fayre and fedde	Together fostered well and fed,
Til thou couthist speke and go.	Until you could speak and go.
Softe the for loue I ledde,	Gently I led you, for love's sake,
Ne dorst I neuere do the wo ...	Not daring ever to do you woe ...
(290–303)	

This extraordinary passage is, in some ways, the poem's point. Seldom is motivation discussed so specifically in the Middle English literature of the thirteenth century. This practically *is* a psychology, one of feudal domination and interdependence. The discourse of pedagogical discipline is here transformed (almost like the transformation that Foucault traces in *Discipline and Punish*, from punishment as spectacle to punishment as the carceral). In place of that which the Body asks for, a pedagogy marked by punishment, the Soul tells a story of training through love.

From its position of powerlessness, the Soul claims to have led the Body gently, not daring ever to do it woe because "to lese the so sore I dredde" (303). Based in this new insight, the Soul goes on to *re*describe the dead knight's life, which it had already described in some detail during the poem's first lines. The new story is of a Body that had been willing to obey its Soul, its confessor, when it was young—a time when it was often beaten; the Body describes itself as having been "betin and birst" (308). Once grown stronger and older and no longer subject to the beatings that a child receives as a matter of course, this Body, a foster-brother, had began to disobey the Soul, and "al thin oune wil thou dist" ("you did all [according to] your [own] will"; 312).

According to its own narrative, the Soul was ultimately doubly powerless, *both* in its impotent position of being borne in the Body's "brest" (320) *and* as a result of the tie of affection binding it to be kind to the Body. The Body seduced it, the Soul claims: "I sau þe fair on fleychs and blod, / And al mi loue on þe I kest" ("I found you fair in flesh and blood / and all my love on you I cast"; 313–14). Is it narcissistic for the Soul to find its own Body beautiful? Here, the relationship really is of a split self, but one that has, at least at some point in the past, been capable of self-love, whether this might be understood as the height of psychological health (as in the modern world) or the depths of deluded sin.

The Body, in its response, does not deny the loving relationship of the narration, but argues only that the Soul ought to have punished it *more:* Had it asserted itself, the Body would have met more of the "soul-nede" (233, discussed previously). Love and discipline characterize the psychology of this poem, which explores so many possibilities of the sinning self's relationship to itself. The word *subject*, in the sense of "subjection" (which was certainly all it meant in Middle English), seems not so strange now as a term to describe this particular representation of psychological theorizing.

To have characterized the relationship between Body and Soul as a queer one, I have shown how the poem figures a series of hierarchies between the two beings as same-sex male relations (when it is not figuring the Body as a beast to be ridden, its own sort of queerness). These homosocial bonds of love do not negate the explicitly named heterosexuality of the knight now dead. The Soul's taunting *ubi sunt* speech mentions the wife as one of the dead knight's losses (the Soul alleges that she will not mourn long), and also implies that the knight might regret the loss of other, extramarital romantic opportunities: "Ne nis no leuedi bright on ble / þat wel weren i-woned of þe to lete, / That wolde lye a night bi þe" ("There is no lady fair of face / that was accustomed to allow you to do so / that would now lie a night beside you"; 249–51). The Soul seems to think that it is the Body that engaged in carnal acts, not itself, and the Body does not argue.

The Body does not discuss ladies or wives. It does, however, offer a speech that echoes very precisely the one made by the Soul to name and ever more precisely characterize the relationship that had existed between them. At this point in the dialogue, the reader may feel that reading the poem is like being stranded in the car with a couple having a spat. The Body redescribes its relationship with the Soul in similar terms:

Were was I bi wode or weyhge	Where was I ever by wood or by way
Sat or stod or dide ought mys,	Sitting, standing or doing amiss,
Þat I ne was ay under þin eyge?	That I was not also under your eye?
Wel ough wost þat soth it ys.	You know well that this is true.
Weder I ede up or doun	Whenever I went up or down
That I ne bar þe on my bac	I bore you always on my back
Als þin as fro toun to toun	I was also yours going from town to town
Alse though me lete haue rap and rac.	Else you would let me have bangs and blows.
Þat tou ne were and red roun	Without you there to advise me
Neuere did I þing ne spac.	Never did I think nor speak.
Here þe soothe se men mouen	Here look at the truth that all men mourn
On me þat ligge here so blo and black.	On me that lies here so black and blue.
For al þe wile though were mi fere	For all the while that you were my mate
I hadde al þat me was ned . . .	I had all that ever I needed . . .
(261–72)	

The difference between the Body saying that it bore the Soul on its back wherever it went and the Soul saying that the Body had borne it about is a slight yet telling one: In the Body's speech, the Soul is rider or ruler, whereas in the Soul's, the Body rules the material world in which the Soul is too crippled to take action by itself. The Soul is the panoptical prison of the Body, according to the Body; the Body is the jail from which the Soul has always dreamed of escaping, according to the Soul. Love and aggression appear in both passages; the Body mourns the loss of "mi fere" ("my mate"; 271), while the Soul regrets that love kept it from sufficiently disciplining its brother.

An analogue to the relationship between the Body and the Soul in "Als I Lay" can be found in one of Foucault's descriptions of his view of power, in a late interview in which Foucault argues against the simplifications of critics who imputed to him a view of power as evil. In his argument, Foucault offers two examples. One is that of the sexual or love relationship, offered as an example of power exercised in a "sort of open strategic game, where things could be reversed." The other example he offers is that of "the pedagogical institution":

I don't see where evil is in the practice of someone who, in a given game of truth, knowing more than another, tells him what he must do, teaches him, transmits knowledge to him, communicates skills to him. The problem is rather to know how you are to avoid in these practices—where power cannot not play and where it is not evil in itself—the effects of domination which will make a child subject to the arbitrary and useless authority of a teacher, or put a student under the power of an abusively authoritarian professor, and so forth. I think these problems should be posed in terms of rules of law, of relational techniques of government and of ethos, of practice of self and of freedom.[36]

There are, therefore, two kinds of relationships based in power imbalances that Foucault offers as instances of "nonevil" relations in this interview—the amatory and the pedagogical. They are ultimately not so very different from one another, and they are certainly, in Foucault's conception, potentially labeled by that slippery, complicated label, "queer." These two kinds of nonevil power relationships, which might actually be one kind, are also the two kinds of relationship being portrayed when the relations between parts of the self are allegorically represented in this thirteenth-century debate poem.

The allegorical structure of "Als I Lay" imposes discipline and confession on a corpse, too late to do much good except as a negative example to others. This belatedness cannot save the Soul from the hell to which it is carried before the poem's end. This leaves the reader to ask whether the poem's didacticism might be conceptually posed as morally endangering. Might the splitting of the self into two quarreling components, and the Soul's "bad" or failed pedagogy, somehow reflect on the fact of pedagogy and its attendant *disciplina* being imperfect ways to mold selves? "In a Thestri Stude I Stod" seems to be more conscious of the always-already-present reality of sin, whereas this poem's focus on the rhetoric of the Body/Soul quarrel displaces the focus from such questions. After several centuries of poems in which Souls lament their sins in life and expect death, does this particular thirteenth-century version of the debate admit to the mode's triteness and underline it as a kind of commentary (either unwitting or deliberate) on the limits of pedagogy?

The Soul suggests that the relationship it had with the Body when they were united as a self was based on love. The Body suggests that their relationship had been pedagogic, including the physical punishments that pedagogy entailed in medieval classrooms. In both cases, the relationship is productive and formative, and not one of domination. The Body is not produced in

36. Michel Foucault, *The Final Foucault*, ed. James Bernauer and David Rasmussen (Cambridge, MA: MIT Press, 1991), 18–19.

response to "the arbitrary and useless authority" of the teaching Soul. Rather, the self is produced as a subject through the encounter between the amatory and the pedagogical, the Body and the Soul. A significant difference from Foucault's account here is that *were* the sexual forms of the love relationship a factor, in the thirteenth century they *may* have been viewed as evil (and would be subject to being confessed)—but the relationships posited in "Als I Lay" imply a kind of innocent connection in which the love is only ever of the entirely *caritas* variety. This relationship is "brotherly," "filial," rather than erotic or even parental (or if parental, it's unclear which is the parent, which the child, since the Soul did the training but the Body did the carrying about). The queer pairing of Body and Soul, useful for depicting their mutual reproaches as both love and aggression, need not be "gay"—it would be absurd to imagine the literal coupling of the self's parts—but it is loving, admiring, and aggressive in ways that tend to characterize romantic love, and here the love is between two male figures who ultimately blame their damnation on the love between them.[37]

What we encounter in tracing the relationships of hierarchy, love, and power in "Als I Lay" are as follows: (1) accusation, remonstration, and beratement for the first 200 lines of the Soul's *ubi sunt* speech; (2) *prosopopeia,* the Body's rebuttal, which describes the relation between Soul and Body in pedagogical terms and poses a retroactive demand for punishments that should have occurred but did not; (3) the Soul's response, which posits a relationship of interdependence through foster brother love—a relationship that is, in essence, kinship without consanguinity, bearing with it an entirely different kind of ethical demand, and a far more equal relationship than that between student and teacher; and (4) the Body's recapitulation of the narrative of love and

---

37. Richard Rambuss offers a comparable understanding of "queer" in "What It Feels Like for a Boy: Shakespeare's *Venus and Adonis,*" in *The Blackwell Companions to Shakespeare: The Poems, Problem Comedies, Late Plays,* ed. Jean Howard and Richard Dutton (London: Blackwell, 2003), 244. Rambuss refuses to see "homoerotic desire [in *Venus and Adonis* as . . .] exclusively, or even primarily, beholden to tropes of gender inversion or reversal, tropes that tend to reinscribe desire onto a heterosexual template (Adonis in the feminine or androgynous role and Venus in the masculine). . . . I find that Adonis can refuse Venus—just as a man may refuse, may turn away from the love of women, and that refusal be neither deviant nor necessarily tantamount to an expression of misogyny" (249). "Queer theory" is often understood as a theory that points out the fluidity inherent in the play of gender and desire; in this article, Rambuss begins to offer a different sort of reading, a new way to understand how and why some individuals are portrayed as preferring same-sex affiliation, perhaps without the misogyny that often characterizes certain strands of queer and LGBT literary analyses. See also Allen J. Frantzen in *Before the Closet: Same-Sex Love from* Beowulf *to* Angels in America (Chicago: University of Chicago Press, 1998), which makes a similar point about male same-sex affection, especially in its second chapter. Of particular note is his analysis of "probably the most intimate moment of intra-male sexual contact in Old English" (101), a discussion between Augustine and the allegorical figure of Reason, who is gendered male and treated with some physical tenderness in King Alfred's translation of St. Augustine's *Soliloquies.*

discipline between Body and Soul, which ends by detailing how lost it is without its mate.[38] By tracing the differences among these relationships and those that are posited in their counterparts, we can see the specificity of Middle English literary approaches to the psychology of hierarchy.

Disputing with Foucault

Disputation is a crucial technique for thought in the pedagogical, philosophical, and literary practices of the Middle Ages. In his *Historia Calamitatum,* Peter Abelard, one of the twelfth century's great philosophers, tells how he "preferred the weapons of dialectic to all the other teachings of philosophy, and armed with these ... chose the conflicts of disputation instead of trophies of war."[39] Abelard then proceeds to narrate a life history marked by constant engagements with and victories over elder masters of argument. Although Abelard's description primarily applies to the university-educated, Thomas Reed, Jr., writing on the institutional context of debate poetry, affirms that "by the middle of the thirteenth century, students were instructed through disputation, examined through disputation, and, upon graduation, obliged to begin their statutory two years of teaching by riding out as presiding master a forty-day flood of disputations."[40] Although the debating style of debate poems in general, and this debate between the Body and the Soul in particular, are far from being records of classroom interaction, this is nevertheless a genre produced by authors who may very well have participated in and witnessed disputation-as-war, and knew how to enjoy—and to produce—a well-made rhetorical point, whether in sermon or in treatise.

"Als I Lay" is a disputation that allegorizes the different emotional stances available to student and teacher, foster brothers, mates. In describing what it means to be subject to classroom discipline (whether sufficient or insufficient), it dramatizes the split and self-berating nature of the confessional self. It, and "In a Thestri Stude I Stod," are both didactic poems, since they threaten damnation with the aim of teaching virtuous living. But in addition to being didactic works, they are also works whose form—the *memento mori* instructions of the Soul in particular—is explicitly pedagogical, as if in the moments

---

38. John Boswell, in *The Kindness of Strangers: The Abandonment of Children in Western Europe from Late Antiquity to the Renaissance* (Chicago: University of Chicago Press 1988), writes about fostering, and mentions medieval complaints that fosterlings sometimes sided with their foster families over their blood kin in conflicts.

39. Peter Abelard, "Historia Calamitatum," in *The Letters of Abelard and Heloise,* trans. Betty Radice (New York: Penguin Books, 1974), 58.

40. Thomas Reed, Jr., *Middle English Debate Poetry and the Aesthetics of Irresolution* (Columbia and London: University of Missouri Press, 1990), 46.

of the Soul's preaching, the audience and the Body are equated, all subjected equally to the discipline of pastoral pedagogy, and therefore brought into the reversible relationship of power enacted in the dialogue.

Works of *sowlehele* are intended to urge proper confession, and to teach layfolk (and those who care for the souls of layfolk) how to organize their own understandings of themselves so that their confession might be effective, thorough, and appropriately contrite. In the thirteenth century, those who grew up to offer pastoral care would have been trained through similar pedagogical methods of discipline and punishment that this poem names as insufficiently administered but necessary. Priests and confessors had been rendered subject to a master's discipline, both internal (in learning to act as docile students) and external (in being punished when internal discipline was insufficient). Inculcating such a stance in others would have seemed an appropriate way to teach them to confess in ways that would seem effective and appropriate to such priests, who both authored poems like the one discussed in this chapter and benefited from their existence in their work on the souls of parishioners. "Als I Lay" is, therefore, a text inscribed with the marks of an author who had undergone a certain kind of pedagogy. With its didactic mode, it functions at the intersection of pedagogy and pastoral care. It describes how the self is trained into selfhood (an analogy to both the teacher/student and the foster brother relationship), specifically through a display of how the sinful self might have trained itself to be better.

The textual production of a comprehensible body by means of a disciplining/disciplined soul cannot but recall the Foucauldian postulate that "the soul is the effect and instrument of a political anatomy; the soul is the prison of the body."[41] For those who have read Foucault and those influenced by him over a period of years, this statement may not seem surprising; it takes a medievalizing gesture to remember that, originally, the body was *supposed* to be seen as

---

41. Michel Foucault, *Discipline and Punish*, 30. In writing this, Foucault is discussing the effects of power on the subjected body of the condemned. The use of the word *soul* is introduced by reference to another thinker (rather than as a term "owned" by the authorial voice of Foucault) "'a non-corporeal', a 'soul' as Mably called it," he writes (29). Foucault takes "Mably's" soul, however, and proceeds to theorize that there are two kinds of souls, distinguishing the "soul represented by Christian theology" (which promptly drops out of discussion) from the soul whose "reality" he seems willing to accept—the soul of the punished man. "It would be wrong to say that the soul is an illusion, or an ideological effect. On the contrary, it exists, it has a reality, it is produced permanently around, on, within the body by the functioning of a power that is exercised on those punished." (30) The soul, here, is exterior to the body as well as interior to it, and entirely a product of power. Here, Foucault has written as if there were only one kind of soul, "the" soul—but in the next sentence, he goes on to write: "This is the historical reality of this soul, which, unlike the soul represented by Christian theology, is not born in sin and subject to punishment, but is born rather out of methods of punishment, supervision and constraint" (30).

the one to imprison the soul. To read Body/Soul debates is to revisit and, to a degree, amplify and revise the Foucauldian approach to the problem of body and soul, knowing that these texts are anterior to the time Foucault is theorizing but wondering whether the structures he finds in the classical prison might not have been established in popular sermonizing poems such as those I consider here.

In "Als I Lay," the Soul is the prison of the Body, literalizing Foucault's gesture, but the Body is also the prison of the Soul, and who imprisons whom cannot finally be decided. Foucault's reversal of something that seems to have been a generally accepted "original" formulation—the Body as prison house of the Soul—is thus only partly accurate as a description of the disciplinary relation of these thirteenth-century poems. His discussion of discipline, however, lacks the dimension of love as the condition of Body/Soul connection that the Soul's discourse introduces, and therefore does not describe the willing subjection to a certain model of the self that the anonymous thirteenth-century poet depicts. The contradictory process of loving self-subjection described in "Als I Lay" and visible in its narrative strategies is illuminated by Foucault's formulations, but, of course, cannot be fully explained in terms of his thinking.

Judith Butler, an astute reader of Foucault as well as herself a critic concerned with the constitution of subjectivity, has written in *The Psychic Life of Power* about the split nature of the subject and its affective relationship to the power that works on and within it. In that study, she examines the paradox of Foucauldian subjection from a psychoanalytic (often, but not exclusively, Kleinian) perspective: In her description, it is characterized by dependence and ambivalence and a kind of helpless love. In her introduction, Butler notes that Foucault writes relatively little about psychic subjection, that he "does not elaborate on the specific mechanisms of how the subject is formed in submission."[42] Her book works to elaborate those mechanisms, which Butler terms *passionate attachments*.[43] Butler writes that:

> power that at first appeared external, pressed upon the subject, pressing the subject into subordination, assumes a psychic form that constitutes the subject's self-identity. The form this power takes is relentlessly marked by a figure of turning, a turning back upon oneself or even a turning on oneself.[44]

Given their didactic intent, it is easy to imagine that works of *sowlehele* were meant to be read over and over again, and so, close to the end of this chapter

42. Butler, *The Psychic Life of Power*, 2.
43. See Butler, 6–10 and beyond.
44. Butler, 3.

about "Als I Lay," let us look back at the poem's beginning. Following the framing, when the narrator has described his or her vision of the Body lying on the bier, he or she turns to the Soul, without describing it except through its behavior as it leaves the Body but cannot truly leave it: "Wan the gost it sholde go / Yt biwente and withstood, / Bihelod the bodi there it cam fro / So serfulli with dredli mod." ("When the ghost should have gone away / It went [instead] and stood nearby / Beheld the body that it came from, / Sorrowfully, with dread-filled mood"; 9–12). The turning of the self upon itself described by Butler, above, is a turn the Soul made at the very beginning of the poem. Its inability to leave might be, to a pious reader, a symptom of its disorder, its excessive love for its Body, but it is also the enabling fiction that initiates the dialogue. Someone rereading the poem—having already experienced its end, this turning in on itself by the Soul, which is both the disciplining power and the object of discipline at the poem's end—might also read the Soul as a figure for how love and interdependence structure this medieval self, in a surprising continuity with the modern subject described by Butler in her rewriting of Foucault, Hegel, Nietzsche, and Freud.

Although Foucault is often read as a theorist positing a hopelessly oppressive and repressive power, his later work emphasized how the self is constituted through language in ways that are not entirely negative—that, indeed, cannot be reduced to poles as simple and opposed as "positive" and "negative." We often forget that, even in *History of Sexuality, Volume One*, Foucault wrote *against* what he called "the repressive hypothesis" (it often seems as if we read Foucault as positing more and more repression when his late arguments' punch line always seemed to be the *productivity* of power relations) and that the discourse of confession was, particularly late in his career, as much about the history of conscious self-construction through language as about oppression by pastoral power. Foucault's late work, and Butler's reading of it, fits better with this chapter's reading of "Als I Lay" and with how this poem does the work of *sowlehele*, although the violence that characterizes the poem's end complicates any straightforward view of "positive" or "productive" power. After all, the person being produced at poem's end is, literally, dead, even as the readers, whose experience of reading is also a disciplinary production, are learning presumably valuable lessons and being "produced" as contrite subjects who imagine the mapping of their selves as bodies and souls just so. The surplus produced alongside such mappings, the queerness at the heart of the Body/Soul relation, might also be installed in these imagined medieval readers along with this contrition, whether it is welcome or not.

Body/Soul debates like "Als I Lay" and its counterparts are tremendously concerned with pedagogy as such as part of their content as well as in their didactic form, and specifically, with the limits of the interpellating power of pedagogical punishment (that of hell as well as that of beatings received by schoolboys). In other words, "Als I Lay" (in this case, differing from its counterparts because it lacks "natural" hierarchies or static noun relationships to fall back on) uses metaphors or analogies, like those of classroom interaction, to tell its didactic story. These analogies are embedded in a narrative that relies on a dialogic rather than a monologic mode to both mourn a wholeness and unity between "mates" and show that such no wholeness may ever have truly existed. Such a mode of *sowlehele* is capable of simultaneously teaching the reader *and* critiquing the scene of teaching. In doing so, the debate represents the processlike nature of *sowlehele* psychological theory as a mode that describes, produces, and disciplines selves in ways intimately implicated in gender and sexuality, even or especially when that gender is male.

"Als I Lay" very clearly intends to preach to both the Body and the reader through the Soul's words, and it ends with the terrified narrator waking up, resolving to live well, and thanking Christ for the mercy that had thus far shielded the narrator from the fate of the punished Soul. Even with this final modeling of reader response for, presumably, its "real" readers, the didactic strength of "Als I Lay" is less than that of other, not so debate-driven, Body/Soul disputations, poems in which the Soul's authority is more definitely established. The poem's narrative drive—the debate genre's demand that both speakers have a chance to make their arguments, the characteristics assigned to the personified beings Body and Soul—complicates the poem's ostensibly didactic intent, because both disputants are given a measure of truth to work with.

The encounter between Soul and Body offers a scene of disputation, accusation, and confession, representing the self as split, self-berating, and negotiating relationships of power and hierarchy between its parts, as we have seen over the course of this and the previous chapters. The self portrayed in Body/Soul debates is one that comes into being through a dialogic splitting, through dialogue rather than through soliloquy (as it had, in a way, for Augustine and would for Hamlet). The relationship between aspects of the self is founded in sharp dispute, and characterized by imperfectly administered pedagogical discipline, the kind of discipline discussed by Butler and the late Foucault, as formative and productive even as it inevitably and perhaps painfully divides the self from itself to enable its rather queer self-understandings.

Although it is true that the body is born of sin in Christian theology, the Body of Body/Soul poetry seems to be born at the moment of death, at the moment of rupture from the Soul. In the narrative of "Als I Lay," it seems as though the Body is a being of arbitrary freedoms, born from the *failures* of punishment, supervision, constraint. This being can never be whole, but cannot exist as just a creature of appetite. The failure of the Soul's punishment is theologically explicable in terms of the philosophical underpinning of Body/Soul debates as a whole, discussed in the previous chapter, but in "Als I Lay" those terms are simultaneously narratively occluded and dramatized (shown rather than told).

The Body's existence within the narrative requires the presence of the Soul, its *failed attempt* at discipline, to be able to come into being and form a self. A simply material body would not qualify as a "self," and can function as a semblance of selfhood only through dialogue with the Soul. If Body and Soul had appeared in a static image or as a metaphor, the discipline imposed on both (abandonment to hell's demons or the cold earth) would function in a simple, complete way. Because the debate has a plot, with characters and personalities, its narrative both disrupts and ornaments its didacticism. The anonymous authors of these works seem to almost take pleasure in showing that one of the narrative possibilities of the dialogue is its capacity to represent a psychology based simultaneously in medieval "common sense" and on a queer relationship of the self to itself.

CHAPTER 4

Defending the Female Self

"SAWLES WARDE" AND *SOWLEHELE*

Commonplace understandings of the relationship between sin and self in the Middle Ages often use the metaphor of the castle keep.1 The Seven Deadly Sins batter at the walls of the self like an attacking army, and the walls either hold or they do not. Implicitly, the body is not only a building of stone; it is also a vessel, delicate, breakable, housing a soul that ultimately belongs to God. The body is a fragile and penetrable barrier between the soul and the evils of the world.

Such metaphors about the relationship of the self to sin have a curious quality, distinguishing what the self is from what it is not through metaphors of place: specifically, through the distinction between what is inside and what is outside the self. This system resembles, without being identical to, the workings of Body/Soul debates—for instance, their figurations of the soul as prison of the body or of the body as imprisoning the soul. The force of the sins and vices pressing on the outside of the delicate vessel that is "man"—or, in the case of the early thirteenth-century prose allegory "Sawles Warde," the subject of this chapter, "woman"—must be counterbalanced by virtues on the inside of that vessel, pressing outward into good works.

---

1. The metaphor of self as castle/vessel can be found in a number of medieval texts that seem to have been written with the aim of spiritual direction. See the excellent and thorough study by Christina Whitehead, *Castles of the Mind: A Study in Medieval Architectural Allegory* (Cardiff: University of Wales Press, 2003), for an extensive discussion of these allegories.

It is a wonder that the vessel doesn't shatter, that the walls so often hold, that the pressures of outside and inside balance one another out day after day after day. That the balance is difficult to maintain is doubly true for women, more susceptible as medieval thinkers consider them to be to temptation, and it may be trebly true for the female hermits known as anchoresses. This category of women was the assumed audience for "Sawles Warde" ("The Guardianship of the Soul"), an allegory about the contents of the self and how the powers between them are resolved—a theme that resonates deeply with *sowlehele*. When the work of producing *sowlehele* turns to describing the female self, the language of subjectivity intersects with the highly gendered discourse of the female body and the difficult work of maintaining its purity.

The source of "Sawles Warde" was not an address to women's souls, although its English translation became one. "Sawles Warde" was adapted from a far shorter Latin homily, attributed in the Middle Ages to St. Anselm as well as, occasionally, to Hugh of St. Victor and called "De custodia interioris hominis." The source homily does not bear any marks of being intended for female readers, or of thinking about female persons, and it is not developed as an allegory, although it uses some allegorical personification.[2] In the process of becoming an English-language work, the homily was transformed into a female-centered allegorical narrative. The religious practice of the anchoress, which involved lifelong enclosure in a cell built into the wall of a church, is precisely the sort of self described by metaphors of assault from without and treasure within: It is plausible to imagine that it is her self being described as a battered but intact vessel.[3] While she is defined by the uniqueness of her chosen isolation, the anchoress's self is offered as a model to be imitated by secular women, who ought to hope to resemble her even if they cannot follow her into the solitude of pure devotion. Placed alongside the other works comprising the Katherine Group, a collection of texts possibly intended for a readership of female religious—particularly alongside the *Ancrene Wisse*, the "Guide for Anchoresses"—"Sawles Warde" is clearly positioned as part of an unusual attempt to address women, and to offer them succor in times of trouble and self-doubt. As such, it is an allegory about the process of guarding ("warde") the female soul.

When Soul and Body talked to each other in now little-known Middle English Body/Soul debates, they split the self in order to provide readers with

---

2. The Latin original is edited and published in R. W. Southern and F. S. Schmitt, eds., *Memorials of St. Anselm*, in *Auctores britannici medii aevi* (Oxford: Oxford University Press for the British Academy, 1969), 354–60.

3. Some scholars avoid the term *anchoress*, since it is a modern invention. The *Middle English Dictionary* suggests *ancre*, which can be applied to female and male anchorites alike. However, anchoress is the term conventionally used in the scholarship about these works, as its gender inflection helps to mark and to circumscribe the gender of these works' addressees.

a didactic—but also dynamically narrative-based—view of the self's components, a model I call *sowlehele*. This psychology, however, was by no means confined to such debates. Better-known allegorical works also offered *sowlehele*, often as an explicit part of their project. This chapter looks at an instance of *sowlehele* from a new angle. Instead of through allegories that eliminate the female figure from within the self, such as "In a Thestri Stude I Stod" and "Als I Lay in a Winteris Nyt," it considers an allegory whose purpose seems to be to anatomize, comprehend, and discipline women by populating the self with primarily female figures. "Sawles Warde" describes and disciplines the female self, and in so doing works out a differently gendered model of *sowlehele*, which can be developed through examining the productive tension between the model of "warding" the soul offered by the allegory's title and the use of the term *sowlehele* within the allegory (spelled, in "Sawles Warde," as *sawle heale*, highlighting the term's similarity to the allegory's title), as well as by examining the work's narrative of a self populated with female figures. This chapter argues that "Sawles Warde" is an allegory about the necessity of guarding the soul as a specifically female-oriented mode of *sowlehele*, that, as a consequence, it provides a way of understanding how gender is performed in medieval psychological thought, and that this work is an allegory for what was being conceived in the Middle Ages as the distinct nature of the female self.

The narrative of "Sawles Warde" begins by describing the self ("seolf the mon") as a household shared by a married pair, Wit and Will.[4] Within the home of the body, the wife, Will, threatens to stir up trouble by encouraging the servants to follow her caprices, while interlopers and occasional visitors from without undermine any sense in which this self might be considered hermetically sealed within its house. The home of Wit and Will, one sees immediately, is less like the anchoress's quiet cell and more like an ordinary layperson's house, with all of the associated problems of maintaining a spiritual life in the context of the bustle of daily comings and goings. To maintain some semblance of order, the home is under the guidance and guardianship of God's four daughters—in this version, Warschipe (Prudence), Gastelich Strengβe (Spiritual Fortitude), Meaβ (Temperance), and Rihtwisnesse (Justice)—lent by God as Wit's helpers. Two visitors arrive and are permitted entry into the otherwise closely guarded keep: Fearlac (Fear) arrives from hell to narrate its horrors, while Liues Luue (Love of Life) details the joys of heaven; both personifications are referred to as "he," and thus add to the allegory's population of male figures, which would otherwise be limited to Wit. Along with the two

---

4. "Sawles Warde," in *Medieval English Prose for Women: From the Katherine Group and "Ancrene Wisse,"* trans. and ed. Bella Millett and Jocelyn Wogan-Browne (Oxford: Clarendon Press, 1990), 86, line 8. Subsequent citations are given in text, and refer to the Middle English text; translations used are by Millett and Wogan-Browne, unless otherwise noted, and appear on the facing page of their edition.

visitors, the long-term guests who are God's Daughters fundamentally disrupt the balance of power in the household, and so unseat Will from her rule over the servants/senses.

This book began with a consideration of female personifications in Latin allegory and the psychological work that they do, and fail to do, in the Middle Ages. Those allegories contained female personifications, but their goal was the rehabilitation of a male narrator (Boethius' *Consolation of Philosophy*) or the salvation of a universal "Mansoul" (the title of Prudentius' *Psychomachia* being "Fight for Mansoul" in Thompson's Loeb translation). These were allegories containing women but intended to discipline the souls and bodies of a mostly male, Latin-literate audience. Two chapters have now examined the ways in which the linguistic possibilities of Middle English caused the personifications that populate *psychomachias* to be remade as male, in at least some Middle English allegorical debates. For two chapters, the marked gender category has been "male," and so has the kind of discipline (that of the schoolroom, for instance) invoked therein. This chapter turns now to an explicitly female allegorical world.

The last two decades have seen a great deal of writing about female readership and Middle English writings addressed to women.[5] This scholarship has often stressed how the rhetoric used in many such texts insists on embodiment as a necessary condition for salvation: It is through the body that the presumed-female audience of such works might sin, but if it does not sin, it is through the deprivations of that same body that this audience will be saved and sanctified. Such thinking relies on the association of women with the

---

5. For a series of useful articles in dialogue with one another about the *Ancrene Wisse*, often in relation to the Katherine Group, see Catherine Innes-Parker, "Fragmentation and Reconstruction: Images of the Female Body in *Ancrene Wisse* and the Katherine Group," *Comitatus: A Journal of Medieval and Renaissance Studies* 26 (1995): 27–52; Sarah Beckwith, "Passionate Regulation: Enclosure, Ascesis, and the Feminist Imaginary," *South Atlantic Quarterly* 93 (1994): 803–24; Jocelyn Wogan-Browne, "Chaste Bodies: Frames and Experiences," in *Framing Medieval Bodies*, ed. Sarah Kay and Miri Rubin (Manchester, UK: Manchester University Press, 1994), 24–42; and Jocelyn Price, "'Inner' and 'Outer': Conceptualizing the Body in *Ancrene Wisse* and Aelred's *De Institutione Inclusarum*," in *Medieval English Religious and Ethical Literature (Essays in Honor of G.H. Russell)*, ed. Gregory Kratzman and James Simpson (London: D. S. Brewer, 1986), 192–208. Recent full-length studies concerned in whole or in large part with the Katherine Group include Elizabeth Robertson, *Early English Devotional Prose and the Female Audience* (Knoxville: University of Tennessee Press, 1990); Anne Clark Bartlett, *Male Authors, Female Readers, and Middle English Devotional Literature* (Ithaca, NY: Cornell University Press, 1995); as well as the classic study that turned medievalists' attention to the psychological importance of the *Ancrene Wisse* as a part of the then-new argument about the "discovery of the individual in the twelfth century," Linda Georgianna's *The Solitary Self: Individuality in the* Ancrene Wisse (Cambridge, MA: Harvard University Press, 1981). Works published prior to 1996 are included in Bella Millett's *Annotated Bibliographies of Old and Middle English Literature Volume II: "Ancrene Wisse," The Katherine Group, and the Wooing Group* (London: D. S. Brewer, 1996).

body as a locus of sin, an association that incarnational theology questioned in works such as the *Psychomachia*, but did not eliminate. It is impossible to read such works as "Sawles Warde" without experiencing this association anew, yet this emphasis on the bodily can draw the attention of present-day readers away from the work's overwhelming emphasis on the soul, that precious thing contained within every single human body, even the distractingly vulnerable bodies of women. Where scholarly disagreement over writings intended to care for medieval women's souls and bodies has existed, it has centered on what it means for a rhetoric concerned with women's bodies to be used in the spiritual address to women: Does it condescend, demean, discipline? Or is it a form of affirmation for women's specific ways of interacting with the bodies they live in? What about women's *souls:* Given that "the soul" has often been figured as female, *anima,* but that the "rational soul" is necessarily male, *animus,* what can writing intended to teach women about their own souls tell us?

This chapter does not choose between the options of resistance and recuperation so often posed in regard to the works of the Katherine Group and *Ancrene Wisse* as much as examine "Sawles Warde" as a work of *sowlehele* and an allegory that performs the workings of the soul within the self. Near its conclusion, "Sawles Warde" gives instructions for its own use: "þus ah mon te þenken ofte ant ilome, ant wið þulliche þoghtes awecchen his heorte, þe i þe slep of gemeles forget hire sawle heale" (106, 33–34).⁶ In the Millet and Wogan-Browne facing-page edition of the poem, these lines are translated: "We should all meditate often on this theme, and with such meditations awaken our hearts, which in the sleep of heedlessness forget the soul's salvation." The phrase used by the anonymous author of "Sawles Warde" and translated as "the soul's salvation," however, is a variant spelling of this study's organizing principle, *sowlehele,* revealing that this allegory's didactic project is of a piece with that of other works discussed in this study, but in a differently gendered mode. Does the allegory of "Sawles Warde" fit with or offer an exception to this book's argument about *sowlehele* as a pastoral, performative mode whose didacticism is somewhat undermined by the exigencies of narrative and of gendering allegories?

A closer look at these lines in context shows that their purpose is to describe the usefulness of "Sawles Warde" to its readers. Certainly, that purpose is pastoral: These lines establish the allegory's purpose through the metaphor of awakening the heart from a dangerous sleep. The soul and the heart

---

6. R. M. Wilson also uses the spelling *sawle heale* (two words) in his edition: The Royal manuscript has the line, in his edition, on page 40, lines 387–88, in the Cotton Titus Ms. 381; the Bodley manuscript breaks off at line 365, the last two leaves of Bodley 34 being lost. Wilson annotates this line only to point out that "*hire* is the correct form, since *sawle* is feminine. C *his* shows decay of grammatical gender" (79).

are to be understood as separate from one another, with the heart identified as the subject of an action and the soul as that action's object. A closer look at these lines, however, also clearly shows that the allegory's didacticism is, even in these closing lines, inextricably intertwined with the complexities of gendered grammar and figural language, including the inadvertent or deliberate use of gender-inflected nouns (discussed in more detail later). In the sentence "βus ah mon te βenken ofte ant ilome, ant wiδ βulliche βoghtes awecchen his heorte, βe i βe slep of gemeles forget hire sawle heale" (106, 33–34), the neutral "mon" is used, and "mon's" heart is "*his* heorte"; yet with the thoughts that awaken this masculine/neutrally male heart, the man must not become too idle to care for the self, a self that is described as "hire sawle." It is unclear whether the feminine pronoun for *sawle* is a retention of the Old English feminine gender for the word, a way of indicating the plural souls of all readers (*hire* can be a feminine singular or a universal plural, so the author could be changing from "his heart" to "their souls") or a referential switch to point specifically toward the soul of the anchoress. This confusion of gendered nouns is being exploited for rhetorical effect, so that *all* persons ("mon," the universal masculine) understand that they must meditate and awaken their hearts so that they might not forget to heal their souls. What we see in the preceding passage may be neither slip nor error, and it cannot be entirely explained as an anachronistic cleaving to the Anglo-Saxon tongue. A discussion of grammar in "Sawles Warde" later in this chapter offers evidence for the possibility that it is linguistic play. "Sawles Warde" was written at a moment when noun gender was both a plaything and a tool for English writers, a possibility for creative invention rather than a rule. "Sawles Warde" is explicitly a work of *sowlehele*—it even tells us that *sowlehele* constitutes its purpose—but it is also a work whose plot, characters, and linguistic play complicate the concept's definition.

As "Sawles Warde" offers *sowlehele* to its readers, it does so with a specific twist that distinguishes it from the similar work of Body/Soul debates: Instead of avoiding figurations of the female as Middle English works tend to do, this one focuses on female figures and addresses its rhetoric to a female audience—at least overtly. Does this exception to the observed tendency in Middle English works to eliminate the female from within the self prove or disprove the existence of that tendency? Reading "Sawles Warde" as a theory of the self as female—which, in the allegory, seems to mean that it describes a self that needs defending as much as it needs healing—one might suppose that it is for women only, segregated from the universal applicability assumed in Body/Soul debates. What does it mean if guarding the explicitly female soul—as the title of the narrative would have it—is actually a method of *sowlehele*? Certainly, "Sawles Warde" shows us what *sowlehele* does that faculty psychology tends not to do—rather than offering a static self, a self in which all the functions are clearly delineated and stable, "Sawles Warde" puts the parts of the self that it describes into dialogue. Although the work may have been intended for anchoresses, as we shall see, it offers a much broader and more provocative view of medieval theories of the self than that seemingly narrow audience would imply, just as the enclosed and seemingly circumscribed life of the anchoress was supposed to open up onto a larger view of eternity.

The Anchoress as Model for the Female Self

Medieval writings for a female readership are frequently addressed to the female recluses called anchoresses, a category of women whose religious devotion made them particularly significant. The anchoress is doubly locked in: She is locked into her cell, in safe but perhaps occasionally claustrophobic enclosure, and she is locked into her female body, inherently sinful within but also assailed by temptation to sin further from without. And yet she is a vessel capable of withstanding attack from outside, so much so that her real work becomes caring for the precious treasure, the soul enclosed by the body. In her solitude, she is powerful, but she is also susceptible to error. The anchoress is in an extraordinary position, as "anchor" of the church in which she dwells, and yet her body, enclosed in its solitary cell, renders literal the metaphor of the self enclosed in its prison house of flesh and becomes a figure for any soul's vulnerability, solitude, and need to resist attacks from temptation and sin. According to this model of the self, sin is not only or always a slip or malfunction within; it is also a failure of defenses without.

The best-known, best-disseminated, and most thoroughly discussed work written for female recluses in the thirteenth century is the *Ancrene Wisse*, the "Guide for Anchoresses," a manuscript accompanied by the works of the Katherine Group, including "Sawles Warde" in one of the collections in which it appears. The *Ancrene Wisse* elaborates the spiritual and institutional circumstances of a group of enclosed women, ones evidently well-known to the clerical male author. While much of the prose treatise consists of direct instruction, describing what the anchoress ought and ought not do, the seventh chapter is an allegory in which the soul is directly figured as a lady who lives "in-with an eorthene castel . . . mid hire fan biset al abuten" ("within an earthly castle," or "within a castle made of earthly materials," who is "beset all around by her enemies"), until she is saved by a "mihti king" who finally dies in the battle against her foes.[7] At this, the narrator puts the question to us, "Nere theos ilke leafdi of

7. *Ancrene Wisse*, ed. Robert Hasenfratz (Kalamazoo, MI: Medieval Institute Publications,

uveles cunnes cunde, yef ha over alle thing ne luvede him her-efter?" ("Would not this lady be of a foul kind of nature, if she did not love him henceforth over everything else?').[8] Because of the thematic and physical relationship between the two manuscripts, the scholarship on the *Ancrene Wisse* sometimes is applicable to "Sawles Warde" as well; "Sawles Warde," however, considers the idea of female selfhood more directly, and thus is more illuminating to my project as an example of specifically female *sowlehele*.

"Sawles Warde" appears in three manuscripts, always grouped with a series of other works also written in West Midlands speech known as the AB dialect, the dialect of the *Ancrene Wisse*, which appears with it in Cotton Titus D 18. In addition to this one appearance with the *Ancrene Wisse*, "Sawles Warde" also shares stylistic features with the longer work that sometimes cause critics to think they had the same author.[9] This group of works associated with the *Ancrene Wisse* is known collectively as the Katherine Group and includes three lives of virgin martyrs (Katherine, Margaret, and Juliana), as well as a prose discussion of why virginity is preferable to marriage, called "Hali Maiβhad" ("A Letter on Virginity" or "Holy Virginity"), and "Sawles Warde." It has been argued that "Sawles Warde" is "the climactic and key work of the group" and that this work "is in some ways a precursor to the morality play in its dramatization of a struggle between Wit and Will and the parallel *psychomachia* between virtues and vices."[10] In its three manuscript appearances, "Sawles Warde" is placed once at the very beginning (Royal 17 A) and once at the very end (Bodley 34) of this grouping, and once at the beginning of the Katherine Group but after a copy of *Ancrene Wisse* (Titus D.18). Critics have speculated that these placements mean that the text played the role of a sort of morality decoder ring in relation to the mysteries of the Group as a whole. In agreeing with this assessment, I understand "Sawles Warde" as a work that tells its readers what they ought to see when they look within, specifying an inner world whose dimensions and inhabitants seem, to the work's author, to be suitable for female readers.

The early thirteenth century, with its efflorescence of writings intended to aid the understanding of the self by laypeople and the clergy who ministered to them, saw a great deal of new writing for and about women. Rather surprisingly, at about the same time as Middle English allegories turned aside

---

2000), pt. 7; 379–80.

8. *Ancrene Wisse*, 380.

9. The manuscripts of the Katherine Group are Ms. Bodley 34, in which "Sawles Warde" appears as ff 72r–80v; Ms. Royal 17. A. 27, in which "Sawles Warde" is ff 1r–10v; and Ms. Cotton Titus D. 18, with "Sawles Warde" on ff. 105v–112v.

10. Diane Mockridge, "The Order of the Texts in the Bodley 34 Manuscript: The Function of Repetition and Recall in a Manuscript Addressed to Nuns," *Essays in Medieval Studies* 3 (1986): 207–18.

from the Latin conventions of depicting all abstract concepts as female figures, more women began to read in Middle English. Even the metaphors of the self as castle or vessel discussed earlier help demonstrate a different way of thinking about women in this period: as beings in need of spiritual counsel and as objects of psychological inquiry, rather than (no matter how subversively) as means to an end for the male narrator seeking self-understanding. This may sound like a move toward treating the female as fully human, rather than as either superhuman, like Lady Philosophy, or somewhat subhuman, as when women are equated with the sinning flesh. However, even as female readers came to be addressed and taken seriously by devotional writings, they were subject to a new, more precise and more stringent discipline. Discipline becomes a means to the end of female self-making, balancing what we might understand as empowerment.

The Fourth Lateran Council's call to confession affected women in particular ways even as it brought about a certain literacy in the language of sin, confession, and penance for all laypersons, regardless of sex or gender. Although the dates for "Sawles Warde" and the Katherine Group as a whole cannot be established beyond a shadow of a doubt, E. J. Dobson's article "The Date and Composition of *Ancrene Wisse*" dates that text to at least "after the Lateran decrees had become known in England, even possibly after the Council of Oxford of 1222."[11] Jacqueline Murray has pointed out that the authors of the "Omnis utriusque sexus" decree saw fit to explicitly state that women as well as men needed to confess, and notes that "women appear to have developed early on a particular affinity for confession and the special relationship which could develop between a woman and her confessor has been attested to in the lives of many medieval saints and holy women," while arguing that confessors were sometimes less than sympathetic to women's concerns.[12] A work like "Sawles Warde," offering a model of the self as an ordinary household, populated by many female figures, would be a useful tool for women thinking about how to understand and organize their own confessional narratives of their impulses and actions.

It is possible that "Sawles Warde" should be read as an address from a confessor to a woman or group of women written for precisely such an end. Such

---

11. E. J. Dobson, "The Date and Composition of *Ancrene Wisse*," British Academy Gollancz Lecture, May 25, 1966. *Proceedings of the British Academy* 52 (1966): 181–208, 206. See also T. P. Dolan, "The Date of *Ancrene Wisse*: A Corroborative Note," *Notes and Queries* NS 21 (1974): 322–23.

12. Jacqueline Murray, "The Absent Penitent: The Cure of Women's Souls and Confessors' Manuals in Thirteenth-Century England," in *Women, the Book, and the Godly*, ed. Leslie Smith and Jane H. M. Taylor (Cambridge, UK: D. S. Brewer, 1995), 13–25, 15. See also Jacqueline Murray, "Gendered Souls," in *Handling Sin: Confession in the Middle Ages*, ed. Peter Biller and A. J. Minnis (York, UK: York Medieval Press, 1998), 79–92.

a reading would account for the way the allegory is framed, as the interpretation of a biblical parable, and it might also account for the first-person plural used repeatedly throughout the work: "Ure Lauerd i þe Godspel leareð us ant teacheð þurh a forbisne hu we ahen wearliche to bitwiten us seoluen wið þe unwiht of helle" ("Our Lord in the Gospel gives us instruction and teaching through a parable on how we should carefully guard ourselves against the Devil of hell and his wiles"; 86, 1–2). The allegory addresses a collective or at least a pair—a knowledgeable "I" who speaks, joined in fellowship by some other who listens.

That use of the first-person plural is repeated throughout the allegory, often pointing out things that the implied audience ought to know about their own selves. For instance, the clamor of the senses within us is described as something we have no direct access to with our own sense of hearing, but that our author knows about and participates in: "þah we hit ne here nawt, we mahen felen hare nurð ant hare untohe bere" ("although we do not hear it, we can feel their din and unruly disturbance"; 86, 21–22). The narrator of "Sawles Warde" includes himself (or potentially herself) in the meditative task at hand, while patiently pointing out something that he thinks his female reader might have missed. If the narrator is assumed to be male, a reasonable assumption given the learned confessor/penitent relationship being figured here, an obvious but unanswerable question is posed: Does "Sawles Warde" describe the workings of a female self *only,* or might it also describe the imagined arrangements of the inner world of the narrator/author? Is "Sawles Warde" generalizable as a description of the human, not just female, self?

A Map of the (Female) Self

It seems clear by now that the variable gender of the body and the soul played an important role in how medieval authors constructed psychological systems. Murray has noted that confessional writings in the Middle Ages aided in the development of "a gendered soul; a soul that while perhaps not explicitly sexed female nevertheless carried with it the implications of being gendered female because it was housed in a female body."[13] Like all the works discussed in this book, "Sawles Warde" aims to name the aspects of the self and set them up in a hierarchical relationship to one another; it does not only ask after the nature of the self; it also describes its moral and physiological impulses, creating taxonomies for and relationships between them. Because "Sawles Warde" is not a dyadic allegory of Body against Soul, or even of Lady Philosophy instructing

---

13. Murray, "Gendered Souls," 80.

Boethius, it sets up a series of complicated, multiple relationships, and this section looks in turn at a number of these, examining the now-familiar concepts of soul and body and will as they are described in "Sawles Warde."

The allegory begins by quoting a parable (Matthew 24:43; Luke 12:39): "If the head of the household knew at what time a thief would come, he would keep watch and not allow his house to be broken into" (87, 1).[14] The object being defended ("warde," here in its sense as guard) in the allegory's title is the soul; the body, if present at all, is present as an inanimate architectural structure that houses Wit, Will, and the Daughters of God. "Sawles Warde" begins by interpreting the biblical parable it started with: "βis hus βe ure Lauerd Spekeβ of is seolf βe mon" ("The house which our Lord is talking about is man himself"; 86, 1). This phrase is as close as "Sawles Warde" comes to mentioning the role of the body in constituting the self: It is the frame within which all the events occur. The choice of phrase used in the allegory's interpretation of the biblical parable, "seolf the mon," is surprising, given the female orientation of the work that will follow: "Sawles Warde" repeatedly uses "mon" ("man") as its universal, and this use returns a number of times, complicating from the outset the argument that this work is specific to women's selves. This phrase also makes a point of distinguishing "selfhood" from "soul," since, as will be shown later, though the soul is contained within the house of the "seolf," it is not identical to it in any way.

Curiously, "Sawles Warde" is an allegory in which both the Soul and Body of the debates discussed in previous chapters are silent, having been rendered inanimate. The flesh, as the negative aspect of the body, does appear in the allegory: It is "flesches licunge" ("physical pleasure"; 96, 7, again on 13), a phrase used to designate the kinds of weapons that the Devil might use to penetrate the house of the self. Later, virgins are praised as particularly blessed because they are capable of overcoming the flesh: "the, libbinde I flesche, ouergath flesches lahe and ouecometh cunde" ("those who, living in the flesh, transcend its law and overcome nature"; 102, 10). Being thus blessed, these virgins are in heaven, and among their pleasures is a miraculous new cooperativeness of the body: "for hwer se eauer βe gast wule, βe bodi is ananriht wiδute lettunge" ("for wherever the spirit may wish to go, the body is at once without any delay"; 104, 27–28). Soul and Body, or rather "gast" and "bodi," are not engaged in a debate here: They are, respectively, the innermost and the outermost layers among the onionlike series of concentric circles that constitutes this allegory, and as such, they are the objects rather than the speaking subjects under discussion.

---

14. In Latin, "Si sciret paterfamilias qua hora fur uenturus esset, vigilaret uique et non sineret perfodi domum suam."

The division of labor within the household (the large middle area between the inanimate body that serves as a penetrable barrier to the outside world and the soul-as-treasure being guarded at the household's center) is explained, briefly and succinctly, at the allegory's beginning:

> Inwith, þe monnes wit i þis hus is þe huse-lauerd, ant te fulitohe wif mei beon Wil ihaten, þat ga þet hus efter hire, ha diht hit al to wundre, bute Wit ase laured chasti hire þe betere ant bineome hire ofte muchel of þet ha walde.

> Inside, man's reason is master in his house, and Will can be described as the unruly wife, who, if the household follows her lead, reduces it to chaos, unless Reason as master disciplines her better, and often deprives her of much she would like. (86, 8–12)

Since what is within the house includes Wit and Will and (as it turns out in the next few lines) a household made up of the senses, it seems that the house is the body, the container for all this activity. The soul, it would seem, is split into many functions, which might be understood as psychological faculties, and the gendering of these faculties establishes both appropriate hierarchy (Wit above Will) and the necessity of discipline, or, as the Middle English word *chasti* implies, chastisement.

The initial phrase, "man's reason is master in his house," is identical to the Latin source: "pater iste familias animus rationalis potest intellegi." The Middle English "Wit" is a translation of *animus* (soul, masculine), a noun that functions in medieval philosophy as the term for the rational part of the *anima* (soul, feminine). In translating and transforming that source, "Sawles Warde" is inconsistent with another work in the Katherine Group, "Hali Maiþhad," in which "Wit" is referred to as "Godes dohter" as part of a discourse about the preferability of virginity: "ure licomes lust is tes foendes foster; vre wit is Godes dohter, and ba beoth us inwith" ("our physical desire is the Devil's offspring; our reason is God's daughter; and both are within us").[15] Wit needs to be male in "Sawles Warde," despite this characterization, in part because "Sawles Warde" is a translation, and in part because this allegory employs a marital hierarchy whereas "Hali Maiþhad" uses a genealogical one. It is, however, the Middle English author's idea to follow this by characterizing the Will as the "fulitohe wif" who reduces the household to "wundre" (86, 9–10). The Will is not named as a character, much less as a female character, in the Latin original being adapted; there, the household of the self, while headed by

---

15. "Hali Maiþhad," in *Medieval English Prose for Women*, 14, lines 4–5.

"animus rationalis," is an undifferentiated grouping of faculties, "cuius multa familia sunt cogitations et motus sui, sensus quoque et actions tam exteriores quam interiors" ("whose large family includes thoughts and emotions, sensations and actions, [which are] exterior as well as interior [in nature])."[16] The inclusion of this married pair does not respond to the necessities of faithful translation, but rather to the conceptual obligation to counterpoise a (negative) characterization of marriage to the anchoritic chastity that, elsewhere in the Katherine Group, has so clearly been established as the desired and superior form of life.

The Latin original posits the interior and exterior forces as an undifferentiated "familia," but "Sawles Warde" imagines a household with servants and masters, reminiscent of (but more multifarious and complex than) the *domina/ancilla* model of the self from "Visio Philiberti." The servants' senses are torn between obeying master or mistress, but the tendency is for those on the outside (the senses) to be described as "under Wit as under house-laured" ("under Wit as the Lord of the house"; 86, 17), whereas the inner servants seem to lean toward obeying the mistress, Will, since they are described as always in the process of trying to please her. It is unclear what aspects of the self these inner servants are, since they are never given names, only the quality of unruliness described here. Somehow managing to think on their own, however, the inner servants "thonc to cwemen wel the husewif agein Godes wille" ("think to please the housewife against God's will"; 86, 20). This line brings up an additional confusion: Will, the wife, is a character in need of chastisement, but "wille" also exists as a quality pertaining to God: "Godes wille" sets itself up as the antithesis of the "fulitohe Wil." At the poem's end, when Will has been thoroughly cowed, the concluding passage sets up her will against her husband's: We ought to act wisely, "nawt efter βat his Wil, βe untohe lefdi, ant his lust leareδ, ah efter βat Wit wule, βe wise husebonde" ("not in accordance with the instructions of Will, the unruly lady, and our desire, but according to what is required by Reason"; 108, 3–5). The translation, in this case, is somewhat deceptive: We are instructed to follow "efter βat Wit wule," or the Wit's will, a complexly contradictory concept.[17] It seems to be impossible to render "will" as entirely negative, much as the allegory establishes the necessity for its chastisement and control; this, too, may be a function of grammar and of grammatical play, in its capacity to serve and undermine didactic narratives in

16. Southern and Schmitt, eds., *Memorials of St. Anselm*, 355.
17. In "Hali Maiβhad," "will" is also used as a figure for sexuality, as part of a warning to women about the demands of the marriage bond: "heo schal his wil muchel hire unwil drehen ... nomeliche i bedde he schal, wulle ha, nulle ha, βlien ham alle" ("she must often submit to his will much against her own will ... especially in bed she must put up with all his indecencies, whether she wants to or not"). "Hali Maiβhad," 28, lines 10, 14–15.

unexpected ways. "Will" is just too necessary a word in the English language, it serves too many functions, to be completely possessed by the willful housewife.

The presence of Will as a character in the allegory stands out against the prolonged conceptual silence about the will in debates between the Body and the Soul, a silence we might understand anew through the word's contradictory uses in "Sawles Warde." Since will is a faculty just as frequently gendered feminine as is the concept of embodiment, it is unsurprising that the psychological allegory about and for women would be the one that contains Will the wife. The association of women with willfulness in "Sawles Warde" parallels and perhaps replaces the common connection of women with the bodily. It is quite clear that medieval women are understood as more thoroughly embodied than medieval men, and that what is meant by "embodied" somehow encompasses the troublesomeness of sexual desire, that which allegories featuring same-sex pairings of forces seem to be trying to circumvent (only to end up with homosocial affection as its replacement). Ruth Mazo Karras's study of John of Bromyard's *Summa Predicantium* and Jacqueline Murray's more general examination of confessors' manuals point out that women appear in such manuals mostly—almost exclusively—in relationship to sexual sins.[18] Perhaps because of the presence of Will the wife as the most feminine of female personifications in the allegory, the abstract body, bodiliness as such, seems strangely irrelevant. The role previously granted the Body of Body/Soul debates has been shifted over to Will and gendered feminine, but just as "the body" could not, for fear of falling into heretical dualism, be portrayed as pure evil, a free "will" is just too important, as an English word and as a philosophical concept, to pertain solely to a female part of the self. In this allegory's explicit consideration of its place, however, "will" and its necessary counterpart "wit" are both located outside (even if beside) the soul.

The Wit/Will pairing functions as a composite of what, in other allegories, might be considered the soul; their conflict is being described as that which guides human action. They are the married pair at the head of the household, ruling the senses and playing host to the Daughters of God. But neither Wit nor Will nor their servants actually constitute the soul as such, and it is not they who need "warde," the defending of the allegory's title. Contained inside the house, a core around which the rest of the narrative revolves, the soul lies silent and inanimate, the English allegory's still center; there is no parallel discussion of the soul in the Latin source.[19] It is an object to be purchased as

---

18. Ruth Mazo Karras, "Gendered Sin and Misogyny in John of Bromyard's *Summa Predicantium*," *Traditio* 47 (1992): 233–58; Murray, "Gendered Souls."

19. Julie Hassel has also pointed out that this is a difference between the Latin and the English texts: in the Latin, "what it is that the household is protecting is never named." Julie Hassel,

well as a treasure to be guarded: "þe tresor þet Godd Zef himseolf fore, þet is, monnnes sawle" ("the treasure for which God gave himself—that is, man's soul"; 86, 87, 26). In the very next line, the value of the treasure is correlated with the price paid for it: The thieves are trying to get access to the treasure "that Godd bohte mid his deað and lette life o rode" ("which God bought with his death and for which he gave up his life on the cross"; 86, 28–29). The soul has a price, and that price has been paid; it is an object whose value is known, but its essence is otherwise outside the discussion at hand.

The soul is an object of exchange and an object to be defended, but it does not have a speaking part. Instead, it works as a kind of surplus or excess. The body of "Sawles Warde" turns out to be an inanimate container, simplifying greatly all the complexities of the speaking body of Body/Soul debate, and, as it turns out, the soul, too, becomes a silent and inanimate quality. For it to be guarded as a treasure by them, it must not be composed of Wit, Will, the senses, or even the qualities of Strength, Justice, and so on, who inhabit the house of the "seolf." It is radically other, deprived of a knowable personality, mysterious and strange, and its precise nature is left undetermined. The language of guarding the soul-as-treasure sounds a great deal like the language of defending a woman's virginity, as when, in the *Ancrene Wisse*, virginity is compared to a balsam carried in a fragile vessel.[20] Rather than speaking, fighting, loving, and regretting, as the souls discussed throughout this study, the soul of "Sawles Warde" is a passive thing to be defended, as unknowable as balsam.

Englishing and Gendered Language

The Latin work that served as the source for "Sawles Warde," "De Custodia Interioris Hominis," was not necessarily written with the confessional subject in mind, but its Middle English revision evidences a strong rhetorical reorientation of the text in the direction of explaining the female self to itself. The differences between the Latin "original" and its reworking run fairly deep. To recapitulate: In the "De Custodia," although the narrative also centers on a household led by Animus Rationalis, there is no wife, much less a wife named Will, to contend with. The Daughters of God are not named as allegorical figures in the Latin; they are merely listed as presences within the self, without the genealogical detail. The soul is not named as an object to be defended, and ought not be, since *animus rationalis* is the term for Wit: The protected object

---

Choosing Not to Marry: Women and Autonomy in the Katherine Group (New York: Routledge, 2002), 88.

20. For a useful analysis of the language of chastity in the *Ancrene Wisse*, see Wogan-Browne, "Chaste Bodies."

of "De Custodia" is the entirety of the house of the self, which might be the reason why the household section is far briefer in Latin. The English author interjected the responses of the listeners into the accounts of both Fear and Love of Life, deepening the characterizations given to the Daughters of God (since each responds very much in character), and there is also an expanded section praising the joys of virgins in heaven, which seems intended to solicit the attention and joyful sympathy of its intended audience of female religious, and a consequent diminution of discussions about the similar joy of virtuous monks from the Latin original.

Many of the differences between "source" and "reworking" can be explained by the fact that the assumed audience of "Sawles Warde" was religious women and the intended audience of the Pseudo-Anselmian homily can be presumed to be clerical and male. The presence of a female character named Will clearly references common misogynist stereotypes about willful wives. Including the badly behaved female will as a character within the narrative invites a kind of negative identification, a dark mirror for women to see into and perhaps recognize or maybe mis-recognize themselves: Either way, description, formation, and, more than that, interpellation are taking place. "Sawles Warde," as an adaptation of "De Custodia Interioris Hominis," does this: It genders the rhetoric of the text, a text that had previously been vaguely universal, gender-neutral. What difference does Englishing the Latin homily make? Was the Latin homily also a work of *sowlehele*? It had the homiletic drive to first anatomize and then offer moral meanings to the self's parts, but it lacks the developed narrative and the even more developed allegorical qualities of the Middle English adaptation.

The strength of the Middle English revision's rewriting is particularly evident with an eye to Dan Michel of Northgate's detailed exposition on the sins, the *Ayenbite of Inwit*, which also contains, at the end, a translation of "De Custodia Interioris Hominis." Dan Michel did not seem aware of the existence of "Sawles Warde" when he was translating the Latin work into his Kentish dialect, but his taxonomy of sin is explicitly intended for a somewhat similar purpose: "uor enlisse men, that hi wyte hou hi ssole ham-zelue ssriue, and maki ham kelne" ("for English men, that they may shrive and make clean their own souls").[21] Any consideration of the post–Lateran IV project of producing

---

21. Dan Michel, *Ayenbite of Inwyt or Remorse of Conscience*, ed. Richard Morris and Pamela Gradon (Oxford: Oxford University Press, EETS, Original Series No. 23, 1866; reissued 1965), 5. Wilson's edition of "Sawles Warde" includes parallel texts of all three manuscripts where the allegory is found (Bodley 34, Royal 17 A 27, and Cotton Titus D.18) as well as the *Ayenbite of Inwit*'s translation of "De Custodia" and the "De Custodia" itself, attributed by Wilson to Hugh of St. Victor. See R. M. Wilson, *"Sawles Warde" and "The Conflict of Wit and Will"* (Leeds, UK: Leeds School of English Language Texts and Monographs), No. 111, 1938–39.

works to instruct layfolk in the care of their own souls would list the *Ayenbite of Inwit* as an example, although it lacks the narrative interest (and popularity) of, for instance, the far more popular *Pricke of Conscience*. However, neither "De Custodia" nor the *Ayenbite*'s version of the story goes about its project of *sowlehele* in as dynamic and interesting a manner as does "Sawles Warde," and neither work deviates from the male-as-universal thinking that has already been discussed in previous chapters of this study. "De Custodia Interioris Hominis" is a homily that happens to be open to transformation into "Sawles Warde," an immanent theory of the female self. It is also open to faithful translation by Dan Michel and, in that translation, becoming vernacular, remaining pastoral and didactic, but not becoming a narrative capable of having its didacticism complicated by its own story and characters. Dan Michel's translation, though clearly intended for ministering to the soul, is not a work of *sowlehele* in the specific ways the term is being used within the present study.

However intimate its ties with its Latin source, "Sawles Warde" marks an interesting point where the cultural moment that produces *sowlehele* intersects with another development that affects English literature and the culture of Britain: the disappearance of arbitrary noun gender from English. In that respect, translating the Pseudo-Anselmian homily into English permitted the translator to take liberties with the flexible tools of a language in transition and to create a genuinely new work (liberties that the *Ayenbite of Inwit* simply did not choose to take with the same source).

Although the English Body/Soul debates, apparently also written in the West Midlands, seem to use the elimination of arbitrary noun gender as a way of rewriting the conventional relationship of soul and body in the language of brotherhood or pedagogy, turning them into dramas about male beings, "Sawles Warde" is very clearly a drama about the relationship between female beings. This is not exclusively a choice played out at the level of allegorical narrative: "Sawles Warde" also bears traces of noun gender, as if some aspect of gendering inanimate or conceptual beings as female or male is retained despite the changes wrought in the language between the linguistic periods that we understand by the terms *Old* and *Middle* English. Interestingly, the author of "Sawles Warde" skews noun gender considerably in the direction of the feminine. There are many reasons why this choice might not have been a choice at all, but rather a set of mistakes or carelessness about language by the author of "Sawles Warde." The retention of certain aspects of arbitrary noun gender may also serve the purposes of this author in his or her rewriting of Pseudo-Anselm's homily into an allegorical story.

Words that have no particular gender connotation in modern English appear in "Sawles Warde" as feminine-gendered nouns. For instance, the house that the thief might break into—despite the fact that "hus" (house) is actually neuter in Old English—is referred to as "hire" [her] house. The language of "breaking into" a woman is, obviously, far from neutral, and indeed evokes a particular kind of violence that can threaten the holy woman as vessel: rape. Wilson, the editor of "Sawles Warde," notes that this "error" appears in all of the manuscripts, and points out that this "hire" might be a reference to "sawle," a feminine noun in Anglo-Saxon, exiting the allegory in order to refer to the "real" thing that the allegory describes.[22] Death is also referred to as "she," as in "cume Deað hwen ha wule, ne βurue we nowðer beon ofdred for hire ne for helle, for ure deað bið deore Godd, ant ingong into heouene" ("let Death come when she will; we need not be afraid either or her or of hell, for our death will be precious to God, and our entrance into heaven"; 94, 19–20).[23] According to R. M. Wilson, although "death" in Old English is masculine, it occasionally appears as feminine in the Katherine Group, possibly because *mors* in Latin and *mort* in French are feminine. The grammatical rules of Latin and Romance languages accounted for how abstractions such as death were gendered in allegories written in those languages, but there is no clear reason to return to the Old English noun gender here, except as a reinforcement of the allegory's rhetoric of being directed to a female audience and creating a female-centered world to do so effectively.

The influence of Latin noun gender on English writing is very clear, and other critics have noted that English authors have struggled with whether to retain conventional allegorical female gender for personified abstractions. Since abstract nouns are feminine in Latin, this has been all the explanation most theories give for the prevalence of powerful female allegorical figures in medieval writing. Both *Ratio* and *Voluntas* are feminine nouns in Latin, which the Pseudo-Anselmian dialogue avoids only by placing an Animus (masculine) that is only modified by "rationalis," *ratio* in its adjectival form compelled to agree with its noun, as the central inhabitant and *pater familias* of his allegory. The author of "Sawles Warde" inserted the plot about the willful wife rather than translating it from the source, so there the allegory is not drawing on its source's use of Latin gender. In Old English, both *wif* and *will* are neuter nouns, which means that our English author had to make a real choice to ren-

---

22. In "Hali Maiβhad," the word *flesch* (neuter in Old English) is *also* referred to as "she."
23. "OE [Old English] 'death' is masc. But it occurs occasionally in our group as feminine. It is to be noted that both L. *mors* and Fr. *mort* are feminine and where the genders of nouns are discernible and yet different from those of OE, they seem to follow Latin or French. This change of gender in our group is hardly due directly to the influence of the Latin original—the above sentence does not occur in the Latin of St. Victor—since it is found also in AW [*Ancrene Wisse*], which is usually allowed to have been composed originally in English. Such confusion of gender, if due to the influence of Latin or French, is more probably a reflection of the general influence of a knowledge of these languages" (Wilson, "*Sawles Warde*," 62, note on line 157).

der them as women, remaking what was neuter in Old English into gendered personification.

The idea of woman as passive doesn't work if Will is a woman, or even if Philosophy is (as I have argued elsewhere). These different choices about English grammatical gender create sexual difference in the Latin homily, where there had been none. If "woman" is not fully passive, there is a contradiction immediately within the walls of the house of the self. Although there is no tradition that follows "Sawles Warde" in coding Will as feminine per se, after "Sawles Warde" it becomes implicated in gender (masculine as well as feminine) in a new way: Will becomes part of the process of *making* gender as such.[24] Though I would insist that this move is significant, I must emphasize that it is not necessarily progressive. "Sawles Warde" is, after all, about how best to keep the willful wife from misbehaving and how best to keep the feminine aspect of the self appropriately imprisoned. This is the contradiction at the heart of "Sawles Warde" as a work of *sowlehele* for and/or about women: It is simultaneously repressive and subversive. At its most basic level, it retains and brings forward the powerful female figures that had characterized Latin allegorical writings, making them useful to a different psychological project from that of Prudentius or Boethius, updating allegory for a new age of self-knowledge—an age of *sowlehele,* for men and, in "Sawles Warde," for women.

"Sawles Warde" and *Sowlehele*

The arrangement of the self as described in "Sawles Warde" draws a great deal from faculty psychology. Both wit and will are faculties in most of the available schemas, and the division of the senses, who function as servants in the allegory, also resembles the workings of faculty psychology. The allegory, however, translated faculty psychology into a psychology for women. As we have seen, the allegory's author/translator/adapter takes up the conventions of Latin and Anglo-Saxon grammar and selects among them for his or her own purposes. At the level of narrative, the allegory does something similar: It uses the understood conventions of Boethian allegory, those powerful female personifications who instruct the hapless narrator, and combines them with the later medieval reimagining of the *psychomachia,* or *sowlehele,* by naming aspects of the self and showing them locked together in an ambivalent mixture of antagonism and love. "Sawles Warde" stages an encounter between Wit and

---

24. See "The Conflict of Wit and Will," also edited by R. M. Wilson, in the same Leeds School of English edition as "Sawles Warde."

Will as a married pair with the theological allegory of the Four Daughters of God, and involves the whole group in a dynamic narrative concerned with futurity and the temporality of sin and confession.

The presence of the Daughters of God within the household of the self transforms the relationships within it. These personified figures, a return to the "allegorical goddesses" discussed in chapter 1, are a fairly common medieval trope, apparently derived from Psalm 85 (Psalm 84 in the Vulgate Bible).[25] They are usually referred to collectively as the Four Daughters of God, which appear in Robert Grosseteste's Anglo-Norman allegory the *Chateau d'Amour,* in late-fourteenth-century *Piers Plowman,* and in the fifteenth-century play *The Castle of Perseverance.* The group normally designated as "God's Daughters" are Mercy, Truth, Justice, and Peace, although, in "Sawles Warde," they are, instead, the cardinal virtues: Prudence, Fortitude, Temperance, and Justice, this last being the only virtue repeated in both quartets.[26] To render them as "daughters" highlights their alignment with religious women as well as their unmarried state.

The Four Daughters of "Sawles Warde" are a harsher, tougher bunch than the original sisters of the Vulgate Bible's Psalm 84: Peace might not have been

---

25. Hope Emily Traver, who wrote the most extensive studies to date about the Four Daughters of God trope, credits this interpretation of the psalm as allegory to a fifth-century Hebrew Midrash, in which a parable is linked with this psalm. In the parable, when God wants to create Adam but asks the counsel of his angels, Love and Justice (here, apparently angels rather than abstractions) speak *for* the creation of Man, and Truth and Peace speak against. See Hope Emily Traver, "The Four Daughters of God: A Mirror of Changing Doctrine," in *PMLA* 40: 1 (1925): 48. See also Traver's monograph, *The Four Daughters of God,* Bryn Mawr Monographs 6 (1907). This is obviously rather outdated research, but it has not yet been superseded by any more recent study focusing on the doctrinal genealogy of the Daughters trope. Mary Immaculate Creek argued that the trope is, instead, derived from a sermon on the Annunciation by St. Bernard, in "The Four Daughters of God in the *Gesta Romanorum* and the Court of Sapience," *PMLA* 57: 4 (1942): 951–65. The sermon in question is edited as "*In annuntiatione Dominica Sermo Primus,*" in *S. Bernardi: Opera,* ed. J. Leclercq and M. Rochais (Rome: Editiones Cistercienses, 1968), V. 13–39. This trope makes several important appearances in medieval literature generally, and in Middle English literature specifically, including the Latin prose *Rex et Famulus,* which may have influenced Grosseteste's Anglo-Norman allegory *Chateau d'Amour.* Both circulated in England, and at least the latter was translated into Middle English several times. In addition, there is the anonymous *De Salvatione Hominis Dialogus* and the *Vie de Tobie* of Guillaume Le Clerc. The Daughters of God trope is genuinely ubiquitous and cross-generic. But it is more than a single continuous trope or motif. In the course of its theological and literary history, it undergoes a significant shift: from being an origin-tale about how God decided to create man to a debate about the nature of the law (Old to New).

26. In the NRSV (which is, of course, postmedieval): "Steadfast love and faithfulness will meet; righteousness and peace will kiss each other," translating, from the Vulgate, "Misericordia et veritas obviaverunt sibi; justitia et pax osculatae sunt." The part where Mercy and Truth are met, in Latin "obviaverunt sibi," has frequently been interpreted as something other than a neutral meeting, but rather as strife, followed by the reconciliation of the kiss between Righteousness (Justice) and Peace.

able to put up much of a fight against thieves trying to steal the soul under her guard, but Fortitude (Gastelich Strengβe), the virtue that takes her place in "Sawles Warde," has no trouble doing so, particularly since, with the adjectival specification that her "strength" is of a "gastliche" nature, she represents an almost physical toughness pertaining to the spirit. "Gast" signifies a kind of embodied power of soul last seen, in its inverse, when the Souls of "In a Thestri Stude I Stod" and "Als I Lay in a Winteris Nyt" were being described as physically suffering at the hands of demons from hell. In "Sawles Warde," the strength of the "gast" lies in its ability to defend the "soul." The conceptual split implied here produces the soul as an inanimate object (a treasure to be guarded) shut away and inaccessible, to some degree, even to the soul's owner, who must defend it without actually interacting with it as one interacts with a personification. "Gastelich Strengβe," on the other hand, is a quality on loan from God; Wit thanks God with "glead heorte of se riche lane as beoð βeos sustren, his fowr dehtren, βat he haueð ileanet him on helpe for te wite wel ant werien his castel" ("with very glad heart for such a rich loan as these sisters are, the four daughters of God, whom he has lent him as a help to guard and defend his castle well"; 98, 6). The silent soul to be guarded in "Sawles Warde" had been bought by Christ's death; "Gastelich Strengβe" was lent, so while both seem to be exchangeable objects, the latter is less firmly in the possession of the human self ("seolf the mon") and perhaps thereby more capable of functioning as a personification, of speaking and taking action.

The sort of female experience being taken up in the rhetorical force of the revisions made to "Sawles Warde" in turning it from a Latin homily into an English allegory calls on the anchoress to choose sides between two discursive constructions of femininity.[27] This is not a new argument: Anne Eggebroten has argued quite persuasively that the central conflict of the text is actually between the wife, Will, and the virgins, the Daughters of God, a conflict between marriage and virginity that is rendered *very* clearly in other works within the Katherine Group. Instead of the Latin version's emphasis on a single *pater familias* ruling over unruly senses, the English version's addition of a married woman, Will, offers the anchoress-as-presumed-reader a negative example (marriage and willfulness), which even a male or married female

---

27. See "Sawles Warde: A Retelling of *De Anima* for a Female Audience," *Mediavalia* 10 (1984): 27–47. Eggrebroten connects "Sawles Warde" directly to the literary tradition of Prudentius' *Psychomachia* and argues that a major difference between the Latin "De Custodia Interioris Hominis" (which she identifies as by Hugh of St. Victor and titled *De Anima*, an attribution that has since been strongly disputed) and "Sawles Warde" is the rich characterization given to the Four Daughters of God, connecting this with the parable of the wise and foolish virgins in Matthew 25: 1–13. Eggebroten's main point is that "the real struggle [of the allegory] is between 'fulitohe wil' (the poorly disciplined will) and the four holy virtues" (Eggebroten, "A Retelling of *De Anima*," 36).

reader would recognize as "bad" in the context given—even a married woman would, presumably, have an anxious time comparing her own behavior in her household with that of Will the unruly wife. The reader is invited to dis-identify from the married woman and choose something other than the push-and-pull of the heterosexual marriage bond between Wit and Will.

This, then, is the topography of the self that "Sawles Warde" offers us, and the anchoress, as a guide to the soul's navigation and its eventual conquest by faith—a theme that appears again and again in the writings of the Katherine Group and in *Ancrene Wisse*, particularly in the allegory of its Book Seven. For all its complexity, the description of all these different powers balancing against one another in joint guardianship over the soul initially seems quite static. Like the maps of different faculties in Aristotle and his commentators, they seem to simply label the various forces that, together, make up the self. But in the course of "Sawles Warde," the allegorical household experiences events that both interrupt and influence the routine of its inhabitants (I discuss the temporal disruption occasioned by these visits later). These events do not ever quite make the work a debate, as the poems discussed in previous chapters, but they do keep it from becoming only and always an enumeration of the self's contents.

The allegory's main action describes visitors who come into the house of the self: Fearlac (Fear) describes in gory detail the suffering of hell; Liues Luue (Love of Life) describes the joys of heaven. As Fearlac begins his speech, he tells the story of Death's coming (while Fearlac is clearly a male messenger, Death is "she" in this allegory): She brings with her "βusent deoflent, ant euchan bereð a gret boc al of sunnen iwriten wið swearte smeale leattres" ("a thousand devils, and each one carries a great book written all over with sins in small black letters"; 90, 10–11). The "gret boc" of this description may resemble the very book that the reader finds before her, or remind her of other books she has read that enumerate the sins and their remedies.

The devils might be said to carry books of soul injury, along with a chain to bind and drag those whose sins, listed in that book, show that they should be taken to hell:

> hwuch se he mei preouin βurh his boc, βat is on euch sunne enbreuet, βat he wið wil oðer wið word oðer wið werc wrahte in all his lifsiðe, bute βat he haueð ibet earβon wið soð schrift and wið deadbote.

> whoever he is able to convict with his book, which contains a record of every sin which that man committed in thought, word, or deed throughout his life, unless he has atoned for it before that time with true confession and penance. (90, 12–14)

These are the kinds of injunctions the Fourth Lateran Council endorses, and this allegory most obviously strives to be the kind of work that reminds its readers to atone, confess, and do penance: *sowlehele,* as always, under threat of eternal punishment.

When, having been frightened by Fearlac's speech, the Four Daughters of God talk about steps they will take to defend the household that is man's self, each speaks in character: Warschipe (Prudence) fearfully prays to God and hopes to do well but fears the devil. Gastelich Strengβe does not fear the devil, but fears temptation, which is not her forte. Meaβ (Temperance) says that they ought to fear both the "hard" force of the devil and the "soft" force of temptation and find a middle way between them. Rihtwisnesse (Justice) sums up her sisters' conclusions and fears and adds remarks of her own. Her job is to pass judgment, and therefore she judges that:

> Nu isriht, βenne, βet we demen us seolf eauer unmihtie to werien ant to witen us oðer ei god to halden wiðoute Godes helpe. βe rihtwise Godd wule βat we demen us seolf eðeliche ant lahe, ne beo we neauer swucche, for βenne demð he us much wurð, ant gode, ant half for his dehtren.
>
> Now it is right, therefore, that we should always judge ourselves helpless to defend and protect ourselves or maintain any virtue without God's help. God, who is righteous, wishes that we should judge ourselves to be worthless and low, even if we are not, for then he judges us to be of great merit, and virtuous, and regards us as his daughters. (96, 30–34)

As the one personification present in traditional allegories of the Four Daughters of God as well as in "Sawles Warde," Justice is particularly significant to this kind of allegory. This study's first chapter discussed Angus Fletcher's and Gordon Teskey's writings on allegory concerning the problems with an allegorical figure of Justice and considered how such a figure might be incapable of taking the contingency and humanity of actions into account and opt for an intolerable rule by absolutes. Here, Justice has said that it is right for "us" to misjudge ourselves, to be unjust, ordering that "we" should judge ourselves incorrectly. She has said that "ne beo we neauer swucche" ("even if we are not") weak, God wants us to misjudge our own powers, and, if we do so, we will earn the right to be God's Daughters, like Prudence and Justice and the rest. This is an aspect of *sowlehele* not encountered in the other works discussed in this study, a demand for humility (even at the cost of untruth) that seems to be directed toward reminding women to be particularly humble. The reason we ought to do so is that a "rihtwise Godd" ("righteous God"; the word is similar to the Middle English name borne by Justice, Rihtwisnesse) wills it thus. Given how negatively the female will has been viewed from the very beginning of this allegory, how strange that what God wills is this mild form of injustice, the pretense of weakness in his own daughters, even though the Daughters of God are clearly shown as quite able to protect the house of man's self. Is the allegorical character, here, undermining her own named nature, or pointing to a deeper (but more arbitrary) conception of justice? (Is it only women who are being told to underestimate themselves, and are we still reaping the effects of such a mindset?) This might be an instance of that very phenomenon discussed in chapter 1, an allegorical personification taking the freedom to be other than what she is: Justice advocating an injustice—although, of course, this injustice is the recommendation to be humble instead of proud.

At its ending, the authoritative voice returns to sum up what ought to have been learned and informs us that "βus ah mon te βenken ofte ant ilome, ant wiδ βulliche βoghtes awecchen his heorte, βe i βe slep of gemeles forget hire sawle heale" ("We should all meditate often on this theme, and with such meditations awaken our hearts, which in the sleep of heedlessness forget the soul's salvation"; 106, 33–34). The use of "sawle heale" (here, because of the vagaries of Middle English spelling, two words spelled somewhat differently) may indicate that *sowlehele* is the goal of "Sawles Warde."[28] However, that general, universal goal is complicated by the allegory's address to women, and "warde" replaces "heale" as the dominant term.

The word *warde* in the allegory's title has a range of meanings: According to the *Middle English Dictionary* (MED), it can mean the relatively neutral "safekeeping" or the more affect-laden "anxious regard, concern, dread" and even "custody, confinement, house arrest, imprisonment." It can mean guardianship in the sense that a child or a woman might be considered "wards," even in modern parlance, and while the MED does not clearly state which of these meanings might apply to "Sawles Warde," the allegory is used as a supporting example for *warde* in the sense of "the action of guarding . . . also, a period of keeping watch."[29] The *warde* in "Sawles Warde" characterizes the self

28. According to Wilson, the title "Sawles Warde" "occurs only in the B[odley 34] Ms. In R[oyal] and C[otton Titus], no title is given and the scribe has started with the text of the homily." Wilson, xxxii.

29. The full MED set of definitions for *warde* in slightly abbreviated form: "1a.(a) Keeping, care, custodial possession; safekeeping, (b) control, rule; stewardship, supervision [occas. difficult to distinguish from (a) and vice versa]; . . . (c) anxious regard, concern; dread, fear; (d) in prep. phrases used adjectivally: [. . .] orderly, well-behaved; . . . hard to maintain or control; not of [. . .] of knights in battle: in disorder or disarray [. . .] 1b.(a) The action of guarding, keeping watch; watchfulness, vigilance; also, a period of keeping watch or guarding, a watch; also in fig. Context [. . .] (b) custody, confinement; house arrest; imprisonment [occas. difficult to distinguish from sense 3.(d)] [. . .] 1c.(a) Formal guardianship of a child, minor, or other such person; also, responsibility for raising and training a young person, tutelage; in ~;(b) control, or the right of control, of the property, with its revenues, of a deceased tenant, often implying

it describes in a paranoid manner, as always awaiting attack, and as a series of layers to be peeled back or penetrated in order to reach the treasure of the soul at its center; the point of the watch-keeping period it describes is that it does not, ought not, end during the lifetime of the allegory's addressee. Somewhere in the tension between "warde" and "heale" lies the specificity of this allegory: Women's souls are more apt to need protection from invasion by sin, making use of a chastity model, rather than subjected to discipline, as in the teacher/student model that dominated allegories about the soul from Boethius through Hildebert of Lavardin and "Als I Lay in a Winteris Nyt."

Allegorical Temporality

"Sawles Warde" brings together the famously static aspects of allegory, its capacity to serve as a kind of anatomical or genealogical chart—here is the will, represented through its marriage with wit—with a more dynamic narrative. In this work, the care for the self is figured through an allegory about kinship and gender dominance; a struggle for power enters into the time of the self. This may be why the work contains odd temporal markers, moments when the eternal present of the self's inner landscape (a static model) gives way to narrative, to event. Ruth Evans, among others, has noted the odd temporal quality of virginity as a category in the Middle Ages. In addition to offering at least a "fantasy of escape from the human condition," she writes, "the strange temporality of virginity shakes the foundations of linear chronology, calling into question the properties of 'before' and 'after.'"[30] The allegory of "Sawles Warde," with its presumed address to virgins, literal or figurative, has a complex relationship with time, in ways both similar to and different from the kind of time depicted in Body/Soul debates discussed in previous chapters.

Following the description of the Daughters of God in "Sawles Warde," something very odd happens to the story. This is approximately fifty lines into the text, and the set-up (house, wife and husband, and servants, Daughters of God) seems essentially stable. The content of the self has been described, and

---

guardianship of the minor heir; also, the revenues derived from the heir's holdings during such guardianship; ?also, control of properties and revenues by knight service; ~ and mariage; ~ mariage, the right to exact a levy upon the marriage of a minor or other dependent, or the revenue thus derived; (c) a child, minor, or other person under the tutelage or formal guardianship of another; a person under the care or control of another; ?also, the subject or vassal of a ruler. 2. A behest, command; a charge, responsibility. 3.(a) A guarded or fortified area, stronghold; a guarded or secured section of a castle; a guard post; also, a fortified encampment; a siege fortification; also in fig. context 4.(a) A body of guards, an armed guard."

30. Ruth Evans, "Virginities," *The Cambridge Companion to Medieval Women's Writing*, ed. Carolyn Dinshaw and David Wallace (Cambridge, UK: Cambridge University Press, 2003), 27.

although it seems clear that Wit and Will are engaged in a continual power struggle, rather than narrating any particular moment of struggle, the allegory has depicted the way in which the presence of the Daughters of God frighten the members of the household into obedience. Just as it seems that the contents of the self have been adequately described, the allegory turns: "As þis is ido þus, ant is al stille þrinne..." ("When this has been completed and all is quiet inside..."; 88, 25).[31] Suddenly, the temporal signature of the allegory shifts away from the eternal present as Time itself seems to enter the scene, in the guise of two messengers warning of the self's future. It quickly becomes clear that the allegory's first fifty lines (expanded from approximately twenty-five in the Latin original) had been a task waiting to be completed in order for the future to enter the allegorical scene. This is the moment when Fearlac (Fear), who has been to hell, arrives to narrate for the household just what happens there to badly guarded souls.

Here, in a tiny throwaway moment, is something really crucial about what works of *sowlehele* can do, with their narrative dynamism and their consequent implication in cause-and-effect temporalities. Rather than offering a completely static self, a self in which all the functions are clearly delineated and stable, "Sawles Warde" begins with a description of what the parts of the self might be, engages those parts in a dialogue with their own future, and then puts them into dialogue with each other. This allegorical shift through time in turn proves capable of influencing the distribution of powers within that initially static self. No matter that this future, described by Fearlac in the lines that follow, could potentially be one of hellish torment (or, as the next messenger, Love of Life, tells the ladies when he appears, it could be a heavenly reward for all the travails of virginity). What is most important is that this self contains its own dynamism. "As this is all done," the text tells us, as if the self has just been adequately arranged and put away for the night through the allegorical description that we have been reading for fifty lines, "and all is still inside," and then Fear enters in, and with Fear enters Time. The verb tenses shift: It is suddenly noticeable that the allegory had, to this point, been written in the present tense, because Fearlac's and Liues Luue's tales of visits to hell and heaven (which are related to the possible futures of the self being depicted in "Sawles Warde") are narrated in the past, but depict the self's possible futures.

There is some argument among the Daughters of God as to whether both visitors can be present within the self. In the aftermath of Fearlac's speech, Will is already utterly cowed ("þe willesfule huswife halt hire al stille," or "the will-

---

31. In Latin, "His ita dispositis...aliquos debet Prudentia introducere nuntios." R. W. Southern and F. S. Schmitt, eds., *Memorials of St. Anselm in* Auctores britannici medii aevi (London: Oxford University Press for the British Academy, 1969), 356.

full housewife remains quite silent"; 98, 9), so the goal of frightening the self into proper behavior is already accomplished. Rihtwisnesse (Justice) argues that it is not right for the house to hold both, since Love of Life should, literally, cast out Fear when he arrives. This view of what comes into the self, fear and joy, is about futurity, since both of the messengers bear tales of what will happen after death.

In an article about the Katherine Group as a whole, Sarah Salih has made the apt observation that "gender in these legends is a continuous process, not a fixed state."[32] What does it mean to talk about gender as a continuous process, and virginity as a disjunctive temporality (one that takes place within or apart from the process of gender)? To use time as a way of understanding gender and the highly gendered concept of virginity in this way is to examine these categories through the theory of performativity. The last decade's developments in the theory of sex and gender have understood it as something that takes place in time because it is intimately involved in temporality as iteration. It can be argued that previous theories of gender, such as the classic feminist distinction between sex and gender that posited sex as biological and fixed whereas gender is contingent and potentially fluid, posited gender, at least, as a category implicated in historical time. To now see both sex and gender as markers of temporality is also to see the temporal work of "Sawles Warde" for what it is: a work of *sowlehele* that uses the specific situation of the female self to explore the tensions between cyclical and eschatological time.

The historical working of gender in "Sawles Warde" has been evident throughout this chapter: The allegory, deeply implicated in the views of gender and spirituality common to its moment, counterpoises the time of virginity (the Daughters of God) with the performance of married conflict within a context that seems, at least initially, to give a static map of the self's workings. Elizabeth Robertson writes that the changes made from the Latin text, the Pseudo-Anselmian homily, to the English version called "Sawles Warde" transform it from "an abstract, hypothetical consideration of the emotions the anchoress must control [into a] pointed example of an emotional process she must repeat daily."[33] "Sawles Warde" has a narrative, not just a description of the self's powers in relation to one another, and its narrative transforms the time of the self from a static situation—that of the anchoress in control of her soul—into an iterative practice, that of the anchoress trying to maintain control. The iterability of this control (which, of course, highlights the many ways in which what must be repeated is also vulnerable to the "broken telephone

---

32. Sarah Salih, "Performing Virginity: Sex and Violence in the Katherine Group," in *Constructions of Widowhood and Virginity in the Middle Ages*, ed. Cindy L. Carlson and Angela Jane Weisl (New York: Palgrave Macmillan, 1999), 111.
33. Robertson, *Early English Devotional Prose*, 128.

effect"—to slippage and error over time) is reflected in the complex temporality of the work. That complex temporality, in turn, codes the specific value of virginity, the ways in which it disrupts regular time.

The movement from a static time of the self to narrative time, and, with it, past and future, over the course of "Sawles Warde" enacts a conception of how the self relates to itself that works to produce *sowlehele* in its audience, among other things by instituting a practice of recursive mediation that returns again and again to the same point but also moves forward in time. It is possible that this conception of meditative time is particularly relevant to the self of an anchoress, whose time, as described in the *Ancrene Wisse,* is supposed to be essentially cyclical, a daily repetition of a set series of devotional tasks. However, it is not only the anchoress who might be accustomed to living essentially in the kind of eternal present created by the cyclical repetition of tasks: Agrarian time functions in a similar fashion, if with variations over the course of the seasons. The cycle, for all, is punctuated by religious holidays, often ones that mark the major events in the life of Jesus Christ, and by exhortations to remember the looming danger of hell and the promise of heavenly reward. "Sawles Warde" captures this rhythm in a way that a strictly philosophical work could not have done.

Self-Defense and Self-Knowledge in the Middle English Tradition of *Sowlehele*

What "Sawles Warde" offers this book's argument is a sort of counterexample: a thirteenth-century English work that most emphatically does *not* exclude women from the inner world. Middle English Body/Soul debates clearly gender both participants as male, and "Sawles Warde," and its *psychomachia*-like figuration of the flux of powers within the self, comes closest to including female participants in an explicitly didactic psychological allegory. Unlike most other works discussed in this study, "Sawles Warde" does not eliminate the feminine or the marital from its arsenal of available metaphors; but also unlike those other works, "Sawles Warde" has the disciplining and educating of female persons as an explicit goal. From early Christianity onward, women were included in the universal category of mankind insofar as they could be considered rational beings. "Sawles Warde" works through that description of women by imagining what would happen if "woman" were to contain Rationality as a personification within her very being. Gender makes a distinctive difference to pastoral care as depicted in "Sawles Warde"; when a psychological allegory does use female-marked beings to figure the relationship of the self to itself, certain kinds of figures, languages, and perhaps temporalities of the psyche emerge into view, complicating the picture of queer male solidarity depicted in previous chapters.

"Sawles Warde" is an allegory in which the self is literally haunted by numerous female figures, but in ways that are significantly different from how earlier Latin allegories, such as Prudentius' *Psychomachia,* depicted such haunting. A central characteristic of the allegory is its depiction of a self that seems to be radically, dangerously permeable—with the implication that, when not invaded, that self has the potential to be a whole, enclosed and protected by the body. Even though the dreaded entry of sins is possible, the defended edifice described in psychological metaphors of enclosure and assault (whether romance metaphors of the lady's castle assailed by the lover or any number of similar religious figures) has a beginning and an ending, a sort of edge for sins to bump up against that is palpable even—perhaps especially—when it is imperiled. Elaborate metaphors like this one tell us about medieval psychologies and the nature of the self they describe by narrating the defensive measures required to protect it. The next chapter looks at *Piers Plowman,* a far better-known work that also contains an allegory of the Four Daughters of God, but in a minor way. The complex theory of the self in that allegory also hinges on allegorical gender in important ways, but, unlike "Sawles Warde," *Piers Plowman*'s Will is gendered male.

CHAPTER 5

Promising the Female, Delivering the Male

TRANSFORMATIONS OF GENDER IN *PIERS PLOWMAN*

A distrust of established pieties is endemic to *Piers Plowman*. Never certain of its own conclusions, repeatedly overturning achieved insights, this work unmakes the very possibility of certainty, even as its protagonist, Will, stubbornly interrogates nearly everyone in his path in search of answers. While Will searches for truths about life on earth, the poem's allegorical frame seems to be on a quest of its own, seeking after a better way to work with the conventions of personification. *Piers Plowman* is largely organized through a series of disputations, encounters between speakers linked through vertical or horizontal relations of power and interdependence, and in this it borrows from the tradition of *psychomachia,* even in the name of its protagonist.[1] It is a far longer work and much more ambitious than

---

1. *Piers Plowman* is in many ways a poem that exceeds any kind of categorization, but examining it as a personification allegory with a narrative organized through a series of debates clarifies some persistent quandaries that the poem poses without ignoring its conceptual difficulty. My concern in this chapter is not whether *Piers* is a debate; it is what happens to personification allegory and to the debate form when Langland tinkers with it. Thinking about debate as one of the genres of *Piers Plowman,* the critic is implicated in almost a century of discussions about the genre of the poem. See the work of T. P. Dunning, *Piers Plowman: An Interpretation of the A-Text* (London: Longman's, 1937), esp. 169–70, and Morton Bloomfield, *Piers Plowman as a Fourteenth-Century Apocalypse* (New Brunswick, NJ: Rutgers University Press, 1962), 10, 21. This chapter's concern with the episodic and generic self-overcoming that characterizes the narrative progress of the poem shares much with an essay by Steven Justice that considers the genres of the "Visio" (the first

the Body/Soul debates discussed in previous chapters. It was also written as much as a century later than they were. However, in its outsized ambitions, *Piers Plowman* takes up and resolves every one of the topics discussed in previous chapters, from the role of allegorical female advisers to the queer relationships within the self. A version of *Piers Plowman* is included in the Vernon manuscript, the one whose scribe labeled it "a book of sowlehele." This chapter examines the poem's work on the self as this entire book has examined it—in terms of gender, desire, the difficulties of establishing stable hierarchies—but although reading *Piers Plowman* helps us understand *sowlehele* psychology, the poem cannot ever be read as any one thing.

Piers Plowman begins by using many female allegorical personifications as interlocutors linked by relations of power with the main character (who himself seems to oscillate unpredictably between being an allegorical figure of "the Will" and being a man named William).[2] But, gradually, the ranks of

---

seven *passus* of B). In it, Justice posits a journey from estates satire to *consolatio* to debate, and then onward to something that resembles confession manuals and a sort of informal typological writing. See "The Genres of *Piers Plowman*," *Viator* 19 (1988): 291–306. For a more precise discussion of the poem as engaged in a project of self-overcoming, see Anne Middleton's "Narration and the Invention of Experience: Episodic Form in *Piers Plowman*," in *The Wisdom of Poetry: Essays in Early English Literature in Honor of Morton W. Bloomfield*, ed. Larry Benson and Siegfried Wenzel (Kalamazoo, MI: Medieval Institute Publications, 1982), 91–122. See also Elizabeth D. Kirk, *The Dream Thought of* Piers Plowman (New Haven, CT: Yale University Press, 1972), 41–42, on the dispute between Conscience and Meed as a formal debate, and Stephen Barney's "Allegorical Visions," in *A Companion to* Piers Plowman, ed. John A. Alford (Berkeley: University of California Press, 1988), 117–33. In a book that treats all of *Piers Plowman* B, James Simpson has a section on "academic debate" in the third vision, examining the way in which these *passus* "deconstruct" academic debate, seeing Will's combative encounter with Scripture as "an inspired act of reading, which underlines the necessity of understanding truth in the self." See James Simpson, Piers Plowman: *An Introduction to the B-Text* (London: Longman, 1990), 136; for the whole discussion, see 132–36.

2. The formal interrogation of how Will functions as both a personification of "the will" and (or, at times, instead of) as a narrator *named* Will seems to have its origins in D. W. Robertson and Bernard F. Huppé's book, Piers Plowman *and Scriptural Tradition* (Princeton, NJ: Princeton University Press, 1951). See also John Bowers, *The Crisis of Will in* Piers Plowman (Washington, DC: The Catholic University of America Press, 1986), especially the chapter titled "Complexities of the Will," which understands the nature of the narrator in terms of the history of the concept of the will in medieval philosophy. For more recent treatments of Will as "will," and the question of Will as subject, see David Lawton, "The Subject of *Piers Plowman*" (*The Yearbook of Langland Studies* 1 [1987]: 1–30); and two essays by Anne Middleton: "William Langland's *Kynde Name*: Authorial Signature and Social Identity in Late Fourteenth-Century England," in *Literary Practice and Social Change in Britain, 1380–1530*, ed. Lee Patterson (Berkeley: University of California Press, 1993), and "Acts of Vagrancy: The C Version 'Autobiography' and the Statute of 1388," in *Written Work: Langland, Labor and Authorship*, ed. Steven Justice and Kathryn Kerby-Fulton (Philadelphia: University of Pennsylvania Press, 1997). See also James Simpson, "The Power of Impropriety: Authorial Naming in *Piers Plowman*," in *William Langland's* Piers Plowman: *A Book of Essays*, ed. Kathleen Hewett-Smith (London and New York: Routledge, 2001), and "Desire and the Scriptural Text: Will as Reader in *Piers Plowman*,"

female characters dwindle, making way for a mostly male cast of personifications. The poem's move to eliminate female interlocutors in favor of male ones raises a larger question, which the poem poses both implicitly and explicitly throughout. This is the question of whether women, as such, might be necessary to men, and *Piers Plowman* leaves open the surprising possibility that women might not, despite their crucial role in propagating the human species, be necessary after all. Ultimately, the poem seems to demonstrate that loving relationships between men are the path to a bearable sort of interdependence. This conclusion opens up many possibilities for interpretation, including that of a queer reading of *Piers Plowman*.

In turning to *Piers Plowman,* I examine a work considered "canonical" in medieval literary studies, unlike the works discussed in previous chapters. However, the difference between *Piers* and the Body/Soul debates of chapters 2 and 3 is not really so great. Each of these works puts different aspects of the self in dialogue with one another, although, more like "Sawles Warde" than "In a Thestri Stude I Stod," *Piers Plowman* is *explicitly* concerned with the specific position of the will in the landscape of the self. Many times longer than any vernacular work discussed in this study, *Piers Plowman* takes up a great many more themes and characters, but the specific stakes of its psychological allegory might actually be comparable to those of "Als I Lay in a Winteris Nyt" or the "Visio Philiberti": Over the broad scope of the entire work, *Piers Plowman* asks the question of the "interlocutor," of what it means to need another being in order to understand something or get somewhere, at both formal and narrative levels. In other words, the allegory can be read as a series of formal experiments in types of allegorical disputation, between aspects of the self as well as between personifications of social and psychological concepts—taking the kinds of questions Body/Soul debates ask in new directions and giving them new scope and scale.

Significantly, for the purposes of this study, the interlocutor being sought in *Piers Plowman* does not seem to be a heterosexual romantic partner or, at least at first, a single partner at all. The author we call Langland is not particularly invested in the conventions of courtly love, and Will's perfect interlocutor is neither a lovely nor a loathly lady, although Lady Meed initially appears to be both. Like the popular debates that shy away from positing Soul and Body as a married couple, and unlike "Sawles Warde," with its married pair of Wit and Will, marriage is *not* a central metaphor in *Piers Plowman*—but, by reason of this allegory's far larger scope, over the course of the narrative there is time to posit marriage as a possible metaphor, and then to reject it. Although

---

in *Criticism and Dissent in the Middle Ages*, ed. Rita Copeland (Cambridge, UK: Cambridge University Press, 1996).

Piers Plowman has sometimes been considered fundamentally uninterested in women because of this marked absence of a love narrative, this is not the case. Gender matters in the poem because it indexes an issue ultimately even closer to the poem's heart: One of the persistent philosophical, social, and economic concerns of *Piers Plowman* is the necessity of dependence on another being.

In both the B and C versions of *Piers Plowman*, the narrator spends several of the early *passus* of the poem seeking knowledge through listening to single speaking figures, such as Holy Church. Then, for several *passus*, we are within the mixed allegorical/"real" world of the field of folk, where Hunger and Truth make their appearances, along with some "real" women voicing worldly complaint. Later, Will debates with a number of allegorical characters, both male and female, many of whom are shown in married pairs. In such cases, one personification represents a particular "power" and the other the object on which the power works; for instance, "Clergy" is the personification of the group whose work is the understanding of Scripture. Scripture, however, represented as a shrewish wife, is among the last of the full-fledged female personifications. As the poem moves into its last third, very few female personifications remain for the narrator to interact with or witness. This is, in part, because the action moves to a clerical high-table scene, the feast of Patience, where women are excluded, and then on to Faith and Hope, who (although typically depicted as the female sisters of Charity) appear here as Old Testament patriarchs. By this point, the logic of the poem has gradually eliminated the need for female persons to serve as Will's interlocutors, creating instead a same-sex economy of recognition.

The major exception to the dwindling numbers of female personifications in the later *passus* of *Piers Plowman* is the appearance of the Four Daughters of God, conventional tutelary figures with a long tradition in medieval writing. Although these are tutelary figures, they do not actually interact with Will. Their gender is also something less than stable. In the aftermath of the Harrowing of Hell and their own reconciliation, Peace sings, Justice speaks, and Truth puts a few remarks in, but Mercy, the first of the Four Daughters, does *not* speak. Instead of her, we hear from Love, a male personification that had previously been referred to as Peace's *lemman* (lover). This replacement of the female by the male could be an oversight, of course (although it occurs in both the B and the C versions of the poem). But it may also be an example, in miniature, of the procedure for eliminating female tutelary figures that characterizes the poem as a whole.

The poem asks its questions about interdependence in a variety of ways. What does it mean to live with the possibility of procreation and the many ethical demands of the "active" (as opposed to the celibate, "contemplative") life? What does it mean to depend on women to continue the human race?

In asking such questions, *Piers Plowman* takes up a psychological insight that was crucial in this study's analysis of the two thirteenth-century Body/Soul debates: that the self as imagined in *sowlehele* psychology is fundamentally split and dialogic, open to its own otherness rather than closed as a windowless monad. *Piers* posits human interdependence as a condition that recurs at every level: between self and God, self and community, self and romantic partner, and, in a profound and surprising way, a relationship of interdependence between different aspects of the self, working with and against one another—a *psychomachia* without, quite, the necessity of battle. The poem's gradual transformation away from female personifications traces the differences between male same-sex and heterosexual love in its persistent search for a less onerous form of interdependence. The transformations of gender in *Piers Plowman*, however, stand for something beyond themselves, as an allegory ought. In addition to commenting on the nature of gender and sexuality, they comment on and complicate psychological understandings of how the self lives its relationship to itself.

The literary form that permits this philosophical experimentation is that of personification allegory. The author of *Piers Plowman* is simply freer than his Latin predecessors to play with the gender of personification. In English, it would not be grammatically odd for his Philosophy to be a man, even if this would depart from the Boethian allegorical tradition. Whether exploiting this freedom deliberately or accidentally, Langland creates an allegory that makes full use of the flexibility offered by the disappearance of what is called "nonnatural" noun gender from the English language. As a consequence, the intersection of grammatical rules (or lack thereof), gender, and interdependence is even more complex and unstable in *Piers Plowman* than in its predecessor allegories.

Inviting, Then Disinviting, Female Personifications

Although critics have often emphasized the view that the literary convention of a female tutelary figure representing an abstraction such as Philosophy or Music is merely an accident of grammar and therefore to be dismissed as *mere* accident, some recent scholarship in *Piers Plowman* studies has considered the implications and meanings of the many female speakers in medieval Latin and vernacular writings.[3] In "Gender and Personification in *Piers Plowman*,"

---

3. For general studies of female tutelary figures in the writings and imagery of the Middle Ages, see Marina Warner, *Monuments & Maidens: The Allegory of the Female Form* (New York: Atheneum, 1985). See also Barbara Newman, *God and the Goddesses* (Philadelphia: University

Helen Cooper noted Langland's tendency to transform abstractions that earlier authors had gendered female into male figures: "[G]iven the freedom to choose what sexual form his personifications will take, over and over again it is the male of the species that he chooses."[4] Even Will, who, in *Piers Plowman,* serves as the narratorial stand-in for the author, could easily have been gendered female and portrayed as a woman—as he actually *is* in "Sawles Warde."[5] Cooper has argued that one reason the personifications are male is that they are faculties of Will's own person—*his* Conscience, *his* Reason—that might be best presented as male figures. Such an analysis understands the grammar of personification in the poem as something other than arbitrary, since recognizing that a male personification is best for representing a male person assumes a motivated connection between allegorical gender and poetic meaning. Whereas Cooper's reading remains crucial, it can be usefully rethought in terms of the poem's process—specifically, in terms of the process by which male personifications become more prevalent over the course of the poem.

The process of inviting the male onto the scene and disinviting the female happens gradually over the course of *Piers Plowman.* It seems that the author chooses to begin with the accepted approach to personification, all the better to demonstrate how it can be changed. The first of the personifications to interact with Will in his dream on the Malvern Hills is Holy Church, the personification of *Ecclesia*—a female tutelary figure very much of the type of Boethius' Lady Philosophy. Holy Church quickly establishes that her job is to personify authority, and immediately takes up a tutelary position toward Will, rebuking and mocking him in a manner familiar from allegories high and low.[6] From the beginning, the poem is in familiar territory for readers

---

of Pennsylvania Press, 2003), and *From Virile Woman to WomanChrist: Studies in Medieval Religion and Literature* (Philadelphia: University of Pennsylvania Press, 1995).

4. Helen Cooper, "Gender and Personification in *Piers Plowman,*" *Yearbook of Langland Studies* 5 (1991): 31–48, 33. It has been a trope in studies of *Piers Plowman* over the past decade that nobody writes on gender in the poem. Be that as it may, Cooper's article began an important discussion, which was continued with a special issue of *The Yearbook of Langland Studies* (Vol. 12, 1998, included many articles cited throughout this essay) and several full-length studies in recent years, all citing Cooper as inspiration and inaugurator of the discussion.

5. Elizabeth Robertson's analyses of the relationship of Will and Study, and of Langland to his Latin antecedent, have implications for any discussion of Will's gender: "By representing the central protagonist of the poem, Will, normally identified as female, as male, one might argue that Langland offers finally Woolf's androgynous vision of the self, one in which male and female are in balance. And when Will is in balance, Will can achieve what Lady Mede cannot: agency as a subject" (Robertson, "Measurement and the 'Feminine' in *Piers Plowman*: A Response to Recent Studies of Langland and Gender," in *William Langland's "Piers Plowman,"* ed. Kathleen Hewett-Smith [New York and London: Routledge, 2001], 192).

6. Ralph Hanna, "School and Scorn: Gender in *Piers Plowman,*" in *New Medieval Literatures* III (Oxford: Oxford University Press, 1999), gives useful historical background to

of Latin or Old French/Anglo-Norman allegory. Although it changes almost immediately, Will's role as a speaker in *Piers Plowman* begins by establishing him within a gendered exchange of tutelary dialogue inherited from the tradition of Latin poetry.

Even as Will begs Holy Church for answers, a contrasting figure appears in response to his expressed wish to "know the false," a figure that both provides partial answers to his questions and serves as a long and important digression. Whereas Boethius' Lady Philosophy drove out the Muses who had been such dangerous distractions for the imprisoned philosopher, Lady Meed appears at Holy Church's direction. Meed is not brought in by Holy Church as an interlocutor for Will—she is, instead, a negative example or object lesson intended to teach Will to "know the false."

Feminist critics have long noted that Meed, whose possible marriage to Fals Fikkel-Tongue threatens the very fabric of the society seen in Will's dream, literalizes discussions of the "traffic in women."[7] Meed actually *is* Woman as an object of exchange, consolidating or threatening the bonds between men, a personification of reward, functioning as currency in exchanges between those in power; as such, she prefigures but does not participate in the homosocial exchange between Will and his Latin-named double, Liberum Arbitrium, discussed in this chapter's final section. Meed is the progeny of the strange

---

understanding the humiliating and difficult position of the male student vis-à-vis the imaginary female instructor-as-disciplinarian, noting that the schoolmaster's whip was often referred to as "the schoolmaster's daughter." Hanna takes note of the rhetoric within surviving schoolbooks about the evils of marriage (which threatens the young cleric with the loss of clerical status). Within this context, Hanna goes so far as to explain the relative sparseness of female figures in the poem following the traumatic encounter with scolding Holy Church as an avoidance, "a swerve designed to suppress the memories of abuse one hears here" (Hanna, 223). I agree with Hanna's conclusion that "the poem's learning is staunchly gendered, as one would expect, as male, but a maleness particularly insecure" (227).

7. Gayle Rubin's influential feminist critique of male social bonds constituted through the exchange of women can be found in "The Traffic in Women: Notes on the Political Economy of 'Sex,'" in *Towards an Anthropology of Women*, ed. Rayna Rapp Reiter (New York: Monthly Review Press, 1975). Discussions of *Piers Plowman* that cite Rubin's work include Clare Lees, "Gender and Exchange in *Piers Plowman*," in *Class and Gender in Early English Literature*, ed. Britton Harwood and Gillian Overing (Bloomington: Indiana University Press, 1994), and Elizabeth Fowler, "Civil Death and the Maiden: Agency and the Conditions of Contract in *Piers Plowman*," *Speculum* 70 (1995). They also include the article by Susan Signe Morrison and Susan Baker, "The Luxury of Gender: *Piers Plowman* B.9 and *The Merchant's Tale*," in *William Langland's "Piers Plowman": A Book of Essays*, ed. Kathleen M. Hewett-Smith (New York: Routledge, 2001), an essay that first appeared in the *Yearbook of Langland Studies* special issue on "Gender and *Piers Plowman*" by the *Yearbook of Langland Studies* (Vol. 12, 1998). Interest in Lady Meed has been so acute that discussions of this figure have formed the bulk of work on gender in *Piers Plowman*, and I suggest that such work would benefit from taking into account where the poem goes with its complicated understanding of the female after its admittedly rich and complex beginning.

coupling of Fals and Amends, a "mixed marriage" of apparent opposites that binds them together as one another's peers: the first instance of how kinship bears a particularly philosophical weight in the poem.[8]

Meed is bound to her named nature, bound to serve as an object of exchange. However, she is also, at least somewhat, a figure imbued with agency: Her consent, like that of any woman entering a marriage, is required by law; she attempts (however incorrectly) to support her argument with scriptural authority; and her will stands as a question within the text. The contrast between Holy Church and Lady Meed is also a contest, since, although only Holy Church directly interacts with Will, and the two female personifications do not directly dispute with one another, they *do* vie for Will's and the reader's memory and attention. The performance and undoing of gender in *Piers Plowman* does not end with this female pair. These two female personifications, rather than serving as basis and structuring trope for the rest of the poem, disappear and are replaced by new interlocutors and debaters for Will. But their pairing does set up the convention of female tutelary figures as a significant aspect of the dream vision. As it turns out, this convention is set up in order to be overturned.

By the end of its first two *passus*, *Piers Plowman* has presented thesis and antithesis, the positive and negative faces of femininity. Although Meed is unusual in being a personification allegory that seems to strive for something like self-determination and ownership of texts and means, the poem has not, by the point at which it leaves her, strayed outside the framework of conventional personification allegory as inherited from earlier Latin authors. It is what the poem does next that retrospectively transforms the beginning of *Piers Plowman* into just one of several in a series of experiments in thinking through the possibilities of gender in allegory.

The presence of both Meed and Holy Church in the allegory gives the reader an opportunity to expect female personifications. And it sets up the reader to experience their removal as a disruption of the norm. The most obvious result of such a disruption is that capital-T "Truth" (this poem's initial quest and question), as well as other large answers, are always kept beyond the narrator's reach—Holy Church can't simply tell Will how to find the truth (or to know the false, his initial, modest goal) in the way Philosophy could tell it to Boethius. Holy Church tells Will to *love* the truth instead, something that

---

8. This issue is usefully summed up by John Bossy, with some reference to *Piers Plowman*, in a much-cited study about marriage and baptism as "rites of passage" in fourteenth-century England. According to Bossy, "one might deduce that, in this society, the kin-relation was taken as the model of all affective social relations." See "Blood and Baptism: Kinship, Community and Christianity in Western Europe from the 14th to the 17th Centuries," in *Sanctity and Secularity: Studies in Church History 10,* ed. Derek Baker (New York: Harper & Row, 1973), 134.

can presumably be accomplished without ownership or attainment. An almost secondary effect of this relationship is that the position of the female tutelary figure as Man's natural Other, the feminine voice to which he can turn for succor as well as discipline, is at first offered as a possibility, then interrogated, experimented and toyed with—and then displaced. Langland gives us female speakers, and Langland takes them away.

Cooper has argued that the choices of gender for Langland's personifications are "never casual," but, instead, reflect his embeddedness in fourteenth-century English life, including its "structures of patriarchal dominance."[9] More recently, Elizabeth Robertson has argued that Langland's representation of gender and personification "exposes the fault lines of gender stereotypes"[10] as much as that representation complies with patriarchy. In other words, he is describing a situation rather than recommending that it continue. She argues that the just society that Langland's poem demands would include women as well as men, undifferentiated, since the significant question for him is not the status of women as such (certainly not as courtly romantic objects or even as personifications) but the proper and appropriate conduct of human society and the search for salvation and connection with the divine.

Given such an understanding, refusing the figure of the female tutelary personification would also mean—although Robertson never quite says this—refusing to elevate Woman just as one refuses to markedly debase her. This view is also implicit in an article by Susan Baker and Susan Signe Morrison, analyzing the role of gender in the poem.[11] A reading extrapolating from Robertson's "just society" or Baker and Morrison's "dissolving gender boundaries" would view Langland's relatively sparse use of female figurations as a pointed refusal to play with what had by then become the easy trope of either debased *or* elevated femininity (sometimes both at the same time), the courtly, philosophic, and didactic examples of which are legion. Although the poem has elements of social satire toward its beginning, these elements gradually give way to other sorts of concerns, and "real" women become gradually less and less relevant, just as female personifications do. By setting up his readers to expect allegorical female figures and then proceeding, for thousands of lines

---

9. Cooper, 46.

10. In "Measurement and the Feminine," Elizabeth Robertson argues that "in his representation of Gluttony, Langland draws on negative stereotypes about the feminine in order to explore the nature of sin; these negative qualities of excessiveness and dilatoriness do have the potential, however, if not to challenge social injustice, at least to call attention to the social definitions of gender roles. Elsewhere in the poem, the potential of the feminine to be liberatory as well as disruptive is more fully articulated" (181).

11. Susan Baker and Susan Signe Morrison argue that, though Langland is not indifferent to questions of gender, the teleology of his vision is that "gender essentially becomes moot, as kinship bonds and gender and class boundaries dissolve" (66).

toward the middle and end of the poem, to have Will dispute with male personifications instead, Langland voids his poem of a certain affective charge. He removes the possibility of a specific sort of flirtation with and within hierarchy, posing for himself the greater challenge of establishing relationships between speakers without reliance on the built-in hierarchies of gender.

Notoriously, *Piers Plowman* never abandons a train of thought; it simply adds another and then yet another. Female personifications do not simply disappear from the poem after the troublesome incident with Meed (and the experiment with female tutelary figures and their doubles) is concluded. Although there are fewer female personifications engaged in disputation than there might have been, the voices of many female figures echo through the poem. There are female speakers who want to know how to help plow the field that Piers must plow for Truth, and wives and mothers who need justice or food. Even female personifications of important abstractions make an eventual return after Will's discussion with Holy Church is concluded.

Becoming Kin
FAMILIES, DYADIC STRUCTURES, AND SPLIT SELVES

Over the course of the poem, relationships between abstractions (and to Will) are established through the manipulation of genealogy rather than through the tutelary dialogue of Holy Church or the debates about Meed's parentage and her marital prospects. A number of abstractions act only as figures marked by relation to other abstractions, and Will is capable of apprehending certain concepts only through understanding the kinship relationships between them.

A striking instance of the way in which genealogy forms relationships occurs in B. V/C. VII, when Piers gives Will and the rest of the pilgrims directions to Truth. As a means of avoiding the Seven Deadly Sins during his quest, Will is advised to *be* or perhaps to *become* kin to the seven virtues, represented as seven sisters who serve as porters and guards in the Castle of Truth:

> And ho is sib to this seuene, so me god helpe
> Is wonderliche welcome and fayre underfonge
> Ho is nat syb to this seuene, sothly to telle
> Hit is ful hard, by myn heued, eny of yow alle
> To geten ingang at eny gate, bote grace be the more.[12]

12. William Langland, *Piers Plowman: The C-Text*, ed. Derek Pearsall (Exeter, UK: University of Exeter Press, 1978; 1994), C. VII, 278–82, very similar to the same passage in B. V, which appears on 625–29. Further citations will appear in brackets within the text, listing version, *passus*, and line number.

What does it mean to be *told* to be kin?[13] Although it might be literally interpreted as just a way of saying that one ought to be on intimately good terms with the virtues, the figure of kinship is a powerful one to invoke in this poem. In this passage, to be kin may mean always-already to have had a kinship relationship with these virtues—to be able to trace distant genealogical connections, figuratively speaking, between one's family and theirs, if we are to think this metaphor through. One of Piers's listeners, a "cotte-pors," is immediately anxious and exclaims, "By Crist, . . . y haue no kyn there" (C. VII, 283). His worry is taken up by one sinner and then another, until Piers attempts to reassure all by promising that Mercy and her son also dwell with these sisters and are related to all who are sinners, and even possess the capacity to urge the guards to let such sinners into the castle of Truth.[14] In the B-text, a "commune woman" (this term is usually understood to mean "prostitute") responds to this reassurance by promising to follow Piers, and avers that "thow shalt seye I am thi suster" an echo of Sarah's words to Abraham as they entered the land of Egypt.[15]

Here, the figuration of kinship has moved from a convenient way of expressing the necessary always-already quality of virtuous living—it must be as natural as blood ties, and as omnipresent—to a figure of radical interdependence and voluntary choice. Sinners need the intervention of Mercy to enter the tower of Truth, just as Will needs his interlocutors to achieve understanding. In both cases, the goal can be achieved only through interaction with another. This way of portraying dependence expresses the poem's interest in human interdependence and describes a self dependent for its capacity to act and to *be* in the presence of another capable of engaging in dialogue and forming ties with it.

It is relatively hard to dream up genealogies where every relevant concept is brother and sister; relations between concepts are often described through the conceptually simpler technology of *making* kin—through marriage. In the poem's third vision, Wit (the husband of Will in most allegories where Will is represented as female, such as "Sawles Warde") appears as a character who is married to Study, and a bit of a shrew. After condemning, with a ferocity that might almost be jealousy, Wit's attempts at teaching Will, Study calms down

---

13. According to the *Oxford English Dictionary*, since the time of *Beowulf*, "sib" in English has meant "related by blood or descent; akin," "kinship, relationship," as well as "peace, amity, concord."

14. In his edition of the C-text (Pearsall, 1978), 144, 289n, Pearsall suggests that Mercy is here being identified with the Virgin Mary.

15. William Langland, *The Vision of Piers Plowman, A Complete Edition of the B-Text*, 2nd ed., ed. A. V. C. Schmidt (London: J. M. Dent, Everyman's Library, 1978; 1995), B. V, 642. Further citations of the B-text appear within the text in brackets, listing version, *passus*, and line number.

and is pleased by Will's words of flattery, ultimately sending Will off to visit her kinsman, Clergy, and his wife, Scripture.

When Will encounters Dame Study, femininity as such—having appeared as motherly Holy Church and whorish Meed, as well as tale-spinning Pride—takes on a third sort of stereotype, that of shrewish wife. Her speech is entirely embedded in the context of her relation to Wit and her kinship to Clergy. The burden of her argument is ultimately that Wit should be careful about showing holy writ to laypeople like Will; in her advice, however, Study makes it very clear that she is bound to thinking in genealogical, relational models, just as those who look at Meed in the first several *passus* of the poem are bound to consider her nature as determined by one branch or another of her parentage, as well as by whom she might marry. Scripture, to whom Study sends Will, is recommended to Will as one who is "sib to the seuene ars and also my suster / And Clergies wedded wyf" (C. XI, 98–99).[16]

Married pairs, such as Scripture with Clergy and Wit with Study, work as one another's foils and best interlocutors. These pairs are not romantic on a *fin amours* model. Instead, it seems that one personification represents a particular "power" and the other the object on which the power works—for instance, the way that Clergy generally works on understanding Scripture. The couple, although somewhat unified in its interaction with Will, is nevertheless a pairing of two disparate (but perhaps difficult to separate) forces, a sort of synergy. In the relationships between Clergy and Scripture, and Study and Wit, the two speakers are very different, but also quite intimately connected, and any attempt to separate them and to measure the differences between them once and for all would be complex, inconclusive, and, very possibly, acrimonious.

These related figures, which are also figures in relation with one another, are significant and respected, but they are also always intermediary and their advice carries Will only so far. The poem's initial tutelary dialogue—between Holy Church and Will—does not bring Will the answers he seeks. Married pairs, the dyadic and heterosexual coupling of two kinds of powers, give him

16. In his analysis of this section in the B-text version of the poem, James Simpson has written that "these figures do form a coherent group; they have a set of relations between themselves which suggests this coherence," and yet he also writes about how insufficient Will finds this group's advice—the B-text version contains an almost 100-line rant by Will about how little he has learned from Scripture and Clergy. "Study represents the grammar school, the preliminary educational system.... Clergy, as "cosyn" to Study, does represent ... the institution of university theological learning" (Simpson, *Introduction to the B-Text*, 1990), 106. Simpson goes on to explain how "clergy" can mean "knowledge, learning, doctrine" according to the *Middle English Dictionary*. "Scripture is being used in a specific way, adduced in academic debate.... [She] occupies a middle ground between ... two extremes of the purely dogmatic instruction and intimate, allegorical understanding; Scripture is being used actively by Will, but the scriptural texts are being used as counters in theological, academic arguments" (107).

directions that lead him forward, but they, too, turn out to be insufficient for his quest's fulfillment.

By creating married personifications (not newlyweds like Martianus Capella's Philology and Mercury, or pairings like Meed's parents, Fals and Amends, or Sloth and Wanhope in C. XXII, but long-term married couples) as a means of thinking through the relationships between institutions of learning and learning within them, Langland works through a new and different way of presenting a sequence of instructors. In this section of the poem, the process of Will's instruction, the narrative progress of the quest, and the encounter between him and the tutelary figures is particularly nonlinear, in a way that Will finds rather frustrating: "'This is a long lesson,' quod I, 'and litel am I the wiser!'" (B. X, 369) he says to Scripture.[17] This encounter with powers that are distinct but joined becomes a recursive and interwoven academic dialogue, one whose complexity partially reflects the entwined nature of these figures' genealogical relationships. Langland's choices in presenting these personifications also reflects a vision of what it means for two or more persons or powers to exist in an interrelated state, as one another's peers and partners within the dialogic situation of horizontal interdependence. Apparently, what it means is that such bonds, and the persons who inhabit lives bounded by such bonds, can be helpful, but are necessarily limited. The problematic, complex interdependence between and within persons modeled by Body/Soul debates is a problem to be solved: Langland solves it by passing through and out of marriage as a model. Here, the version of *sowlehele* psychology enacted in the poem becomes the work of finding independence even in contexts of radical dependency.

Nearer the poem's end, Liberum Arbitrium in *passus* XVIII of the C-text shows Will the Tree of Charity. It is clear that the apple representing virginity is sweeter than that which represents marriage, even though marriage seems to be required of adult human beings who are not committed to the clergy (C. XVIII, 80–100).[18] Marriage is depicted, typically, as problematic—the wicked

---

17. James Simpson discusses Will's response to Scripture in "Desire and the Scriptural Text: Will as Reader in *Piers Plowman*," in *Criticism and Dissent in the Middle Ages*, ed. Rita Copeland (Cambridge, UK: Cambridge University Press, 1996). For him, this moment is a particular instance of Will as reader, and of Langland's "voluntarist hermeneutics," and a turning point away from the despair that characterized Will's response to many of his interlocutors' teachings in earlier *passus* of the poem.

18. Late in the poem, when he encounters the Tree of Charity, Will sees three kinds of apples on that tree and asks his guide, Liberum Arbitrium, "sethen ther aren but tweye lyues / That oure lorde alloweth, as lered men us techeth, *Activa Vita* and *Contemplativa Vita*" (C. XVIII, 81–83). Liberum Arbitrium replies that the apples affirms the existence of three states—virginity, widowhood, and marriage; in his notes to the text, Pearsall point out that Will's question reflects ignorance (either strategic or real) about the third option, the "mixed" or "apostolic" life. Given the three apples and the trinity of Dowel, Dobet, and Dobest, the tension introduced

wife is listed as one of the three things that are capable of driving a man from his home. This appearance of the wicked wife trope is part of an extended simile of the temptations of the world, the flesh and the devil, and the wife is presented as a stand-in for "oure wikkede flesche" (C. XIX). Here, the femininity of the flesh is assumed and utterly conventional. To be bound in marriage is to be bound to the flesh—as Actif demonstrates when he refuses to follow Piers on a pilgrimage to truth, using the excuse that he has recently wedded a wife, in C. VII. That trope of "uxorem duxi" as harmful excuse names the potential drawback of the married state. Even as the married state is understood to be necessary for the propagation of kind, it remains profoundly troubling to Will and to many of his interlocutors—even, to a degree, his married ones. Interdependence is terribly important in this poem; it is also, as these *passus* make very clear, terribly problematic—particularly the kind of interdependence produced by the married state, which seems, at best, a transitional state, a phase out of which the maturing self must grow.

Kynde
THE GODDESS NATURE AND THE PROBLEM OF SEX

Will's stipulated ignorance, his position as a curious and almost naïve narrative center, is presented early in the poem when Will admits that he has "no kynde knowing" (C. I, 136). His lack of "kynde knowing" directs the poem's narrative development as a series of imperfect understandings amended by an ever-growing cast of irritated tutelary figures.[19] It might also stand in for Will's inability to think about his own psychology in purely academic terms, his

---

by Will's pointedly *ignorant* assertion of two kinds of life is an interesting one—possibly a void demanding to be filled, like so many of Will's frustrating questions are, and possibly, also, a way of putting thinking organized in threes up against thinking organized in twos (which the disputational situation of the text *tends* to be but isn't always).

19. Mary C. Davlin writes that "kynde knowing" is best translated as "divine wisdom," arguing that "in *kynde*, with its wealth of 'natural' connotations, Langland found an array of interacting meanings perfectly though paradoxically suited to suggest the kind of knowledge called *gnosis sapientia* in the Church tradition." See Davlin, "*Kynde knowing* as a Middle English Equivalent for 'Wisdom' in *Piers Plowman* B," in *Medium Aevum* 50 (1981): 8. Elizabeth Kirk disagrees, seeing the term *kynde knowing* as "an attempt to coin a vernacular equivalent for the theological term 'natural knowledge.'" See Kirk, "*Kynde Knowing* as a Major Theme in *Piers Plowman* B," *Review of English Studies* n.s. 22 (1971): 1–19; 37–38, fn. 18. In "Langland's *Kynde Knowing* and the Quest for Christ," *Modern Philology* 80 (1982): 242–55, Britton J. Harwood discusses the concept of kynde knowing as a version of "*notitia intuitiva*, one of the terms essential to philosophy for the previous hundred years" (245), a concept that Harwood describes as "intuitive cognition": "'Notitia intuitiva' included the certain, immediate knowledge of the mind's own acts." See also Harwood's Piers Plowman *and the Problem of Belief* (Toronto: University of Toronto Press, 1992).

need to develop his own version of psychology—a personal, individual take on *sowlehele* in the context of confessional culture as a whole—out of the givens of quotidian existence, particularly of the natural world represented by the term *kynde*. Sometimes, the problem of lacking "kynde knowing" becomes, in the way of personification allegory, the problem of not yet having been introduced to the character named Kynde.

Kynde, one of the crucial personifications in this poem, appears in the immediate aftermath of Will's encounter with the two married pairs.[20] As a character, he is an important instance of Langland's pointed refusal to rely on "allegorical goddesses": This father figure clearly takes on the role that allegories from Martianus Capella through Alan of Lille's *Plaint of Nature* and Chaucer's *Parlement of Foules* assigned to a female character, a goddess of bountiful fertility named Nature.[21] Here, Langland is making a different point

---

20. Kynde as a personified character is referred to repeatedly throughout the text but appears with a speaking role only three times. In *passus* IX, it is he who encloses the soul in the castle of the body, an allegory that will be discussed in a later section. In addition to the section where Kynde offers the vision of Mydelerthe, he is also called on in *passus* XX when the Antichrist comes and Conscience counsels all to shelter in Holy Church and cry out to Kynde to defend them. Hugh White has made a full-length study of notions of "kynde" in *Piers Plowman* in *Nature and Salvation in "Piers Plowman"* (Cambridge, UK: D. S. Brewer, 1988), which examines this character (and the notions of *kynde knowing* and *kynde wit*) far more carefully than the scope of this chapter permits.

21. J. A. W. Bennett surveys the literature about Natura and Kynde in his appendix, "Natura, Nature, and Kind," to *The Parlement of Foules*. He notes that Chaucer's use of "kinde" for "natura" may reflect "the example set by the Alfredian translator of Boethius." See Bennett, *The Parlement of Foules: An Interpretation* (Oxford: Clarendon, 1957), 207. Mary Clemente Davlin has a very useful discussion of Langland's use of Kynde instead of Natura, and of the word's etymological connections: "The Natura of earlier literary and philosophical convention is the intermediary of God, and with him the creator of earthly things. . . . In *Piers Plowman*, the personification is no longer named 'Natura,' but the Middle English equivalent, Kynde (a word related to 'genus,' 'genealogy,' 'generation' and 'gender' as well as 'generous' and 'genial'; to French *genre* and Italian *gentilezza*.) Kynde is conventionally associated with creation, fertility, growth, sex, experience, love, Reason, and God, and with nature in the sense of birds, beasts, grass, and flowers. . . . [I]t is associated with sickness and death as well as with creation. . . . Moreover, Langland makes two major changes in the convention, by changing the sex of Nature from feminine to masculine and by identifying Nature (*natura naturans*) with God Himself. Whereas previously Natura was 'vice regent' or 'vicaire of the almighty Lord,' Kynde in *Piers Plowman* 'under one aspect' is God Himself." Mary C. Davlin, "*Kynde knowyng* as a Middle English Equivalent for 'Wisdom' in *Piers Plowman* B," in *Medium Aevum* 50 (1981): 5–17. See also Brian Tierney, "Natura id est Deus: A Case of Juristic Pantheism?" *Journal of the History of Ideas* 24 (1963): 307–22, an article that contains useful background material about the philosophical and political theories that undergird the medieval understanding of "Nature" as another name for "God." Hugh White (1988) discusses the influence of and differences from the Chartrian and the juristic understandings of Natura manifested by Langland's Kynde, but argues that Langland's character "is indeed something rather strange and apparently new in medieval poetry" (67) because it leaves no space between God (who is always good) and Nature (which at least occasionally manifests in defective beings or behaviors). White notes that the conflation of the two in Kynde make questions about the provenance of evil particularly sharp, particularly in the vision of Mydelerthe, discussed in this section of my chapter. For White's analysis of how

than his predecessor-allegorists, even as he is dealing with some of the same questions. He has taken up that character and removed her neo-Platonic history, reattaching the powers of Natura to a creation deity who is the Father.

Kynde appears to Will in a dream within his dream to show him the wonders of the natural world.[22] Through him, Will is granted access to a vision that permits him to witness the rational design by which the world is run, and he is all the more dismayed and surprised by the irrationality of human behavior—specifically, human mating—in comparison with the orderly mating of beasts.[23] The schematics of faculty psychology would not help explain this irrationality, since, in that schema, the appetitive faculty (the one getting human beings into sexual trouble) is one that is shared by animals and humans. Within the dream of Kynde, Reason appears to tell Will that "no creature under Crist can formen hymselven" (B. XI, 387). The word *formen*, here, emphasizes the simple fact that creatures are made, and reminds Will that they are made by God.[24] Although formen denotes the creation of a self in the context of divine omnipotence, however, it can also mean that creatures are doomed to have been formed as a consequence of sexual congress. Human beings are thus doubly made, both by God ("under Crist") and by the potentially sinful interaction of their parents.

The problem of interdependence is not just located within human society; it is also inherent in the human relation with the divine. In addition to needing one another in life, sublunary creatures are fundamentally dependent on the intervention of a power that, while intensely personal, is inexorably located outside the self of any single being. In its larger context within Will's dream

---

Langland creates and partially resolves these questions, see 73–78.

22. The context for Kynde's appearance in the poem varies in the two versions that include it: In the B-text version of the poem, this appearance immediately follows a speech by the Emperor Trajan, the "righteous pagan." In the C-text version of the poem, the vision of Kynde and Mydelerthe takes place when Kynde comes to Clergie's rescue. In the C-text, the vision is seen *by* Clergie, not Will, although it is Will who responds to it. Since in that version, the vision comes in the context of Will's discussion with Rechlessnesse, Will may be having this dream of Kynde under the aegis of that character.

23. This is the section of the poem that most resembles the garden of the *Parlement of Foules*, where Chaucer sees the natural mating of birds on the day prescribed by Nature. Will sees birds and beasts, each paired with their "make." In Chaucer's allegory, complications arise in the mating of a higher class of birds, in a transparent allegory of social hierarchy. In the natural world shown by Langland's Kynde, the mating of beasts and their mates is entirely unproblematic. These beasts do not seem to take on an anthropomorphic role or stand in for human behaviors, except insofar as they are being compared to humankind and described as exemplary.

24. In the *Middle English Dictionary*, this line is used to gloss one of the meanings of the verb *formen*, in a case where the verb is taken to mean "(b) to give life to (someone), create (a person, a soul)." Other lines of *Piers Plowman* define related meanings: "5. To inform or instruct (someone), to train or educate, to guide or advise; to give instructions; to develop (manners or habits), to learn," and also, "6. To be constituent parts of (a whole), to form." Both (5) and (6) offer examples from *Piers Plowman* B to demonstrate their meaning.

vision, this phrase participates in a continuing concern about the fact that all creatures are formed by one another: influenced by one another, mated with one another, and born of mothers. This is the very concern evinced in "Als I Lay in a Winteris Nyt" over the interdependence *within* the self, which can now be understood, as perhaps it always ought to have been, as worry about interdependence in general, in a context where—to simplify greatly—the kind of individualistic selfhood touted as that of the Enlightenment subject coexists and uncomfortably clashes with other models of the self, inducing a kind of vertiginous sense that the subject somehow ought to be independent but cannot find a way to live cut off from others.

The discussion of human and animal formation that follows this description of human interdependence confirms that human beings have a particularly troubled relationship with one another and with the divine. "Man and his make [mate] y myhte se bothe" (C. XIII, 138) characterizes in the singular the relationships between human beings, emphasizing the centrality of the male subject and the secondary quality of "his" (necessarily female?) mate. Two lines later, however, we are thrust out of the imaginary dyad's brief domestic bliss, and human interrelatedness is once again subjected to critique: Now in the plural, "men" are the ones who "mede toke and mercy refusede" (C. XIII, 141). The world of "men" is situated in opposition to the world of beasts and characterized by an unnatural refusal of mercy. But there's more to this passage still: Both "meed" and "mercy," qualities to which "men" are said to have a relationship, have appeared as characters in the poem prior to this *passus*. Indeed, Lady Meed herself appeared amid a complicated marriage plot. Consequently, what men "toke" or "refusede" in line 141 can be understood as both a set of qualities and a bride. The poem has moved from a singular "man" to a generalized "men," and from the initially idyllic dyad of "man and his mate" to a refusal of mercy, which can be understood as an unreasonable rejection of dependence on the grace of an omnipotent God, or even a rejection of the often surprising capacity for grace inherent in one's fellow human beings—a refusal of "men's" capacity for dependence on an Other.

In Will's vision of Kynde, the ideal natural world necessitates strict gender segregation, untainted by unseasonable desire. It is governed by time, divided into "mating time" and "non-mating time," a sort of natural universal that humans ignore. Nonprocreative sexual urges are, surprisingly, products of advanced culture, not of nature, and beasts live more sexually orderly lives than man does in this version of the human/animal divide:[25]

25. This is an important trope about animal purity: M. Teresa Tavormina, in *Kindly Similitude: Marriage and Family in 'Piers Plowman'* (London: D. S. Brewer, 1995), cites Jerome's *Adversus Jovinian* 1.49 (PL 23:293–94), Lombard's *Sentences* 4.31, and Gratian's *Decretum* C.32 q.4 c.5, because each contains "a model of animal restraint in sexual matters... the model especially stresses animal abstinence during pregnancy" (181).

> Resoun y sey sothly sewe alle bestes
> In etynge and drynkyng, in engendrure of kynde.
> Aftur cors of concepcion noon toek kepe of other,
> As when their hadde roteyed anon they reste aftur;
> Males drow hem to males amorwenynge by hemsulue,
> And females to femeles ferddede and drowe.
> Ther ne was cow ne cow-kynde that conseyued hadde
> That wolde bere aftur bole, ne boer aftur sowe.
> Ther ne was no kyne kynde that conseyued hadde
>
> That ne lees the lykynge of lost of flesch, as hit were,
> Saue man and his make; and thereof me wonderede
> For out of resoun they ryde and rechelisliche taken on,
> As in derne dedes, bothe in drynkyng and elles.
> (C. XIII, 142–54)[26]

The beasts highlight a tension in human beings between the active and the contemplative lives, in other words, between family life and the sex-segregated (but not procreative) lives of monks and nuns. Beasts can manage to be wholly virtuous and sex-segregated, mating only in the prescribed and appropriate seasons, even when living the active life. Among animals, unlike humans, a life of heightened virtue is accessible to all, rather than only to members of the leisured elite or religious groups. All animals are capable of withdrawing into same-sex groupings, and living in those groupings is the natural way. Homosociality, in other words, is more natural than lustful heterosexuality. The option of choosing pure homosociality interrupted only by necessarily procreative mating with the opposite sex, as animals do here, seems not to exist for human beings.

Here, man—particularly the dreamer, Will—suffers over how beings are formed in a way that beasts need not, because man knows that what he is doing is wrong, whereas the beasts neither do anything wrong, nor know what wrong is. The poem seems to take the view that "man" alone is constituted so as to be able to experience his own contingency, to know himself as needy and mortal in ways unavailable to beasts. Hence man's awareness of the source of his misery is, at the same time, his joy and liberation from bestial "kynde."

Witnessing with envious dismay the rational order of animals, and under the sponsorship of misbehaving Rechlessnesse, Will turns to reproach Reason

---

26. Pearsall notes Kane-Donaldson's reading of "amorwenynge" (in the morning") in their edition of the B-text is "al mornyng," (all mourning), "referring to the notion *post coitum est omne animal triste*" ("after intercourse every being is sad") but disagrees with this "anthropomorphic view of animal sexuality" (Pearsall, 229, 149n).

(oddly, not Kynde, although he is witnessing Kynde's showing) for not having watched over human beings more firmly and kept their activities more rational. Reason angrily replies that it is his, Reason's, job to be patient with things as they are and to endure, and that therefore he shouldn't be criticized by Will. Within this angry retort, Reason insists that "no creature under Crist can formen hymselven" (B. XI, 387), emphasizing the fact that humankind ought not blame its misfortunes on Reason or on Kynde because man's suffering self had been created by God for a reason (but in no way *by* Reason). According to Reason, the unchanging reality of existence is that man is made to suffer because he cannot either make or mate with his own self.

In the way of this poem's progress through digression, the vision of Kynde and of mating briefly becomes a discussion of salvation, but then, of necessity, returns to the problem of *kynde* from another angle, moving from the spectacle of beasts to the question of that which God requires from man. God, according to Reason,

> . . . bad every creature in his kynde encreesse,
> Al to murthe with man that moste wo tholie
> In fondynge of the flesh and of the fend bothe.
> For man was maad of switch a matere he may noght wel asterte
> That some tyme hym bitit to folwen his kynde.
> Cato acordeth therwith—*Nemo sine crimine vivit!*
> (B. XI, 398–402)

In this passage, the necessity of procreation among creatures in general and man in particular is cause to pity man's inability to escape both temptation and the injunction to procreate. The sexual union is expected to comfort man in his temptation-ridden existence, even as "the flesh" appears as one of those temptations that cause his woe. Here, Langland indicates that the procreative urge is not a curse but, as for other beasts, a pleasurable mitigation of one's mortal state, which is simply misused and perverted by human beings. Although this natural process is a basic need and comfort humans and animals share, its unnatural mistiming by human beings threatens to become, with the citation of Cato, a sinful, almost criminal (*crimine,* as in line 402 above) activity, although one of a criminality that is almost universal. Man is simultaneously free and compelled; made so that he cannot escape sin, he nevertheless chooses the moment when he will follow and take pleasure in his particular *kynde,* committing his own particular crime, which enables him to propagate his own kind in a manner that follows Kynde's universal injunction.

Here, Kynde becomes a governing aspect of humankind, something internal rather than external to the self; this figure represents species, natural principle, and a temptation of the will all at the same time. Within the poem, realization of these words' truth awakens Will, blushing, from his dream within a dream. The fact that man was made of "swich a matere" binds him to *kynde*, forcing man to participate in marriage and procreation, even if marriage is always inherently viewed as a problematic state of being. Though the married state is understood to be necessary for the propagation of kind, it remains profoundly troubling to Will and to many of his interlocutors, even, to a degree, his married ones. Celibacy would be a blessed relief, but given the inescapability of interdependence, it seems to be an option for only a privileged few. In other words, women cannot be eliminated from life as from the poem, but their presence can be diminished. In a work that acknowledges the necessary demands of *kynde* even as it rails against them, the necessity of female tutelary figures—a necessity that generations of Latin writers had established as a formative fiction—is both very obvious and, over the course of the poem's progress, radically questioned.

Piers Plowman is more interested in gender as a primary mode of structuring relationships of interdependence between persons (as in hierarchies between men and women, kinship and marriage relations, and so on) than in the categories of male and female in and of themselves. Gender is interesting only insofar as it dictates the kinds of interdependence available to a given person or persons. Langland is particularly concerned with how human beings, possessors of rationality, act irrationally: Those whose work involves careful attention to the seasons somehow fail to mate in the correct seasons. The separation of female and male beasts can also be read in relation to a question about who might be the best interlocutor posed by the poem. The ethical injunction to keep "male" and "female" in separate spheres within the specific discourse of Kynde is, in a general way, reflected in how disputations change over the course of the poem. Ultimately, the male narrator, like the male animal, will also find his best company in chaste communion with others who are most like himself, likely those of his own sex: Although homosexuality is normally coded as utterly unnatural in medieval writings and in commonly held interpretations of the Bible—and is often even called "unkynde," the very opposite of the Kynde dominating this section of the poem—*Piers Plowman* has shown here that human heterosexuality is comparatively unnatural as well.

The tutelary figures that largely structure the narrative progression of *Piers Plowman* are gradually fragmented by the impact of the poem's narrative in increasingly complex ways—ways that this chapter, indeed, this book, can only begin to survey. The shifting of interlocutors as Will struggles toward knowledge does more than offer multiplicity and keep at bay the quest's end. Will's journey gradually fragments the very nature of the disputational scene.

Toward the end of the poem, recognizing the limits of the dialogue form, the most conventional mode of literary instruction in the Middle Ages, Langland dissolves it, opting for something more radical: He represents the monologue of man speaking with himself.

Will's Soul and His Doubles
B-TEXT AND C-TEXT

Many of the personifications who teach and harangue Will resemble him in some way. In fact, they act as his mirrors, reflecting back at him some of his own qualities in a somewhat distorted way, from their position as separate beings. Others can be understood (as Helen Cooper, among others, has argued) as faculties of Will's own soul, essentially the same as he but capable of independent functioning; indeed, Will himself could be a faculty of some other, unnamed soul. In this work, faculty psychology functions usefully as a generator of personifications to advance the narrative: *Piers Plowman* incorporates faculty psychology, but cannot ultimately be limited to it. This work, which contains multitudes, manages to contain both distinct traces of faculty psychology and the performative, didactic, pastoral, and gendered qualities that comprise *sowlehele* psychology.

To get to the poem's end and the partial fulfillment of his quest that this end and its vision of Christ represent, Will must engage figures that are increasingly *like* him in their nature. Will's most perfect interlocutor is one so completely suited to him that his appearance can only be described as "soothly but as myself in a mirour" (B. XV, 162). This figure is so close to Will that he even, in the C-text version of the poem, shares Will's name, with a Latin twist. Only a figure of that sort—Will's other self, his clearest mirror image—seems capable of leading Will *out* of the deepest quagmire of his confusion, toward the Tree of Charity and the vision of the coming of Christ. As Teresa Tavormina has written, "love and likeness go hand in hand for Langland. In fact, the ambiguity of the phrase 'lik to hymselue' may be intended precisely to unite the two syntactic possibilities."[27] Will's best interlocutor, this other self, will prove "same" enough for narcissistic self-love and "other" enough to permit the homosocial relationship in which learning happens best. As it turns out, given the gradual disappearance of female personifications and the troubling character of marriage and procreation within the poem, Will's most significant double, the self outside his self that is nevertheless nearest to him, *has* to be male.

---

27. Tavormina, 54.

That which is within or equal to the self, as it turns out, ought not be female (although at times it seems as though it is). The transformations undergone by the figure of "the soul" help explain this principle of self-sameness. In describing the structure of the soul, Langland follows in miniature the poem-wide pattern described in this chapter: He first offers a structure of conventional, female-personified allegory, and then disrupts it, setting the stage for a male interlocutor to arrive. The first model of the soul that appears in *Piers Plowman* is a static, architectural allegory—Castle Caro, where Anima, the Soul, dwells under the tutelage and guidance of Dobest and the protection of Inwit. The castle itself is made of earth, air, wind, and water joined together. Together, these elements constitute the generalizable human body. The logic of this allegory describes that body as essentially inanimate—the elements joined together stand for the stones and other materials that make up a castle's walls, while the body represented by these walls is merely a thing, like wind, water, or the walls themselves.[28] This body seems to be genderless—but it is inhabited by figures both female and male.

Within the enclosure of the body dwells its animating principle, a female personification complete with kinship and social ties. Anima is the lover of Kynde, the power that joins man with woman in such endlessly problematic ways. Anima, the soul, is coupled with the very principle of coupling—an indication of how deep the significance of interdependence, of sexuality and reproduction, goes in the poem. Within the presumptive solitude of the soul, within the very core of the body, dwells the necessity of interdependence, just as it dwelt at the place where Body and Soul met in the earlier poems. The passage describing Anima, this grammatically feminine and dramatically female soul, is placed within a *passus* that seems entirely concerned with marriage and the importance of gender. The (female-gendered) Soul is joined with Nature, although a female same-sex coupling of these principles has been avoided by turning the goddess Natura into the male Kynde. A female Anima, capable of heterosexual union with Kynde, is clearly an authorial choice. Grammatically,

28. Tavormina's observation about the relationship between Kynde and Anima encapsulates an idea that informs this chapter's approach to the poem as a whole: "Important to Wit's characterization of Kynde's love for Anima is the phrase 'lyk to hymselue,' since it can be taken to modify either 'lemman' (Anima is a lemman like Kynde himself) or 'louith' (Kynde loves Anima as he loves himself). Although the two possibilities are logically distinct, they may well not be mutually exclusive.... In fact, the ambiguity of the phrase 'lik to hymselue' may be intended precisely to unite the two syntactic possibilities" (54). This ambiguity characterizes much of the poem, and in particular Will's relationship to Liberum Arbitrium, who is also very much "lik to hymselue." For a consideration of the relationship between Inwit and Anima, the reason and the soul, and how both relate to the will in the Castle Caro allegory, see Bruce Herbert, "A Will with a Reason: Theological Developments in the C-Revision of *Piers Plowman*," in *Religion in the Poetry and Drama of the Late Middle Ages in England: The J. A. W. Bennett Memorial Lectures, Perugia, 1988*, ed. Piero Boitani and Anna Torti (Cambridge, UK: D. S. Brewer, 1990).

the option of the Latin noun *animus* (m) always exists. The marriage metaphor allows Langland to describe two things that are related to and dependent on one another, but fundamentally separate, and to dramatize the interdependence of concepts and persons alike. As always, however, he finds that interdependence, no matter how necessary, is also limiting, and moves away from this vision of the radical dependence on the Other, this radical dependence on the female.

After hundreds of lines, Will encounters Anima once again. This time, instead of living as a lady with a lover within castle walls, Anima is represented as an almost hallucinatory image:

> I seigh, as it sorcerie were, a sotil thing withalle—
> Oon withouten tonge and teeth, tolde me whider I sholde,
> And wherof I cam and of what kynde.
> (B. XV, 11–14)

Anima's knowledge turns out to be soul-knowledge rather than mind-knowledge. Anima (rather than, say, Reason) is the one who tells Will where he's from and where he's going, and reveals his own "kynde" to him. Anima is transformed from the female lover of Kynde (a sort of female tutelary personification without a speaking part) into something entirely different, this incredibly odd, almost ghostly thing. She goes from being an embodied and romantically placed concept to being disembodied or very differently bodied.

Perhaps, doctrinally speaking, the soul *ought* to be incorporeal and not a lady in a castle, but the phrase used to describe this incorporeality of the new Anima is a complexly suggestive one. For instance, the word *anima* is a feminine noun in Latin, but is this thing being described still female? This Anima is referred to as a "thing" on line 11, and it seems to have become a male personification ("hym" and "he") by lines 14 and 15. Even then, however, Anima is only partially male, since (as we shall see later) its names for itself include a number of traditionally female ones. Given the indeterminacy of the figure's gender in terms of pronouns used about it and the names it gives itself, it seems possible to read Anima as, among other things, a lower bodily orifice. James Paxson has argued that Anima's toothless speech is that of a phantasmagoric vagina, although it could just as easily be interpreted as an anus, although Paxson doesn't entertain this rather queer possibility.[29] Perhaps

---

29. See James Paxson's "Gender Personified, Personification Gendered, and the Body Figuralized in *Piers Plowman*," *The Yearbook of Langland Studies* 12 (1998): 65–96, 85. In this article, Paxson sets up a series of provocative equations that work to describe the cultural context in which the personifications of *Piers Plowman* were created, offering a new model to explain the gender of allegorical personification.

what is important to draw from any interpretations of Anima as some part of the human anatomy is that Anima's is a type of allegorical body or object that seems radically and challengingly open. Whether ghostly disembodied creature or orifice, Anima seems to have the capacity to shift from signifying femininity (as Kynde's *lemman* and as penetrable orifice) to becoming a masculine thing, marking the place where male figures and bodies supplant female ones, by, among other things, encompassing the feminine and then moving beyond it.

Will's peculiar vision of the personified soul does not turn into a tutelary figure like Holy Church or Dame Study. Instead, it seems to speak for and as the soul (though whether as Will's soul, the soul of "mankind," or some abstraction that is neither, is uncertain). Though it possesses a voice, Anima is, in effect, shapeless; it is composed entirely of essential functions distinctively human without seeming to be human itself. When Will interrogates this figure, honestly unsure whether it is a friend or foe, Anima offers a long series of names that describe him/it:

> "The whiles I quykne the cors," quod he, "called am I *Anima*;
> And whan I wilne and wolde, *Animus* ich hatte;
> And for that I kan and knowe, called am I *Mens*;
> And whan I make mone to God, *Memoria* is my name;
> And whan I deme domes and do as truthe techeth,
> Thanne is *Racio* my righte name—'reson' on Englissh;
> And when I feele that folke telleth, my firste name is *Sensus*—
> And that is wit and wisdom, the welle of alle craftes;
> And whan I chalange or chalange noght, chepe or refuse,
> Thanne am I *Conscience* ycalled, Goddes clerk and his notarie;
> And whan I love leely Oure Lord and alle othere,
> Thanne is 'lele Love' my name, and in Latyn *Amor*;
> And whan I flee fro the flesh and forsake the careyne,
> Thanne am I spirit spechelees—and *Spiritus* thane ich hatte.
> Austyn and Ysodorus, either of hem bothe
> Nempnede me thus to name."
> (B. XV, 23–38)[30]

In this list of Anima's names (which are essentially the same as those of Liberum Arbitrium in the C-text, as I discuss later), the authoritative naming is

---

30. A. V. C. Schmidt's article "Langland and Scholastic Philosophy" (*Medium Aevum* 38 [1969]: 134–56) contains an appendix that examines each of the names of Anima in the B-text, tracing the differences between the Latin and the English versions and what these might mean.

in Latin while the description of function is largely in English. The litany of names has a probable source in Pseudo-Augustine's *De Anima,* but, here, it has been moved into the context of a personification allegory where, as a series of names spoken by a character, it takes on an entirely new set of meanings: What does it mean for a single voice to personify so many concepts? Some of the names seem female, or would be female were this a Latin poem, and others seem male. The retention of Latin nouns in what is largely a translation of a Latin text genders the proceedings, highlighting gender instability as part of what seems to be a project of highlighting instability and multiplicity as such.

In the B-text of *Piers Plowman,* where the speaker of these multiple names functions under the general rubric of "Anima," this act of multiple self-naming crafts a transition from the previously female character of Anima (the one in the Castle Caro), a more traditional allegorical figure resembling didactic allegories such as that of the *Ancrene Wisse,* to a different, perhaps entirely new, allegorical mode. After all, embodying its name is what a personification does. But how can any being remain a personification and at the same time embody so many names? The multinamed complexity of this figure marks the Soul within man as something other than purely female—as containing a composite of masculine, feminine, and neuter nouns. Will, our one particular "man," is confused by all of this and persists in asking questions until he is accused of being one of Pride's knights for wanting to know "the cause of all hire names" (B. XV, 45; note that "hire" is "her," temporarily specifying Anima's gender as female). It is as if delving into these names, and with it, Will's or the reader's descent into the very stuff of personification allegory, is not an admirable or a useful task to take on. This very rejection of analysis is, in itself, a final farewell to a traditional approach to personification allegory. Paxson has written that the character of Anima is "a metapersonification—an embodiment of the idea of embodying abstractions."[31] I agree, and would argue that this way of "doing personification" in the poem actually signals nothing less than the most profound and basic transformation of how the gender of personification allegory works: not exactly androgynous, but somehow male, female, and both all at once. The figure of Anima changes the nature of the kind of body an allegorical figure can possess, dissolving the necessity that the process of personification involve some sort of embodiment.

The role of this strange new Anima is to direct Will beyond himself, toward Charity. In response to Will's boundless curiosity, he replies:

"Therefore by colour ne by clergie knowe shaltowhym nevere
neither thorugh wordes ne werkes, but thorugh wil oone,

---

31. Paxson, 85.

> And that knoweth no clerk, ne creature on erthe
> But Piers the Plowman."
> (B. XV, 209–12)

Charity, the object to be known according to this passage, is an allegorical character that never speaks for itself but can be described by Anima. This character is never properly personified, never becomes Will's interlocutor, but it does appear later in the poem as a tree, a manifestation of a different kind of allegorical genre altogether. Only through the will can charity be known (not through any act of speaking, arguing, or learning), and, of course, Will is the one privileged to see the Tree of Charity in his dream, on his readers' behalf.

In the B-text version of the poem (and not in the C-revision, which contains Liberum Arbitrium as Will's double, as I discuss later), Will's knowing and the knowledge adduced of Piers are connected in a circular relationship that relies on Will's double nature, as person and as personification. As a person, Will needs Piers in order to know Charity, and the content of Piers's knowledge, the "fre liberal wille" (B. XV, 150), is "the will." Will, in responding to this definition, finally names himself: "[M]y name is Longe Wille" (B. XV, 152). What Will asks, while naming himself, is where he might find someone who can teach him about Charity: "Where sholde men fynde swich a frend with so fre an herte?" (B. XV, 151). Anima responds that Will can find such a friend in Piers: "Ac Piers the Plowman parceyveth moore depper / What is the wille, and wherfore that many wight suffreth" (B. XV, 199–200). What Piers knows seems to be the nature of Will, which Will himself doesn't yet know, but somehow must come to know. This is a relationship of epistemological interdependence that recalls Reason's admonitory words: "[N]o creature under Christ can formen hymselven" (B. XI, 387).[32] Instead of organizing knowledge and the goal of a narrator's quest through an amatory model (as when Christ woos the Soul in many allegories or as the moment when whom Meed marries truly matters), here Langland has rewritten the organization of the literary/spiritual quest as a search for reciprocation: for a peer, and not for a wife as such. The kind

---

32. James Simpson has written about this ambiguous interdependence, albeit with a different set of questions in mind; he has considered this passage in terms of its biblical context: "[T]he logic of the passage is strangely circular, however: Will can know charity (which Anima has defined as a 'fre liberal wille') only by knowing Piers, since Piers knows the will. Will, that is, can know charity only by knowing the figure who knows him. Has Langland simply lost his way? Not at all: the biblical text from which Langland takes his inspiration here, I Corinthians 13, is as much concerned to define what charity is as to define how one might know it; Paul defines full understanding in terms of knowing to the degree that one is known by a principle outside the self.... Just as Paul, then, defines perfect knowing as knowing to the degree that one is known, so too does Anima define the knowing of charity as being both active and passive, or as active in being passive" (Simpson, *Introduction to the B-Text*, 185).

of interdependence that Will needs is, ultimately, to join with another male figure. Although interdependence is unfortunately necessary, the harshness of that necessity can be mitigated by finding a free-hearted friend.

Whereas in the B-text, Will encountered Anima in all its hallucinatory, orifice-like dimensions, the C-version offers instead Will's meeting with Liberum Arbitrium, who changes roles from B, giving up his work at the Tree of Charity (see B. XVI, 16–17) and instead assuming Anima's very own lines.[33] But who is this Liberum Arbitrium, this even-more-purely-male character, uncontaminated by association with Anima, the girl in the castle?[34] He is Will, but with a twist: He now incorporates a faculty that our Will lacks. He says so himself—he is "a will with a resoun."[35] Perhaps it is the Latinity of his name

---

33. In a study of the changes between the B- and the C-text versions of *Piers*, E. Talbot Donaldson argues that Liberum Arbitrium has his origins in Bernard of Clairvaux's views (or someone influenced by that school), being "that part of man which bears the impress of the image of God to which man was created" (*Piers Plowman: The C-Text and Its Poet* [New Haven, CT: Yale University Press, 1949], 189). This enigmatic character seems to have been particularly popular with medieval audiences in his C-text incarnation, despite Donaldson's assertion that Liberum Arbitrium "would win no popularity contest for characters in *Piers Plowman*" (188). According to Kerby-Fulton and Justice, "medieval readers, for reasons unknown to us today, were particularly taken with this passage in Langland: the scribe John Cok extracted it for John Shirley; the Anglo-Irish artist of Douce 104 chose to illustrate it, and in Book III of the *Testament* Usk attempted to combine this image of *liberum arbitrium* as a spiritual lover with the image of the secular lover, a combination awkward indeed (at least in Usk). But the Douce 104 artist did exactly the same thing when confronted with the passage: he portrayed Langland's Liberum Arbitrium as a handsome young lover"; see Kathryn Kerby-Fulton and Steven Justice, "Langlandian Reading Circles and the Civil Service in London and Dublin, 1380–1427," in Wendy Scase, Rita Copeland, and David Lawton, David, eds., *New Medieval Literatures* (Oxford: Clarendon, 1997), 67–68. Although Kerby-Fulton and Justice do not give a reason for Liberum Arbitrium's popularity, they note the fact that it is sometimes extracted with fragments of *Troilus and Crisyede* also concerned with the question of the freedom of the will.

34. Britton Harwood offers the possibility that Liberum Arbitrium is simply a figure for the soul, and offers five ways of conceiving Liberum Arbitrium as a concept: Two of these notions regard Liberum Arbitrium as being of either will or reason, notions that he rejects for their incompleteness. Liberum Arbitrium in *Piers Plowman* makes it quite clear that he functions as a will *with* a reason, after all. Other options include Liberum Arbitrium as a separate faculty, a faculty that serves "to account for choice by coming between the reason's judgment of the good and the will's desire for the good—yet one composed of reason and will" (*Piers Plowman and the Problem of Belief*, 105). Yet other possibilities suggest that Liberum Arbitrium represents all of the powers of the soul lumped together and, as the image of God in humankind, also as a kind of *habitus*, not merely as a power of volition.

35. Schmidt highlights two possible understandings of *liberum arbitrium*, "the theory that *liberum arbitrium* is one faculty of the soul and the theory that it is all faculties of the soul" ("Langland and Scholastic Philosophy," 139). The correspondence between Anima's speech and Liberum Arbitrium's convinced Schmidt that, in both cases, it is the soul speaking; he understands the revision as, in the B-version, "one term served for the part and the whole"; in C, however, "Liberum Arbitrium, while remaining quite clearly a part of the soul, becomes the spokesman for the whole soul." Schmidt argues that Langland had come to see Liberum Arbitrium as the "essence" of human nature—a sort of synecdochal logic by which Liberum

that gives Liberum Arbitrium the extra gift of "resoun" that renders him capable of serving as a guide for Will.[36]

Whatever the cause, his is a Will that incorporates another allegorical character, Reason, someone we have been hearing from since the early *passus* of the poem (he would normally be a female figure, as in the *Roman de la Rose*, but is represented as male in *Piers Plowman*). Liberum Arbitrium appears in the C revision as the more reasonable, more knowing equivalent of the narrator, himself split into as many pieces as Will might be if he were a human self with a variety of competing, complex faculties, incorporating more powers than Will has been able to include within himself. The C-text version of *Piers Plowman* offers Will tutelage by his closest male double, his slightly more masculine and Latinate superior.

It is as Will's double that Liberum Arbitrium can expound to Will the meaning of charity and lead him, ultimately, to the poem's climax, which includes the coming of Christ and the Harrowing of Hell. Will is led to the poem's end, in the C-version, by his other self. In Langland's consideration of how gender and interdependence works, this self cannot be associated with the female: the term *liberum arbitrium* is neuter, neither entirely masculine nor feminine. Escaping the gender seesaw of Anima/Animus, Liberum Arbitrium achieves a perfect balance. But since English grammar demands that a personified, neuter abstraction become either a "he" or a "she" through the act of speaking, this Latin-neuter person becomes a "he" when he functions in a Middle English poem, as in Will's response to the character's first words: "Thenne hadde y wonder what *he* was, that Liberum Arbitrium . . ." (C. XVI, 161, my emphasis). Although Boethius presents the voice of his own innermost philosophical reason, his calmest and most transcendent faculty, as a stern female speaker, centuries later, Langland shies away from incorporating

---

Arbitrium is the part permitted to stand in for the whole. This has come to be one of the ways in which critics deal with this character's confusing growth in significance between B and C. Lorraine K. Stock suggests that Langland renames the character between the B- and C-versions because "Langland's emphasis on the negation or submission of one's will in order successfully to achieve the contemplative state required in C an allegorical personification of that correct direction of the *voluntas*, who would vividly exemplify that principle of spiritual reform for the character Will, here standing for the universal human will" (Lorraine Kochanske Stock, "Will, Actyf, Pacience, and *Liberum Arbitrium:* Two Recurring Quotations in Langland's Revisions of *Piers Plowman C Text*, Passus V, XV, XVI," in *Texas Studies in Literature and Language* 30 (1988): 461–77, 472.

36. Schmidt's commentary on Liberum Arbitrium suggests that Langland may have thought the term *liberum arbitrium* untranslatable into Middle English, just like *anima*. However, it might also be possible that Langland was employing the rhetoric of untranslatability deliberately; to think about why Langland uses Latin in this way (whether for alienation, authority, the impression of striving for philosophical accuracy, actual striving for philosophical accuracy, or to take his manipulation of Latin-and-English personification to another level) would be another study altogether.

the female as an essential aspect of the male. Will's most useful and intimate Other turns out to be, and *must* be, a Latin-named Will.

Piers Plowman concludes with the male allegorical figure of Conscience heading off to seek out Piers the Plowman, perhaps thereby to repeat the cycle of seeking and finding the double, the perfect interlocutor who, alone in all the world, can lead one to knowledge of the ultimate. Although the alternative offered to active heterosexuality throughout *Piers Plowman* is, of course, celibacy, that state is envisioned by the poem as a relationship between a man and his (male) double. This double might represent a quality that is already to be found within the male seeker, but the goal of the quest that he has undertaken is to find a way to externalize, then encounter, and then begin to love this previously internal quality: to eject an aspect of the self in order to learn to internalize it all the more thoroughly. Such a relationship entails a homosocial, nonsodomitical, probably asexual avoidance of the female rather than an active desire for the male. The female to be avoided is, of course, "merely" any female personification, but now that gender has been revealed as a dramatic factor in allegorical plot, avoidance of female personifications may indeed mean something about avoidance of female persons, and vice versa. This interpretation of *Piers Plowman,* like that of "Als I Lay in a Winteris Nyt" in chapter 3, insists that putting something into the category of "queer" does not necessitate an insistence on anything resembling contemporary formations of gay or lesbian desire.

Piers Plowman sets up a system in which the question of the Will is centered on a male narrator and his masculine alter egos. And yet, the poem is not only or merely exclusionary. Rather, it seems to struggle with its own desire to exclude the feminine. After all, *Piers Plowman* is structured in such a way that we begin and end with female personifications (Holy Church, Lady Meed, and, close to the end, the Four Daughters of God) and with the problems of Kynde and *kynde,* of what it means to live in the world as a sexed and gendered being, in an interdependent relationship with one's fellow creatures. Langland gradually disentangles himself from these female personifications, but he also starts out by tangling with them at great length. At first, we are set up to expect female personifications like those we would see in all the other great medieval allegories. Undermining that tradition with the apparent goal of moving toward a better and more reasonable way to live and love, *Piers Plowman* proceeds from that inaugurating moment to offer us an alternative to the conventional tutelary dialogue. In its stead, the poem offers its readers the silence of the soul in communion with itself, a silence broken only by the monologue of man communing with his own male self.

CONCLUSION

The selves discussed in Body/Soul debates are always dead. That's why they find themselves capable of separating from one another enough to engage in debate. Indeed, to study the Middle Ages at all is always to study writings by and about people who are centuries dead. We reach back in time and find only disembodied words. And yet, these words speak to us about the very stuff of embodied life: love, sex, hunger, dirt, death, decay. To study medieval literature, in this context, can cause us to fantasize more than a little bit about access to those long-gone bodies, to dream that they will someday look up and speak to us in their groaning, ghostly voices, as the Body in "Als I Lay" does in response to the Soul's accusations. We may imagine that these words about what the body speaks might grant us access to bodies themselves, but of course they do not—our knowledge is, as ever, mediated by and produced through discourse, including the discourse of mind/body dualism.

When I started writing this book, an important goal was to critically interrogate the colloquial understanding that medieval persons strongly divided the concept of "body" from that of "soul." I was hoping, thereby, to push against casual or unthinking contemporary views that support such dualism, up to and including earlier feminist affirmations of the "woman = body" equation, an equation that threatens to strand "femininity"—and, conceptually, woman—on one side of a rigid binary. To write about debates within the self, thus, seemed, paradoxically, to be a way of actually affirming that self's wholeness, its unalienated totality.

As I continued to work on this project and realized that, in examining medieval psychological thought, I was encountering the medieval psychological practice of *sowlehele,* it became particularly important to acknowledge the complex role of love and interdependence within the self as a crucial aspect of *sowlehele* narratives. The body had to be something other than a prison for the soul in order for the two to ever have functioned as one; it had to be loved as well as disciplined. That, at least, is how the medieval story goes when a tale has to be told about the relationships between interrelated aspects of the self. Rather than writing against dualism, then, I came to produce a book about the difficult integration of the material world with the world of the immaterial (I hesitate to call on "the spiritual") when both are available to us only through narrative and its various conceptual limitations.

Since beginning this book, I have also had occasion to confront the meaning of just how separate body and soul can be from one another, something I might have denied during the early years of my research. When this manuscript was essentially complete, my father suffered a massive stroke that left him effectively brain dead. Walking into the hospital room where he lay, I was overwhelmed by the sense that he was gone although his heart continued to beat with the help of machines. I would have said that the things about him that mattered, my father's personality, his gallant spirit, were gone and that what remained was nothing at all. He had urged us to let him go without a fancy send-off: After all, he wouldn't be there to enjoy it, he would say. Encountering his empty body, I was overwhelmed with the need to fit my hand inside his, as he had held it safely when I was a little girl. In that hospital room, what I experienced were both the terribly harsh reality of a separation between spirit and flesh *and* their ultimate inseparability—the way in which the beloved body encodes memory and love even absent mind, soul, and voice. To encounter such a paradox is not to resolve it but rather to accept its inevitability. To have been able to understand this was, for me, the single most useful piece of *sowlehele* that this book could offer me, as its author.

Debate poetry takes up topics of vast theological or philosophical importance, and renders them as narratives, with all the ambivalences, twists, and turns that narrative imposes. The poems discussed in this study should not be understood as simply equivalent to philosophical or theological treatises, or to works of self-help. Rather, they should be read as representing the sea change that both philosophy and didactic discourse undergo when both encounter the dual forces of narrative-driven personification allegory and Middle English vocabulary. The works discussed in this study show that the form taken by a philosophical/didactic endeavor can (perhaps must) inflect its content.

The process by which medieval allegory grants the Body speech is a result of the allegorization of what had perhaps started out as a sermon example: the movement from a static moment ("imagine how your soul will address you after you're dead") to a dramatic narrative. Granting the body speech gives the philosophical thinker behind the poem a fair amount of pause: If the body is capable of consciousness, whatever is the soul for? Then again, who is it that generates the voice, that essential feature of the allegorical scene? Is it the (corporeal) vocal cords or the (incorporeal) soul? How can the self be divided in half if something as simple as speech is so intimately implicated in both the physical and the spiritual? The seeds of body/soul dualism's breakdown are contained within its more literal and explicit manifestation, leaving the field open for works such as *Piers Plowman* to push the implications of the debate tradition to their logical extreme.

At the outset, in this book's Introduction, I set out a series of criteria for *sowlehele:* adapting this term to a broader set of texts rather than cataloguing instances when it was being used by medieval authors. *Sowlehele,* I argued, acts on the soul rather than describing it, and in this emphasis on action, it differs in subtle and significant ways from medieval psychology or psychologies. A work of *sowlehele* is an act of performative speech, enacting (or at least promising to enact) the soul-healing it describes. It is a didactic and pastoral work, more use-oriented than theoretical, yet many works of *sowlehele* discussed in this book are interesting precisely because their narrative drive and strange conventions around gendering aspects of the self seem to undermine or at least complicate any simple understanding of their didactic mission. This was particularly true in the works discussed in the two chapters about Middle English Body/Soul debates and the chapter on "Sawles Warde," works whose very explicit intent was to frighten readers about hell, encourage them to dream of heaven, and cause them to consider the relationships between different aspects of their own selves.

The three chapters on shorter Middle English psychological allegories are bookended by considerations of better-known medieval allegories, from Prudentius' fourth-century *Psychomachia* to William Langland's fourteenth-century *Piers Plowman*. This rather too teleological arrangement encourages this book's readers to imagine a plastic, malleable object, "personification allegory," inserted into didactic discourse around the time of Prudentius and then molded and transformed by centuries of works like the Body/Soul debates into a work as odd and surprising as *Piers* . . . and perhaps to insert their own favorite works of personification allegory and test them according to the criteria of *sowlehele* discourse as outlined here, to see how other works might push against or fit tidily within this framework. *Piers Plowman* may conclude this study, but its many words are by no means the very last (chronologically or otherwise) on how gender, allegory, and psychology intersect. Your mileage in seeking other works of *sowlehele,* other ways of approaching the divisions of the self in medieval allegory, may vary, but the attempt will reveal its own possibilities, limitations, and innovations, I am certain.

The book's concluding chapter on *Piers Plowman* recapitulates the argument as a whole. The poem begins using classic female personifications, very much as the representations of allegorical women in chapter 1, and then gradually eliminates them, with certain key exceptions, over the course of its unfolding narrative. In medieval personification allegory, from Boethius and Prudentius onward, the balance of power between disagreeing interlocutors is figured through gendered hierarchies, with female tutelary figures as men's superiors, as midwives to men's thought. As Jean de Meun's Reason reminds us by offering herself flirtatiously to *her* allegorical pupil (as discussed in chapter 1), this is not necessarily a neutral situation. Despite Jean's coy Reason, however, no poem before *Piers Plowman* pushes the implications of allegorical gender in the scene of disputation as far: *Piers* literalizes the formal difficulty of debating with a female personification as part of its narrative mechanism. Although it would be impossible to argue direct influence (whether in terms of the influence of the Katherine Group or the Body/Soul debates discussed in earlier chapters), it is implicit in this study's structure that something *happens* to English-language allegory in the thirteenth century, something that pushes the working of psychological personification in a new direction, that, even if it does not enable or cause *Piers Plowman* to come into existence, permits that work to make sense to its immediate audience.

The presence of the transformed and transformational figure of Anima/Liberum Arbitrium in *Piers Plowman* is a particularly fraught example of the tendency in some medieval allegories to foreground the inherent contradictions of figuring abstract ideas in and through female bodies. From the violent ladies of Prudentius' *Psychomachia* to the contrast between Will-the-wife in "Sawles Warde" and Langland's multiple Wills, a sort of lineage might be traced, an increasing consciousness (among English-language writers most particularly) of the literal meaning of all those women's bodies and voices that populate medieval psychological allegory. Indeed, the most basic of this book's conclusions, its feminist core, is that the works of *sowlehele* that it has selectively traced gradually come to eliminate women as men's double even as they worry that heterosexual interdependence with women is mankind's inevitable fate.

A complex, not at all necessarily sexual version of a queer reading of *Piers Plowman* and of this book as a whole can be offered to complement this feminist reading.[1] On this account, *Piers* and works such as "Als I Lay" offer a way

---

1. The first to offer a queer reading of *Piers Plowman,* James Paxson, argues that if "sod-

out of human heterosexuality's misogynist dilemmas: not the same-sex love of Gay Pride or of the fight for gay and lesbian marriage, but homosociality.² Unfortunately for feminists and for the female figures in allegory, Langland's homosociality, at least, seems to be a vision of the soul's development without the need for women to triangulate the bonds between men—a recognition of the same, or the mirror, as the beloved.³ This homosociality is duplicated in the Middle English works discussed in this book, and it seems clear that the exclusion of women does create a space of tenderness between men, or at least personified male beings, that possesses its own beauty.

Although this book has argued that one of its goals is the gradual marginalization of what had previously been imagined as female aspects of the self, its examination of how dualism is gendered does not simply indict the works discussed as misogynist. These are, rather, imaginative documents sternly accurate to their time and place, insistent on the unalterable and difficult "fact" that woman is not really in a position to be man's Other, despite the necessity of mating, discussed in such detail in *Piers Plowman* at least, and of engaging in relations of *kynde*. That last work examined in this study documents an anxiety about interdependence, especially with women, and offers an alternative, one that had already been present, to an extent, in the thirteenth-

---

omy might be taken as the most palpable sign of the queer—just as personification is often taken as the most palpable sign of allegory . . . personification and body-centered allegory can be viewed as queer semiotic enterprises" (Paxson, 91). Although my argument in this book, like Paxson's, is that it is possible to perform a queer reading of medieval works, I am not entirely persuaded by his provocative series of equations, wherein he slips between a generally accepted equation, "medieval allegorical personification = women," into a new equation, "multiplicity of personifications = queer," which relies on an extremely loose understanding of this term, as well as ignoring the boundary between a world populated by female personifications and one in which they have been excised. Instead of seeing feminist and queer readings as complementary, as Paxson seems to, I find only conflict when I try to read as a feminist (tracking the misogyny that goes into the making of female personifications) *and* as a queer theorist (tracking male same-sex affection in the context of a fundamental exclusion of women). See Paxson, "Gender Personified," 1998.

2. David Halpern, in *How to Do the History of Homosexuality* (Chicago: University of Chicago Press, 2002), has argued for a series of different approaches to characterizing same-sex affection, in order to avoid anachronism and overstatement. Halpern offers and discusses four provisional "pre-homosexual categories of male sex and gender deviance . . . (1) effeminacy (2) paederasty or 'active' sodomy (3) friendship or male love, and (4) passivity or inversion" (109). In tracking the movement away from female personification in most English works discussed by this book, I am looking at how they manifest relevance to Halpern's third category. "Queer" is not the same as "homosexual," of course, and Paxson's work on the queerness of multiplicity does not fit any of the categories above.

3. In *Between Men: English Literature and Homosocial Desire* (New York: Columbia University Press, 1985), Eve Kosofsky Sedgwick argued that women as the putative objects of love poetry, particularly in their role as the apexes of "love triangles," actually mediate and help consolidate homosocial male desire. In arguing thus, she opened up a field of inquiry into the complexities of a same-sex desire that does not necessarily express itself through sex or explicit sexual longing.

century Body/Soul debates: love for and recognition by one's male other, one's other self. Allegorical gendering becomes, in the hands of English writers, a flexible tool for conceptualizing the complexities of interdependence.

One of the crucial abilities of medieval allegory, as it turns out, is its capacity to literalize the relationship between the material and the nonmaterial in the making of persons, who are imagined as the combination of base flesh with spiritual spark. Personification allegory gives a body to a spirit or concept, literally reenacting "the Word made flesh," but also working through the implications of making flesh out of a "word," of the Body and Soul of a dead knight, for instance. This book examines works that literalize body/soul dualism by staging disputations between the crucially interdependent characters, Body and Soul, in terms of some of their influential antecedents and successors as well as the philosophical and psychological work that these poems did and continue to do. Although many medieval and later thinkers have taken body/soul dualism for granted to some degree, it is not an inevitable way of dividing up the parts of the self. The more commonsense and "real" body/soul dualism feels, the more suspicious of it we might want to be. This book does not, *could* not, have the undoing of body/soul dualism as its purpose. Its far more modest intention has been to look at a crucial moment in the history of representing that particular variety of dualism to see how it was set up, reiterated, and reinforced.

Much work has been done in the last decades on the history of the body, about how fundamentally different the experience of embodiment has been in different centuries and different places. To return to the Middle Ages is also to return to the notion of the soul. We have not studied the soul in the way that we have studied the body—not recently. It has been a transhistorical universal or it has been an outdated ideological construct. One might argue that the humanities, as a whole, are ceaselessly engaged in examining the many permutations of what it means to possess a soul, an inner life, a narrative of oneself. But the fact remains that the story of the soul as a historical construct has largely been left implicit in the histories of subjectivity's emergence, which insist, instead, on imposing a term like *subject*—a term that encompasses body, mind, spirit, and social standing—on a time that strictly distinguished these things and thought incessantly about how they might be distinguished even more finely. This book has attempted to put the "soul" back into "body studies," not just through recourse to psychoanalytic theory but by examining the cultural work accomplished by the relationship between soul and body in literary and scientific works, beginning, here, with the medieval literature of *sowlehele*.

APPENDIX

In a Thestri Stude I Stod
(I Stood in a Dark Place)

TRANSLATION BY MASHA RASKOLNIKOV

Standing in a dark place, I heard a little argument, 1
All about a body that was ungood, lying there upon the bier.
Thus spoke the spirit, with sorrowful thoughts and all downcast:
"May woe befall your flesh, your foul blood; why are you now lying here?

"While you were still in life, you were keen to sit in judgment 5
Passing false decrees, profiting by trading two for five;
Now it's clear to me that we will never be worthy of heaven's bliss
Sorely may I make complaint, then, about our long time together."

Then spoke the body, so dismal, to the wretched spirit:
"I had thought that my worldly bliss would last forever, at least for me; 10
I had no [thought] of the sins that now bind me so tightly;
[But] the shackles that hold me now heavily pull me down into the earth."

Then spoke the spirit, with right counsel after foul indeed:
"Where is your overweening pride, your richly-trimmed garments and
    your furs,
Your palfreys and your steeds and your purple opulence? 15
Will you bring none of these along, wretch, to the place where you will lie?"

Then spoke the body, with envy of heart, lying there shrouded in sin:
"Now is this day come upon me, woe has indeed overwhelmed me.
My hands are bound, my eyes are covered up,
I think that I will remain here, in this evil that has happened to me." 20

"Body, you have lived too long; may evil befall you [who are] so treacherous;
All too often, you have turned right into wrong.
While you were in this world, your words were false and treacherous;
The one thing you can be sure of now are future torments, hard and strong."

"Go away now, wretched spirit, how long must this wrangling last? 25
As we argue, worms are holding their own debate, rendering their own firm judgment,
They are casting their lots for my flesh;
Many noble bodies will rot, I shall not be the last."

"Body, you may not leap up now to play or rage,
To beat wild bears or to bind savage lions to your will, 30
Or threaten poor men, despoil them of their inheritance,
You must have fallen very low, for all your high birth."

"Wretched spirit, oh go away, all you know is how to chide.
I know well that I must rot here for all my pride;
Worms must eat my throat and my pale, white side, 35
My own flesh they must eat and under earth it hide."

"I was no wretch at all except through your evil counsel.
Oh, I have such shame thinking of your sins and all your evil deeds.
For a while you were wild, now I dread you very little.
To Christ must I call now; may he remedy now my need." 40

"Go away now, wretched spirit, with your long tale,
I have plenty of pain without you to upbraid me.
I know truly that the worms must eat me;
Yes, I know my deeds have drawn me from my proper place into this deep pit."

"Body, where are your sunny rooms and all your towers, 45
Your beautiful clothes and fancy vestments?
So low must you fall for all your high bowers.
Now all I can do is call out to Jesus; may he be my salvation."

"Wretched spirit, now go away, and journey where you must journey;
My pain is truly enough now, my sides are cold and bare; 50
My house is made of clay, the walls are also cold and bare;
Though you chide night and day, I will say nothing more to you."

"Body, why did you never think, while you might have been able to,
About Him who made us all out of naught, and what you owe Him?
For our sins and not for His, He sold His flesh; 55
Bloody was He made on the cross, as the prophet told us.

"Body, if you now wish to listen, I will tell you
About two miracles and five that must happen before Judgment Day.
The man who is alive, he may see them then:
Then will the man be fortunate who contrives to escape.   60

"On the first day shall come a red dew;
It shall take away from us our joys and pleasures.
The green tree shall bleed that our Lord saw:
Then will the man be fortunate who ever had been true.

"On the second day, fire shall burn all that stands before it,   65
No water will be able to quench it, nor will anything else that comes up against it,
All this world shall be overwhelmed, all the wide lands:
Then shall our Lord see who honored his wounds.

"On the third day, flood waters will inundate all the world,
Both those who are low and those who are high will be swept away in their
    abundance.   70
Higher than any hill [is] will they be [sent] miles into the earth.
Fortunate is the one who has been faithful all along.

"On the fourth day, a wind shall blow; it will blow so long
That castles and high towers shall fall down.
The forest will fall right onto the moor against the fierce blasts;   75
There shall each man know his [fate], and we shall know our own.

"On the fifth day it will be light; again the wind will blow,
And, I don't think it's good to needlessly expand this tale;
The woods will fall into the earth, the hills into the valleys
I hold him lord and sire who can survive all seven of these days.   80

"On the sixth day at the ninth hour, four angels shall appear,
And blow so hard with the horns in their hands that all the earth shall shake;
If any thing proves to be still alive in water or upon the land,
There it must rise and go to its judgment.

"On the seventh day, so the book told us,   85
From their graves every one, both young and old, must rise,
And come into the hall, to stand for harsh judgment:
It will be well for the man who has done any good.

"It won't help you at all to argue or to carp that these judgments are harsh;
For angels must tremble whom Christ made with his own hands,   90
And the twelve apostles who once dwelled in this land,
And our dear Lady, who never loved any wrong.

"Then our Lord will call upon Saint Mary,
To bring him the rood that stood upon Mount Calvary;
They will see where his feet stand, that his side is all bloody; 95
For our souls' food, he knowingly suffered death.

"Then our Lord will call out, without any rebuke:
'Come, blessed children scattered all over the world;
You shall all [go] to paradise, as the prophets told us,
Whoever comes into this hall, with bliss he shall be led there.' 100

"Then our Lord will call upon Satan the rude:
'Fly away, foul creature, with your accursed gang.
Fly away hence, don't stay here a minute,
But ever without end [go] down into the pit of hell pit.'"

Then the spirit said, "alack," and after that "alas!" 105
"Woe was that moment, Body, when you were born."

BIBLIOGRAPHY

All citations from the New Testament are from the New Revised Standard Version Bible (NRSV) in an edition called *The New Testament and Other Early Christian Writings: A Reader*, 2nd ed. Ed. Bart D. Ehrman (Oxford: Oxford University Press, 2004).

Abelard. "Historia Calamitatum." In *The Letters of Abelard and Heloise*. Trans. Betty Radice, 11–57. New York: Penguin Books, 1974.

Ackerman, Robert W. "*The Debate of the Body and the Soul* and Parochial Christianity." *Speculum* 37 (1962): 541–65.

Adams, J. N. *The Latin Sexual Vocabulary*. Baltimore: Johns Hopkins University Press, 1982.

Aers, David. "A Whisper in the Ear of Early Modernists: Or, Reflections on Literary Critics Writing the 'History of the Subject.'" In *Culture and History, 1350–1600: Essays on English Communities, Identities, and Writing*. Ed. David Aers, 177–202. Detroit, MI: Wayne State University Press, 1992.

Alford, John A. *A Companion to "Piers Plowman."* Berkeley: University of California Press, 1973.

———. "The Role of the Quotations in *Piers Plowman*." *Speculum* 52 (1977): 80–99.

Alfred. *King Alfred's Version of the Consolations of Boethius Done into Modern English, with an Introduction*. Trans. W. J. Sedgefield. Oxford: Oxford University Press, 1900.

Allen, Michael J. B., and Daniel G. Calder, eds. and trans. *Sources and Analogues of Old English Poetry: The Major Latin Texts in Translation*. Cambridge, UK: D. S. Brewer, 1976.

Althusser, Louis. "Ideology and Ideological State Apparatuses (Notes Towards an Investigation)." In *Lenin and Philosophy*. Trans. Ben Brewster, 177–83. London: New Left Books, 1971.
Anderson, Marcia Lee. *What Time Is It? And Other Poems*. Memphis, TN: Stafford Books, 1997.
Arendt, Hannah. *The Life of the Mind*. New York: Harcourt Brace Jovanovich, 1978.
Aristotle. *Aristotle's* De Anima *Books II, III*. Trans. D. W. Hamlyn. Clarendon Aristotle Series. Oxford: Clarendon, 1968.
———. *Aristotle's* De Anima *in the Version of William of Moerbeke and the Commentary of St. Thomas Aquinas*. Ed. and trans. Kenelm Foster and Silvester Humphries. London: Routledge and Kegan Paul Ltd., 1951.
———. *Basic Works of Aristotle*. Trans. Richard McKeon. New York: Random House, 1941.
———. *On the Generation of Animals*. Trans. A. L. Peck. Loeb Classical Library. Cambridge, MA: Harvard University Press, 1953.
———. *The Politics*. Trans. Stephen Iverson. Cambridge, UK: Cambridge University Press, 1988.
Augustine. *City of God*. Trans. Henry Bettenson. London: Penguin Books, 1972.
———. *Confessions*. Trans. R. S. Pine-Coffin. New York: Penguin Classics, 1961.
———. *Confessionum libri tredecim*. CL.0251. Corpus Christianorum, Series Latina. Turnhout, Belgium: Brepols, 1954.
———. *De civitate Dei*. Ed. B. Dombart and A. Kalb, 2 vols. Stuttgart: Teubner, [1981] 1993.
———. *Sermons on Selected Lessons of the New Testament*. Trans. R. G. Macmullen. A Library of Fathers of the Holy Catholic Church, vol. 2. Oxford: 1845.
Baker, Joan, and Susan Signe Morrison. "The Luxury of Gender: *Piers Plowman* B.9 and *The Merchant's Tale*." In *William Langland's* Piers Plowman: *A Book of Essays*. Ed. Kathleen M. Hewett-Smith, 41–67. New York: Routledge, 2001.
Balint, Bridget K. "Hildebert of Lavardin's 'Liber de querimonia' in Its Cultural Context." PhD diss., Harvard University, Cambridge, MA, 2002.
———. *Ordering Chaos: The Self and the Cosmos in Twelfth-Century Latin Prosimetrum*. Boston: Brill Academic Publishers, 2009.
Barney, Stephen. "Allegorical Visions." In *A Companion to* Piers Plowman. Ed. John A. Alford, 117–33. Berkeley: University of California Press, 1988.
Barnum, Priscilla Heath, ed. *Dives and Pauper*, 2 vols. EETS no. 275. London: Oxford University Press, 1976.
Bartlett, Anne Clark. *Male Authors, Female Readers, and Middle English Devotional Literature*. Ithaca, NY: Cornell University Press, 1995.
Batiouchkof, Theodore. "Le Débat de l'âme et du corps." *Romania* 20 (1891): 1–55, 513–78.
Baugh, Nita Scudder, ed. *A Worcestershire Miscellany, Compiled by John Northwood, c.1400. Edited from British Museum Ms. Add. 37, 787*. Philadelphia, 1956.
Beckwith, Sarah. *Christ's Body: Identity, Culture and Society in Late Medieval Writings*. London: Routledge, 1993.
———. "Passionate Regulation: Enclosure, Ascesis, and the Feminist Imaginary." *South Atlantic Quarterly* 93 (1994): 803–24.

Bennett, J. A. W. *The Parlement of Foules: An Interpretation.* Oxford: Clarendon, 1957.
Bernardus Sylvestris. *Bernardus Sylvestris' Cosmographia.* Ed. Peter Dronke and trans. Winthrop Wetherbee. New York: Columbia University Press, 1973.
———. *S. Bernardi: Opera.* Ed. J. Leclercq and M. Rochais. Rome: Editiones Cistercienses, 1968.
Bernauer, James, and David Rasmussen, eds. *The Final Foucault.* Cambridge, MA: MIT Press, 1991.
Bestul, Thomas. *Satire and Allegory in Wynnere and Wastoure.* Lincoln: University of Nebraska Press, 1974.
———. *Piers Plowman as a Fourteenth-Century Apocalypse.* New Brunswick, NJ: Rutgers University Press, 1962.
Boethius. *Anicii Manlii Severini Boethii Philosophiae consolatio.* Ed. Ludovicus Bieler. Corpus Christianorum, Series Latina, no. 94. Turnholt: Brepols, 1957.
———. *Boethius: The Theological Tractates and the Consolation of Philosophy.* Ed. E. K. Rand and trans. H. F. Stewart and S. J. Tester. Cambridge, MA: Harvard University Press, 1973.
———. *The Consolation of Philosophy.* Trans. V. E. Watts. London and New York: Penguin Books, 1969.
The Book of Vices and Virtues. Ed. W. Nelson Francis. EETS Original Series 217. Oxford: Oxford University Press, 1942.
Bossy, John. "Blood and Baptism: Kinship, Community and Christianity in Western Europe from the Fourteenth to the Seventeenth Centuries." In *Sanctity and Secularity: The Church and the World.* Ed. Derek Baker, 129–43. Studies in Church History 10. New York: Harper & Row, 1973.
———. "Medieval Debates of Body and Soul." *Comparative Literature* 28 (1976): 144–63.
Boswell, John. *The Kindness of Strangers: The Abandonment of Children in Western Europe from Late Antiquity to the Renaissance.* Chicago: University of Chicago Press, 1988.
Bowers, John M. *The Crisis of Will in* Piers Plowman. Washington, DC: The Catholic University of America Press, 1986.
Boyle, Leonard. "The Fourth Lateran Council and Manuals of Popular Theology." In *The Popular Literature of Medieval England.* Ed. Thomas Heffernan. Knoxville: University of Tennessee Press, 1985.
Brown, Peter. *The Body and Society: Men, Women, and Sexual Renunciation in Early Christianity.* New York: Columbia University Press, 1988.
Bullough, Vern. *Sexual Variance in Society and History.* Chicago: University of Chicago Press, 1976.
Butler, Judith. *Bodies That Matter: On the Discursive Limits of "Sex."* London and New York: Routledge, 1993.
———. *Excitable Speech: A Politics of the Performative.* New York: Routledge, 1997.
———. *Gender Trouble: Feminism and the Subversion of Identity.* New York: Routledge, 1990.
———. *The Psychic Life of Power: Theories in Subjection.* Stanford, CA: Stanford University Press, 1999.

———. *Undoing Gender*. New York: Routledge, 2004.

Bynum, Caroline Walker. "Did the Twelfth Century Discover the Individual?" In *Jesus as Mother: Studies in the Spirituality of the High Middle Ages*, 82–109. Berkeley: University of California Press, 1982.

———. *Fragmentation and Redemption: Essays on Gender and the Human Body in Medieval Religion*. New York: Zone Books, 1992.

———. *The Resurrection of the Body in Western Christianity, 200–1336*. New York: Columbia University Press, 1995.

Cannon, Christopher. *The Grounds of English Literature*. Oxford: Oxford University Press, 2004.

Carrette, Jeremy R. *Foucault and Religion: Spiritual Corporality and Political Spirituality*. New York: Routledge, 2000.

Carruthers, Mary. *The Book of Memory: A Study of Memory in Medieval Culture*. Cambridge, UK: Cambridge University Press, 1990.

Cartlidge, Neil. "Aubrey de Bassingbourn, Ida de Beauchamp, and the Context of the 'Estrif de deus dames' in Oxford, Bodleian Library Ms. Digby 86." *Notes and Queries* 47; 4 (2000): 411–15.

———. "In the Silence of a Midwinter Night: A Re-Evaluation of the *Visio Philiberti*." *Medium Aevum* 75; 1 (2006): 24–46.

Chaucer, Geoffrey. *The Riverside Chaucer*, 3rd ed. Ed. Larry D. Benson. Boston: Houghton Mifflin, 1987.

Conlee, John W. *Middle English Debate Poetry: A Critical Anthology*. East Lansing, MI: Colleagues Press, 1991.

Cooper, Helen. "Gender and Personification in *Piers Plowman*." *Yearbook of Langland Studies* 5 (1991): 31–48.

Copeland, Rita. *Rhetoric, Hermeneutics and Translation in the Middle Ages: Academic Traditions and Vernacular Texts*. Cambridge, UK: Cambridge University Press, 1991.

———, and Marjorie Curry Woods. "Classroom and Confession." In *The Cambridge History of Medieval English Literature*. Ed. David Wallace, 376–406. Cambridge, UK: Cambridge University Press, 1999.

Corrie, Marilyn. "Further Information on the Origins of Oxford, Bodleian Library, Ms. Digby 86." *Notes and Queries* 46; 1 (1999): 430–34.

Creek, Mary Immaculate. "The Four Daughters of God in the Gesta Romanorum and the Court of Sapience." *PMLA* 57 (1942): 951–65.

Dan, Michel. *Ayenbite of Inwyt or Remorse of Conscience*. Ed. Richard Morris and Pamela Gradon. EETS Original Series No. 23, 1866. Oxford: Oxford University Press, 1965.

Davlin, Mary Clemente. "*Kynde knowyng* as a Middle English Equivalent for 'Wisdom' in *Piers Plowman* B." *Medium Aevum* 50 (1981): 5–17.

de Lorris, Guillaume, and Jean de Meun. *The Romance of the Rose*. Trans. Charles Dahlberg. Princeton, NJ: Princeton University Press, 1995.

———. *Le Roman de la Rose*. Ed. Felix Lecoy. Paris: Librarie Honoré Champion, 1985.

De Man, Paul. "The Epistemology of Metaphor." In *Aesthetic Ideology*, 239–62. Minneapolis: University of Minnesota Press, 1996.

Dobson, E. J. "The Date and Composition of *Ancrene Wisse.*" The British Academy Gollancz Lecture, May 25, 1966. *Proceedings of the British Academy* 52 (1966): 181–208.
Dolan, T. P. "The Date of *Ancrene Wisse:* A Corroborative Note." *Notes and Queries* 21 (1974): 322–23.
Donaldson, E. Talbot. Piers Plowman: *The C-Text and Its Poet.* New Haven, CT: Yale University Press, 1949.
Dreyfus, Hubert, and Paul Rabinow, eds. *Michel Foucault: Beyond Structuralism and Hermeneutics.* Chicago: University of Chicago Press, 1982.
Dudley, Louise. *The Egyptian Elements in the Legend of the Body and the Soul.* Bryn Mawr College Monographs No. 8. Bryn Mawr, PA: Bryn Mawr College, 1911.
Du Méril, Edélstand, ed. *Poésies populaires latines antérieures au douzième siècle.* Paris, 1843.
Duncan, J. Robert. "The Textual Context of the Vernon Manuscript." PhD diss., University of Saskatchewan, Saskatoon, Canada, 2000.
Dunning, T. P. Piers Plowman: *An Interpretation of the A-Text.* London: Longmans, 1937.
Eggebroten, Anne. "Sawles Warde: A Retelling of *De Anima* for a Female Audience." *Mediavalia: A Journal of Medieval Studies* 10 (1988): 27–47.
Evans, Ruth. "Virginities." *The Cambridge Companion to Medieval Women's Writing.* Ed. Carolyn Dinshaw and David Wallace. Cambridge, UK: Cambridge University Press, 2003.
Fein, Susanna "Herbs, Birds, and Cryptic Words for English Devotional Readers." *Essays in Medieval Studies* 15 (1998): 35–44.
Felman, Shoshana. *The Scandal of the Speaking Body: Don Juan with J. L. Austin or Seduction in Two Languages.* Trans. Catherine Porter. Ithaca, NY: Cornell University Press, 1983.
Finch, Casey. "Introduction," in *The Complete Works of the Pearl Poet.* Berkeley: University of California Press, 1993.
Fletcher, Angus. *Allegory: The Theory of a Symbolic Mode.* Ithaca, NY: Cornell University Press, 1964.
Foucault, Michel. *Discipline and Punish: The Birth of the Prison.* Trans. Alan Sheridan. New York: Vintage Books, 1979.
———. *The History of Sexuality: Volume One, An Introduction.* Trans. Robert Hurley. New York: Vintage Books, 1978.
———. *Religion and Culture: Michel Foucault.* Selected and ed. Jeremy R. Carrette. New York: Routledge, 1999.
Fowler, Elizabeth. "Civil Death and the Maiden: Agency and the Conditions of Contract in *Piers Plowman.*" *Speculum* 70 (1995): 760–92.
Frantzen, Allen J. *Before the Closet: Same-Sex Love from* Beowulf *to* Angels in America. Chicago: University of Chicago Press, 1998.
Furnivall, F. J., ed. *The Minor Poems of the Vernon Manuscript.* 2 vols. EETS Original Series Nos. 98, 117. London: Kegan Paul, Trench, and Trubner, 1901.
Galen. "The Soul's Dependence on the Body." In *Selected Works.* Ed. and trans. P. N. Singer, 150–76. Oxford: Oxford University Press, 1997.
Galloway, Andrew. "Intellectual Pregnancy, Metaphysical Femininity, and the Social

Doctrine of the Trinity in *Piers Plowman*." *The Yearbook of Langland Studies* 12 (1998): 117–52.

Gardner, John. *The Alliterative Morte Arthure, The Owl and the Nightingale and Five Other Middle English Poems.* Carbondale: Southern Illinois University Press, 1973.

Gatens, Moira. *Imaginary Bodies: Ethics, Power and Corporeality.* London and New York: Routledge, 1996.

Gaunt, Simon. "Bel Acueil and the Improper Allegory of the *Romance of the Rose*. In *New Medieval Literatures,* vol. 2. Ed. Rita Copeland and David Lawton, 65–93. Oxford: Clarendon, 1999.

Georgianna, Linda. *The Solitary Self: Individuality in the "Ancrene Wisse."* Cambridge, MA: Harvard University Press, 1981.

Grosseteste, Robert. "Chateau d'Amour." In *The Middle English Translations of Robert Grosseteste's Chateau d'Amour.* Ed. Kari Sajavaara. Mémoires de la Société Néophilologique de Helsinki, 32. Helsinki, Finland: Uusfilologinen yhdistys, 1967.

Grosz, Elizabeth. *Volatile Bodies: Toward a Corporeal Feminism.* Bloomington: Indiana University Press, 1994.

Guibert of Nogent. "Monodiae." In *Self and Society in Medieval France.* Ed. and trans. John F. Benton. Medieval Academy of America Reprints for Teaching. Toronto: University of Toronto Press, 1984.

Halpern, David. *How to Do the History of Homosexuality.* Chicago: The University of Chicago Press, 2002.

Hanna, Ralph. "School and Scorn: Gender in *Piers Plowman*." In *New Medieval Literatures,* vol. 2. Ed. Rita Copeland and David Lawton, 213–27. Oxford: Clarendon, 1999.

Harvey, E. Ruth. *The Inward Wits: Psychological Theory in the Middle Ages and the Renaissance.* London: Warburg Institute, 1975.

———. "Langland's *Kynde Knowing* and the Quest for Christ." *Modern Philology* 80 (1982): 242–55.

———. Piers Plowman *and the Problem of Belief.* Toronto: University of Toronto Press, 1992.

Hasenfratz, Robert, ed. *Ancrene Wisse.* Kalamazoo, MI.: Medieval Institute Publications, 2000.

Hassel, Julie. *Choosing Not to Marry: Women and Autonomy in the Katherine Group.* New York: Routledge, 2002.

Heningham, Eleanor K. *An Early Latin Debate of the Body and Soul.* Menasha, WI: George Banta Publishing Company, 1937.

———. "The Precursors of the Worcester Fragments." *PMLA* 55 (1940): 291–307.

Herbert, Bruce. "A Will with a Reason: Theological Developments in the C-Revision of *Piers Plowman*." In *Religion in the Poetry and Drama of the Late Middle Ages in England: The J. A. W. Bennett Memorial Lectures, Perugia, 1988.* Ed. Piero Boitani and Anna Torti, 149–61. Cambridge, UK: D. S. Brewer, 1990.

Hildebert of Lavardin. *Hildeberts Prosimetrum De Querimonia und die Gedichte eines Anonymus.* Ed. Peter Orth. Vienna: Osterreichische Akademie der Wissenschaften, Arbeiten zur mittel- und neulateinischen Philologie, 2000.

———. *Les Mélanges poétiques d'Hildebert de Lavardin.* Ed. Barthélemy Hauréau. Paris: Pedone-Lauriel, 1882.

Hillman, David, and Carla Mazzio, eds. *The Body in Parts: Fantasies of Corporeality in Early Modern Europe*. New York: Routledge, 1997.
Hobbes, Thomas. *Leviathan*. Ed. C. B. MacPherson. London: Penguin Books, 1982.
Hodgson, Phyllis, ed. *The Cloud of Unknowing*. EETS. London: Oxford University Press, 1955.
Hume, Kathryn. *The Owl and the Nightingale: The Poem and Its Critics*. Toronto: University of Toronto Press, 1975.
Huppé, Bernard F., and D. W. Robertson. Piers Plowman *and Scriptural Tradition*. Princeton, NJ: Princeton University Press, 1951.
Innes-Parker, Catherine. "Fragmentation and Reconstruction: Images of the Female Body in *Ancrene Wisse* and the Katherine Group." *Comitatus: A Journal of Medieval and Renaissance Studies* 26 (1995): 27–52.
Jacobs, Nicholas. "Typology of Debate and the Interpretation of *Wynnere and Wastoure*." *Review of English Studies* 36 (1985): 481–500.
Johnson, Barbara. *The Wake of Deconstruction*. Oxford: Blackwell, 1994.
Jones, Charles. *Grammatical Gender in English: 950–1250*. London: C. Helm and Methuen, 1988.
Justice, Steven. "The Genres of *Piers Plowman*." *Viator: Medieval and Renaissance Studies* 19 (1988): 291–306.
———, and Kathryn Kerby-Fulton. "Langlandian Reading Circles and the Civil Service in London and Dublin, 1380–1427." In *New Medieval Literatures*. Ed. Wendy Scase, Rita Copeland, and David Lawton, 59–83. Oxford: Clarendon, 1997.
Kantorowicz, Ernst H. *The King's Two Bodies: A Study in Medieval Political Theology*. Princeton, NJ: Princeton University Press, 1957.
Karras, Ruth Mazo. "Gendered Sin and Misogyny in John of Bromyard's *Summa Predicantium*." *Traditio* 47 (1992): 233–57.
Kay, Sarah. "Women's Body of Knowledge: Epistemology and Misogyny in the *Romance of the Rose*." In *Framing Medieval Bodies*. Ed. Sarah Kay and Miri Rubin. Manchester, UK: Manchester University Press, 1994. New York: St. Martin's Press, 1994.
Kelly, Douglas. *Internal Difference and Meanings in the "Roman de la Rose."* Madison, WI: University of Wisconsin Press, 1995.
Kenny, Anthony, Norman Kretzmann, and Jan Pinborg, eds. *The Cambridge History of Later Medieval Philosophy: From the Rediscovery of Aristotle to the Disintegration of Scholasticism 1100–1600*. Cambridge, UK: Cambridge University Press, 1982
Kirk, Elizabeth D. *The Dream Thought of* Piers Plowman. New Haven, CT: Yale University Press, 1972.
———. "Kynde Knowing as a Major Theme in *Piers Plowman* B." *Review of English Studies* 22 (1971): 1–19.
Kurath, Hans, Sherman M. Kuhn, Robert E. Lewis, and John Reidy, eds. *The Middle English Dictionary*. Ann Arbor: University of Michigan Press, 1952–present.
Langland, William. *"Piers Plowman" by William Langland. An Edition of the C-Text*, ed. Derek Pearsall. 1978. Exeter, UK: University of Exeter Press, 1994.
———. *The Vision of* Piers Plowman: *The B Text*. 2nd ed. Everyman's Library. Ed. A.V.C. Schmidt. London: J. M. Dent, 1978; 1995.
Lapidge, Michael. *Anglo-Latin Literature 600–899*. London: Hambledon Press, 1996.
Lawton, David. "The Subject of *Piers Plowman*." *The Yearbook of Langland Studies* 1 (1987): 1–30.

Lees, Clare. "Gender and Exchange in *Piers Plowman*." In *Class and Gender in Early English Literature*. Ed. Britton Harwood and Gillian Overing, 112–30. Bloomington: Indiana University Press, 1994.

Leicester, H. Marshall. *The Disenchanted Self: Representing the Subject in the Canterbury Tales*. Berkeley: University of California Press, 1990.

Lerer, Seth. *Boethius and Dialogue: Literary Method in the Consolation of Philosophy*. Princeton, NJ: Princeton University Press, 1985.

Linow, Wilhelm, ed. "þe Desputisoun between þe Bodi and þe Soule." *Erlanger Beitrage zür Englischen Philologie* I (1889).

Lochrie, Karma. "Desiring Foucault." *Journal of Medieval and Renaissance Studies* 27 (1997): 3–16.

Machosky, Brenda. "The Face That Is Not a Face: The Phenomenology of the Soul in the Allegory of the *Psychomachia*." *Exemplaria* XV; 1 (Spring 2003): 1–38.

Macrobius, Ambrosius Theodosius. *Commentary on the Dream of Scipio*. Trans. William Harris Stahl. New York: Columbia University Press, 1952.

Malamud, Martha A. *A Poetics of Transformation: Prudentius and Classical Mythology*. Ithaca, NY: Cornell University Press, 1989.

Mannyng, Robert (of Brunne). *Handlyng Synne*. Ed. F. J. Furnivall, EETS Nos. 119 and 123. London: Kegan Paul, Trench, and Trubner, 1901–3.

Martianus Capella. *Martianus Capella and the Seven Liberal Arts, Volume II: The Marriage of Philology and Mercury*. Trans. Richard Johnson, William Harris Stahl, and E. L. Burge. New York: Columbia University Press, 1977.

McEvoy, James. "Grosseteste on the Soul's Care for the Body: A New Text and New Sources for the Idea." In *Aspectus et Affectus: Essays and Editions in Grosseteste and Medieval Intellectual Life in Honor of Richard C. Dales*. Ed. Gunar Freibergs, 37–56. New York: AMS Press, 1993.

McGinn, Bernard, ed. *Three Treatises on Man: A Cistercian Anthropology*. Cistercian Fathers Series: No. 24. Kalamazoo, MI: Cistercian Publications, 1977.

Middleton, Anne. "Acts of Vagrancy: The C Version 'Autobiography' and the Statute of 1388." In *Written Work: Langland, Labor and Authorship*. Ed. Stephen Justice and Kathryn Kerby-Fulton. Philadelphia: University of Pennsylvania Press, 1997.

———. "Narration and the Invention of Experience: Episodic Form in *Piers Plowman*." In *The Wisdom of Poetry: Essays in Early English Literature in Honor of Morton W. Bloomfield*. Ed. Larry Benson and Siegfried Wenzel, 91–122. Kalamazoo, MI: Medieval Institute Publications, 1982.

———. "William Langland's 'Kynde Name': Authorial Signature and Social Identity in Late Fourteenth-Century England." In *Literary Practice and Social Change in Britain, 1390–1530*. Ed. Lee Patterson, 15–82. Berkeley: University of California Press, 1993.

Millett, Bella. *Ancrene Wisse, the Katherine Group, and the Wooing Group. Annotated Bibliographies of Old and Middle English Literature*. Vol. II. London: D. S. Brewer, 1996.

———, and Jocelyn Wogan-Browne, eds. *Medieval English Prose for Women: Selections from the Katherine Group and "Ancrene Wisse."* Oxford: Clarendon, 1992.

Mills, Robert. "Seeing Face to Face: Troubled Looks in the Katherine Group." In *Troubled Vision: Gender, Sexuality, and Sight in Medieval Text and Image*. Ed. Emma Campbell and Robert Mills, 117–36. New York: Palgrave Macmillan, 2004.

Minnis, Alastair J., and A. B. Scott, eds., with assistance of David Wallace. *Medieval Literary Theory and Criticism, c. 1100–1375: The Commentary Tradition.* Oxford: Clarendon, 1988.

Mirk, John. *Instructions for Parish Priests.* Ed. Edward Peacock. EETS. London: Kegan Paul, Trench, and Trubner, 1868.

Mockridge, Diane. "The Order of the Texts in the Bodley 34 Manuscript: The Function of Repetition and Recall in a Manuscript Addressed to Nuns." *Essays in Medieval Studies* 3 (1986): 207–18.

Moffat, Douglas, *The Soul's Address to the Body: The Worcester Fragments.* East Lansing, MI: Colleagues Press, 1987.

———, ed. and trans. *The Old English Soul and Body.* Cambridge, UK: D. S. Brewer, 1990.

Morris, Colin. *The Discovery of the Individual 1050–1200.* London: SPCK, 1972.

Morris, Richard, ed. *The Pricke of Conscience.* Berlin: A. Asher, 1863; London: Philological Society, 1863.

Murray, Jacqueline. "The Absent Penitent: The Cure of Women's Souls and Confessors' Manuals in Thirteenth-Century England." In *Women, The Book, and the Godly.* Ed. L. Smith and J. H. M Taylor, 13–25. Cambridge, UK: Cambridge University Press, 1995.

———. "Gendered Souls in Sexed Bodies: The Male Construction of Female Sexuality in Some Medieval Confessors' Manuals." In *Handling Sin: Confession in the Middle Ages.* Ed. Peter Biller and A. J. Minnis, 79–92. York, UK: York Medieval Press, 1998.

Muscatine, Charles. "The Emergence of Psychological Allegory in Old French Romance." *PMLA* 68 (Dec. 1953): 1160–82.

Newman, Barbara. *God and the Goddesses: Vision, Poetry and Belief in the Middle-Ages.* Philadelphia: University of Pennsylvania Press, 2003.

———. *From Virile Woman to WomanChrist: Studies in Medieval Religion and Literature.* Philadelphia: University of Pennsylvania Press, 1995.

O'Daly, Gerald. *The Poetry of Boethius.* Chapel Hill: University of North Carolina Press, 1991.

Ong, Walter. "Latin Language Study as Renaissance Puberty Rite." *Studies in Philology* 56 (1959): 103–24.

Pantin, W. A. *The English Church in the Fourteenth Century.* Toronto: University of Toronto Press, 1955.

Pasnau, Robert. "Human Nature." In *The Cambridge Companion to Medieval Philosophy.* Ed. A. S. McGrade. Cambridge, UK: Cambridge University Press, 2003.

Patterson, Lee W. "Chaucerian Confession: Penitential Literature the Pardoner." *Medievalia et Humanistica* 7 (1976): 153–73.

Paxson, James J. "Gender Personified, Personification Gendered, and the Body Figuralized in *Piers Plowman.*" *The Yearbook of Langland Studies* 12 (1998): 65–96.

———. *The Poetics of Personification.* Cambridge, UK: Cambridge University Press, 1994.

Pearsall, Derek, ed. *Studies in the Vernon Manuscript.* Cambridge, UK: D. S. Brewer, 1990.

Perraud, Louis, and Ian Thomson, eds. and trans. *Ten Latin Schooltexts of the Later Middle Ages: Translated Selections.* Lewiston, NY: E. Mellen Press, 1990.

Philips, Helen. "Dreams and Dream Lore." In *Studies in the Harley Manuscript: The Scribes, Contents, and Social Contexts of British Library Ms. Harley 2253*. Ed. Susanna Fein. Kalamazoo, MI: TEAMS, 2000.

Plato. *Collected Dialogues of Plato*, Bollingen Series LXXI. 14th printing. Ed. Edith Hamilton and Huntington Cairns. Princeton, NJ: Princeton University Press, 1989.

———. *Timaeus*. Trans. Francis M. Cornford. New York: Macmillan, 1959.

Price, Jocelyn. "'Inner' and 'Outer': Conceptualizing the Body in *Ancrene Wisse* and Aelred's *De Institutione Inclusarum*." In *Medieval English Religious and Ethical Literature: Essays in Honor of G. H. Russell*. Ed. Gregory Kratzman and James Simpson, 192–208. London: D. S. Brewer, 1986.

Prudentius. *Psychomachia*. Loeb Classical Library. Ed. and trans. H. J. Thomson. Cambridge, MA: Harvard University Press, 1949.

Pseudo-Cicero. *Rhetorica ad Herennium*. Loeb Classical Library. Trans. Harry Caplan. Cambridge, MA: Harvard University Press, 1954.

Pugh, Tison. *Queering Medieval Genres*. New York: Palgrave Macmillan, 2004.

Purdon, Liam O. "'Als I Lay in a Winteris Nyt' and the Second Death." In *Mindful Spirit in Late Medieval Literature: Essays in Honor of Elizabeth D. Kirk*, 45–56. New York: Palgrave Macmillan, 2006.

Quintillian. *Institutio Oratoria*. Loeb Classical Library. Trans. and ed. H. E. Butler. Cambridge, MA: Harvard University Press, 1920.

Rambuss, Richard. "What It Feels Like for a Boy: Shakespeare's *Venus and Adonis*." In *The Blackwell Companions to Shakespeare: The Poems, Problem Comedies, Late Plays*. Ed. Jean Howard and Richard Dutton, 240–58. London: Blackwell, 2003.

Raymo, Richard. "Works of Religious and Philosophical Instruction." In *A Manual of the Writings in Middle English, 1050–1500*. Ed. Albert Hartung, 2255–378. New Haven: Connecticut Academy of Arts and Sciences, 1986.

Reed, Thomas, Jr. *Middle English Debate Poetry and the Aesthetics of Irresolution*. Columbia and London: University of Missouri Press, 1990.

Rhodes, Jim. *Poetry Does Theology*. Notre Dame, IN: Notre Dame University Press, 2001.

Robertson, Elizabeth. *Early English Devotional Prose and the Female Audience*. Knoxville: University of Tennessee Press, 1990.

———. "Measurement and the 'Feminine' in *Piers Plowman*: A Response to Recent Studies of Langland and Gender." In *William Langland's Piers Plowman: A Book of Essays*. Ed. Kathleen M. Hewett-Smith, 167–92. New York: Routledge, 2001.

Root, Jerry. *"Space to Speke": The Confessional Subject in Medieval Literature*. New York: Peter Lang, 1997.

Rubin, Gayle. "The Traffic in Women: Notes on the Political Economy of 'Sex.'" In *Towards an Anthropology of Women* Ed. Rayna Rapp Reiter, 157–210. New York: Monthly Review Press, 1975.

Rubin, Miri. *Corpus Christi: The Eucharist in Late Medieval Culture*. Cambridge, UK: Cambridge University Press, 1991.

Salih, Sarah. "Performing Virginity: Sex and Violence in the Katherine Group." In *Constructions of Widowhood and Virginity in the Middle Ages*. Ed. Cindy L. Carlson and Angela Jane Weisl, 95–112. New York: Palgrave Macmillan, 1999.

Sawles Warde and "The Conflict of Wit & Will." Ed. R. M. Wilson and Bruce Dickins.

Leeds, UK: Titus Wilson of Kendal, School of English Language at the University of Leeds, 1938.
Schiebinger, Londa. "Introduction." In *Feminism and the Body*. Ed. Londa Schiebinger. Oxford: Oxford University Press, 2000.
Schmidt, A. V. C. "Langland and Scholastic Philosophy." *Medium Aevum* 38 (1969): 134–56.
Schmitt, F. S., and R. W. Southern, eds. *Memorials of St. Anselm in Auctores britannici medii aevi*. London: Oxford University Press for the British Academy, 1969.
Schroeder, H. J. *Disciplinary Decrees of the General Councils: Text, Translation and Commentary*. St. Louis: B. Herder, 1937.
Sedgwick, Eve Kosofsky. *Between Men: English Literature and Homosocial Desire*. New York: Columbia University Press, 1985.
Simpson, James. "Desire and the Scriptural Text: Will as Reader in *Piers Plowman*." In *Criticism and Dissent in the Middle Ages*. Ed. Rita Copeland, 215–43. Cambridge, UK: Cambridge University Press, 1996.
———. *Piers Plowman: An Introduction to the B-Text*. London: Longman, 1990.
———. "The Power of Impropriety: Authorial Naming in *Piers Plowman*." In *William Langland's Piers Plowman: A Book of Essays*. Ed. Kathleen M. Hewett-Smith, 145–65. New York: Routledge, 2001.
———. *Sciences and the Self in Medieval Poetry: Alan de Lille's Anticlaudianus and John Gower's Confessio Amantis*. Cambridge, UK: Cambridge University Press, 1995.
Smalley, Beryl. *The Study of the Bible in the Middle Ages*. Oxford: Clarendon, 1941.
Solterer, Helen. *The Master and Minerva: Disputing Women in French Medieval Culture*. Berkeley: University of California Press, 1995.
Southern, R. W. *Medieval Humanism and Other Studies*. Oxford: Blackwell, 1970.
Spade, Paul Vincent, ed. and trans. *Five Texts on the Mediaeval Problem of Universals: Porphyry, Boethius, Abelard, Duns Scotus, Ockham*. Indianapolis, IN: Hackett Publishers, 1994.
Spelman, Elizabeth. "Woman as Body: Ancient and Contemporary Views." *Feminist Studies* 8; 1 (1982): 109–31.
Stock, Lorraine Kochanske. "Will, Actyf, Pacience, and Liberum Arbitrium: Two Recurring Quotations in Langland's Revisions of *Piers Plowman* C Text, Passus V, XV, XVI." *Texas Studies in Literature & Language* 30 (1988): 461–77.
Tavormina, M. Teresa. *Kindly Similitude: Marriage and Family in Piers Plowman*. Cambridge, UK: D. S. Brewer, 1995.
Teskey, Gordon. *Allegory and Violence*. Ithaca, NY: Cornell University Press, 1996.
Tierney, Brian. "Natura id est Deus: A Case of Juristic Pantheism?" *Journal of the History of Ideas* 24 (1963): 307–22.
Traver, Hope Emily. *The Four Daughters of God*. Baltimore: Bryn Mawr Monographs 6, 1907.
———. "The Four Daughters of God: A Mirror of Changing Doctrine." *PMLA* 40; 1 (1925): 44–92.
Usk, Thomas. *The Testament of Love*. Ed. R. Allen Shoaf. Kalamazoo, MI: Western Michigan University (TEAMS), 1998.
Utley, Frances L. "Dialogues, Debates and Catechisms." In *A Manual of the Writings in Middle English*, vol. 3. Ed. A. E. Hartung, 669–745. Hamden, CT: Connecticut Academy of Arts and Sciences, 1972.

Varnhagen, Hermann, ed. "Der Altesten Altfranzosische Bearbeitung Des Streites Zwichen Leib Und Seele." In *Erlanger Beitrage zür englischen Philologie*, vol. 1. Leipzig: 1889.

Vogel, Sister Mary Ursula. *Some Aspects of the Horse and Rider Analogy in "The Debate Between the Body and the Soul."* Washington, DC: Catholic University of America Press, 1948.

von Karajan, Theodor Georg, ed. *Frühlingsgabe für Freunde alterer Literatur.* Vienna: 1839.

Wallace, David, ed. *Cambridge History of Medieval English Literature.* Cambridge, UK: Cambridge University Press, 1999.

Walther, Hans. *Das Streitgedicht in Der Lateinischen Literatur des Mittelalters.* Vol. 5, pt. 2 of *Quellen und Untersuchungen zür Lateinischen Philologie des Mittelalters.* Munich: 1920.

Warner, Marina. *Monuments & Maidens: The Allegory of the Female Form.* New York: Atheneum Press, 1985.

Warner, R. D-N., ed. *Early English Homilies from the Twelfth Century Ms. Vesp. D. XIV.* EETS No. 152, 1917. New York: Kraus Reprint Co., 1971.

Wetherbee, Winthrop. *Platonism and Poetry in the Twelfth Century: The Literary Influence of the School at Chartres.* Princeton, NJ: Princeton University Press, 1972.

———. "The School of Chartres." In *A Companion to Philosophy in the Middle Ages.* Ed. Jorge J. C. Gracia and Timothy B. Noone, 36–44. Oxford: Blackwell, 2003.

White, Hugh. *Nature and Salvation in* Piers Plowman. Cambridge, UK: D. S. Brewer, 1988.

Whitehead, Christina. *Castles of the Mind: A Study in Medieval Architectural Allegory.* Cardiff: University of Wales Press, 2003.

Whitman, Jon. *Allegory: The Dynamics of an Ancient and Medieval Technique.* Cambridge, MA: Harvard University Press, 1987.

Wogan-Browne, Jocelyn. "Chaste Bodies: Frames and Experiences." In *Framing Medieval Bodies.* Ed. Sarah Kay and Miri Rubin, 24–42. Manchester, UK: Manchester University Press, 1994.

Wright, Thomas. *The Latin Poems Commonly Attributed to Walter Mapes.* London: Camden Society, 1841.

Wynnere and Wastoure and The Parlement of the Thre Ages. Ed. Warren Ginsberg. Kalamazoo, MI: Medieval Institute Publications, Western Michigan University (TEAMS), 1992.

Yates, Frances A. *The Art of Memory.* Chicago: University of Chicago University Press, 1966.

Zacher, Samantha. *Preaching the Converted: The Style and Rhetoric of the Vercelli Homilies.* Toronto: University of Toronto Press, 2009.

Zink, Michel. "The Allegorical Poem as Interior Memoir." Trans. Margaret Miner and Kevin Brownlee. *Yale French Studies* 70 (1986): 100–126.

INDEX

Abelard, Peter, 133
Ackerman, Robert, 13, 110–11, 112
Alfred, King, 47n34, 49
allegorical characters: acting beyond limits of names, 38–39, 47; embodiment of, 48–49; female tutelary figures, 49, 54n47, 68, 171, 172; limited by their names, 38–39, 48, 50, 53–54, 175. *See also* "Als I Lay"; body; Body/Soul; *Consolation of Philosophy*; "In a Thestri Stude"; "Liber de Querimonia"; *Piers Plowman*; *Psychomachia*; "Sawles Warde"; soul; "Visio Philiberti"
allegories, 3–5, 74n4, 199; definitions of, 5n4; hierarchies present in, 7, 20–22, 74; and philosophy, 35, 44, 54; psychological, 56. *See also* Body/Soul debates; personification allegories
"Als I Lay in a Winteris Nyt," 3–4, 29, 108–21, 124–38; Body and Soul both male, 124, 126, 127; Body and Soul's relationship, as brotherly, 132; Body and Soul's relationship, as enmeshed, 115, 119–20, 121, 128, 130, 135, 138; Body and Soul's relationship, as pedagogical, 131–32; Body and Soul's relationship, as queer, 124, 129; Body and Soul's relationship, as self-love, 124, 129; Body and Soul's relationship, Soul as loving teacher, 128–30; Body as beast, 118–19; Body's voice, 115–17, 119, 120–21; compared to "Visio Philiberti," 111, 125–26; compared to "Un Samedi Par Nuit," 124–25, 126–27; compared to Foucault, 130–31, 134–36; as disputation, 133, 137; as epitome of Body/Soul debates, 109, 111; as pedagogy, 133–34, 136–37; *prosopopeia* in, 116, 118, 121; as psychological realism, 112; publication history, 108–9,

Index

110; punishment in, 114; responsibility for sin, 114, 117–18, 127–28, 129; as *somnium,* 113; Soul turning in on itself, 136; as *sowlehele,* 111, 137; summary, 109, 112, 132–33; *ubi sunt,* 115–16

anchoresses, 140, 145. *See also* "Sawles Warde"

ancilla/domina, 62n64. *See also* "Liber de Querimonia"; "Visio Philiberti"

ancre or *ancrene. See* anchoresses; "Sawles Warde"

Ancrene Wisse, 142n5, 145–46

Anderson, Marcia Lee. *See* "Debate of the Body and Soul: A.D. 1949"

anima, animus. See soul

Anglicus, Bartholomaeus, 120

Aquinas, Thomas, 90n22

Arendt, Hannah, 96n31

Aristotle, 15–16, 20n36, 53, 120; separability of soul and body, 15, 26, 90–91

Augustine, Saint, 16–17, 21, 88n19; on the soul, 93–94; on the will, 97, 98

Austin, J. L., 67

Ayenbite of Inwit (Michel of Northgate), 154–55

Baker, Susan, 176

Balint, Bridget Kennedy, 43n25, 58, 59n59, 60, 62n64, 64

Barney, Stephan A., 47n33

Batiouchkof, Theodore, 6n6, 56n51

Bennett, J. A. W., 182n21

Boethius, Anicius Manlius Severinus. *See Consolation of Philosophy, The*

body or Body: as beast, 118–19; capable of speech, 199; as castle or house, 2, 58, 139, 149, 189; as discursive, 27; as feminine, 25–26, 28, 52–53, 59, 61, 142, 148; guilt of, 86–87; as locus of sin, 142–43; other words for, 61; as prison of soul, 42, 145; as vessel of soul, 139, 153. *See also* "Als I Lay"; "In a Thestri Stude"; "Liber de Querimonia"; *Piers Plowman;* "Sawles Warde"; self; "Visio Philiberti"

Body/Soul: dualism, 4, 13, 22, 198–99, 202, 203; feminist criticism of, 25–26; and gender, 5, 7–8, 21–23, 67–68, 166, 197, 201; hierarchy of, 7, 15, 22, 68, 90–91; love/hate relationship, 124. *See also* "Als I Lay"; body; "In a Thestri Stude"; "Liber de Querimonia"; soul; "Visio Philiberti"

Body/Soul debates, 2–4, 74, 98, 103, 112; in Anglo-Saxon, 3n2, 86–87; emergence of, 97; in Middle English, 3n2, 6; in Old English, 6, 56; popularity, 18, 71–72; prefigured in *Psychomachia,* 42; as *sowlehele,* 13, 99

body studies, 8, 27

Bossy, Michel-Andre, 63, 65

Bossy, John, 175n8

Boswell, John, 133n38

Bowers, John, 94n27, 169n2

Butler, Judith, 7n11, 26–27, 108n8, 121, 135

Bynum, Caroline Walker, 8n13, 21, 88–89

Cannon, Christopher, 113n16

Carruthers, Mary, 18

Cartlidge, Neil, 63, 64n67, 64n69, 65, 85n13

Chaucer, Geoffrey, 45n28, 47, 182n21, 183n23

Chrysostom, Saint John, 98n35

Cicero, Marcus Tullius. *See Rhetorica ad Herennium*

confession, 11–12, 17, 18–19, 107, 147; and the classroom, 122; of homosexuality, 19n34

Conlee, John, 84, 85n16

Consolation of Philosophy, The (Boethius), 28, 40, 41n19, 43–49; authorial position, 45, 46; free will, 47–48,

49; influence of, 51, 58; Lady Philosophy, 40, 43–49; *prosimetrum* style of, 43n25, 46n30
Cooper, Helen, 7–8, 173, 176, 188
Copeland, Rita, 47n32, 121–22
Creek, Mary Immaculate, 158n25

Daughters of God, 153–54, 158. See also *Piers Plowman;* "Sawles Warde"
Davlin, Mary C., 181n19, 182n21
"De Custodia Interioris Hominis," 153–55
De Spiritu et Anima, 61
"Debate Between the Body and the Soul, The." See "Als I Lay in a Winteris Night"
"Debate of the Body and Soul: A.D. 1949" (Anderson), 1, 2
Digby, 86, 85, 86
disciplina, 122–24
Dobson, E. J., 147
domina. See *ancilla*
Donaldson, E. Talbot, 194n33
dream visions, 76, 113. See also "Als I Lay"; "In a Thestri Stude"; *Piers Plowman*
dreams, classification of, 113n15

Eggebroten, Anne, 159
Evans, Ruth, 163

faculty psychology, 14, 15, 19, 87–88, 157, 183, 188
Fein, Susanna, 9
Finch, Casey, 40n18
Fletcher, Angus, 13–14, 48
formen, 183, 193
Foucault, Michel, 24–25; on confession, 107; on formation of the self, 105–7, 136; on power in relationships, 130–31; on the soul, 27, 107–8, 134

Four Daughters of God. See Daughters of God; *Piers Plowman;* "Sawles Warde"
Fourth Lateran Council, 11, 72, 112, 147, 161. See also confession
Frantzen, Allen J., 132n37
free will. See will

Galen, 15–16
Galloway, Andrew, 17n30
gender-inflected nouns, 7–8, 33, 155–56; body and soul, 20–23, 61–62, 73, 127, 148; death, 156; feminine, 12, 22–24, 32–33, 36, 52. See also "In a Thestri Stude"; "Liber de Querimonia"; *Piers Plowman; Psychomachia;* "Sawles Warde"
gost, 77n8
Grosseteste, Robert, 64, 103n39

"Hali Maiþhad." See Katherine Group, The
Halpern, David, 201n2
Hanna, Ralph III, 122–23, 173n6
Harley Lyrics, 85
Harvey, E. Ruth, 16n28
Harwood, Britton J., 181n19, 194n34
Hassel, Julie, 152n19
Heningham, Eleanor K., 56n51, 57n53
Hildebert of Lavardin. See "Liber de Querimonia"
homosexuality. See homosocial relationships; *Piers Plowman;* queer
homosocial relationships, 24, 29, 68, 74, 201. See also *Piers Plowman;* queer
humoral theory, 15–16

"In a Dark Place I Stood." See "In a Thestri Stude I Stod"
"In a Thestri Stude I Stod," 28, 70–104, 203–6; Body/Soul, 77–84, 99–100; Body/Soul, both masculine, 71,

73–74, 81; Body/Soul, hierarchy of, 81, 89; confounds traditional philosophy, 88, 89, 90–91; as drama, 76n7, 77; as dream vision, 76; Jesus Christ in, 100–101; Judgment Day, 101; as mutability literature, 81; narrator, 75–76, 78, 79–80; personification, 83; manuscript history, 84–86, 102; responsibility for sin, 80–82, 86, 87–88, 89–90, 92; and the self, 79, 83–84, 87–99, 103–4; as *sowlehele*, 72, 73, 80, 99; structure of, 74–75, 77; summary, 80–83; translation issues, 95–96; will, 89–90, 92, 94–97, 98
individuality, 55. See also Foucault; self
Isagoge (Porphyry), 50

James of Venice, 90n22
Jerome, Saint, 20–21
Johnson, Barbara, 31–33, 68–69
Jones, Charles, 23n40
Justice, Steven, 45n29, 168n1, 194n33

Karras, Ruth Mazo, 32n2, 152
Katherine Group, The, 146; "Hali Maiβhad," 150, 151n17, 156n22. See also *Ancrene Wisse*; "Sawles Warde"
Kay, Sarah, 53
Kenny, Anthony, 44n26, 118n21
Kerby-Fulton, Kathryn, 194n33
Kirk, Elizabeth, 181n19
Kittredge, George, 109

Langland, William. See *Piers Plowman*
"lede," 115n17
"Lestrif de ii dames," 85n13
"Liber de Querimonia" (Hildebert of Lavardin), 28, 57–63; Anima, 62; Body as the Soul's *ancilla*, 62, 64; and gender, 59–60, 62; *prosimetrum* style of, 58; queerness, 60; sexuality, 62–63

liberum arbitrium, 47, 92, 95, 96, 195. See also *Piers Plowman*
Lochrie, Karma, 105n2
de Lorris, Guillaume. See *Roman de la Rose*

Machosky, Brenda, 37n11, 41
Macrobius, Ambrosius Theodosius, 113n15
Malamud, Martha A., 36n9
de Man, Paul, 118
Mapes, Walter, 63n66
McEvoy, James, 98n35
McGinn, Bernard, 93n24
de Meun, Jean. See *Roman de la Rose*
Michel, Dan, of Northgate. See *Ayenbite of Inwit*
Middle English Dictionary, 9n14, 96n31, 100, 115n17, 140n3, 162, 179n16, 183n24
Middleton, Anne, 95n28, 169n1, 169n2
Minnis, Alastair, 44
Morrison, Susan Signe, 176
Murray, Jacqueline, 147, 148, 152
Muscatine, Charles, 12–13
mutability literature, 81

Nature, 182–83
Newman, Barbara, 13n22, 33n7, 59n58, 61
"Nuper huiuscemodi." See "Royal Debate"

Ong, Walter, 122
Orth, Peter, 58

Pasnau, Robert, 98
Paul, Saint, 4, 14, 15, 20n36, 21, 98, 193n32
Paxson, James, 5n5, 7n9, 32n3, 36n9, 38n14, 116n19, 190, 192, 200n1
Pearsall, Derek, 185n26
pedagogy. See *disciplina*

personification allegories, 5–8, 35, 38n14, 67, 69, 192, 202; and Christ's incarnation, 36, 40; and philosophy, 43, 45–46. *See also* allegories
Phillips, Helen, 74, 76n6, 79n9, 81
philosophical dialogues, 44, 46
Piers Plowman (Langland), 5, 7, 10, 17n30, 30, 49, 91–92, 168–96, 200–202; Anima, 189–92; B-text, 171, 178, 192–94; body, 189; C-text, 171, 180, 194–95; Charity, 192–93; compared to other medieval allegories, 170; dream vision, 183–87; dwindling of female figures, 170, 171, 172, 173, 176–77, 187, 196; female tutelary figures in, 173, 175, 176; Four Daughters of God, 171; gender of personifications, 173, 176, 189, 190n29, 191–92; gender-inflected nouns in, 172–73, 184, 189, 190–91, 192, 195–96; grammar as metaphor in, 23; Holy Church, 173–74, 175; homosociality, 185, 187, 196, 201, 202; human relation to the divine, 183–84; interdependence, 171, 172, 178, 180, 181, 183–84, 187, 189, 190, 193–94, 201–2; kinship, 175, 177–78; kynde or Kynde, 181–84, 186–87, 189; Lady Meed, 174–75; Liberum Arbitrium, 174, 180, 189n28, 191, 193, 194–96; married pairs of figures, 179–80; marriage as problematic, 180–81, 184, 187; mating, 183, 184–85, 186–87; Piers the Plowman, 193; as *psychomachia*, 168, 172; queer reading of, 170, 196, 200–201; Reason, 185–86; Scripture, 179; soul, 189–92; as *sowlehele,* 169, 180, 181–82, 188; Study, 178–79; summary, 171; three states of life, 180n18; Will, 168, 169, 173–74, 183, 185–86, 188, 193–94; Will's gender, 173, 196; Will's ignorance, 180n18, 181; Will's interlocutors, 170, 187–88, 190–92, 194–96; Wit, 178–79; women as less essential, 170, 187, 201
Pinborg, Jan, 44n26, 118n21
A Pistil of Susan, 126n35
Plato, 25, 107
predication, 49–50
prosopopeia, 38n14, 116, 118
Prudentius, Aurelius. See *Psychomachia*
psychological realism, 13, 35, 112
psychology, 8, 10; and allegories, 13–14; Augustinian Trinitarianism, 16–17; and philosophy, 35. *See also* faculty psychology; *sowlehele*
psychomachia, 36n10, 37, 69, 168
Psychomachia (Prudentius), 28, 35–43; acts that contradict personification's character, 38–39; Chastity, 38–41; female personifications, 36, 38; soul's supremacy, 37; transformative power of the virgin birth, 39–40, 41; warring aspects of self, 37–38, 42
Pugh, Tison, 60
Purdon, Liam O., 60, 110n11

queer, 131, 132n37. *See also* "Als I Lay"; homosocial relationships; "Liber de Querimonia"; *Piers Plowman*

Rambuss, Richard, 132n37
Reed, Thomas, Jr., 71, 133
Rhetorica ad Herennium (Cicero), 116
Rhodes, Jim, 11n17
Robertson, Elizabeth, 13, 165, 173n5, 176
Roman de la Rose (de Lorris and de Meun), 32n4, 35n8, 50–54, 200
Root, Jerry, 12
"Royal Debate," 57
Rubin, Gayle, 174n7

Salih, Sarah, 165

Salus Anime. See *sowlehele*
same-sex relationships. See "Als I Lay"; homosocial relationships; "Liber de Querimonia"; *Piers Plowman*; queer
sawle heale. See *sowlehele*
"Sawles Warde," 13, 29, 139–67; as address from a confessor, 147–48; anchoress, 165; audience, 140, 144, 145, 147–48, 163; body, 149; as conflict between marriage and virginity, 159–60, 165; Fear, 164; focus on female figures, 141, 144, 166; Four Daughters of God, 154, 158–59, 161–62; gender-inflected nouns in, 144, 150, 155–57; hierarchy of figures, 150; instructions for women, 157, 161, 162, 163; Justice, 161–62, 165; manuscript history, 140, 146, 153–55; self as house, 149, 150–51, 155–56, 160, 167; soul, 152–53, 159; as *sowlehele*, 141, 143, 144–45, 157, 161, 162, 164, 165; summary, 141–42, 160–61; temporal shifts, 163–66; *warde*, 162–63; Will, 141, 150–52, 154, 157, 164–65; Wit, 141, 150–52
Scarry, Elaine, 27
Schiebinger, Londa, 25–26n43
Schmidt, A. V. C., 61n63, 191n30, 194n35, 195n36
Sedgwick, Eve Kosofsky, 201n3
self, 197–98; definition of, 8; formation of, 105–7, 136; performative theory of, 29, 67, 73, 77, 79, 99, 199; as split, 2, 42, 76, 89, 102, 123, 137, 140, 172; turning on itself, 135–36. *See also* body; "In a Thestri Stude"; *Psychomachia*; "Sawles Warde"; "Visio Philiberti"
"sellen," 100
Simeon manuscript, 6n7
Simpson, James, 56, 95n29, 169n1, 179n16, 180n17, 193n32
Smalley, Beryl, 93n24

Solterer, Helen, 33n6, 44n27
somnium. See dream visions; "Als I Lay"; "In a Thestri Stude"; *Piers Plowman*
soul or Soul, 8, 16n28, 41, 93–94, 202; bodily torments of, 88–89; as dominant over Body, 37, 68, 134; female, 148; other words for, 37n11, 61, 73, 77, 95, 144, 149, 150, 191–92, 194; as prison, 107–8, 134–35; as treasure, 153, 159. *See also* "Als I Lay"; Aristotle; Augustine; *gost*; "In a Thestri Stude"; *liberum arbitrium*; *Piers Plowman*; *Psychomachia*; "Sawles Warde"; "Visio Philiberti"
soule-heil. See *sowlehele*
sowlehele, 5–8, 69, 80, 141, 198, 199; as aid in confession preparation, 11–12, 18, 134, 147; definition of, 9–11, 20, 35, 36; as process of individualization, 106; and time, 164, 166; works for layperson, 10, 11, 18, 72, 134. *See also* "Als I Lay"; "In a Thestri Stude"; *Piers Plowman*; "Sawles Warde"; "Visio Philiberti"
Stock, Lorraine K., 195n35

Tavormina, M. Teresa, 184n25, 188, 189n28
Teskey, Gordon, 48, 74n4, 116n18
Tierney, Brian, 182n21
Traver, Hope Emily, 158n25
Trinity College Ms. B.14.39, 85n15

ubi sunt, 64, 81, 85, 103. *See also* "Als I Lay"
"Un Samedi Par Nuit," 124–25, 126–27
Usk, Thomas, 96
Utley, Francis Lee, 3n2, 6n8

Vernon manuscript, 6n7, 9–10, 169
virga, 123, 124

virginity, 163, 165
"Visio Philiberti," 28, 63–66, 88, 102n39, 111; Body as the Soul's *ancilla*, 64, 81, 125; compared to "Als I Lay," 125; same-sex hierarchy, 64, 65–66; Soul seduced by Body, 66; as *sowlehele*, 65; warring aspects of self, 64
Vogel, Sister Mary Ursula, 118n22
voice, 116, 120, 121
voluntas. See will

Walther, Hans, 63, 64n67
warde, 162–63
White, Hugh, 182n21
Whitman, Jon, 5n4, 35n9, 40n18
will, 46–47, 49, 92–98; *voluntas*, 95–96, 156. *See also* "In a Thestri Stude";

Consolation of Philosophy; *Piers Plowman*; "Sawles Warde"
William of Ockham, 50
Wilson, R. M., 143n6, 154n 21,156, 156n23, 157n24
women: and confession, 147; depicted in allegories, 31–32, 33–34, 45n27, 142; problematic partners to men, 200; readers in the thirteenth century, 146–47
Woods, Marjorie Curry, 121–22
"wrecche," 81
Wright, Thomas, 6n6

Yates, Frances, 18

Zink, Michel, 35n8, 36n10, 43n24

INTERVENTIONS: NEW STUDIES IN MEDIEVAL CULTURE
ETHAN KNAPP, SERIES EDITOR

Body Against Soul: Gender and Sowlehele *in Middle English Allegory*
Masha Raskolnikov

www.ingramcontent.com/pod-product-compliance
Lightning Source LLC
Chambersburg PA
CBHW030135240426
43672CB00005B/138